Ethnopsychoanalysis

GEORGE DEVEREUX

Ethnopsychoanalysis

PSYCHOANALYSIS AND ANTHROPOLOGY AS COMPLEMENTARY FRAMES OF REFERENCE

UNIVERSITY OF CALIFORNIA PRESS

BERKELEY   LOS ANGELES   LONDON

BF
698.9
.C8
D4813

University of California Press
Berkeley and Los Angeles, California
University of California Press, Ltd.
London, England
English edition copyright © 1978 by George Devereux
Other editions copyright by Flammarion, Paris
ISBN 0-520-02864-3
Library of Congress Catalog Card Number: 74-16708
Printed in the United States of America

To
Claude Lévi-Strauss

Contents

Preamble ix

The Argument (1972) 1

1. A Conceptual Scheme of Society (1940) 20

2. Inside and Outside: The Nature of Stress (1966) 48

3. Culture and the Unconscious (1955) 63

4. The Logical Foundations of Culture and Personality Studies (1945) 86

5. Two Types of Modal Personality Models (1961) 113

6. Ethnic Identity: Its Logical Foundations and Its Dysfunctions (1970) 136

7. Ethnopsychoanalytic Reflections on the Notion of Kinship (1965) 177

8. Antagonistic Acculturation (1943) 216

9. Dream Learning and Individual Ritual Differences in Mohave Shamanism (1957) 249

10. Cultural Thought Models in Primitive and Modern Psychiatric Theories (1958) 265

11. Time: History vs. Chronicle. Socialization as Cultural Pre-Experience (1975) 297

Permissions and Bibliographic Indications 313

Name Index 315

Index of Geographical Names and Peoples 319

General Index 323

Preamble

THE essays constituting this volume outline and exemplify the substantive aspects of my complementaristic approach to the study of Man.[1] That theory constitutes the infrastructure even of those of my publications which contain no explicit reference to complementarity (*1, 2*).

Owing to circumstances which need not be discussed now, I became aware of some of the key problems examined here already during my adolescence (1924), though I first got a glimpse of one of the solutions (Chapter 2) only some six years later. As further insights emerged, my intellectual situation came to resemble that described by the great mathematician K. T. Gauss: "I have had my results for quite some time now, but do not know as yet how I would reach them."[2]

The long evenings of eighteen months of fieldwork amongst the Sedang of Indochina (1933–35)—a period of incessant preoccupation with concrete data—gradually enabled me to fit more and more of my insights and conclusions into the framework of scientific method. I still consult the countless notes and outlines which I jotted down at that time, whenever I tackle a theoretical or methodological problem (Chapter 11).

1. The epistemological and methodological aspects of my theoretical scheme are presented in another volume (*3*).
2. "Meine Resultate habe ich schon längst; ich weiss nur noch nicht wie ich zu ihnen kommen werde."

However, the gradual crystallization of my theoretical and methodological outlook inevitably isolated me from the thoughtways which dominated the Sciences of Man at that time. Hence, at times three or four decades elapsed between the drafting of a theoretical book (*3*) or article (Chapters 2 and 11) and its acceptance for publication.

Thus, it is only near the end of my career that I could assemble in a volume those of my papers which formulate explicitly the core of my theoretical work.

The magnitude of my debt to Monsieur Fernand Braudel, Professor at the Collège de France, is therefore self-evident. As President of the Ecole des Hautes Etudes en Sciences Sociales[3] he first urged me to revise and to prepare for publication, under the auspices of the Ecole, a book (*3*) whose first draft had been gathering dust in my files for more than thirty years. Next, he made me select, revise and make ready for publication (in French) the present volume of my basic theoretical papers.[4] I complied with Professor Braudel's requests with some misgivings, for my appraisal of my chances of getting a hearing at last was less accurate than his: he had sized up current trends far better than I did. Indeed, shortly after the publication of the first book he had commissioned, and which was subsequently translated into French, German, Spanish and Italian, four of my first five books were reprinted and the present work, as well as another (*4*), appeared in four languages. Even my first book-length venture into the field of Greek Tragedy (*6*), commissioned by Basil Blackwell Publishers, Oxford, had the good fortune of being published simultaneously in America by the University of California Press.

The publication of this book in English was made possible largely by the initiative of Ronald Davidson and Richard Day who, ever since they first contacted me in 1974, devoted

3.   Formerly: Ecole Pratique des Hautes Etudes, VI[e] Section.
4.   Subsequently Professor Braudel also commissioned other volumes of my essays, two of which are already available (*5, 7*).

much time, energy and enthusiasm to making my work known. Little did I realize, when they first telephoned me from America to arrange for my participation in a symposium on Psychoanalysis and Anthropology,[5] how decisively their dedicated interest in my work would contribute to a long hoped for turning of the tide.

The dedication of this book to Professor Claude Lévi-Strauss gratefully acknowledges the debt I owe to him for many kindnesses over a period of more than thirty years.

My late friend, Dr. Edwin M. Loeb, authorized me, shortly before his death, to include in this volume Chapter 8, which we wrote in collaboration.

A visiting Fellowship at All Souls College, University of Oxford, enabled me to draft at leisure *The Argument*, which greatly benefited by the suggestions of my friend and colleague, Professor Alain Besançon.

In connection with the first (French) edition of this book, I owe thanks to Monsieur René Hess, of the Editions Flammarion, Paris, to Madame Tina Jolas and Monsieur Henri Gobard, who had translated into French also one of my earlier books (*4*), and to Mademoiselle Claude Briand, who helped me translate Chapter 6 into French.

Miss Judith Aspinwall copy edited the English version of this book with exceptional perceptiveness and care.

I also wish to thank the Journals, Publishers and Scientific Organizations listed in the Bibliographic Appendix, who permitted me to include these essays in the present volume.

I conclude by noting that so many details of all chapters were improved before they were translated into French that I had to translate back into English even the eight chapters published originally in that language. Since, in so doing, I made further minor improvements, as of now the present English version is the definitive one. As for Chapter 11,

5. American Anthropological Association, Annual Meeting (1974), Mexico City, D.F.

which was outlined more than forty years ago, but published only after this book had already appeared in French, Spanish and Italian, it could be incorporated only into the present edition.

GEORGE DEVEREUX
Paris, July 1976

Addendum 1977 : Because one reviewer of the French edition (inexplicably) managed to read into Chapter 5 an advocacy of psychological reductionism, I rewrote the end of that chapter to make such a misinterpretation impossible.

Bibliography

(*1*)   Bastide, Roger: Preface to (*4*).
(*2*)   Idem: *Sociologie et Psychanalyse*, 2nd ed. Paris: Presses Universitaires de France, 1972.
(*3*)   Devereux, George: *From Anxiety to Method in the Behavioral Sciences*, Paris and The Hague: Mouton, 1967.
(*4*)   Idem: *Essais d'Ethnopsychiatrie Générale*. 3rd ed. Paris: Gallimard, 1970, 1972, 1977.
(*5*)   Idem: *Tragédie et Poésie Grecques*, Paris: Flammarion, 1975.
(*6*)   Idem: *Dreams in Greek Tragedy*, Oxford: Blackwell; Berkeley and Los Angeles: University of California Press, 1976.
(*7*)   Idem: *Femme et Mythe*, Paris: Flammarion (in press).

The Argument (1972)

ACCORDING to Henri Poincaré (*13*), if a phenomenon admits of one explanation, it will admit also a certain number of other explanations, all as capable as the first one to elucidate the nature of the phenomenon in question. I, for my part, specify that in the study of Man (but not only in the study of Man) it is not only possible but mandatory to explain a behavior, already explained in one way, also in another way,—i.e., within another frame of reference. The obligation to hold an (explanatory) "double discourse" is not imposed upon us by the fact that human behavior is "overdetermined," but by certain considerations which will be enunciated further on. The simple fact is that a human phenomenon which is explained in one way only is, so to speak, not explained at all (*8*) and is therefore not fully exploitable, and this even—and, in fact, chiefly—if this phenomenon's first explanation has made it perfectly comprehensible, controllable and foreseeable in terms of its own specific frame of reference.

Moreover, it is precisely the possibility of a human phenomenon being explained "completely" in at least two (complementary) ways which proves, on the one hand, that the phenomenon in question is both real and explainable and, on the other hand, that *each* of these two explanations is "complete" (and therefore valid) within its own frame of reference. In short, the double discourse makes possible a double predictability of the phenomenon, for each of the two means of predicting it makes it "inevitable" within the explanatory system one uses.

However, before explaining why these two (explanatory) discourses, each of which must (at least in principle) be enunciated—though this double discourse can never be enunciated (nor even "thought") *simultaneously* (by the same researcher) and even though there exists a complementarity relationship between the two—I must discuss first the implications of this principle for the fundamental classification of the sciences of Man. I specify from the start that the principle of the double discourse unconditionally repudiates all "*inter*disciplinarity" of the additive, fusioning, synthetic or parallel type—in short every "hyphenated," and therefore "simultaneous," discipline. Thus, authentic ethnopsychoanalysis is not interdisciplinary but *pluri*-disciplinary, since it performs a double analysis of certain facts, within the framework of ethnology on the one hand and within the framework of psychoanalysis on the other, and enunciates also the nature of the (complementarity) relationship between these two systems of explanation. I thus oppose to traditional interdisciplinarity—which is useful only on a rather rough-and-ready practical level—a non-fusioning and "non-simultaneous" pluridisciplinarity: that of the mandatory double discourse.

Authentic pluridisciplinarity—which has recourse successively to two "pure" sciences[1]—need not be "created." It is sufficient to take cognizance of the existence—and methodological inevitability—of pluridisciplinarity and to draw from it all the conclusions which this finding necessitates. Now, the first and most important of these conclusions is the need to postulate the total *interdependence* of the sociological datum and of the psychological datum (precisely because, starting from the same *raw* fact, each of

1. Gorer's review of my *Mohave Ethnopsychiatry* (3) highlights well how completely I separate ethnological facts and reasonings from psychiatric facts and reasonings in that book.

these data is *created* by the *manner* in which that fact is considered)—but also the (conjugate) need to postulate, at the same time, the autonomy of both the sociological and the psychological discourse, precisely by showing that these discourses are *complementary*. It is hardly necessary to add that it is precisely the independence and complementarity of these two discourses which makes all "reductionism"—the one which seeks to reduce ethnology to psychoanalysis or vice versa—absolutely illusory.

Classification of the Sciences of Man

There exists a number of disciplines concerned with Man, each of which is capable of making understandable, in its own manner, any human fact whatever—and this to the point of representing it as inevitable. But, on a more abstract level, each of these disciplines belongs either to "psychology" or to "sociology," whose specific natures will be explained further on.[2]

Deeming it self-evident that the very basis of all science is the study of our sense data—and this even for those who, like Chomsky, profess to be "mentalists"—I begin by defining the observable, that which is "the observed" in the science of Man.

"The observed" is, in the last resort, *the individual*. He alone is the source of those data of our senses which are relevant here, *and that even if* the individual seems to disappear—to become "non-identifiable"—in the crowd. It is hardly necessary to add that the same is true of the "invisible" molecule, which is part of a drop of water. [*Addendum 1974:* In other cases, the source of our sense data may be the atom which is part of the molecule, or the electron, etc., which is part of the atom. But the electron, etc., cannot be the source of the data of our senses when we consider the

2. Sometimes it is the biological study of the *species* which can stand in a complementarity relationship with psychology, but there is no need, in the present context, to take that possibility into account.

molecule, nor the atom when we consider the drop of water. This specification has a logical import greater than that of the definition of "the observed." It formulates very strictly the *range* of globalities that can be constructed out of a particular set of sense data, while delimiting the *range* of sense data a global construct may presuppose.]

Thus, the starting point even—and above all—of the most uncompromising sociologism is always the individual. Moreover, even as one pretends (*argumenti causa*) to know nothing of the individual (qua person), this sociologism must, nonetheless, attribute to the individual a *human* individuality—a personality which is "typically" (uniformly) human only because it *differs* from the individuality (which is *also* human and therefore *equally* differentiated) of every other human being (see Ch. 1). I will indicate further on that, were it otherwise, all sociological laws would be untrue.

I hasten to add that the conception of society and of the person which underlies my reasoning is totally incompatible with the notion that the human species is a *social* species in the sense in which the termite is a social species. Mankind is only a *gregarious* species, which exploits its innate plasticity in order to *constitute* a society for itself. To the morphological specialization of various *types* of termites living in "society," Man substitutes the differentiation of the *person*. It replaces the constraint of instincts, tropisms, etc., by custom, which, in the sociological perspective, is external to the person. "Social" communication by means of gestures, or even by means of swallowed and then regurgitated food, is replaced by symbolic communication. In fact, the only human instinctual need whose full gratification requires the conjugate cooperation of another being, which is *morphologically* differentiated from the subject, is the *genital* sexual drive.[3] But I must add that this drive does give rise

3. Indeed, it is possible that a baby, bottle-fed by a loving father, could become a normal adult—as a puppy, bottle-fed by a human being, becomes a normal dog.

to, and insures the cohesion of, *only* interpersonal relations of such intensity that society formerly felt itself threatened by them. This is what Freud hints at when he points out to what extent enlaced lovers decathect the society to which they belong (*10*).

In short, whereas the "sociality" of certain social insects is an imperative of their genetic patrimony, the "societality" of the human species (which is only gregarious) is but an actualization, always only possible, though always realized, of the possibilities which are part of Man's genetic patrimony. The actualization of this potential includes the capacity to state:

1. "I am an *X*" and/or: "I am not a *Y*."
2. "Our customs (imperative mood) are such"; "people belonging to our ethnic group behave (indicative mood) thus."

I note, finally, that when one observes an individual, that which, for the psychologist, is "inside" of that individual, is "outside" him when the sociologists considers him qua member of the ensemble to which he belongs.[4]

Since the considerations which I have just advanced indicate that the nature of the psychological explanation differs from that of the sociological explanation, it seems easiest to distinguish between them first on a purely practical level.

The *separation* of these two types of discourse can be effected in two fairly simple ways:

1. *The Criterion of Yield:* When a supplementary explanatory effort made by the psychologist ceases to produce a supplementary yield proportional to his supplementary effort—in short when it ceases to be profitable—the time has come to resort to sociological explanations, and vice versa (see Ch. 4).

4. It is sufficient to think, on the one hand, of Aischylos' very personal language and, on the other hand, of the Greek language in which Aischylos expressed himself—in his own way—and then to note the imprint which his very personal manner of handling Greek left on the "absolute" Greek language.

2. *Definition of the Observer qua Source of Constraint:*

a) *In sociology* the observer is, by definition, outside the subject. This observer can be public opinion, a policeman (see Ch. 1), an ethnologist and even, quite simply, an unconcealed camera (7).

b) *In psychology* the observer is, by definition, located within the subject. This observer is often simply the Ego, acting on behalf of the Superego, of the Ego Ideal, or even of the reality principle which contributes powerfully to the development of what I call the "temporal Ego" (5). It is this temporal Ego which guarantees (subjectively) "the coherence of the sequence of ideas," and (objectively) "the coherence of the sequence of behaviors." Thus, it is the temporal Ego which persuades the subject that he is indeed the one who uttered a certain word (promise) or performed a certain action yesterday—and is responsible for it today, even (and above all) when, *today*, the subject wishes he had acted differently *yesterday*. Finally, this internal observer appraises and continues to appraise the various activities of the subject in a relatively uniform manner. Within the framework of a truly autonomous psychology, these activities of the Ego, and above all of the temporal Ego, thus constitute an ("experimental") "constraint" as real as the constraint a policeman, an ethnologist or even a psychoanalyst imposes within the framework of an autonomous sociology.

Thus, there is always "constraint"—which means behavior *partly* triggered by the observation (*infra*). Therefore "spontaneous" or "free" behavior—*l'acte gratuit* of which poets of all kinds never cease to dream—is, on the theoretical level, just barely a hypothesis and is altogether illusory on the practical level in psychology. And it is even less than that in sociology.[5] But all that matters here is the *existence of a complementarity relationship between the psychological*

5. It is hardly necessary to specify that even "creativity," as conceived by Chomsky, unfolds itself under this constraining "surveillance."

explanation (involving an internal observer) and the sociological explanation (involving an external observer).

Although this finding is, in a certain sense, the keystone of my argument, I must once more postpone my explanation of the concept of complementarity in order to discuss first the much simpler problem of the difference between explanations concerning the individual (the person) and those which concern either the group (to which this individual belongs) or a certain individual considered chiefly qua member of some group.

At this stage of my argument I must specify just what I mean by a "group" or "society." These terms denote an ensemble of individuals which is sufficiently large to *prevent* the personality (in the psychological sense of the term) of a given individual from exerting a great influence on group processes *without the support of a social status* (king, president, chief, sorcerer, leader). I mean by "small group" a set of individuals sufficiently small to *permit* the (brilliant, aggressive, neurotic, etc.) personality of one of its members to influence radically the group processes *without the support of a (particular) social status*. In the present study I do not take into account the existence of small groups which one can study with the same degree of precision—*though never simultaneously*—in the psychological manner and in the sociological manner. This does not mean that the small group is a kind of "wasteland" or "no man's land" situated "between" the domain of psychology and that of sociology. The problems it creates become puzzles only when one tackles them in a quibbling and Byzantine manner. The small group corresponds, in a way, to a system made up of a sufficiently small number of particles to permit one to study it with sufficient precision by the method of theoretical mechanics and yet large enough for the laws of statistical mechanics to foresee, with sufficient exactness, the behavior of the whole system.

This remark enables me to tackle a fact belonging to the domain of physics which, *without* exemplifying authentic

complementarity, permits one to demonstrate that the
behavior of a single system can be analyzed in two perfectly
distinct ways. I state at once that, for present purposes, the
example I will discuss *need* not be *in any way* analogous with
the data of psychology or with those of sociology. I cite it
only in order to prove that there is nothing disconcerting
about the fact that the nature of psychological explanations
and that of sociological explanations are not the same.

The (irreversible) global phenomena which occur in a
"closed" system and which thermodynamics and statistical
mechanics explain in *their manner*—that is, as a drifting or
sliding of the system from a mathematically less probable to
a mathematically more probable state[6]—presuppose a perfect applicability of theoretical mechanics to each individual
molecule of the system,[7] precisely because these laws concern *reversible* phenomena and *utilize* the notion of force,
which the analysis of the drifting of a system toward the
state of entropy *does not utilize.*[8] In fact, if the molecules
in question violated the laws of theoretical mechanics, all
the laws of thermodynamics and of statistical mechanics
(which concern the system as a whole) would turn out to
be false.

Now, it is important to recall emphatically that in the
study of this kind of system it is *exclusively* our *incapacity*
to analyze mathematically, with absolute precision, the behavior of more than two particles in relative motion to each
other which has compelled us to invent the reasoning of
thermodynamics and of statistical mechanics, whose formulations and explanations differ entirely from those of theoretical mechanics. If a great mathematician ever manages to

6.   One may think, for example, of the uniform diffusion of the particles
composing a drop of ink throughout a glass of water.
7.   It suffices to think in this context of the collisions and ricochets of a
small number of billiard balls, moving about in a very small enclosure.
8.   I note in passing that the absence of the notion of "force" in the explanation of this kind of drift renders absurd certain speculations which seek to
link a (primary) "death instinct" with entropy.

solve completely the so-called "problem of three bodies," the global behavior of a system of molecules (of a volume of gas, for example) would become *totally* explainable also in terms of the laws of theoretical mechanics. I note in passing that it is this fact which shows that the explanations of theoretical mechanics and those of statistical mechanics are not "complementary" in the strict sense of this term.

I hold, on the other hand, that even the most perfected psychology that may exist one day would never permit us to formulate sociological laws,[9] just as the most perfect sociology would never be able to formulate authentically psychological laws.

By now, I have mentioned complementarity often enough to be obliged to tackle it at last frontally.

The Notion of Complementarity, of Bohr (*1*), represents a generalization of the principle of indeterminacy (or uncertainty) enunciated by Heisenberg, who sought to clarify a fundamental problem of quantum physics. This principle states that it is impossible to determine (measure) *simultaneously and with the same precision* the position and the momentum of an electron. Indeed, the more precisely one measures the position of an electron (at a given instant) the more one's determination of its momentum becomes imprecise—and vice versa, of course. Thus, everything happens *as if* the experiments to which one subjects it "forced" the electron to have either a *precise* position or a *precise* momentum.

By extending his field of observations to biology, Bohr was able to identify the manifestations of the principle of complementarity also in that domain. His "principle of destruction" (*Abtötungsprinzip*) concerns a fact which is as simple as it is striking: any experimental study of the phenomenon "life" which is *carried too far* destroys precisely that which it seeks to define too precisely: Life. In short, it is

---

9. And this *not only* because such a psychology could be created only if the *Abtötungsprinzip* (*infra*) did not exist.

the experiment which transforms living flesh into butcher's meat.[10]

Now, I have already briefly noted a fact I discuss at length in another publication (7): the behavior which a human being actualizes in the presence of an observer (*lato sensu*) is not the behavior which he would have actualized while not being observed. In a way he actualizes an "experimental" behavior—one of constraint—even when the observer is the subject himself.

Better still, the principle of complementarity can manifest itself in a very striking manner even in self-observation, in which either the "observer" or the "observed" (which can be simply a behavior) is subjected to the *Abtötungsprinzip*. In order to prove this, I will cite an observation which I discussed in detail elsewhere.

1. A fully experienced orgasm produces a clouding of consciousness which makes the self-observation of the orgasm imprecise.

2. If, in order to observe it better, one makes an effort to prevent this clouding of consciousness, that which one observes will no longer be a true orgasm, experienced in all its plenitude, but simply a physiological spasm which culminates in an ejaculation (7).

Finally—and it is this that matters most in the present study—there exists an *inevitable* complementarity relationship between the psychological explanation and the sociological explanation of the same phenomenon. Since I analyze this phenomenon at length in Chapter 5, I subject here to a double analysis only one small raw fact, which I describe in detail elsewhere (4).

The Raw Fact: The Mohave witch Sahaykwisā incited her two lovers to kill her.

---

10. I note in passing that, when a laboratory animal is reduced to what certain people call a "preparation," the experiments to which this "preparation" is subjected furnish informations which are *fully* valid only for the preparation; they are only *partly* valid for the intact organism.

1. *Psychological Explanation:*

a) *Operant Motive:* Sahaykwisā's self-destructiveness was so great that she would have managed to get herself murdered in any society;

b) *Instrumental Motive:* Qua Mohave witch, persuaded that it is only by getting herself murdered that she could perpetuate her hold on the shades of her (beloved) victims, she *proclaimed* herself a witch. In the Mohave socio-cultural setting this made her murder inevitable.

2. *Sociological Explanation:*

a) *Operant Motive* = instrumental motive of the psychological explanation.

b) *Instrumental Motive* = operant motive of the psychological explanation.

It is hardly necessary to specify that it is because these two explanations concern the same raw fact that the two discourses cannot be held simultaneously. This implies that there exists a complementarity relationship, in the strict sense of the term, between these two discourses. But it is perhaps useful to recall that a raw fact does not belong, from the start, either to the domain of sociology or to that of psychology. It is only through its explanation (within the framework of one or the other of these two sciences) that the raw fact *is transformed* either into a psychological or into a sociological datum (7). One is even inclined to think that just as in quantum physics it is the experiment which, so to speak, "forces" an electron to have either a *precise* position or a *precise* momentum at a given moment, so it is the manner in which one proceeds to explain it which "forces" the raw fact to "become" either a psychological or a sociological datum. There exists no imaginable explanation capable of "forcing" the raw fact to become a datum pertaining *simultaneously* to these two domains of the sciences of Man. Thus, the principle of complementarity seems to operate already on the level of the raw fact's transformation into a datum pertaining to one or the other of these two sciences.

But the psychological and the sociological discourses are not the only ones that are mutually irreducible and between which a complementarity relationship obtains. The same reciprocal irreducibility and the same complementarity relationship can exist also between two perspectives or two theories. The perspective which permits Lévi-Strauss to discover the *structural* (logical) invariants of a group of variants of a given myth, and that which enables me to discover the invariance of the affective content in the variants of another myth (6)—where this invariance is guaranteed precisely by the transformation of (psychoanalytically defined) symbols which express that affective content—are reciprocally irreducible and the relationship between them is, likewise, a complementarity relationship. This implies that structuralism is true because psychoanalysis is true—and vice versa. Similarly, there exists a complementarity relationship between the notion of the innate structure of human thought (Lévi-Strauss), or of grammar (Chomsky), on the one hand, and my notion, on the other, that what is characteristically most human is not the ensemble of innate invariant structures (whose existence I do not deny) but the capacity of the mind to effect transformations in the course of which certain structures remain invariant.[11] I believe, however, that my theory ablishes, at least in principle, one of the main difficulties of Chomsky's theories: the "excessive power" of his transformational grammar. Indeed, it suffices to insist on the fact that all human activity—including the "creativity" which Chomsky discusses—implies also an antecedent "structured selection" (see Ch. 6; 9, Ch. 2) of a number of structures which it will subject to transformations and a *rejection*, also *structured*, of other structures which are quite as innate and (in principle) quite as possible, *but only for the species in its entirety*.

---

11. It is hardly necessary to specify that this manner of considering things has nothing in common with Boas' interesting views concerning the significance of the diversity of real grammars.

It therefore seems necessary to determine, on the one hand, the structure which governs the "selection" of certain innate structures for the purpose of involving them in a group of transformations which does not affect their invariance and, on the other hand, the structure which governs the simultaneous (concurrent) "rejection" of certain other innate structures. I admit that I would not in the least be surprised if there turned out to exist a complementarity relationship between the structures governing "selection" and those which govern "rejection."

The fact that two theories (which are explanations) can stand in a complementarity relation with each other is as natural as the fact that two sciences (psychology and sociology) should be able to stand in such a relationship to each other. Indeed, "society" (and "culture") and "psyche" are at first simply seeds of explanations. But, once these explanations—which, in the last resort, define only perspectives—are "constructed" (without being reified in the process), they, too, can constitute explanatory frames of reference, which are both autonomous and valid, but only if one never loses sight of their explanatory "origin."

To conclude, I must once more return to the *Abtötungsprinzip* and to the role which it plays not only in laboratory experiments but also in "thought experiments" (*Gedankenexperimente*), which involve no manipulation of the subject —in short, in explanation (*3*).

I deem evident the equivalence of an actual experiment pushed too far and of the overly minute explanation of a phenomenon within the framework of a *single* explanatory system. In both instances the "experiment" *destroys* the phenomenon which it seeks to study too meticulously. In the case of an explanation pushed too far, it is this "experiment" which *explains away ("escamote")* that which it seeks to explain too well. This view, be it noted in passing, is fundamentally different from Foucault's remark, which proclaims the death of Man qua possible object of science.

What I assert is much more concrete than this maxim. I

simply establish the fact that, as far as any results or conclusions are concerned, they are the same whether one *actually* destroys the "centers of reflection" of an animal, or if one simply assumes the *theoretical* position that all that matters is visible behavior, in the most platitudinous and pretentious behavioristic sense. In both cases the conclusions shall be valid only for the "preparation" or for its conceptual equivalent: for the "stat. rat" (statistical rat). In both instances that which one seeks to explain ceases—precisely *because* of this explanation—to be what one professes to explain. Thus, the *Abtötungsprinzip* intervenes—creating a complementarity situation—not only in research *through acts* but also in research *through explanation* which is at once too ambitious and too obstinately attached to a single frame of reference, even—and chiefly—at the point where it almost ceases to be productive.

Thus, when the sociological explanation of a fact is pushed beyond certain limits of "profitableness" (*rentabilité*), what occurs is not a reduction of the psychological to the sociological, but a disappearance of the very object of sociological discourse. What appears in its place is that which is the most psychological in Man. What survives the *total* sociological explanation of the behavior of a given man —when all he does is reduced to the actualization of his various social roles—is, e.g., the counteroedipal impulse which he actualizes qua father, the neurotic aggressivity which he manifests qua soldier, etc.

The situation is the same in the case of overly ambitious psychological explanations: the object of the authentically psychological discourse disappears and leaves in place only materials whose *totality* has pertinence only for sociology: the statuses of father, of soldier, etc., that the individual in question may possess.

Lastly, as my friend Alain Besançon pointed out to me, all explanation that goes to excesses becomes in the last resort tautological. The raw fact transforms itself into a mere conceptual token belonging to a particular theory, and this, inevitably, opens the way to a supposed "verification" of the said theory in terms of itself and in terms of its own consequences. It is hardly necessary to add that such an (unjustifiable) procedure must not (as it often is) be confused with a (legitimate) testing of the *coherence*—of the non-self-contradictory character—of a theoretical system; for the later procedure does, in fact, require that the system of postulates be put to a test in terms of itself.

Thus, the views I have just expressed define also the boundary of *one* particular discourse. This boundary is located at the very point at which, when the explanation is pushed too far, its object "disappears" and is automatically replaced by an object pertaining exclusively to the complementary discourse. In fact, this boundary is *created* by the disappearance of the object which actually pertains to the discourse one is enunciating and by the appearance, in its stead, of an object pertaining to the complementary discourse.

It seems unnecessary to discuss here all the characteristics of this boundary, which is constantly being created by the crossing thereof, for its characteristics are exactly the same as those enumerated briefly in Chapter 2 and which I analyze elsewhere in great detail (7).

Having come to the end of my account, I think I must forestall two types of criticisms and to repudiate a third one.

One kind of criticism might assert that the double discourse constitutes a vicious circle (*A* explaining *B*, and vice versa), without any possibility of determining which of the two discourses is prior to the other. Such a criticism is possible only if one loses sight of the fact that these two discourses can never be held *simultaneously*. In fact, were it possible to hold them simultaneously (which is *totally excluded*), it would be indispensable that a vicious circle should come into being, for it is only on this condition that each of these two discourses, enunciated successively, and also the method of the double discourse itself, can be valid.

The other criticism might conclude that my constant use

of Russell's solution of the "Epimenides" type paradoxes (see Ch. 6) implies some kind of a relationship between the theory of the double discourse and the theory of "mathematical types" (the class of all classes not members of themselves). It is hardly necessary to specify that, since these two discourses are unfolding on the *same* level of abstraction, whereas a statement concerning all statements is not applicable to itself (*inter alia* because that statement is on a *different* level of abstraction than is every other statement), there is no relation whatever between complementarity and Russell's theory of mathematical types.

As for a third type of criticism—one that might impute to me a "physicalistic" manner of proceeding—*that* criticism fails to distinguish between an appeal to the *general consequences* (logical as well as methodological) of facts which were discovered and explained first by physicists and the slavish and nearly always absurd imitation of the technical "façades" of physics, which belong exclusively to that science.

[*Addendum 1976:* Certain considerations, which need not be mentioned here, make it necessary to indicate that situations explainable only in terms of the complementarity principle do not occur only in the domain of quantum physics.

As regards biology, Bohr's repeatedly cited *Abtötungsprinzip* suffices to demonstrate this.

As regards psychology and especially psychoanalysis, the situation is, if possible, even more striking. The relevant factual observations were made by Josef Breuer and published, in a book he wrote jointly with Freud (*2*, pp. 34–35), in 1895, i.e., about six years before the word "quantum" was used by a physicist (1901).

Breuer's observations were subsequently generalized in psychoanalytical terms by Freud. The theoretical formulation of Freud—which is "strikingly reminiscent" (*12*, p. 248) of Bohr's thesis—was published in 1917, that is: ten years or more before Heisenberg enunciated the indeterminacy principle and Bohr the principle of complementarity.

This is proven by a remark of one of Bohr's most distinguished followers, the theoretical physicist and epistemologist Pascual Jordan, though he did not underline the chronology mentioned in the preceding paragraph.

Breuer made the following clinical observations:

1. As long as there is an [observable and conscious] symptom, the meaning of the symptom is unconscious [and not observable].

2. When the meaning of the symptom becomes conscious [observable]—and is linked with the symptom—the symptom disappears.

Before I quote in full Jordan's relevant remarks, I specify that I had to translate from the German the Freud sentence which he cites, because its translation in the *Standard Edition* (*11*, p. 279) is not only inaccurate, but also amounts to a manifestly erroneous statement. The chief difficulty in translating that sentence is that the German word *Vertretung* has no precise English equivalent; the Standard Edition's "inseparable relation" does not even approximate its real meaning. The noun *Vertretung* denotes the act whereby, or the situation in which, for example, the head of a state is represented at a ceremony by a delegate or proxy, to whom "head of state honors" are rendered on that particular occasion.

Speaking of the fact that a psychoanalytic intervention makes the meaning of the symptom conscious and, in so doing, causes the symptom to disappear, Jordan (*12*, p. 247) writes: "Thus, we have here, once again, a situation similar to that in quantum physics: it is not possible actually to execute the observations which, in terms of deterministic conceptions, would be needed in order to provide the bases [the supporting evidence] for the prediction without producing thereby, in the observed conditions, a modification which utterly overthrows their whole predetermination."

This sentence is immediately followed by Jordan's (*12*, p. 248) crucial remark: "Freud described the '*psychological complementarity'* which appears here in a formulation that reminds one in a truly striking manner of Bohr's statements: 'The meaning of the symptoms is not only consistently unconscious; there exists also a relationship of representation [*Verhältnis von Vertretung*] between this unconsciousness [of the meaning of symptoms] and the possibility for the existence of symptoms." (*11*, p. 279 English, p. 316 German.)

Jordan's statement is so clear as to require no comment. But it is useful to underline, for present purposes, that the psychoanalytic intervention which makes the meaning of the symptom conscious and thereby causes the symptom to disappear, is a mere explanation or insight. This justifies my earlier assertion that a certain manner of viewing an organism is the conceptual equivalent of its *Abtötung*, and that a complementarity relationship may obtain between two ways of explaining a given phenomenon.]

I note in conclusion that complementarism is not a "theory" but a methodological generalization. Complementarism excludes no valid methods or theories; it coordinates them. Last, but not least, complementarism does not stand in a complementarity relation with *non*-complementarism—an anti-method which the acrobats of the Word will no doubt soon try to invent.

Bibliography

(*1*)   Bohr, Niels: Causality and Complementarity, *Philosophy of Science* 4:289–298, 1937.

(*2*)   Breuer, Josef and Freud, Sigmund: *Studies on Hysteria, Standard Ed.,* vol. 2, London, 1957.

(*3*)   Devereux, George: Discussion, *Psychosomatic Medicine* 32:65–67, 1960.

(*4*)   Idem: *Mohave Ethnopsychiatry*, Washington, D.C., 1961 (2nd augm. ed. 1969).

(*5*)   Idem: Transference, Screen Memory and the Temporal Ego, *Journal of Nervous and Mental Disease* 143:318–323, 1966.

(*6*)   Idem: The Exploitation of Ambiguity in Pindaros *0*.3.27, *Rheinisches Museum für Philologie* 109:289–298, 1966.

(7) Idem: *From Anxiety to Method in the Behavioral Sciences*, Paris and The Hague, 1967.

(8) Idem: La Naissance d'Aphrodite (in) Pouillon, Jean and Maranda, Pierre (eds.): *Echanges et Communications* (*Festschrift* for Claude Lévi-Strauss), 2 vols., Paris and The Hague, 1970.

(9) Idem: *Essais d'Ethnopsychiatrie Générale*, Paris, 1970, 1972, 1977.

(10) Freud, Sigmund: *Group Psychology and the Analysis of the Ego, Standard Ed.*, vol. 13, London, 1955.

(11) Idem: *Introductory Lectures on Psychoanalysis* (Part iii), *Standard Ed.*, vol. 16, London, 1964. (See, for the original German text of the newly translated Freud sentence, *Vorlesungen zur Einführung in die Psychoanalyse*, 3rd ed., Leipzig, Wien, Zürich, 1920, p. 316.)

(12) Jordan, Pascual: Quantenphysikalische Bemerkungen zur Biologie und Psychologie, *Erkenntnis* 4:215-252, 1934.

(13) Poincaré, Henri: *Electricité et Optique*, Paris, 1901.

1

A Conceptual Scheme
of Society (1940)

THE concept "society" can be introduced into sociological discourse in three ways.

1. As a metaphysical "reality." This is scientifically meaningless.

2. As a working hypothesis or as a concept. This is permissible. It precludes, however, the possibility of making sociological statements with respect to the individual. The definition of the individual or of individual process with reference to, or in terms of, a society of which he is a part is a nonpredicative statement. Such statements lead to vicious circles (7).

3. As a conceptual scheme, derived from individual data. One can "describe given and possible aspects, or elements, without considering the problem of their subjectivity or independent reality" (21).

The introduction of the conceptual scheme "society" into scientific discourse is a matter of manipulatory convenience and of conciseness of expression. The same may be said of the conceptual scheme "space." Both are constructed inductively from concepts derived from sense data concerning individuals. It is desirable that these concepts should be operationally definable (4). It permits one to think of society as a conceptual scheme. One can then study its implications, including those referring to the individual.

The relationship between the individual and society is the central problem of sociology. Three types of approaches to this problem exist.

1. *The Theory of Emergence* has been summarized by White: "Each forward integration emerges into a field of entirely new possibilities, which cannot be forecast by the understanding of the previous state. [This new state] is an *emergent* ... a new being with laws of action unpredictable on the basis of the preceding lower stage of development" (*43*). The "emergent" is obviously introduced not as a concept but as a reality. This method is exemplified by the theories of Le Bon (collective mentality, genius of the race), Durkheim (collective representation), McDougall (group mind), etc. The solution offered is purely formal. Poincaré would say that it labels the problem instead of solving it. The "emergent" is nowhere derived from individual data. It is considered an independent reality, which is metaphysical and therefore meaningless, though this does not necessarily imply that it is useless in practice (*infra*).

2. *The Organismic Theory* has been presented in the shape of Gestalt and field theories. Inspired by the works of Neurath (*28*) and Lewin (*23*), it has been elaborated by J. F. Brown: "The whole includes the parts. . . . [That which] occurs at any given position within the *whole* is determined by the structure of the *whole*" (*5*). This is a nonpredicative statement. The social "field" is nowhere derived from the (inter-) individual hypothetical social field. Brown studies the dynamics of individual motion in the hypothetical social field. Methodological objections notwithstanding, both the emergence and the field hypotheses are more or less useful working hypotheses.

3. *The Method of Contrasts* does not pretend to be a theory. The concepts "individual" and "society" are introduced almost simultaneously into the scientific discourse. The methodological utility of the concept "society" is explained as follows. The *sum total* of individual behavior cannot be explained in terms of biopsychological theories

only. From this total behavior one subtracts those parts which are more or less understandable in terms of biology, psychology, etc. The residue is then "explained" by introducing the concept "society." Only such properties as are necessary to explain this residue are ascribed to society. Actually, the most rigorous authors do not "subtract" but "differentiate," which is a far better procedure. All concepts are used as working hypotheses. The scientific self-restraint and the simplicity of this procedure make it the practical method par excellence. It works by analogy, enumeration, exemplification and contrast. It permits one to discover a wealth of new data. A good example of this approach is the work of Linton (*25*). Unlike some self-styled empiricists, he never confuses hypotheses with objective reality.

According to Meyerson (*26*), to explain a natural process means to recognize it as rational, to reduce it to identical things in space and time and to present the diversity of temporal change as only apparent. The explanation is, thus, always partial, since we cannot pursue the chain of causes ad infinitum. I differ from Meyerson—and this is probably the only major point on which we disagree—in believing that the unknowable or irrational substratum is not the proper subject matter of scientific discourse; its existence is a metaphysical pseudo-problem (*Scheinproblem*). I shall therefore start with sense experience, from which I derive operationally definable concepts. I refuse to look for explanations beyond these concepts. The existence of even more "ultimate" causes—or their nonexistence—is meaningless to the working scientist.

The concepts selected are not further analyzable. They are mutually independent. One can change the meaning of any one of them without thereby changing that of any or of all of the other concepts. They are sufficient for my purpose. From them a number of productive propositions can be deduced. The choice of the basic concepts is, of course, always arbitrary. Any other set of basic concepts from which the same set of propositions can be deduced is equivalent to my set of basic concepts (*34*). The ultimate test of a conceptual scheme is its coherence and internal compatibility, as well as the facility with which one can manipulate it for predictive purposes.

Two concepts suffice to define society: the individual and the relative positions of individuals. This recalls Osvald Veblen's starting point for geometry: the point and order (cf. also Leibniz: Time is the order of events; space is the order of bodies). A third concept is necessary for the analysis of social process. I call it for the moment: change. (According to J. C. Maxwell, kinetics differs from geometry in that time is explicitly introduced into it as a commensurate quantity.) I need no further concepts in the present context.

The individual can be defined operationally. One can measure his age, his weight, his wealth, etc. (see Ch. 6). One can state that he has mass.

The relative position of individuals (order of individuals) can also be defined operationally in terms of transitive, asymmetrical relations. Consider individuals *A*, *B* and *C*. If individual *A* is the ancestor of *B*, and *B* the ancestor of *C*, then it follows that *A* is not only not *C*, but also that he must be *C*'s ancestor. The same is true if one substitutes to the relation "ancestor of" the relation "superior to," "richer than," etc.[1] In some cases other orders exist. If the relation is "loves," the resulting proposition is not necessarily transitive and asymmetrical and *may* not indicate "order" (*22*, p. 115).

Change, too, is operationally definable. It involves the dimension "time." If *A* takes a trip, ages a minute, becomes more learned, etc., he has changed. It is only by definition that one agrees to consider individual *A* of whom one had a sense experience at 1:59 P.M. the same *A* of whom one has

---

1. It is always important to verify whether an asymmetrical relationship is also transitive. As a result of the vicissitudes of conquest, one finds for example that in Fijian society, *A* can be the vassal of *B*, *B* the vassal of *C*, and *C* the vassal of *A*.

a sense experience at 2:00 P.M. One can agree on some sort of operation whereby one ascertains that the two sources of stimuli are the same person. One can ask A to tell his name at 1:59 P.M. and also at 2:00 P.M. One may also take his fingerprints on both occasions. One may, if one wishes, use a motion picture camera, which follows and records all his movements, etc., between 1:59 P.M. and 2:00 P.M. Hereby one concedes to individual A a measure of permanence. One assumes that A, when he comes in contact with B, does not coalesce with the latter into a single continuum. Weyl's definition of the atom also applies to individuals: "If a given individual occupies a specific place at a specific time, then after a sufficiently small interval there is one individual who occupies a space which differs less than any assignable amount from the space occupied by the given individual at the earlier time" (*42*). The operation whereby one defines a concept is not important in itself, as long as there exists a conventional operation which permits one to recognize and accept A's identity through every change. One may call change "motion." This tallies with the terminology adopted by Sorokin (*36*) and Brown (*5*). I mean thereby that if individual A changes in any way, his position with respect to other individuals also changes. (Example: A has become richer than B; B has become the husband of C; etc.) Thus, one must revise the initial nomenclature and call the third fundamental concept: "motion."

One can now define society as the order of individuals. One defines social process as the order of successive orders of individuals (cf. the Leibnizian definition of space and time, supra).

In sociological discourse it is entirely legitimate not to attempt to explain individual change or motion in terms of psychology, biology, biochemistry, or physics. Bohr formulates the problem as follows:

"Every experimental arrangement suitable for following the behavior of the atoms constituting an organism in an exhaustive way as implied by the possibilities of physical observation and definition would be incompatible with the maintaining of the life of that organism. . . . Those essential features of living organisms which are brought to light only under circumstances which exclude an exact account of their atomic constituents are laws of a nature which stand in a complementary relationship to those with which we are concerned in physics and chemistry" (2).

In other words, it is impossible to determine operationally with any precision the internal ("atomic") motivation of the motion of living organisms without killing them (*Abtötungsprinzip*). Vice versa, the complete description of a corpse yields no complete clues to processes in living organisms. Hence "motivation" must be excluded from the present analysis. But I must so formulate my conceptual scheme as to leave me free to assume anything whatever with respect to individual processes. Thus, I may assume that there are causes for any motion, while leaving the nature of these causes undefined. I can assume, if I wish, that any motion "proves" predestination, free will, divine guidance, mechanism, vitalism, reversibility of individual processes (Lewis [24], Jeans [17]), irreversibility of individual processes (Ehrenberg [14], Donnan [11], Donnan and Guggenheim [12]), quantic indeterminism and discontinuity of individual processes (Jordan [18; 19, pp. iii–ix, 217–319]), or any other theory. Although the nature of individual processes (motion) does not concern one here in the least, since it cannot be defined operationally, certain considerations of Bohr (2), Jordan (18, 19) and Blum (1) make it appear useful, though not necessary, to think of individual processes as irreversible (9).

I am now confronted with the difficulty of accounting for social processes without knowing anything of individual processes. Assume for a moment that one could account causally for the motions of every individual. One would still be confronted with the calculatory difficulty of solving the problem of a great number of bodies in relative motion to one another. One must therefore ignore individual processes and account for social processes in terms of laws independent of the validity of mechanics (*24*, p. 140). The very attempt to account at all for social processes implies that they must be reduced to some sort of regularities. I thereby query, for the time being, the very existence of regularities, since I have renounced the possibility of deriving them from individual regularities of which I know nothing —not even that they exist. On the other hand, there could be no sociological laws if there were no regularities permitting generalizations. Now, there could be no regularities without some cause, which, as will be shown further on, may very well be only a cause of a statistical kind. I must therefore analyze the meaning of "causality" and of "law." I must look especially for causes which contain no specifications concerning individual processes and yet result exclusively from individual processes.

According to Petzoldt, there are two types of causality: simultaneous and succedaneous. Simultaneous causality implies the coherence of spatial structures. It is exemplified by organization (structure). The belief of Cuvier in simultaneous causality is expressed in his attempt to reconstruct an animal from a single vertebra. Succedaneous causality implies the coherence of temporal structures. It is exemplified in processes. The belief of Newton in succedaneous causality is expressed in his attempt to predict the successive positions and velocities of a freely falling body.

Unless otherwise specified, by "causality" I mean here succedaneous causality. I must therefore analyze on precisely what grounds I assume causal connectedness between two events. Let it be assumed that event *B* always succeeds event *A* and never occurs without being preceded by event *A*. Event *A*, however, can and does occur without event *B* occurring also. I tacitly assume that the initial conditions under which *A* occurs are always the same. This is only an ideal possibility. In theory, however, one can approximate the initial conditions as closely as one wishes. One repeats the experiment several times. One then enunciates the law:

"Event *A* is the cause of event *B*." According to Schrödinger: "From the idea of special regular connectedness, we
come to the idea of general necessary connectedness . . . as
an abstraction from the mass of connections as a whole"
(*35*, p. 135). He further states that "the constancy of the
laws of nature is guaranteed to us only by experience" (*35*,
p. 40). This is obvious. One cannot repeat an experiment at
all places, at all times, an infinite number of times. One
simply assumes that the repeated recurrence of the same
sequence of phenomena in a finite number of experiments
guarantees, by extrapolation, the recurrence of the same
sequence of events always and everywhere. This tallies with
Hume's view that it is very difficult, if not impossible, to get
at the root of causal connectedness. This being so, the difference between true causality (cause and effect) and false
causality (*post hoc, ergo propter hoc*) is—or could be—one
of degree only. It could consist in the greater and probably
more uniform repetitiveness of sequences accounted for in
terms of "true causality." So formulated, the problem of
causality involves extrapolation and statistical induction
only, which can be more or less valid. As to the modern
theory of "functional causality," it introduces the concept
of function, which is not defined with perfect clarity. I must
therefore admit that, for the observer at least, nothing
guarantees the absolute, universal, permanent, uniform and
infinite "repeatability" of a given sequence of phenomena.

[*Addendum 1966:* In practice, one may not content oneself with so vague a definition of causality, expressed exclusively in terms of probability. One must *also* demand that *A*
should not be treated as the cause of *B*, save only if one's
present knowledge allows one to link *B* to *A* by means of an
intelligible mechanism. This procedure has certain advantages. It permits one to treat the (statistically significant)
results of Rhine's card guessing (*32*) as purely fortuitous,
simply because Rhine is unable to postulate an intelligible
mechanism which links the subject's ("clairvoyant") utterances with the presentation of certain cards. One must

concede, however, that the insistence of the necessity of specifying the *nature* of the connection is a purely heuristic requirement, justified only by the praxis of scientists and by experience, which shows that the requirement that the connection be specified does actually produce results (8).]

A law is a verbal, mathematical, or any other formulation of observed regularities and of the probability of the recurrence of the same regularities. I state explicitly: "Event *A* is always followed by event *B*." I state implicitly something different: "It is observed that usually the above sequence takes place under given conditions. I therefore think it highly probable that by duplicating said conditions the same sequence of events will recur."

These and similar considerations have long troubled physicists. They have attempted to distinguish statistically between degrees of probability. In the wake of Boltzmann (3), Gibbs and others have developed modern statistical mechanics. Statistical analysis has been substituted for causal analysis. This method of inquiry does not involve belief or lack of belief in ultimate causality; it only implies a refusal to deal with what cannot be interpreted scientifically and defined operationally. Physicists limit themselves to defining operationally the probability of various events and successions of events. They have thereby been enabled to make very accurate predictions, to formulate simple and coherent systems of laws, etc., without overburdening their schemes with unnecessary ideologies. Their chief triumph, however, was the fact that they not only could foresee deviations but could also assign a limit to these deviations. The importance of this argument has been clearly seen by Schrödinger (35, p. 46). Physicists have accounted for causality by saying, with Schrödinger, that "chance lies at the root of causality" (35, p. 43).

The cause-and-effect concept involves the concept of direction. According to Schrödinger, "all laws relating to irreversible natural processes are now known definitely to be of a statistical kind" (35, p. 64). The second law of thermodynamics, "*which plays a role in positively every physical process* . . ., is very intimately connected with the typical one-directional character of all natural processes. . . . . Although . . . by itself . . . [it] is not sufficient to determine the direction in which the state of a material system will change in the next instant, it always *excludes certain directions of change*, the direction exactly opposite to the one which actually occurs being always excluded" (*35*, p. 141).

According to W. S. Franklin (*15*), one is aware of the fact that time has a "direction" only because all fundamental processes in the universe are irreversible. (Local processes involving but one particle, like a pendulum, etc., are reversible. The particle, on the other hand, can be a closed system in which irreversible thermodynamic processes do take place.) Summing up, in Lenzen's words, "macroscopic laws express the probable sequence of phenomena" (*20*, p. 131).

Statistical mechanics starts with two additional concepts: It is assumed that the molecules obey Hamiltonian dynamics and that all molecules of the same kind are equal in most respects. The operational position taken *here* is that, since one knows nothing of individual processes or individual nature, one can dispense with these concepts. For the observer who, for methodological reasons, chooses (for the moment) to be ignorant, individuals can be either perfectly alike or perfectly different, and individual movement wholly random. One is, nevertheless, able to obtain, on a purely statistical basis, all the basic propositions of sociology which, in one form or the other, have obtained universal assent.

THEOREM I—History is an irreversible social process.

1. A society possesses a large number of states, each of which is characterized by a social structure, which is defined as the order of positions which it is possible for individuals to occupy in that society.

2. If the social structure characterizing a state is not materially modified when at least two individuals exchange positions, then we may say for brevity's sake that that

society is in equilibrium with respect to certain aspects of social mobility. For reasons stated in The Argument this is almost never the case as regards small groups.

3. An exchange of positions between two or more individuals which does not involve important changes in the existing social structure may be denoted as a "change of phase within a given state." The situations obtaining before and after such changes (of phase) are called "phases." (Example: The United States in 1928 and in 1929. "Le roi est mort, vive le roi!")

4. The number of phases possible within a given state assigns a probability value to that state and is a measure of that state's stability. The number of phases pertaining to a given state is usually large.

5. If a society, while in phase *a* of state *A* is disturbed, then it is highly probable that, after a certain lapse of time, it will return to a different phase *x* of state *A*, or else to some phase of another state, *B*, which is not too radically different from phase *a* of state *A*. This corresponds to the conception that homeostasis implies fluctuations within set limits (see Ch. 2). (Example: The United States in 1933 and after the NRA was declared unconstitutional.)

This definition of "equilibrium" appears to blend the somewhat divergent views of Cannon (*6*), Henderson (*16*) and Sorokin (*37*) and assigns a meaning to Donnan's statement (*13*) that society is a hereditary (chronoholistic) system.

Because of the large number of individuals involved, and also because of the large number of variables on which human motion depends, social process is an irreversible process.

Corollary 1—Once the state of equilibrium has been reached by a closed system composed of particles having a high degree of freedom, the system will change of phase, but usually not of state (Pareto's law: Change is illusory; circulation of the elites [cf. the static cultures of the populations of Cape York, Kesar Island and Pitcairn Island]).

Corollary 2—When particles or energy, or both, are added to a system, the equilibrium is disrupted and the system *slowly* proceeds toward another state of equilibrium of a higher degree of stability. When particles or energy or both are extracted from the system, the equilibrium is disrupted and the system *rapidly* proceeds toward a state of equilibrium of a lesser degree of stability.

The stability of a state of equilibrium (its relative probability) depends on the number of particles involved. A system composed of six particles will more often be found in a 3:3 distribution than a system composed of four particles will be found in a 2:2 distribution.

Examples: Immigration, sudden industrialization, etc. Depopulation, economic crisis, failure of crops. Both sets of events disrupt the existing social equilibrium and cause societies to find a new equilibrium.

Corollary 3—The degree of stability of an equilibrium may be greater or smaller than, or equal to, that of one or more other states of equilibrium which the same system may possess under other conditions. A system is in an unstable equilibrium when the least change causes it to proceed toward a state of equilibrium of a higher degree of stability. Consider the first and the second halves of the reign of Louis XIV.

Corollary 4—By multiplying the specifications of what constitutes an equilibrium, it is possible to consider that no system is in equilibrium at any time in all its parts or with respect to all processes which occur within it.

Durkheim's law: The degree of polysegmentation of a given society is the measure of its capacity to change (progress); compare the threefold segmentation of the Ancien Régime (three estates) to the polysegmentation of the Third, Fourth or Fifth Republic.

Corollary 5—From the knowledge and observation of any given phase it is impossible to infer the nature of the phases through which the observed phase has been reached.

Reformulation of Durkheim's law: It is impossible, from

the knowledge of an event, to infer by induction or deduction the nature of the preceding event. It is impossible therefore to reconstruct *statistically* the unwritten culture history of a group, or of a culture area, only whose present state is known.

Corollary 6—From the knowledge of the present event it is impossible to make anything but gross predictions concerning the next event or future events in general. (Compare insurance rates for individuals and for groups.)

Corollaries 5 and 6 can be blended as follows:

Theorem II—The path of a system is not uniquely determined until the system has already covered the path.

Expressed mathematically, the path of a society is neither analyzable a priori nor reconstructible a posteriori by means of differential equations or of equations reducible to differential equations. This view fits, I think, Volterra's (*40*) and Donnan's (*13*) integro-differential analysis of life phenomena, which will be mentioned later on.

Two hypotheses have been implicitly introduced in the preceding discussion. Neither of them has been completely validated by logic. Both have been found useful.

The theory of ensembles has been made fruitful by Gibbs. According to Tolman, we do not really discuss the "behavior of a single system, but rather the behavior of a *collection* of systems, containing an enormous number of sample systems identical in nature with the one of interest" (*39*, p. 39).

The ergodic hypothesis (principle of continuity of path) means, according to Tolman, that "we shall have to assume that the results obtained by selecting a collection of systems at random from such an ensemble are practically the same as would be obtained by considering the given system at random times" (*39*, p. 39). (See also Ch. 3).

Two invalid objections and one valid objection may be raised against this analysis. It will be objected that the behavior of molecules can be described in terms of three generalized coordinates and three momenta, while the individual apparently possesses a large number of degrees of freedom. It should be remembered, however, that in statistical mechanics all demonstrations are made with respect to particles of n degrees of freedom. As Lewis (*24*, p. 157 and passim) has pointed out, nowhere is the irreversibility of processes more obvious than in the destruction of living matter and the works of man. The fact that individuals have a large number of degrees of freedom makes the validity of my considerations highly probable. It may be objected that I do not measure but count—but "counting" is also a general character of modern geometry. Last of all, one may stress that certain recurrent regularities in individual processes apparently exceed our mathematical expectations based on the study of molecules. These regularities are usually explained in terms of "structure" or "heredity," "culture" or "tradition," etc. As a matter of fact, these entities appear to lie at the root of the absolutistic metaphysical conception of "society." This makes it doubly necessary to explain these structures in terms of sense data obtained through the observation of individuals.

At this point of my argumentation, I wish to analyze, at least briefly, the problem of time, and especially the problem of social time, for a confusion between metaphysical "absolute time" (in the Newtonian sense) and "physical time" underlies the distinction Sorokin and Merton (*38*) draw between "social time" and "physical time." Leibniz, who holds that Newtonian time is but an ideal possibility, correctly defines time as the order of succession of events. Time does not exist apart from events. As noted, W. S. Franklin (*15*) has shown that we are aware of time only because of certain unidirectional processes which take place in the whole universe, in accordance with the second law of thermodynamics.

Sorokin and Merton have shown that social time is not synchronous with physical time and perhaps not even ratable in Richmond's sense (*33*), but this does not imply that they differ in nature.

We cannot measure time—or space. We can only measure the "distance" between two events or two bodies, respectively. The fundamental concept of the measuring processes is that of *equality*; in the case under consideration, the equality of intervals between events. I will neglect here the relativistic interpretation of simultaneity and will concern myself only with the problem of the equality of the duration of two successive events.

Consider a clock which is being photographed by a motion picture camera, between 1:00 P.M. and 1:10 P.M. Let the finished film be then projected on the face of the clock, the hands of the clock having been set back to 1:00 P.M. If the film is projected at the proper speed, the image of the hands will at every instant fall exactly on the actual hands of the clock. If the film is projected in slow motion, the image of the hands will trail behind the actual hands of the clock. Thus, by the real clock, which I have arbitrarily chosen as a standard, the other (photographic) clock is slow. Vice versa, if the slow-motion projection of the film is selected as the standard, the actual clock is fast. These are mutually independent clocks. But there is no clock running independently of the rate at which the universe runs down. Hence one has no means of observing any acceleration or deceleration in the rate at which the universe runs down. It is therefore only by hypothesis and definition that two seconds, two days, or two years have an equal duration, just as it is by hypothesis and definition that in non-relativistic physics one assumes that a standard measuring rod does not change its length when transported from New York to Newark. One states that a lapse of time from t_0 to t' is equal to any other lapse of time from t' to t'' if roughly the same number and type of events take place during both intervals.

If roughly the same type and amount of social change takes place between two presidential elections or two coronations, one is entitled, *in sociology*, to consider them as equal intervals.[2] It may not be possible to synchronize this social clock with any physical clock which is "regular" —although Milne (27), for instance, has shown that one can build up a theory of relativity with irregular clocks (which may, if one wishes, be synchronized with such social clocks). The choice of units for measuring time is a matter of pure convenience.

Social dates are significant, as Sorokin and Merton have shown. So are physical dates. A significant event is simply one emerging from its context with distinctness (to the human mind), even if it is not distinct in any way in nature itself. One reckons the year from New Year's Day, and the oscillations of the pendulum from an extreme lateral or from the vertical position, but these are matters of convenience.

Two social time systems are not necessarily synchronous. Similarly, it is possible to construct two physical clocks which are not mutually ratable. Hutton Webster's (41) study of intervals between market days can be paralleled by thermodynamic clocks. Consider two containers of one litre each, one filled with water at 5° C, and the other at 70° C. Drop in each container five grams of salt. The two "clocks" start. They stop when all the salt is dissolved. Obviously, the hot water dissolves the salt faster than does the cold water. Here one has two thermodynamic clocks which are not synchronous (in the usual sense), although the same type and number of events take place in each of them. Instead of selecting different temperatures, one may select liquids of different viscosities, containers of different sizes, etc. If one measures thermodynamic time by the percentage of salt dissolved, one will have an analogy to social time, though neither of the clocks may tally with the astronomic clock. The basic difficulty of synchronizing social

2. I show elsewhere (9) that all battlefields on which Christendom and Islam affronted each other in the course of history constitute, when taken as a whole, a spatially conceived Jordan curve.

and physical time is due to the fact that the first is measured
—figuratively speaking—by a thermodynamic clock (statis-
tical-mechanics or irreversible-process clock) and the other
by a mechanical clock (reversible-process clock).

The unexpected fact that it is not possible to postulate a
fundamental difference between social and physical time
adds rather than detracts from the value of Sorokin and
Merton's researches for a unification of the sciences.

Having elucidated those aspects of time which are of
interest in the present context, I now pass from kinetics to
statics, by eliminating motion and time. It is known since
Faraday, Lord Kelvin and Maxwell that statics is a branch
of kinetics and not vice versa.

Peirce (*30*) comes as near as possible to asserting that
chance is a metaphysical reality. This would transform the
calculus of probability into the epistemological branch of
the philosophy of chance. I dissent from this view. No one
knows whether chance "exists," for chance is not observable. Hence, I nowhere introduce chance, either as a concept
or as a hypothesis. I state only that one observes a number
of events which one does not know how to analyze in detail.
As far as the present analysis is concerned, the whole world
cound function with the precision of a clock, provided one
agrees that one knows nothing about the mechanism of the
clock. Speculations on the nature of chance, or on the existence or nonexistence of chance, are neither germane to my
discussion nor the proper subject matter of scientific discourse.

Science makes an "arbitrary" classification of sense data
according to similarities which are thought to be "significant" for no better reason than that they are convenient.
Statistics enumerates the recurrence (the number) of sense
data in each of the arbitrary classes. The calculus of probability compares the number of recurrent sense data of one
class to the number of recurrent sense data in another class
and then assigns relative probability coefficients to each of
the two classes of sense data. If one changes the system of
classification, one changes the coefficients of probability of

each class. This is simply a modification of Mach's principle of variations.

Consider a hypothetical example: Assume that there are as many people in New York City as there are in the rest of New York State. The probability of finding John Doe in New York City is equal to the probability of finding him at any other place within the state. One can say: "New York City equals the rest of New York State." In what way? In population. It is possible to construct a perfectly valid and coherent "geometry" in which the volume (or area) of New York City is equal to the volume (or area) of the rest of the state. If one has constructed such a system or geometry, one can say that the density of individuals is the same per unit-volume throughout New York State (including New York City). This is meant when one says: "The density of population in New York State (including New York City) is x persons per square mile." One thus dispenses with "force" in accounting for any empirically nonhomogeneous distribution.

If one keeps the volume constant, one assigns various coefficients of probability to various elements of volume (or area). It is not necessary to go into the causes of these differences. One assigns the coefficients statistically a posteriori, or expresses one's mathematical expectations a priori. Only in the latter case must one consider causes (or forces). Thus one can say: "In a fertile country like Hungary, the probability of finding individual A living in the city is x, while the probability of finding him living on the land is, let us say, $3x$." In mountainous Switzerland or industrial Cook County the probability would perhaps be $4x$ against x. These coefficients may be calculated from statistical data (census).

Summing up, if people move at random, only activated and oriented by the special structure of their environment, their motions can still be accounted for exclusively in terms of statistical mechanics and the calculus of probabilities. It suffices to assign various coefficients of probability to various elements of space. The same proposition can be stated inversely, in terms of the number of individuals.

Given John Doe, what is the probability of his being at a given time within an area of a hundred square yards, a square mile, the state of Texas, the United States, North America, etc.?

This, I think, is the analysis, in terms of probability and statistical mechanics, of the purely environmentalist theory of behavior.

Consider now the theory that society or culture or tradition is an emergent. One must derive social structure from individual data and individual relations only. This can be done in several ways, proving once more Poincaré's contention (*31*) that if a phenomenon admits of one mechanical explanation it admits also of a number of others which are equally satisfactory.

1. *Method of the Least Path:* Consider three men on the sidewalk in front of a house. The first is the owner of the house; the second, the butler; the third, the burglar. Which is, for each of them, the least path (the easiest, the least risky) to the dining room, where the silver is kept? For the owner it is through the front door; for the butler, through the service entrance; for the burglar, through the second-story window, via the elm tree. The "least path" is here the path of least resistance. One can even say that social space is "curved" in a different way for each of them. Or else, one may say, with Weyl, that in a very general geometry the path of displacement will influence the "shape" of the displaced figure. One can link either explanation with probability. As a rule, the burglar enters by the window. What is the probability of finding him at (*a*) the window, (*b*) the service entrance, (*c*) the front door? The application of the "free-path method" to sociology was first attempted by J. F. Brown (*5*).

2. *Method of Transformations:* One specifies for each group in geometry what characteristics of the figure are to remain unchanged (invariant) in a given set of transformations. In the same way one can consider society as a special type of group, wherein all transformations maintain certain characteristics invariant. (The word "group" is used here in

its mathematical sense.) Thus, one can say: "The Constitution of the United States is the invariant characteristics of all statutes," or: "In whatever way an American changes, he may not have more than one wife at the same time."

3. *Quantum-Mechanical Method:* Consider a burglar. He is burgling the house which is within the beat of Officer Donovan. The law covers the whole beat uniformly. Officer Donovan may, however, be found in any place at the time when the burglar makes his unlawful entry. Consider, within the officer's beat, the unit of volume called "shouting distance." The center of it is the house which is being burglarized. Let this element of volume be 1/10 of the whole beat. The burglar does not know where Officer Donovan is at time t. He bets 10:1 that he is not within the element of volume, "shouting distance," at time t. It will be objected that the law is everywhere. But as long as Officer Donovan is not within shouting distance, one can measure only the force, the impulse of the law—its moral restraint. This moral restraint is—or can be operationally defined as—a function of the 10:1 bet and its influence upon the burglar's "better self"—upon his Ego Ideal or Superego. One may say: "Officer Donovan is *distributed along the law.*" When Officer Donovan is absent, one can measure the moral force of the law. When he is present one can measure only the struggle between the officer and the burglar. Hence the problem, "Are there moral values independent of sanctions?" is meaningless. Between moral values and sanctions there exists an uncertainty or complementarity relation, similar to Heisenberg's principle of indeterminacy, which forms the basis of Bohr's (2) theory of complementarity. When one member of a pair of complementary entities is present and measurable, the other is not, or just barely.

It may be objected that in all these cases I have taken custom and society for granted and have therefore made nonpredicative statements. That is true. I have done so for reasons of expository simplicity. I must now *construct* the social field inductively, from individual data only.

According to Mach, the metrical properties of space are
determined by the presence of bodies having mass. Gravitational fields do not exist without bodies being present. Is
there a gravitational field when only one body is present?
The question is meaningless, for one cannot answer it operationally. Hence I start with two bodies. Consider two
bodies, whose respective masses are M_1 and M_2. A mutual
attraction exists between the two. Let d be the distance and
G the gravitational constant. The two bodies "pull" together, according to the formula GM_1M_2/d^2. The acceleration (force) is GM_1/d^2 (pull of M_1) per unit mass. If the mass
of the "directing" body is very large, this suffices to explain
the "directed" motion of other bodies. To this it will be
objected that a hundred-and-forty-pound dictator rules
(directs) a huge populace. I therefore introduce here the
operationally definable, conventional concept "social
mass." A slim millionaire has a greater social mass than a
penniless pugilist; a pretty but poor girl, a greater social
mass than a wealthy frump. One can establish standards and
measure these social masses. These gravitational theories of
society tally with my earlier remarks on the nature of gravitational fields in general. Social mass does not exist without
two bodies being present. Consider the social mass of a
millionaire on Wall Street and compare it to the social mass
he would have were he suddenly alone with his millions in
the Sahara. In the latter case he would have no social mass,
for, in the absence of a second social mass (body), he and
his wealth could not generate a social field.

It may now be objected that I have introduced social force
into my discourse. I can eliminate this force easily. Maxwell
stated that we are able to express physical processes in
mathematical formulas because the laws of bodies *happen*
to parallel the laws of numbers. I will therefore now attach
a system of coordinates to every individual. One need not
puzzle how one can attach coordinates to individuals. One
does so every day when one plots learning curves, growth

curves, etc. In daily practice one assumes that learning has a dimension and can be assigned a Cartesian coordinate. Consider two individuals. The formulas describing the properties of the gravitational field parallel closely the formulas for the transformation of the individual coordinates. Einstein stated that gravitational fields result (symbolically) from the transformation of coordinate systems. Instead of saying, "Body X attracts body Y," he says, "By transforming a system of coordinates one obtains a space so curved that the least path for body Y will be the one passing near body X." In the same (purely symbolic) way a social gravitational field can result from the transformation of all individual coordinates of a group of people. This field will then direct and restrict the motions of the individual and can be called "custom" or "morals." If one does not wish to use the concept of force, one may say that the social field is "curved" (theory of the least path; cf. the expression "keeping to the right side of someone"). One can give custom a Rousseauan contrat social meaning by resorting to the theory of quantum mechanics, which states that the law is everywhere, but also that the representatives of law "are distributed along the law" (cf. the popular expression "the law" = policemen). This group theory is implicit in the gravitational field theory, which is based on the theory of groups in mathematics. Any transformation belonging to a group shares certain invariant characteristics with other members of that group. All members of a society share the invariant characteristic "obedience to law."[3] When one no longer possesses it, one ceases to be a member of the body social (group): one is incarcerated, deported, exiled or killed. In geometry, this simply means that, having lost his invariant characteristic, that person is no longer a member of the given (selected) group of transformations.

3. It is hardly necessary to stress that an *intentional* violation of a law implies not only an awareness of the existence of that law, but also a (negativistic) orientation of behavior with respect to Law (*10*, Ch. 3).

This theory may shock certain readers.[4] Yet Leibniz, the father of topology, suggested (in his correspondence) that topology (the science of point-to-point transformations) is especially applicable to the study of living beings. According to Pareto (*29*), the great mathematician Volterra was puzzled by the reluctance of sociologists to operate with formally conceived individuals, like *Homo oeconomicus*, who have no real counterpart in nature. Yet theoretical mechanics operates with ideal rigid bodies, having likewise no counterpart in nature. In the same sense, one need not imagine men with *concrete* coordinate systems attached to their bodies. I say only that one can account for human customs and traditions, as well as for the motion of material particles in gravitational fields, by this methodological artifice. In short, I did not state concrete facts. I only proposed a new method of inquiry and of representation.

Let me now extend this field concept to social process and show its implications. What are the implications of the conceptual scheme: "Society is the order of individuals in a structured space"? To answer this query, one must return to the concept of equilibrium. I have shown that it is always possible to imagine at least one process with respect to which *no* system is in equilibrium, even though it is in equilibrium in all other respects.

The meaning of these considerations can be laid down in a general theorem, which is, implicitly, also a definition both of social process and of stability and tradition.

THEOREM III—A society will, when external forces are applied to it, tend to maintain its structure. It can do so only by modifying certain other of its characteristics. The less rigid the structure, the smaller the changes in the other characteristics. If its structure is very rigid, no modification it can make will suffice to maintain it when large forces impinge on it.

---

4.   [*Addendum 1966:* This prediction, made in 1938, did not come true. My opinions shocked no one, for no one paid any attention to them.]

Example: In a war, a nation loses many of its citizens, puts itself on a war basis, etc., in the hope of maintaining invariant its structural identity. If the structure is very rigid, the changes to be made are small if the external forces are not very large. A war with Luxembourg would cause less upheaval in a totalitarian state than it would in a democracy. If, on the other hand, the structure is very rigid and the forces operating on it are very large, the structure will break down from lack of adaptability. Compare the breakdown of the rigid Pawnee culture and the continuous easy adjustment of the flexible Comanche culture after the establishment of American rule. Compare also the well-known fact that, as a rule, democracies easily survive defeat, while dictatorships survive only on victories.

This concept can further be linked with the theory of hysteresis in physics, which, with certain modifications, has recently penetrated also certain areas of biological thought. The magnetization of a bar of iron is interpreted as a rearranging of minute magnets in a new pattern. A brisk shock will once more disarrange this pattern and "jam" the small magnets. During these operations, as well as during the process of remagnetization, a certain lag (hysteresis) may be detected. Similar social lags are familiar to everyone (Example: "The Bourbons have learned nothing and have forgotten nothing").

A few words should be said with respect to the mathematical treatment of hereditary or historic systems. Volterra (*40*) and Donnan (*13*) have suggested that they should be described in integro-differential equations instead of in mere differential equations. Schrödinger—cited by Donnan (*13*)—further specifies that these equations should not be reducible to differential equations by any amount of differentiations, since that would imply a "one-point memory." I add, for my part, that these equations must use statistical macroparameters. These approaches have been found useful in the study of evolution, conditioning and heredity in biology and in population studies. This makes it likely that until statistical hereditary mechanics are evolved it will be impossible to use mathematical formulas in the exact socio-logical analysis of social *processes*. This suffices to show that it is emphatically not my intention to suggest that the formulas of statistical mechanics as such be taken over into sociology. The illusion of precision is fatal to science.

I have simply suggested that it is possible to construct a conceptual scheme of society based upon three concepts only, all of which are derived from sense data and are opera-tionally definable. I have shown that one can profit even by one's ignorance (9) by using the reasoning processes— though not, for the time being, the formulas—or statistical mechanics and of the calculus of probabilities.

Social theory may be compared to the investigation of the "metrical" properties of social space. Many social theories exist, and, provided that they are coherent, all of them are valid. I recall once more that, according to Poincaré (31), if a phenomenon admits of a mechanical explanation, it will admit of an infinity of others which will account equally well for all the peculiarities disclosed by experiment. I have not proposed a social theory. Rather have I tried to elucidate the nature of some of the fundamental hypotheses of soci-ology and also attempted to define the subject matter of sociological discourse. My studies no more contradict any imaginable coherent social theory than Riemann's geo-metry contradicts those of Euclid, Bólyai or Lobachevski— or vice versa. It does contain, however, other social theories as "limiting cases."

The scope of a truly scientific sociology is best expressed in the words of a great mathematical physicist, R. C. Tolman:

"Inspite the impossibility of precise observation and pre-diction, . . . [the sociologists] have not been deterred from [their] labors. . . . Even if they can not follow or predict the *exact* behavior of individual elements, they can observe and predict with remarkable surety the *gross* behavior of their systems as a whole. . . . Each time there is a war, the sociologist can predict that rich men will profiteer and poor men die. These complicated phenomena do not lie beyond the realm of law and predictability" (*39*, p. 17).

In conclusion, it should be stated that the fact that I used physical examples and laws to formulate social laws must not be construed to imply that sociology is a branch of physics. The whole problem of hierarchy—the question of which field is the general case and which is the special case —is not touched upon in this study, if for no other reason than because my conclusions would startle some social scientists, although they would probably be deemed self-evident by most thinking physicists. This problem is, more-over, too involved to be discussed in this study. Everyone is therefore free to assume that I have discussed social laws in terms of physical laws only in order to save space and to avoid ambiguities due to the penumbras surrounding most sociological concepts and terms.

Résumé

Society is not an emergent. It is introduced into sociological discourse by subjecting sets of sense data pertaining to in-dividuals to logical analysis in terms of the basic concepts of probability and of statistical mechanics. Sociology needs only three operationally definable basic concepts: "in-dividual," "order," and "motion." Social equilibrium is defined with respect to social mobility. Units of social space and the concept of social mass were defined and some basic theorems of social process enunciated. It was shown that, after an external disturbance, society cannot return to its previous state, but only to a related one, since society is a hereditary system. Culture was defined in terms of the principle of the least path, of groups of transformation, and of the Heisenberg-Bohr uncertainty principle. It was shown that social space has certain properties of a curved space. Statistical and other formulas are almost useless in an analysis of social *process*, since they are incapable of describing hereditary processes which are statistical rather than mechanical. The logico-meaningful procedures of scientific method must be applied in, and adapted to the purposes of, systematic sociology.[5]

Bibliography

(*1*) Blum, H. F.: A Consideration of Evolution from a Thermodynamic View-Point, *American Naturalist*, 69:354–369, 1935.

(*2*) Bohr, Niels: Causality and Complementarity, *Philosophy of Science*, 4:289–298, 1937.

(*3*) Boltzmann, Ludwig: *Vorlesungen über Gastheorie*, 2nd ed., Leipzig, 1910.

(*4*) Bridgman, P. W.: *The Logic of Modern Physics*, New York, 1927.

(*5*) Brown, J. F.: *Psychology and the Social Order*, New York, 1936.

(*6*) Cannon, W. B.: *The Wisdom of the Body*, New York, 1939.

(*7*) Carnap, Rudolf: Die logizistische Grundlegung der Mathematik, *Erkenntnis*, 2 (Nos. 2–3), 1931.

(*8*) Devereux, George: Extrasensory Perception and Psychoanalytic Epistemology (in) Devereux, G. (ed.), *Psychoanalysis and the Occult*, New York, 1953, 1970.

(*9*) Idem: *From Anxiety to Method in the Behavioral Sciences*, Paris and The Hague, 1967.

(*10*) Idem: *Essais d'Ethnopsychiatrie Générale*, Paris, 1970, 1972, 1977.

(*11*) Donnan, F. G.: Activities of Life and the Second Law of Thermodynamics, *Nature*, 133:99, 1934.

(*12*) Donnan, F. G., and Guggenheim, E. A.: Activities of Life and the Second Law of Thermodynamics, *Nature*, 133:530, 869; 134:255, 1934.

(*13*) Idem: Integral Analysis and the Phenomena of Life, *Acta Biotheoretica*, Serie A, 2:1–11, 1936; 3:43–50, 1937.

(*14*) Ehrenberg, Rudolf: *Theoretische Biologie, vom Standpunkte der Irreversibilität des elementaren Lebensablaufs*, Berlin, 1923.

(*15*) Franklin, W. S.: On Entropy, *Physical Review*, 30:766–775, 1910.

(*16*) Henderson, L. J.: *Pareto's General Sociology: A Physiologist's Interpretation*, Cambridge, Mass., 1935.

(*17*) Jeans, Sir James: Activities of Life and the Second Law of Thermodynamics, *Nature*, 133:174, 612, 986, 1934 (cf. *12*, *13*).

5. Professors L. B. Loeb and V. F. Lenzen, of the Department of Physics of the University of California at Berkeley, were kind enough to provide advice and criticism. I also derived profit from an exchange of letters with Professor F. G. Donnan, of the University of London. Without the help of these scientists the precise formulation of a certain number of problems would probably have been impossible.

(*18*) Jordan, Pascual: Quantenphysikalische Bemerkungen zur Biologie und Psychologie, *Erkenntnis*, 4:215–252, 1934; idem: Ergänzende Bemerkungen über Biologie und Quantenmechanik, *Erkenntnis*, 5:348–352, 1935.

(*19*) Idem: *Anschauliche Quantentheorie*, Berlin, 1936.

(*20*) Lenzen, V. F.: Statistical Truth in Physical Science, *University of California Publications in Philosophy*, 10:119–140, 1928.

(*21*) Idem: The Nature of Geometrical Relations, *University of California Publications in Philosophy*, 13:101–123, Berkeley, Calif., 1930.

(*22*) Idem: *The Nature of Physical Theory*, New York, 1931.

(*23*) Lewin, Kurt: *Principles of Topological Psychology*, New York, 1936.

(*24*) Lewis, G. N.: *The Anatomy of Science*, New Haven, 1926.

(*25*) Linton, Ralph: *The Study of Man*, New York, 1936.

(*26*) Meyerson, Emile: *De l'Explication dans les Sciences*, Paris, 1921.

(*27*) Milne, A. E.: Some Points in the Philosophy of Physics: Time, Evolution and Creation, *Smithsonian Report for 1933*, pp. 219–238, 1935.

(*28*) Neurath, Otto: *Empirische Soziologie,* Vienna, 1931 (cf. idem: Soziologie im Physikalismus, *Erkenntnis*, 2:293–341, 1931).

(*29*) Pareto, Vilfredo: Anwendungen der Mathematik auf die Nationaloekonomie (in) *Encyclopaedie der Mathematischen Wissenschaften*, 1 (No. 2):1094–1120, 1904.

(*30*) Pierce, C. S.: *Chance, Love and Logic*, New York, 1923.

(*31*) Poincaré, Henri: *Electricité et Optique*, Paris, 1901.

(*32*) Rhine, J. B. et al.: *Extra-Sensory Perception After Sixty Years*, New York, 1940.

(*33*) Richmond, C. A.: The Measurement of Time: A First Chapter of Physics, *Philosophy of Science*, 4:173–201, 1937.

(*34*) Rougier, Louis: *La Philosophie Géométrique de Henri Poincaré*, Paris, 1920.

(*35*) Schrödinger, Erwin: *Science and the Human Temperament*, New York, 1935.

(*36*) Sorokin, P. A.: *Social Mobility*, New York, 1927.

(*37*) Idem: Le Concept d'Equilibre est-il Nécessaire aux Sciences Sociales? *Revue Internationale de Sociologie*, 44:497–529, 1936.

(*38*) Idem and Merton, R. K.: Social Time: A Methodological and Functional Analysis, *American Journal of Sociology*, 42:615–629, 1937.

(*39*) Tolman, R. C.: *Statistical Mechanics*, New York, 1927.

(*40*) Volterra, Vito: Principes de Biologie Mathématique, *Acta Biotheoretica*, 3:1–36, 1937.

(*41*) Webster, Hutton: *Rest Days*, New York, 1916.

(*42*) Weyl, Hermann: *Was ist Materie?* Berlin, 1924.

(*43*) White, W. A.: Psychiatry and the Social Sciences, *American Journal of Psychiatry*, 7:729–747, 1928.

2

Inside and Outside:

The Nature of Stress (1966)

SEEN in a purely historical manner, the socio-cultural fact is of external origin and part of the "outside." It is therefore able, in this very circumscribed sense, to elicit a stress, to initiate a dialogue between the Self and the Others, between the "inside" and the "outside," in the same sense in which this can be done by a coconut which falls on one's head and bruises or smashes it.

However, as soon as one abandons this historical—and simplistic—conception of things and proceeds to a functional analysis, the "cultural fact" ceases being outside. Transformed into psychical material or structure, into Superego, Ego Ideal and Ego—in short into a thing learned, produced or constructed—it is internal: it is inside. Thus, I indicated a quarter of a century ago (see Ch. 1) that it is impossible to attribute an operational meaning to the Superego, which forbids theft, as long as a policeman is present, just as it is impossible to attribute an operational meaning to the policeman (social agent) whenever he is absent— except perhaps in the sense of a calculation of the probability of his appearing on the scene while a theft is taking place. In a strictly sociological sense—within the framework of a "pure" sociological explanation—the Superego can momentarily be treated as the product of an appraisal of the probability that the policeman will materialize at the right moment, permitting him to arrest the thief or to prevent the theft. For the weak Superego this probability is very slight; for a strong Superego this probability is great.[1] I stress again that I am speaking here in a purely sociological manner; within the framework of psychological explanations I define the Superego in the sense which Freud ascribed to it. Nonetheless, I stress that the Superego is specifically the residue, the precipitate, of all experiences which, at the time these experiences occurred, the child was unable to master by means of its own resources (4).

This manner of considering matters creates a theoretical problem: that of the relations between the individual and his environment—his ecological milieu. These relations always express themselves by means of a stress of variable amplitude; this leads in a straight line to the fundamental problem of the distinction between what is inside and outside, between that which is "person" and that which is "environment." This distinction seems simple, but is not, precisely because of the kind of problem with which the external origin of the subsequently internalized Superego confronts us.

In topology it is easy to draw a closed curve—called a "Jordan curve"—and to say afterwards: This is inside the curve, that is outside it; everything which is not inside the curve is outside it and vice versa. This operation is infinitely more difficult in the human sciences, chiefly because, at every moment, the person is "subject" to himself and "environment" to the Others; all that is inside for the subject is outside for the Other. In addition, in order to become a social being, one must learn to view oneself as being, in certain respects and above all with respect to the Others, as

1. In order to simplify the problem I do not take account here of the sadistic Superego which sometimes urges on the criminal to commit a crime in order to be punished for it. I note, however, that I have described the psychopathic personality (character disorder) as one which is tyrannized not by the instincts—by the Id—but by the Superego (6, Ch. 7).

outside—*as the milieu of the Other*. In fine, I have proven elsewhere that one can envisage the (non-psychoanalytic) "I" as *being* a frontier and not as *having* a frontier between the inside and the outside, and that this frontier is mobile at each instant. A thing which at instant t_0 is inside may, at the instant $t_0 + \Delta t$, be outside (5). Similarly, that which was formerly outside can, later on, be inside. That which at the moment when it is perceived was outside, and therefore "environment," is later on "souvenir"—that is, inside— and functions thereafter as an "inside," since, as Donnan (7) indicates, the living being is a chronoholistic system, whose behavior (or state) at time t_0 does not permit the prediction of his behavior or state at time $t_0 + \Delta t$. In order to predict that, one must know all of its history (7).[2]

I note, in conclusion, that the very fact that the subject knows that he is part of the outside—of the "environment"—of the others is a constituent element of the subject's inside. It is thus easy to see why it is so difficult to draw Jordan curves in the sciences of Man. I can dispense here with the analysis of this problem, having examined it with all the necessary precision elsewhere (5).

Now, from the medical, and above all from the psychosomatic, point of view, the problem of the inside and of the outside is directly linked with the problem of the "endogenous" and of the "exogenous." I must therefore stress from the start the fundamental difference between the pathological consequences of the direct impact of the "charge"— of the "load"—upon the person and the pathological effects of the organism's reaction to this impact or stress. I must examine very carefully the G.A.S. (General Adaptation Syndrome) and also the other extreme reactions of the organism to an exogenous impact which, objectively, is minimal, as is minimal, for example, the quantity of matter which produces a fatal anaphylactic (allergic) shock, or as

2.   Which, mathematically, means that one can describe an organism only by means of integro-differential equations of a type which cannot by means of differentiation be reduced to simple differential equations.

are minimal the few quanta of light which can trigger a flight reaction in a hunted man. This capacity of the organism to amplify enormously the impact of objectively minimal forces is, according to Niels Bohr (*1*) and Pascual Jordan (*10*, *11*),[3] a basic characteristic of every state of life.

I have held, ever since 1931, that the problem of the exogenous and the endogenous is susceptible of being formulated in almost mathematical terms. In the simplest cases one can speak of an endogenous pathology whenever a minimal modification (or impact) of the environment triggers radical upheavals in the organism which, because of its own characteristics, tends to amplify this type of modification. Consider the case of a virtuoso who loses a finger joint. The greatness of his reaction—which constitutes precisely its pathology—is determined by endogenous factors: by his selective sensitiveness to this particular kind of stress—a sensitiveness comparable to that of an allergic person.

I have specified elsewhere (*6*, Ch. 1) that in psychiatry, as in medicine, the notion of trauma must be defined not, as is usually done, in terms of the objective intensity of the impact but in terms of the defenses of which the "traumatized" person disposes, defenses which enable him to cope with a stress of external origin—i.e., enable him to dis-amplify (to reduce) its effects. The fact that the rays of the sun kill lice—traumatize them fatally—has a meaning only if one considers it in conjunction with the fact that these rays do not kill man. It is only when the organism lacks the means of dis-amplifying (muting) the impact of a force that a genuine trauma can occur.

Now, paradoxically, even this capacity to dis-amplify impacts (which, in principle, are harmful) can, in certain respects, be envisaged as being of external origin. Smallpox killed countless American Indians, who had no resistance against this virus. However, resistance to smallpox—the

3. One should not confuse Pascual Jordan with the inventor of the Jordan curve.

capacity of *not* being killed by it, hence the capacity to dis-
amplify its impact—is, it would seem, due to a resistance
which, at least in part, is inherited from ancestors who have
had smallpox. As regards our own resistance to—our im-
munity at least to the fatal effects of—smallpox, is it external
or internal? In the same sense, how should one view certain
seemingly endogenous vulnerabilities? It is well known that
dogs are much more susceptible to the toxic effects of
strychnine than are rats. I even seem to remember that morphine puts dogs to sleep but excites cats. If this is so, we are
dealing with differences in the effects the same drug has on
various species.

I therefore define as endogenous also conditions in which
a trifling spontaneous change, occurring in the organism,
produces a considerable change in the environment. This
happens almost exclusively when a slight initial change was
already pre-amplified by the organism itself. This hypothesis
can be easily linked with the chronoholistic conception of
the organism, for the totality of the (often exogenous) experiences of its past can produce cumulative vulnerabilities
in it. In the first approximation, one deals here with a process comparable to that which permits the last drop of water
to cause a vessel to run over—needless to say, in the proverbial sense. In such a case all the phenomena of habitu-
ation intervene. One can think in this context also of the
kind of process made evident by the therapeutic administration of strychnine. Too little strychnine has no therapeutic
efficacity. Too much strychnine kills. Between these two
extremes is located the so-called "manageable zone" (*zone
maniable*), which can be efficaciously exploited for therapeutic ends.

Phenomena of this kind manifest themselves also on the
psychical level: the drop that makes a vessel run over, the
few quanta of light which cause a tracked man to flee, function in this manner because of the significance which one
ascribes to them. It is not the extremely small energy of a
few quanta of light which sets in motion the body of a man

weighing 70 kilograms, it is the *sense* which he *attributes* to these quanta of light.

In the time dimension, one can thus speak of an accumulation which is possible only because an organism is a chronoholistic system. This accumulation can, in the end, attain a "critical mass." Ten times in a row the father tells his noisy child to be quiet; the eleventh time a slight additional noise triggers an explosion of rage in the parent. Though objectively small, the last noise triggers an important modification in an already sensitized subject, for the cumulative effect of noise has reached a critical mass. This triggering of a massive reaction can be explained only by means of the mobilization of the *residue* of a large number of earlier small impacts, which were internalized and acccumulated. Should one, in such cases, speak of exogenous stress or endogenous stress? This reaction—of the "last drop" or, better still, of the critical mass type—can, I think, be mathematically quantified by means of the method of the "Dedekind cut" (5), whose psycho-physical equivalent seems to be the Weber-Fechner law.[4]

Should this last drop—this sensitizing material added to the earlier accumulation—be situated inside or outside of the Jordan curve which separates the subject from his milieu? Since the reaction is great, I must—in accordance with my basic criteria—situate the cause of the stress inside the subject but consider that drop as exogenous. This notion is not in the least paradoxical since, in the last resort, it is the critical mass attained and not the last drop per se which causes the massive reaction.

This situation, which seems hopelessly complicated, can

4.   One can determine only approximately the "value" (magnitude) represented by the symbol $\sqrt{2}$, which is an irrational number. This is done by constructing two series: one begins with 1 and increases little by little; the other begins with 2 and slowly diminishes; $\sqrt{2}$ is located where these two series come closest to each other without, however, "touching" each other. As early as 1938, I suggested to a specialist of mathematical biophysics this mathematical method for the representation of the Weber-Fechner law.

fortunately be greatly simplified; in ecology it is sufficient to say that it is not indispensable to situate anything whatever, *definitively and forever*, either outside or inside. What matters, from both the theoretical and the practical point of view, is what happens when the last drop creates a critical mass.

I therefore propose the following solution: From the operational point of view, this drop plays the role which the cloture element plays in Gestalt psychology. It is this element which *organizes*, in a practically irreversible manner, the ensemble of significant and pertinent *previous* stimuli and attributes to them a stable meaning. In so doing, it co-ordinates them, thereby constituting a structure which is henceforth capable of being mobilized in its totality—qua structure—whereas previously it could only be mobilized in a fractional manner. The principal effect of this consolidation is precisely the capacity of an objectively minimal impact to set in motion a mass reaction which, according to my criteria, is an endogenous occurrence, even though it is, *in appearance*, triggered by this drop. Indeed, the great action potential of this drop dwells not in that drop itself but in the already accumulated material, which it organizes and saturates until a critical mass is attained. It will be shown subsequently that this chain reaction is logically linked with the phenomenon of amplification.

I hasten to add that such a consolidation can occur either in a beneficent or a harmful manner, i.e., depending on the manner in which that consolidation is brought about. A series of rhymes is not a poem; it is difficult to learn it by heart and impossible to appraise it qua (good or bad) "work of art," *before* these rhymes are attached to the ends of incomplete lines. Similarly, someone who has perfectly mastered the *prime*, the *tierce* and the *quarte*, but does not know the *seconde*, is not a good fencer, for he is vulnerable to attacks which call for a parry by means of the *seconde*. It is the mastery of the whole gamut of these parries which makes a good fencer.

What matters from the viewpoint of the magnitude of this reaction is, thus, not the simply additive—though perhaps delayed—manifestation of the countless earlier drops; what does matter is, precisely, the organization of these (previously isolated) drops into a structured "atomic pile" which, having attained a critical mass, is capable of producing and of maintaining a chain reaction.

One gains direct access to the domain of the behavorial sciences as soon as one asks whether this structuring occurs within the subject or pre-exists in the external world. As regards the noisy child, one may say—*grosso modo*—that this organization takes place within the parent. In other instances, this amplifying structure is socially and culturally pre-established. Man, as a being conditioned by his sociocultural milieu, reacts maximally to certain stimuli which, objectively, are minimal and sometimes even simply allusive or indirect.

One can think in the present context of the fact that a small object placed near a small lamp casts a big shadow on the wall. The magnitude of this shadow is determined by the entire structure. And yet, all that is really present at this moment is the "last drop"—the cloture element. Thus, reliable sources (*8, 12*) report that a single Mongol was able to terrify a whole Mohammedan village in Khwaresm simply because behind this lone Mongol one could sense the immense army of Genghis Khan's empire (*3*). He was the element that indicated, that *revealed*, the existence of the structure in its totality. The terrified Mohammedans therefore did not react to the (objectively minimal) mass of a single Mongol horseman, but to the enormous structure which he incarnated. In this case one can certainly speak of a pre-amplification taking place in the environment itself. One gets a glimpse of the same kind of pre-amplification in the commotion which the shout "Fire!" stirs up in a town built of wood. The Mongol horseman exploited this social pre-amplification of his mass exactly as a Malayan bandit-prince exploited the social pre-amplification of the exclama-

tion "Amok!"—a word he shouted in order to paralyze
with fright people in the gambling den which he wished to
plunder (2).

The role of our senses—of our organs of perception—is
simply that of bringing to us stimuli which are often
minimal. The role of the central nervous system is to sort
these stimuli in order to determine if that with which one is
dealing is exclusively *this* minimal "charge" or a great
massive structure of which this small charge is only an
element.

Let us suppose, for example, that the colonel of a regiment observes the approach of an enemy company. Though
he knows that a single company represents no immediate
danger for his regiment, he will seek to determine whether
this company is simply a reconnaissance force or the van-
guard of a general attack. Moreover, even if he decides that
these soldiers are only scouts, he will nonetheless understand that an enemy army which can afford to send out a
whole company on a mission of reconnaissance must be
infinitely more numerous than his regiment. Hence, that to
which the colonel will react will *not* be this small company,
but the *big* enemy *army* whose presence the great size of the
scouting party permits him to infer.

In such cases a minimal "charge" can provoke a very
great reaction, because it is socially pre-amplified—because
a single element conjures up the whole structure. It goes
without saying that in the majority of cases of this kind the
organism which perceives this isolated element must be *pre-
conditioned* to the total structure to which this element
belongs. It must be able to imagine the entire police force
behind a single policeman—which presupposes an adequate
manipulation of the notion of time and the capacity to
consider the future as "real."

This situation differs sufficiently from the model of the
last drop—from the model of the *internal* accumulation
which tends toward the structure capable of producing a
chain reaction—to justify treating pre-amplified and pre-

structured stimuli as exogenous. It is, in fact, precisely the tendency to neglect this difference which leads to certain, partly unjustifiable, affirmations according to which a minimal charge can trigger a considerable *stress reaction*.

Let me now pass to the exploration of total and segmental systemic reactions and begin by noting a paradoxical fact. The most rigidly structured organisms are also the most archaic ones. An amoeba always reacts totally; it is incapable of experiencing segmental upsets; its non-segmented reactions are biochemically structured and directed. By contrast, paradoxical as it may seem, the nervous system, which centralizes and structures our behavior was, originally, not in the service of unification but of segmental autonomies. Thus, when one stimulates one of the halves of a sea anemone (*coelenterata*) with blotting paper soaked in bouillon, one sooner or later "teaches" this half—*and only this half*—that blotting paper is not edible. The other half of that organism *does not profit from this lesson*. One must teach that lesson to it separately and by the same means. I readily admit that what occurs in such a case is not solely "learning" but also—and perhaps even chiefly—a nervous exhaustion of the stimulated half. But it seems to me that there are many forms of learning which can also be interpreted as exhaustion. In short, the networklike—non-axial —nervous system of the sea anemone permits one to teach something to one of its halves (chosen and defined arbitrarily, since this organism is round), without the other half being able to profit by it.

The appearance, the formation, of "systems" within the organism goes hand in hand with the appearance of an autonomous centralizing system superordinated to the behavior's biochemical unification, which, *at the start*, does not constitute a "system" within (inside) the organism. In primitive forms, each segment tends to have its own individual neural organization, as is the case with the earthworm. In simple organisms these subsystems are more independent of each other than they are in complicated organisms, which seems to explain two facts:

1. Simple organisms are capable of partially regenerating themselves, as lizards regenerate their tails.

2. Specialized tissues tend to become de-specialized when one makes them survive outside the organism. Thus, it is known that the chicken hearts which Carrel kept alive transformed themselves in the end into non-specialized connective tissue, pure and simple.

It would therefore seem that the specialization of tissues can be *maintained* (preserved) only *inside* a complex system.

It is only fairly late in the evolution of segmentary systems that their subsystems become fully coordinated. I recall here that certain great prehistoric reptiles had two "brains": one in the head and one at the root of the tail. It is only in fairly highly developed beings that the central nervous system plays a genuinely centralizing role, and it seems to play this role primarily because it constitutes, itself, a system within the total system. The role of the central system is no longer the resultant of the accumulation of parallel subcentralizations, examplified by the fact that each ring of the earthworm does approximately what the two rings between which it is located also do. In this sense, each segment of these primitive organisms is also a *bridge* between the segments which surround it. The fact is that the central nervous system *first* creates a center, and it does so in creating *itself*: the center is there where it is located.

Hence, it is more "natural," but also more archaic, for an organism to react totally rather than segmentally and to do so by biochemical means rather than by the means of the nervous system.

It is, no doubt, for this reason that when the organism is stimulated by a considerable charge, it manifests more affectivity than reasoning, more total motility of great amplitude (or a greater inhibition of motility) than diversified and *coordinated* partial reactions; hence, more non-discriminating than discriminating reactions. In fact, it is only when the charge has already been internalized, when the subject has already adapted himself to it and has already structured it internally—by attributing a "meaning" to it— that one observes either a rational and efficient behavior or else a truly psychiatric symptomatology. These two types of reactions—and, above all, the psychiatric symptoms—are, moreover, conjugated and coordinated with an infrastructure of fundamental and polysystemic organic reactions.

Within the framework of this theory, the finding of Hinkle and Wolff (9) that every period of tension between the being and its milieu produces also organic ailments and, specifically, illnesses which attack simultaneously several systems, was at once foreseeable and inevitable. If, in a situation of this kind, an illness caused by stress attacks only a single system, this means that the load was already subjected to a previous internal structuring. A monosystemic stress illness would therefore be a segmental reaction, which would imply that one had already attributed to the stress— at least unconsciously—a "meaning," for example a meaning which links it to such-and-such a system (digestive, circulatory, etc.) and hence, to some fundamental process of the organism. I mention here only in passing a case of inhibited and, incidentally, justifiable anger which involved the wish of the subject to see his foe die in a very particular manner. This aggressive wish could, despite a lack of any organic predisposition, trigger in the angry subject the very symptoms which he wished upon his foe, who *did* have a genuine organic predisposition for that kind of symptom.

It goes, moreover, without saying that an absolute segmentation of the illness, whatever it may be, is always fictitious, since whenever one of the systems is affected, the stability of the others is necessarily also affected. This destructive process usually unfolds itself specifically on an infra-neural, that is, biochemical, unifying level.

Another fact which deserves study is the margin of the organism's normal functioning, as well as its relation to the margin of safety of its reactions to the charge which it must endure. I mean by "margin of normal functioning," for

example, the fact that the beats of a normal heart can, even
without external stimuli, vary between such-and-such numbers per minute. I mean by "margin of safety," for example,
the limits between which the heartbeats can vary without
catastrophic results either in response to an internal charge
or in response to an external charge. A careful analysis of
these two types of margins would contribute a great deal to
the formulation of a better definition of stress.

Having advanced fairly bold hypotheses, I would like to
conclude with a statement of a methodological kind.

The terrain of medical ecology is situated neither within
nor outside the Jordan curve. The study of medical ecology
is thus comparable to the study of osmosis and even more
to that of quantic jumps. The real locus of the phenomena
which it should study is precisely this curve which "divides"
in theory, but "unifies" in practice, Man and his milieu. It
is the "I"—it is the events and processes whose *locus geometricus* is (and creates) this imaginary line of demarcation
(5)—which concerns the psychosomatician. What happens
entirely on the inner side of the line can be studied by the
physician; what happens on the other—external—side, by
the sociologist. In fact, I believe more and more that the
principal difference between the externalist and the internal-
ist is that the former says that the phenomena of interaction
are *produced on* this curve, whereas the latter says that it is
the perceived phenomena of interaction which *create*—and
are—this curve. The very variable events which *take place*
on this curve itself and which, in fact, *create* this curve are,
despite the exiguousness of the terrain, of the greatest importance. But after all, even though Athens is much smaller
than the Sahara, its historical importance was considerably
greater. A concern with the study of events located on this
curve—the study of events which, in one sense, create and
constitute this curve—would permit the psychosomatician
to open new avenues for all the sciences of Man and even of
Life itself.

Résumé

What separates the "inside" from the "outside" is not an ordinary Jordan curve, but a curve which is established by means of a kind of "cut" related to that of Dedekind. This curve is, in a way, "mobile"; operationally it creates *itself*, *de novo*, at every instant. The events which take place *on* this curve—or, better still, which *create* and *are* this curve—are those which concern the psychosomatician. This conception requires a precise definition of the meaning of "inside" and of "outside." A quantitatively minimal stimulus, coming from without, which triggers a massive reaction in the organism is a source of endogenous stress; a minimal impulsion which comes from the organism and triggers a massive reaction in the milieu is a source of exogenous stress. In both cases the minimal stimulus is the cloture element of a configuration (*Gestalt*); it organizes and structures a series of previous predispositions and attributes a meaning to them, which permits them to be mobilized *en bloc*. This fact is of a capital importance for the understanding of the functioning of the central nervous systems, which, paradoxical as it may seem, is basically a decentralizing system. The organism usually reacts to stress by a complex illness which affects several systems. When it affects one system only, this proves that the stress has already been assigned a pre-established meaning *by* and *for* the organism. This implies that homeostasis, far from assuring the perfect stability of the organism, simply regulates its variations within certain limits, in terms of the situation which it is obliged to face.

[*Addendum 1977:* Any impression that I am contradicting myself on the matter of endogenous and exogenous disappears if due attention is paid to the nouns to which these adjectives refer.]

Bibliography

(*1*) Bohr, Niels: *Atomic Theory and the Description of Nature*, Cambridge, Eng., 1934.

(*2*) Clifford, Sir Hugh: The Experiences of Râja Haji Hamid (in) *The Further Side of Silence*, New York, 1922.

(*3*) Devereux, George: Catastrophic Reactions in Normals, *American Imago*, 7:343–349, 1950.

(*4*) Idem: *Therapeutic Education*, New York, 1956.

(*5*) Idem: *From Anxiety to Method in the Behavioral Sciences*, Paris and The Hague, 1967.

(*6*) Idem: *Essais d'Ethnopsychiatrie Générale*, Paris, 1970, 1972, 1977.

(*7*) Donnan, F. G.: Integral Analysis and the Phenomena of Life, parts 1 and 2, *Acta Biotheoretica*, Serie A, 2:1–11, 1936; 3:43–50, 1937.

(*8*) Grousset, René: *L'Empire des Steppes*, Paris, 1941 (citing Mohammed Nessawi).

(*9*) Hinkle, L. E., Jr., and Wolff, H. G.: The Nature of Man's Adaptation to His Total Environment and the Relation to His Illness, *Archives of Internal Medicine*, 99:442–460, 1957.

(*10*) Jordan, Pascual: Quantenphysikalische Bemerkungen zur Biologie und Psychologie, *Erkenntnis*, 4:215–252, 1934.

(*11*) Idem: Ergänzende Bemerkungen über Biologie und Quantenmechanik, *Erkenntnis*, 5:348–352, 1935.

(*12*) Lamb, Harold: *The March of the Barbarians*, New York, 1940 (citing Ibn Athir).

3

Culture and the Unconscious (1955)

> No fantasy so mad can fall into human imagination, that
> meets not with the example of some public custom.
>
> Montaigne

I N THIS essay I formulate and prove two fundamental
propositions:

1. *A Methodological Thesis:* The intensive analysis in
depth of the context and implications of one institution in a
single tribe or of the still proverbial Viennese neurotics can
—as both Durkheim and Freud indicated—yield universally
valid conclusions. Conversely, the selfsame propositions
can also be derived from a study in breadth of the variations
of the same culture trait or institution in a large number of
societies. This general methodological proposition may, as
far as *practical* implications are concerned, be thought of as
the equivalent of the mathematician's ergodic hypothesis
(See Ch. 1 and *infra*). It justifies simultaneously, and by
identical means, both studies in depth and cross-sectional
studies in breadth and even the use of illustrative examples
(*14*, Ch. 16).

2. *A Substantive Thesis:* Were anthropologists to draw
up a complete list of all known types of cultural behavior,
this list would overlap, point by point, with a similarly complete list of impulses, wishes, fantasies, etc., obtained by

psychoanalysts in a clinical setting, thus demonstrating, by identical means and simultaneously, the psychic unity of mankind and the validity of psychoanalytic interpretations of culture, both of which have hitherto (1954) been validated only empirically.

Although I seek to prove these propositions in general terms, a paradigmatic value will be assigned to data on abortion, which I have assembled elsewhere, and which were derived at first from three hundred and fifty (*10*) and then from approximately four hundred (*11*) primitive societies, for, so far as I know, no one has ever studied a cultural item in so many societies. In the context of this discussion the *differences* between the study based on three hundred and fifty and that based on four hundred societies are particularly relevant.

Although it must be admitted that the concrete topic (abortion) was chosen more or less accidentally, it so happens that it is ideally suited for demonstrating the above theorems. In the first place, the number of theoretically possible modes of abortion behavior is sharply limited by the fact that biological factors automatically place a limitation upon an indefinite proliferation of culturally devised techniques and attitudes. At the same time, the fact that abortion always involves trauma and stress and is closely linked with areas of conflict between Superego, Ego and Id, renders it particularly suitable for psychoanalytic study. Last, but not least, the fact that—for obvious reasons— abortion does not occupy anywhere a focal position in culture and that a good many possible actions and attitudes related to abortion are, in Linton's terminology, either cultural alternatives or optional elements (i.e., patterns of behavior which are, to an appreciable extent, individually motivated and shaped) compensates implicitly for the usual lack of adequate and specific psychological data concerning named individuals, which bedevils every student of the psychological dimensions of primitive cultural behavior. In other words, given the nature of data usually found in anthropological works, it would be almost impossible to write a major depth psychological study about—to take an example at random—primitive potters in general, simply because in pottery work most of the behavior observed is fairly rigidly standardized and therefore, except in the few areas where pottery has become an art, yields no really significant clues as to *individual* choice and motivations.

Since the foregoing propositions are validated in this work on a rather large scale, it is hoped that they will prove to be useful as basic propositions also in other comparative studies which combine the cultural with the depth psychological approach.

In the final accounting, the chief purpose of this work is to add another inch to the bridge which one day will inevitably link the social and the psychological sciences and weld them into an indissoluble whole, precisely through the principle of complementarity.

The Methodological Thesis

The chief difficulty is to find a society or social group whose conscious and unconscious attitudes toward abortion have been reported exhaustively and analyzed in detail. No single primitive people has been sufficiently studied in this respect to provide the research worker both with complete data and with a careful analysis in depth of these data. The same seems to be true of all other non-European and great historical cultures, with one exception so obvious that it took me a long time to notice the forest which was hidden from my sight by the trees.

Even nowadays everyone who pretends to offer an "irrefutable" critique of psychoanalysis falls back upon the argument that, as a science or body of theory, it speculates, on the basis of an intensive clinical study of a number of (culturally admittedly distinctive) middle-class Viennese neurotics, or their equivalents. The opponents of psychoanalysis as a scientific theory, or only of its applicability to all mankind, have sought to exploit this objectively correct statement in a manner which necessarily obscures the very important fact that, in its simplest and most literal sense, psychoanalytic theory is probably the most penetrating set of conclusions ever drawn from the intensive study of a single social class, living at a certain point in history, in a distinctive cultural milieu, which is not even remotely duplicated in intensity or exhaustiveness by the very best existing ethnographic field reports.

We are therefore entitled to turn the tables on those who sneeringly assert that psychoanalytic theories are fully applicable only to an effete and neurotic Viennese bourgeoisie of the turn of the century, living at a given point in history and carrying on in an amiable atmosphere of waltzes, Graustarkian court ritual, Hollywoodish uniforms, "Heuriger" wine and good-natured "Schlamperei." This we may do by "accepting" their views—but only in order to indicate that psychoanalytic theory, inductively derived from an incomparably intensive study of such individuals, is equally applicable to all mankind.

The polemical aspect of my logical position is, therefore, wholly subsidiary to the methodological point which postulates the equivalence of conclusions derived from extensive studies in breadth on the one hand and intensive studies in depth on the other—which is precisely the *implicit* view of both Durkheim and Freud.

Hence, I am not postulating a priori the universal validity of psychoanalysis. *As a methodological device*, I will therefore even go so far as to deny—but only for reasons of expository convenience—that there is a science of psychoanalysis in the sense in which there is a science of physiology, and postulate instead that what goes under the name of "psychoanalysis" is simply a set of socio-psychological conclusions derived from the intensive study of the pre-World War I Viennese middle class. For the same reason, I will view Freud, *in this context*, not as the founder of a new science, but as an exceptionally thorough sociologist and social psychologist, who did his field work among the natives of Vienna, and who formulated a series of general conclusions about the Viennese *only*.

If, however, even after this methodological position is assumed, it can *nonetheless* be shown that Freud's conclusions about the Viennese have a universal applicability, both because they help one understand (*verstehen*) data pertaining to abortion in primitive societies (7) and because these primitive phenomena almost automatically fall into the categories which constitute the conceptual framework of psychoanalysis, my thesis may be considered as proven.

I wish to add that this procedure and methodological device is neither illegitimate nor specious, and cannot, in fairness, be viewed as a simple rhetorical tour de force. Indeed, ever since Abel, mathematicians have used a method of proof which "inverts the problem," by taking as known that which is unknown and working back from that point to what is, in fact, already known and established. If this procedure meets the standards of mathematical reasoning, then the burden of proof that a similar procedure is *not* legitimate in the human sciences rests upon the self-appointed critic. Indeed, in the last resort, I have done nothing more than ask a question in an *answerable* manner, which means in the *correct* manner. For the great mathematician Georg Cantor proved long ago that it is more important to ask a question correctly than it is to answer it —presumably because a correctly asked question already implies its own answer.

This approach does more than take the wind out of the sails of those who keep harping on the "Viennese background" of psychoanalytic theory. In other words, I "meekly" accept their criticism, and then turn the tables on them by means of the hypothesis—already *implicit* in both Freud and Durkheim—that a single detailed study in depth can yield universally valid conclusions. This actually provides a logical basis for the assertion that psychoanalysis has a universal validity, which has hitherto either been simply affirmed or else has been proven only empirically by means of numerous examples. Needless to say, the confirmation of the universal validity of psychoanalytic theories by means of examples, however numerous, can only create a *presumption* in favor of their universal validity, since it can always be suggested that eventually someone will turn up some data from the X tribe which (allegedly) "disprove" some aspect of psychoanalytic theory. This kind of "refutation" does not, as a rule, prove anything more than that the critic is too unfamiliar with psychoanalytic theory to realize that, just as the law of gravitation is not disproven by the existence of airplanes—which counteract the force of gravitation by means of buoyance (the law of Archimedes) and momentum, without, however, abolishing it—so the absence, *on the conscious and culturally implemented level*, of some phenomenon which, in the view of psychoanalysts, is a universal one, calls for nothing more than a description of the psychodynamic processes which keep that factor or phenomenon *in a state of repression*. I have made this point so often that it seems superfluous to discuss it once more in the present context (*9*; *14*, Ch. 15).

One conclusion to be drawn from all this is that it is sometimes useful to pay attention even to seemingly senseless criticisms, for their apparent illogicality and bias often simply disguise the fact that the critic has unwittingly hit upon a potentially productive problem, but was able neither to formulate it constructively nor to solve it meaningfully.[1]

Certain attempts to interpret inferential psychological processes in individual primitives, whom the would-be interpreter has never seen in person, are open to almost the same type of criticism which can be advanced in regard to

1. I have shown elsewhere (*13*) that, by accepting the biased view that the psychoanalyst "directly influences" his patient, one can prove, even more conclusively than has already been done, that psychoanalysis is an experimental and inductive science and that its procedures and problems are similar to those of other sciences dealing with almost imponderable phenomena.

interpretations of the motivation of *successful* suicide.[2] In both instances interpretations have to be based upon inferences and are always open to criticism, either on the score of overinterpretation or on that of underinterpretation. At this point, one can engage in a nice game of intellectual tag, productive—to paraphrase Bertrand Russell—of heat rather than light, which gratifies little more than the scholar's obsessive impulses masquerading as methodological rigor.[3] Methodology itself cannot point the way out of such methodological impasses. That can be done only by common sense, which—almost intuitively—warns the scholar when his quest for insight begins to deteriorate into an exhibition of subtlety.

Broadly speaking, two attitudes are possible in regard to

2. Data based on the study of persons who have *unsuccessfully* attempted suicide do yield some clues but are open to criticism on the score that a really determined person can kill himself even when restrained and under constant supervision. Almost any psychiatrist can confirm this from his own experience. In this sense, then, the range of phenomena, from threats of suicide motivated by the desire to create a sensation or to blackmail someone, etc., to seemingly bona fide suicidal attempts which were frustrated at the last moment through the "chance" intervention of some external agency, forms a continuum. However, a caveat must be entered at this juncture against complete interpretative nihilism. Thus, if many last-minute "chance" rescues are admittedly suspect of having been unconsciously engineered, one is equally entitled to ask precisely how many actually successful suicides were originally intended simply as exhibitionistic attempted suicides, which "happened" to succeed through a "chance" failure of the rescuer to appear at the proper moment. Of course, at this point one may say that this chance failure of the rescuer to arrive was also a contrived one and that the suicide was therefore a genuine one, and so on, ad infinitum (*12*). One is caught here in the very midst of an Epimenides type paradox (*32*). Due allowances being made for Lagrange's apt dictum that nature is not concerned with the analytical difficulties confronting the mathematician, *somewhere or other* a boundary must be drawn between excessive and obsessive methodological refinement-mongering, and naïve generalization-mongering.
3. Everyone knows obsessive methodologists, who can cite only the reasons why a certain thing cannot be done, but never think of the reasons which make it possible to do it.

attempts to interpret psychological factors in abortion in primitive society. One is represented by the Durkheim-Freud attitude, which implies that the meticulous analysis in depth of a single social or psychological phenomenon can yield universally valid results. The other underlies the attempt to derive valid generalizations from the statistical analysis of sets of data derived from a large sample of cultures.

It is my methodological thesis that differently formulated, but (in the last resort) identical conclusions, can be derived from both these procedures. In order to justify this view, I will now construct the sociological and psychological equivalent, or counterpart, of the ergodic hypothesis of mathematicians, which postulates—on the basis of experience and convenience rather than on the basis of a generally accepted formal proof—that the score of a large number of consecutive tosses with one coin is identical with the score of a large number of simultaneous tosses with many identical coins. In the realm of human behavior—i.e., in the field of social and psychological sciences—the analogue of this hypothesis would be the assertion that information in breadth (the cross-sectional or comparative method) yields results or inferences comparable to information in depth (by means of a full analysis of all implications of a single item or set of items) (Durkheim and Freud). Also, the errors caused by the hyper-specificity of information in depth are comparable to the errors due to the non-comprehensiveness of cross-sectional hypo-information in breadth. A corollary of this view—that we can treat as "free associations" to our main topic relevant data from other segments of the culture one of whose specific traits is being investigated, and/or comparable data from other cultures pertaining to the identical segment or trait—will be justified further on.

As regards positive results, both data in depth and data in breadth necessarily lead one to a general theory of human society and of human nature—regardless of whether one chooses to recognize or to ignore this fact. The *particular* theories to which one is led by such data are partly dependent on such existential and *wissenssoziological* factors as the investigator's training and personal biases, both conscious and unconscious (*13*). These factors and biases should be stated, but need not be justified otherwise than by a display of one's results—if any.

The Substantive Thesis

It is always desirable that a new major insight be generally accepted. However, there are ways and ways of accepting a new generalization. One can accept it wholeheartedly and make it one of the leitmotifs of one's thinking. But one can also "accept" it consciously, and yet be so ambivalent about it unconsciously that the very manner in which one "accepts" it sterilizes the new insight. When a new major truth is transformed either into a dogma or into a commonplace, one can be certain that it has undergone a process of sterilization and degradation precisely in the minds of those who consciously profess to have accepted it but unconsciously resist it to the uttermost.

The view that impulses, wishes, fantasies and other products of the human psyche which are completely repressed in one society may be fully conscious and even culturally implemented in another society is, today, almost a scientific commonplace. This means that, instead of being an axiom, it has become a dogma or even a platitude. In undergoing this metamorphosis, the insight in question has, in fact, lost its provocative and thought-provoking character and has consequently failed to stimulate attempts to explore all of its deeper implications.

What facilitated the degradation and sterilization of this axiom was its apparent simplicity and obviousness which—somewhat along the lines of Edgar Allan Poe's *Purloined Letter* device—concealed the magnitude and depth of the problems which lay hidden behind its deceptively simple façade. It is therefore chiefly in this context that one must bear in mind a great mathematician's warning: "Seek simplicity, but distrust it!"

Two examples drawn from theoretical physics well exemplify the tendency to "accept" a new theory for the wrong reason.

1. *The Indeterminacy Principle*, formulated by Heisenberg, is simply the enunciation of an experimentally verifiable fact and its formulation in theoretical terms: the more precisely one determines (measures) the position of an electron, the more indeterminate (non-determinable) becomes its momentum *at the same instant*, and, vice versa, of course. Yet the pseudo-ambiguousness of the word "indeterminacy," which, as Russell (*33*) has shown, pertains solely to problems of measuring, was promptly exploited by those who wished to undermine the principle of causality (determinism). Incidentally, Russell noted ironically that whereas one eminent physicist based his argument in favor of the existence of God on the fact that electrons *do* obey the laws of arithmetic, another based his on the fact that electrons *do not* obey these selfsame laws. As a result, the logical consequences of Heisenberg's principle of indeterminacy were not clarified by those who, impelled by irrational needs, misunderstood the meaning of "indeterminacy," but by Niels Bohr (*3, 4*) and by his disciple Pascual Jordan (*20, 21, 22*). These two scientists formulated the principle of complementarity, which turns out to be applicable also to the social and psychological study of human behavior (see Chs. 1 and 5).

2. *The Second Law of Thermodynamics* (law of entropy), which is manifestly anxiety arousing, incited certain eminent physicists to postulate that this law is reversed in certain segments of the universe or at least that living matter in general, and Man in particular, is not subject to its sway (*26*). The controversy between Jeans (*18*), on the one hand, and Donnan and Guggenheim (*15*), on the other, is particularly illuminating in this context.

These examples show that important scientific principles can be accepted superficially and yet encounter unconscious resistances and undergo distortions for affective reasons. It is in this manner that the theory that certain items which are repressed in one society are culturally implemented in another was degraded and sterilized by an overly hasty (and therefore too ambivalent) acceptance, which actually impeded the exploring of its deeper implications. That is why I propose to analyze here first certain fundamental principles, so as to clear the ground for an investigation of the complex problems hidden behind the seemingly simple façade of this far-reaching theory.

The *"Principle of Limited Possibilities,"* formulated by Goldenweiser (*17*), states that the customs of tribe *A* in regard to a certain matter may resemble the customs of a distant tribe *B* in regard to the same matter simply because there are just so many ways, and no more, of doing certain things. This simple and sound principle promptly fell into complete oblivion, chiefly because it seemed to threaten some of the major logical foundations of a certain attempt —which I prefer not to mention by name—to reconstruct unwritten culture history statistically, directly from the *present* geographical distribution of various culture traits. Now, Goldenweiser's principle in no way concerns this particular procedure, which is inadmissible for altogether different reasons (see Ch. 1). The theory which underlies the calculus of probabilities implies that the *present* distribution of mobile elements in space is unable to furnish clues which would permit one to retrace the *paths* which the individual elements took in order to reach their present positions and the system as a whole took so as to attain its present phase or state. The fact that those who attempted these statistical reconstructions were less naïve in their practices than in their theoretical stance and were therefore able to formulate a certain number of plausible conclusions, does not diminish in the least the basically fallacious character of their theoretical positions.

Only three considerations militate in favor of the diffusion hypothesis:

1. *Logically*, this hypothesis is parsimonious—and it was the *naïve* diffusionists' use of this principle which Golden-weiser sought to supplant by another conception of this principle.

2. *Psychologically*, its chief argument is Herbert Spinden's seductive rhetorical question: "Does man think, or merely remember?"

3. *Empirically*, one can contrast the few examples of demonstrably independent invention with countless, fully documented, instances of diffusion and acculturation.

Another source of resistance to Goldenweiser's principle may well be its (purely external) similarity with Bastian's *Elementargedanken* theory (2) which, though irritatingly presented by its author, is an imaginative extension of the generally—and far too easily—admitted theory of the psychic unity of mankind, which scientists are quite ready to accept, provided no one compels them to draw certain awkward conclusions from it.

Though Bastian spoiled by his argumentation what was potentially a defensible thesis, his theory was not rejected because it seemed evident that certain *Elementargedanken* did not manifest themselves in every case in which, according to his own theories, similar external conditions favored their appearance. It was rejected because Bastian did not indicate—and, in 1881, *could not* indicate—that, in a given ethnic group, a particular idea can surface consciously and be culturally implemented, while in another one it occurs only on the *unconscious* level and finds no direct *cultural* expression. It was only when Freud's work had come into being that Ernest Jones and Géza Róheim could reach this conclusion, which I took over and elaborated further elsewhere (*14*, Ch. 16). In short, it is precisely because of its incompleteness that Bastian's theory turns out to be scientifically fertile and stimulating.

There remains the question why psychoanalysts failed to

revive Bastian's views, which in many ways dovetail so admirably with the principle of the psychic unity of mankind—without which, as I have shown elsewhere (*8*), psychoanalysis as a general human science, rather than as a special science pertaining exclusively, as some of its specious opponents still maintain, to Viennese neurotics, becomes unthinkable. The classical psychoanalysts' neglect of Bastian's views may be partly due to the fact that, in its foggier implications, it shows an unfortunate kinship with Jung's mystical theory of archetypes and of a racial unconscious. Perhaps it was in a praiseworthy attempt to avoid all resemblance with Jung that psychoanalysts—by means of a process which E. M. Loeb and I call "antagonistic acculturation" (see Ch. 8)—have, as regards Bastian, "thrown out the baby with the bath" and have lapsed instead into the kind of paleopsychological speculation which I have called "pseudobiologia phantastica." In addition, they have failed to state *sufficiently often* and *sufficiently clearly* that the psychic unity of mankind is a cornerstone of psychoanalytic theory since, without this axiom, all psychoanalytic extrapolations from clinical data to cultural material remain idle speculations: empty tours de force of no great consequence.

I cannot, in this place, restate again and in extenso the argument that the human mind functions pretty much the same way everywhere, and never more strikingly so than in situations of stress, when tensions strip off the prostheses of culture and the "old Adam" emerges more or less in his pristine condition (*8*). It was this latter finding which induced me to affirm elsewhere that a neurotic or (a fortiori) a psychotic Cheyenne Indian or Maori resembles an American neurotic or psychotic *more* than a normal Cheyenne or Maori resembles a normal American (*14*, Ch. 15). I simply note here that this view does not presuppose the theory of archetypes or the need to engage in paleopsychological fantasies. Thus, Feldman has shown that paleopsychological attempts to explain, e.g., the universality of the Oedipus complex, are worse than false; they are *unnecessary*, since

each child's *personal* experience is sufficient to account for
it (*16*). Even less does it enable one to ignore the influence of
the specific cultural setting, since the same impulse or fundamental fantasy can be stimulated by various cultural influences and, conversely, can use equally well a great variety
of cultural outlets and fields of action. Above all, the cultural setting is decisively important in determining which
impulse or fantasy will receive direct cultural implementation, which will receive indirect or substitute cultural implementation, which will be actualized only in a subjective
manner, and, finally, which will remain altogether unconscious, being kept in a state of repression either by means of
culturally provided repressive devices or by means of idio-
syncratically evolved repressive devices unsupported by
culture (*14*, Ch. 1).

Nothing said here can disprove the theory of diffusion. In
fact, it is specifically one of my basic theses that the universal
process of diffusion itself presupposes at least one universal
uniformity of the human mind : the capacity to learn, and to
integrate knowledge so acquired with the rest of one's
psychic material, in a manner determined, on the one hand,
by the specific ethos of the borrowing culture, and, on the
other hand, by the ethnic personality structure of the
members of the borrowing group.

The following discussion rests on three basic postulates:

1. The psychic unity of mankind, which includes its
capacity for extreme variability,

2. The principle of limited possibilities, and

3. The finding that something which is out in the open
and is even culturally implemented in one society is often
repressed in other societies.

The foregoing postulates lead to one inescapable conclusion:

If all psychoanalysts were to draw up a complete list of all
impulses, wishes, and fantasies elicited in a clinical setting,
this list could be matched point by point by a list of all

known cultural beliefs and devices drawn up by anthropologists.

This conclusion is necessarily true, since fantasies and cultural items alike are products of the human mind and, therefore, should be acceptable—at least as a working hypothesis—to all who deem self-evident the uniformity of the human mind, and particularly of the unconscious human mind; though ultimately little more is required in practice than a belief that the science of human psychology is distinct from the science of, e.g., bird or rat psychology. This basic distinction, even if it be only a quantitative one, is tenable—and this regardless of whether or not one concedes that beyond a certain point quantitative differences become (or can, *in practice*, be treated as) qualitative differences.

Simple as this principle is, it must be proven empirically, even if it is admittedly altogether beyond the powers of any individual, or group of individuals, to develop a typology of all forms of human cultural behavior and to match it with a typology of all fantasies recorded in psychoanalytic literature. Even the Human Relations Area Files (H.R.A.F.), which are the product of the joint efforts of a large team of investigators, covered in 1954 only some 200 groups.[4] Furthermore, if many workers have already established the fact that valid studies can be made with the help of data pertaining to only 200 tribes, my book on abortion (*11*) has shown that even without resorting to unnecessarily fine distinctions, the typology which could have been constructed by means of the data found in the Human Relations Area Files in 1954 would *not* have covered the full range of the *finer shadings* of phenomena listed in the typology which I developed on the basis of some 350 tribes (*10*). In fact, even after completing my typological study on the basis of 350 tribes, in looking up data on some 50-odd additional tribes, bringing up the number of ethnic groups to 400, some

4. It now covers more than 450 groups and continues to expand.

further typological variations came to light, although it must be admitted that, after the 200 H.R.A.F. tribes were covered, the principle of diminishing returns manifestly began to operate.

In brief, the typology of practices, etc., pertaining to abortion, which I could establish on the basis of data concerning 400 societies, turned out to be reasonably exhaustive. This leads me to conclude that no additional important data and insights of interest in the present context would have emerged had I covered 1,000 instead of "only" 400 tribes.

Now, it seems logically legitimate to suppose that, had my typological study concerned a topic which anthropologists study routinely, instead of one which is of relatively marginal interest to most of them—as is shown by the fact that the H.R.A.F. data contained information on abortion for only some 125 tribes—it is very probable that 200 tribes would easily have sufficed for the construction of a complete basic typology. This is best shown by the fact that there is only a limited number of types of kinship systems (*24*), though kinship systems are certainly far more complex than are abortion patterns and, being less limited by biological imperatives, might, in theory, be expected to show a much larger range of variations. In fact, for perhaps 90 percent of the tribes, information on abortion is spotty in the extreme: witness the fact that wherever one possesses adequate information on a tribe (Fiji, Masai, etc.) the data would have sufficed by themselves to define a fair number of the major categories of my typology. By contrast, differences *seem* to be largest between tribes on whom information on abortion is extremely fragmentary or one-sided.

If this hypothesis is correct—and, on the basis of my data, I have but little choice in believing it correct—then there is a real justification, *even on this basis alone*, for my approach, which consists in an attempt to analyze the real, *though latent*, meaning of the customs of one tribe with the help of data reported preferably from neighboring, but sometimes also from quite remote, tribes. I already justified this interpretative technique on another basis, namely, by suggesting that data pertaining to a *definite* and *limited* cultural trait, such as abortion, which, moreover, is closely linked to biology, may be interpreted by treating:

a) the rest of that culture, and

b) traits pertaining to abortion in other cultures,

as "free associations" to the specific tribal practice under consideration.

I can justify this procedure by two findings reported in more detail elsewhere: a Sedang Moi girl's *lie* about her abortion corresponds to Persian abortion practices (*30*), and a female Aleut abortionist, seeking to *evade* the anthropologist's questions about abortion, began to talk about the weaving of baskets—i.e., of objects which often symbolize the female reproductive organs (*11*).

These facts explain why, in the interpretative chapters of my book on abortion (*11*), I exploited chiefly material obtained from a limited number of people, for whom information about abortion is relative exhaustive.

Another convincing—though admittedly indirect—proof also supports my view that even material derived from 350 tribes constitutes an adequate sample, at least for the formulation of a typology and for interpretative purposes. I found that the data from my original 350 groups did not contain a single example of attempted abortion by means of the *deliberate* violation of a taboo for which the penalty is *involuntary* miscarriage. Nonetheless, I envisaged this *possibility* in my typology (*10*). Subsequently, I found that precisely this means was resorted to by Maori women wishing to rid themselves of an unwelcome pregnancy (*11*).

I will now briefly demonstrate my main thesis that material repressed in one society—our own—can be conscious —and culturally implemented—in another, even though it may seem superfluous to demonstrate for psychoanalysts that one and the same fantasy can spontaneously emerge in very different persons and that it usually has a culturally implemented counterpart in some society.

I will cite three examples only:

1. *Feces-Eating Monsters*. Miss Ruth Faison Shaw reported to me that, after making a finger painting, a child told
her that it represented certain monsters living in the plumb-
ing, to which the child had to make daily food offerings of
feces.[5] Some time later I came across an identical fantasy in
one of Ernest Jones's clinical papers (*19*). So far, Jones's
case material is the only published example of such a fantasy
I have come across in my fairly extensive readings of
psychoanalytic literature. But I can add to this clinical finding a personally observed cultural fact: among the Sedang
Moi of Indochina, whenever a baby soils itself, its mother
calls one of the village dogs—which live largely on human
feces—to cleanse with its tongue the baby's buttocks and the
blanket in which it is wrapped. This observation acquires a
particular significance in light of the fact that—like many
other Circum-Pacific groups (*23*)—the Sedang profess to be
descended from the mating of a woman with a dog. Last,
but not least, a white, living in the Moi country, who had
an outhouse with a small opening beneath and behind the
seat so as to permit the periodic removal of the excrements,
discovered that, as soon as anyone used the outhouse, the
village dogs and pigs rushed in through this small opening
and devoured the feces on the spot.

2. *The Fantasy of the Inverted Penis*, as well as the practices and beliefs connected with it, are discussed elsewhere
(*14*, Ch. 16) in sufficient detail to make a further discussion
unnecessary in the present context.[6]

5.   Ruth Faison Shaw invented "Finger painting." Instead of a brush, the
subject uses his fingers, hands, etc. On the clinical level, both the way such a
painting is executed and the painting itself can be used for diagnostic (*9*),
and at times even for psychotherapeutic, ends.

6.   I wish to complete one finding recorded in that work by the following
datum: The psychotic German, who inverted his penis, had lived for quite
a while in Japan—that is, in a country where, according to rumor, *sumo*
wrestlers learn to retract their testicles before the wresting bouts. By contrast, the *koro* neurosis is found neither in Japan nor even in Northern
China, and it is quite unlikely that this relatively primitive person would,

3. *The Myth-Fantasy of Human Beings Without an Anus* (*28*), as well as relevant clinical and ethnographic data, are analyzed elsewhere (*13*). Both Plinius the Elder (*29*, 7.9 ff) and Aulus Gellius (*1*, 9.4.6. ff) seem to have derived their information from Aristeas of Prokonnesos (*5*). Loukianos (*27*, 1.22), who ascribes this trait to an imaginary people, has, I believe, furnished a model for Cyrano de Bergerac (*6*). Ploutarchos (*31*, 19) even speaks of a bird lacking an anus. In the meantime, Lévi-Strauss made available further materials on this myth-fantasy and subjected it to a structural analysis (*25*), which stands in a complementarity relationship to my psychoanalytical interpretations of the same data. This permits me to mention here this myth-fantasy only as a reminder.

In my book on abortion (*11*), I have therefore examined a series of clinically observable and theoretically explainable attitudes and fantasies, which seem to play a role in the motivation and justification of abortions. It may, of course, be argued that I should have proceeded inductively rather than deductively, *first* examining and presenting my set of data, and *then* reaching these broader formulations by induction. However, such an expository procedure would have been technically impossible and wholly spurious as well—even to the point of being little more than an empty gesture—since one cannot simply forget everything one knows (except, perhaps, when using the philosophical tabula rasa, and even that is far from certain).[7] As a psychoanalyst, I cannot simply pretend never to have heard of the Oedipus complex, for such a procedure would be disingenuous in the extreme and, what is worse, also wholly

---

during his stay in Japan, have accidentally heard of so unusual a fact. This hypothesis seems substantiated by the fact that the repeated inversion of his penis—which, in the end, caused his death—was but one of several weird and sadistic manipulations to which he had subjected his sex organ.

7. It goes without saying that this difficulty arises only in the course of interpretative work. When the patient is on the analytic couch, one must know only what the patient himself (herself) says.

inappropriate in a study which specifically seeks to establish
that the productions of patients, which emerge from their
unconscious, are duplicated elsewhere by customs, beliefs
and traditional action patterns. I did, however, use major
psychoanalytic concepts simply as *initial* classificatory devices, and, from that point onward, proceeded inductively.
This is proven by the fact that, on the basis of primitive data,
I was able to reach some *new* theoretical conclusions regarding the unconscious background of abortion and certain
related matters which, as far as I am able to recall, I have
not found mentioned anywhere in the literature (*11*). I also
confidently believe that the few fantasies I inferred will
eventually turn up in the analysis of patients who have
aborted or have been indirectly connected with some abortion or miscarriage and probably also in cultures not included in my book on abortion. I believe this precisely for
the same reason which induced me to mention in my original
(350-tribes) typology the *possibility* of someone attempting
to abort by the deliberate violation of a taboo for which the
penalty is miscarriage—a practice which, as noted above,
did turn up, in precisely this form, in some very reliable
Maori material.

It is evident that no one could list all fantasies reported in
psychoanalytic literature and then match them one by one,
perhaps in alphabetical order, with some equivalent cultural
practices. In my abortion book I deemed it sufficient to
arrange the discussion of the psychological motivations of
abortion under a few broad headings, confident that if the
available ethnological data fitted these broad—but not
vague—concepts perfectly, they would also fit specific
variations thereof. So far as I was able to ascertain, the
ethnological data did not contain any trait which did not
have its counterpart in some clinically reported and theoretically explained fantasy—which is precisely what I sought
to demonstrate. If this assertion should seem inacceptable
to anyone, the data contained in the third (sourcebook)
section of that book should enable him to elaborate, with a

minimum of effort, a theory which, in his opinion, contradicts my central thesis. I admit that I would watch that attempt with a good deal of malicious pleasure.

Perhaps the best proof of the fact that my approach to ethnological data was unmarred by preconceptions is the fact that, originally, I only meant to write a simple typological study. However, shortly before the completion of the sourcebook section of this work, two eminent colleagues asked me precisely what *problem* I sought to solve in that book. Only then did I grasp that something more than a simple typology was expected from me. It is only when— spurred on by these queries—I re-examined my material, casting about for a clue to a suitable problem on which to focus that book, that it began to dawn on me that my material was ideally suited for the demonstration of the thesis which I presented in the preceding pages.[8]

If the manner in which the central problem of my book on abortion was found is not a specimen of the process of induction, then I do not know what genuine induction means.

Bibliography

(*1*)   Aulus Gellius: *Attic Nights.*
(*2*)   Bastian, Adolf: *Der Völkergedanke im Aufbau einer Wissenschaft vom Menschen und seine Begründung auf ethnologische Sammlungen,* Berlin, 1881.
(*3*)   Bohr, Niels: *Atomic Theory and the Description of Nature,* Cambridge, Eng., 1934.
(*4*)   Idem: Causality and Complementarity, *Philosophy of Science,* 4: 289–298, 1937.
(*5*)   Bolton, J. D. P.: *Aristeas of Proconnesus,* Oxford, 1962.

8.   As stated above, the material is ideally suited for this purpose, both because it is a relatively limited one and because it is fairly closely linked to basic psychophysiological processes. This does not mean, however, that— given sufficient time and patience—precisely the same point could not be established also by means of, e.g., an exhaustive study of religious beliefs, or of some other item.

(6)   Cyrano de Bergerac, Savinien de: *L'Autre Monde ou les Etats et Empires de la Lune*, 1649.

(7)   Devereux, George: Mohave Indian Infanticide, *Psychoanalytic Review*, 35:126–139, 1948.

(8)   Idem: Catastrophic Reactions in Normals, *American Imago*, 7:343–349, 1950.

(9)   Idem: *Reality and Dream: The Psychotherapy of a Plains Indian*, New York, 1951 (2nd augm. ed., 1969).

(10) Idem: A Typological Study of Abortion in 350 Primitive, Ancient and Pre-Industrial Societies (in) Rosen, H.: *Therapeutic Abortion*, New York, 1954.

(11) Idem: *A Study of Abortion in Primitive Societies*, New York, 1955 (2nd augm. ed., 1976).

(12) Idem: *Mohave Ethnopsychiatry*, Washington, D.C., 1961 (2nd augm. ed., 1969).

(13) Idem: *From Anxiety to Method in the Behavioral Sciences*, Paris and The Hague, 1967.

(14) Idem: *Essais d'Ethnopsychiatrie Générale*, Paris, 1970, 1972, 1977.

(15) Donnan, F. G.: Activities of Life and the Second Law of Thermodynamics, *Nature*, 133:99, 1934; idem and Guggenheim, E. A.: Activities of Life and the Second Law of Thermodynamics, *Nature*, 133:530, 869; 134:255, 1934.

(16) Feldman, S. S.: Notes on the "Primal Horde" (in) Róheim, Géza (ed.): *Psychoanalysis and the Social Sciences*, 1:171–193, 1947.

(17) Goldenweiser, Alexander: The Principle of Limited Possibilities in the Development of Culture, *Journal of American Folklore*, 26:261–290, 1913.

(18) Jeans, Sir James: Activities of Life and the Second Law of Thermodynamics, *Nature*, 133:174, 612, 986, 1934.

(19) Jones, Ernest: *Papers on Psychoanalysis*, 3rd ed., New York, 1923.

(20) Jordan, Pascual: Die Quanten-Mechanik und die Grundprobleme der Biologie und Psychologie, *Naturwissenschaften*, 20:815–824, 1932.

(21) Idem: Quantenphysikalische Bemerkungen zur Biologie und Psychologie, *Erkenntnis*, 4:215–252, 1934; idem: Ergänzende Bemerkungen über Biologie und Quantenmechanik, *Erkenntnis*, 5:348–352, 1935.

(22) Idem: *Anschauliche Quantentheorie*, Berlin, 1936.

(23) Koppers, Wilhelm: Der Hund in der Mythologie der Zirkumpazifischen Völker, *Wiener Beitrage zur Kulturgeschichte und Linguistik*, 1:359–399, 1930.

(24) Lévi-Strauss, Claude: *Les Structures Elémentaires de la Parenté*, Paris, 1949 (2nd ed., Paris and The Hague, 1967).

(25) Idem: *Mythologiques*, III: *L'Origine des Manières de Table*, Paris, 1968.

(26) Lewis, G. N.: *The Anatomy of Science*, New Haven, 1926.

(27) Loukianos: *A True Story*.

(*28*)   Norbeck, Edward: Trans-Pacific Similarities in Folklore: A Research
        Lead, *Kroeber Anthropological Society Papers*, no. 12:62–69, 1955.
(*29*)   Plinius (Maior): *Natural History*.
(*30*)   Ploss, Heinrich, Bartels, Max, and Bartels, Paul: *Das Weib in der
        Natur und Völkerkunde*. New ed. by Reitzenstein, F., Baron von,
        3 vols., Berlin, 1927.
(*31*)   Ploutarchos: *Life of Artaxerxes*.
(*32*)   Russell, Bertrand: *Principles of Mathematics*, vol. 1, Cambridge,
        Eng., 1903 (2nd ed., New York, 1938).
(*33*)   Idem: *The Analysis of Matter*, New York, 1927.

4

The Logical Foundations of Culture and Personality Studies
(1945)

IT IS usually advisable to begin the discussion of the logical foundations of a science with a definition of the author's own "philosophical" position. This procedure enables one to avoid numerous misunderstandings. It is, furthermore, a highly economical procedure. Definitions can be stripped of a lot of verbiage whose sole purpose is the avoidance of types of ambiguousness resulting from a lack of understanding of the author's position with regard to some of the fundamental concepts and problems of philosophy, e.g., the object's reality versus its subjectivity. My own position is close to Poincaréan (*36*) conventionalism and also to Russell's conceptions regarding certain points of pure logic (*37, 38*).

1. I believe that the following two statements are equivalent:

   a) "The external world exists," and

   b) "It is more convenient to assume that the external world exists."

2. It is possible to describe given and possible aspects of a phenomenon without raising the issue of the independent reality or subjectivity of that phenomenon.

3. Two sets of postulates from which the same conclusions can be drawn are equivalent.

4. If a phenomenon admits of one explanation, it will also admit of any number of other explanations, all equally satisfactory (*35*). The term "explanation," as understood here, denotes the process whereby a given phenomenon is reduced to a series of other phenomena (*34*). All explanations are partial ones, since the complete explanation of a phenomenon implies denying the phenomenon to be explained, by reducing it entirely to other, more "basic," phenomena.

In fact, I shall nowhere concern myself with the problem of the existence of anything; I simply intend to avoid the culturalist fallacy, which is obviously untenable.

My modus operandi is equally simple with regard to methodology. On the practical level a scientific method may be considered either as:

a) a means of doing things efficiently, or

b) a means of proving that nothing feasible is worth doing, since all that *can* be done is not worth the trouble.

Conceived in the second manner, scientific method has all the characteristics of an obsessive symptom—of a kind of self-serving (quasi autotrophic) doubt (*12*)—for the only operation that those who propose this definition consider valid is, paradoxically, the operation which pretends to establish that no operation is valid in any possible case. One could, perhaps, appeal in connection with this notion to Russell's (*37*) theory of mathematical types,[1] though Russell himself would hardly appreciate an application of his theory to this particular case.

Nearly all culture and personality studies appear to rest upon the basic assumption that culture influences personality. This assumption distinctly implies that there "exists" a sui generis phenomenon, *A* (culture), which acts upon another sui generis phenomenon, *B* (personality).

However, neither this assumption, nor its obvious

1. A fruitful application of this theory to the study of behavior is discussed in detail in another work (*16*).

implications are methodologically necessary in the pursuit of such studies.

I have offered elsewhere a definition of the methodology of culture and personality studies which does not rest upon this assumption: "If, at any stage of the individual's life, we correlate our findings concerning his individual configuration *at* that time with the structure of the field wherein the individual has moved *up to* the time to which our formulation of his personality refers, we have made a significant statement concerning the interrelation of culture and personality" (*6*). Although this statement is clear enough as it stands, I have taken further precautions against any attempt to read Platonic idealism into the above statement by previously defining culture as a highly structured and patterned field within which the individual has a certain mobility (*6*). How such a field is generated is discussed in Chapter 1.

In fact, culture and personality studies are, in a sense, merely a subdivision of general studies in conditioning or learning. If, in the following pages, I discuss certain suitable definitions of culture and of personality, I do so defensively, because every time the conception of culture as a phenomenon sui generis is ejected by the front door, it is invariably smuggled in once more by the back door, in a more or less transparent disguise.

The pitfalls of the "culturalist fallacy" in culture and personality studies have been clearly formulated by Hallowell: "It is hard to see how culture—an abstract summation of the mode of life of a people—can exert an influence except as it is a definable constituent of the activities of human individuals in interaction with each other. In the last analysis, it is individuals who respond to and influence one another" (*22*). Culture, as Bidney (*3*) has pointed out, "is not an efficient cause and does not develop itself, hence it is not capable of interacting with any other entity." To argue otherwise leads to what he calls the "culturalist fallacy," which is based on the assumption that "culture is a force that may make and develop itself and that individuals are but its passive vehicles or instruments."

This statement formulates with great precision the basic problem of culture and personality studies. Actually, it is probable that the difficulties arising from the correctness of the Hallowell and Bidney statements may—at least unconsciously—be at the root of all attempts to consider culture as a phenomenon sui generis, having independent reality.

Three erroneous reactions to the Hallowell and Bidney position are possible:

1. It makes culture and personality studies entirely impossible. The concrete accomplishments of students of culture and personality, including those of Hallowell himself, make such an interpretation preposterous.

2. The Hallowell and Bidney statements abolish the autonomy of the field of culture and personality studies and transform this discipline into a branch of social psychology. Such an interpretation is probably incorrect on the one hand, and, on the other, makes no particular difference.

3. The meaning of these statements can be distorted in such a manner as to make them appear to instance what F. Kluckhohn (28) calls the "psychological fallacy," and which I prefer to call the "psychologistic fallacy" (i.e., the inability to see the forest for the trees). Such an interpretation is obviously erroneous, both in terms of the Hallowell and Bidney statements and in terms of F. Kluckhohn's definition of the psychological fallacy.

The way out of this predicament is already implicitly indicated in Hallowell's own formulation of the problem. I refer to the term "abstract summation" and to his reference to a "definable constituent of the activities of human individuals in interaction with each other."

Let me consider, first, the concept "abstract summation." It can be subdivided into two parts, each part being an abstract summation in its own right:

1. It is possible to offer an abstract summation of the social and cultural norms of a suitably selected group of persons.

2. It is likewise possible to offer an abstract summation of the prevalent concrete modes of behavior of a suitably selected group (of persons). It is usually possible to push this operation even further and to construct an even more abstract *quasi*-summation of the two special summations in question, but *only* on the methodological level (see Ch. 5).

The principle underlying this distinction is partly implicit in Linton's distinction between overt and covert culture (*29, 30*) in C. Kluckhohn and W. H. Kelly's (*26*) distinction between implicit and explicit culture, and in Bidney's (*2*) distinction between theory and practice.

This first distinction, between two types of abstract summations, was made in terms of the subject matter (*lato sensu*) of the summations.

Another useful distinction may be made in terms of the type of person who performs the act of summation:

1. Human beings can and, in fact, do, perform such abstract summations of the norms (i.e., "this is our custom") and of the practices (i.e., "our people act in this manner") characteristic of their own group.

2. Human beings in general, and social scientists in particular, can, and in fact do, perform such abstract summations of the norms (i.e., "Mohave Indian descent is patrilineal") and of the practices (i.e., "the Mohave family is highly unstable") characteristic of, or arbitrarily imputed to, the outgroup. (Hostile stereotypes of the opponent or of the despised are of this type.)

The first of the two types of summations just mentioned is presumably the one to which Hallowell refers in speaking of the "definable" constituents of human behavior. Human beings do develop a conception of their own culture and then reify this conception and respond to this *collective representation* (in Durkheim's sense) in a highly distinctive manner, i.e., when the Hopi characterize socially inacceptable or manifestly deviant behavior as "ka-Hopi" (un-Hopi) (*39*), just as, in America, one speaks of un-American activities.

This means, in fact, that scholars and research workers are not the only ones to respond differently to trees and to the forest. We all do this, regardless of the level of perception on which we place ourselves. It suffices to think, for example, of the differential effects of referring, in a poem, either to trees or to a forest.

The psychological process of reification, and of differential response to such a reification, is by no means unique. It resembles the process whereby the child transforms his father into a Superego. In this context one must define the "father" and the infantile Superego into which the child transforms "him" as the abstract (but incoherent) summation of the residues and precipitates of all the experiences the child has not been able to master with his own limited (because infantile) means at the very moment in which he experienced these events (*11*). It is to be noted that this represents, in a way, an internal apprehending of the situation. Indeed, the moment one considers the same phenomenon "from the outside," one must take it for granted that the father, too, has a Superego which determines the *kind* of father (i.e., "typically Mohave" or "atypically Mohave") he makes. In this sense, the father is but an agent of society, or, to be more specific, of his *particular* abstract summation of his own socio-cultural setting. Hence, it is sometimes more profitable to emphasize the "transformation" of society into the father, than to stress the "transformation" of the father into the Superego (*19*, Ch. 3). Since no chain of arguments of this type is profitably prolonged beyond a certain point, technical expediency alone will decide which of these two sequences one emphasizes in a given context.

Here, I think, one is on sound psychological ground, and Hallowell's thesis may be considered as proven.

An abstract summation of this type is present in the psychological makeup of every individual, regardless of whether it was handed to him ready-made by his "mediators of culture," or whether he has developed it independently. Likewise, it is of no importance whatever in *this* context whether or not he realizes that he (or some mediator of culture) has evolved this abstract summation on the basis of a study of concrete individuals, either in his own lifetime or on some past occasion (*10*).[2]

Thus, it is not necessary even for the student of culture and personality to reify culture. The members of the society which he studies have already performed this task for him. It is, perhaps, this pre-reified abstraction which is precisely *that* "culture" which influences the behavior and "personality" of the individuals composing that group, both directly, as part of any given individual's makeup, and indirectly, through the concrete behavior of other individuals who have likewise introjected the same norms and whose behavior our subject refers back to that reified abstraction, precisely in the manner in which he refers back his own actions, sometimes in a negative manner (*19*, Ch. 3), to the norms and practices of his group.

I can now turn to abstract summations made by outsiders and, more specifically, by behavioral scientists. The latter have an advantage over the student of gases. Gas molecules do not enunciate the laws of probability, nor the kinetic theory of gases, nor the laws of statistical mechanics. That is to say, they in no wise inform the physicist of their "normative" behavior. By contrast, the members of a given society, which the behavioral scientist studies, do precisely that whenever they perform the operation known as abstract summation on their own culture and enunciate its result in the form: "This is our custom," or "Our women tend to be flighty." Better still, the *expressing* of enunciative propositions concerning one's own culture or of its statistically prevalent behavioral patterns is, in itself, a cultural act. Thus, when one says "After Sokrates the Greeks

2.   It goes without saying that, on the psychiatric level, the situation is different: the subject's tendency to perceive—or not to perceive—the cultural (and therefore external) origin of a given item is of the greatest importance in all intercultural diagnostic investigation and even in meta-cultural diagnostic studies (*19*, Ch. 2).

became more and more interested in the description and analysis of cultural and personal behavior and in the function of the πόλις (City)," one makes a statement about Greek culture. What is more, this Greek cultural interest— exhibited *by* the Greeks toward Greek culture and behavior —probably had important cultural repercussions. It might explain, at least in part, their obsessive and self-destructive attempt to preserve, regardless of cost, the autonomy of each City even though, in view of the growing power of the Macedonians, the unification of Greece became a matter of life and death for every Greek and for every City that wished to remain Greek.

Sometimes, however, the student of culture and of society is called upon to perform a further operation of his own. He may find it expedient to evolve a special type of abstract summation in connection with a given culture. Such an abstract summation would be a conceptual scheme establishing a functional nexus between the norms and actual practices of a given group. (Chapter 6 offers a conceptual scheme of this type.) Similarly, the student of personality may have to evolve a conceptual scheme to create a functional nexus between what the individual says he ought to do (or thinks he does) and what he does in fact. (This problem is studied in Chapter 5.)

There is probably always a need for such a conceptual scheme or abstract summation. In certain special instances, recourse to it is indispensable. This is the case, for example, whenever theory and practice diverge very sharply—when the individual has to go rather frequently to great lengths to rationalize his actual behavior.[3] It is also necessary whenever, due to various causes, mostly historical, the norms of a given group are contradictory, discontinuous and constitute nothing more than an unstable pseudo-totality, weakly and artificially integrated and full of gaps.

3. In cases of this kind one creates a "forced (and therefore altogether artificial) compendence" (linkage) between a behavior and its justification (*19*, Ch. 16).

Last, but not least, it is necessary to develop such a conceptual scheme or abstract summation whenever—as in Sparta (*14*)—norms and practices vary extensively between the several segments of a complex society.

Societies whose study calls for further summations of this type are, with the exception of the genuinely polysegmented ones, generally more or less disorganized or in a state of flux, the chaos increased even further by the effort to compensate this unbalance by means of a hyper-structured rigidity, which, through its very excesses, runs counter to the goal pursued.[4] In such instances the *technical* difficulties of evolving appropriate conceptual schemes or abstract summations are usually considerable, but do not, as a rule, involve fundamental problems of a *logical* order.

One is, however, confronted with certain special problems in the analysis of polysegmented societies. Polysegmentation—especially in the form which Durkheim (*20, 21*) calls "organic"—presents complex problems of its own, which are present in a simpler form in every single society differentiating between the members of the group on any basis whatsoever, i.e., in terms of age, sex, status, etc. In strongly polysegmented societies these problems are sufficiently complex to necessitate a defining of the exact limits of the usefulness of the *specific* "basic personality" conceptual scheme developed by Kardiner (*24, 25*), though they appear to create no dilemmas regarding the *partial* validity of the special techniques pertaining thereto.

In fact, the problems raised by polysegmentation are so complex that they cannot be tackled without first defining "personality."[5]

4. One is dealing here with the vicious circle which characterizes the functioning of every pathological organism or system.
5. I do not take here into account the hypothesis that culture is an emergent, for, as already indicated in Chapter 1, it is *unnecessary* to consider society an emergent. The same logical procedure can prove also that there is no need to envisage culture as an emergent. Now, I deem it scientifically legitimate to lose interest completely in a hypothesis as soon as it is shown that it does not satisfy any real need.

Definitions of personality are, of course, very numerous. One of the best known is that of Mark A. May (*33*), whose usefulness for culture and personality studies has been shown by C. Kluckhohn and Mowrer (*27*). Like most really useful definitions it is a simple one: "Personality is the social stimulus value of the individual." This definition has several advantages: it avoids any reification of personality; it results from inductive reasoning; it implies that different observers will be differently stimulated by a given subject and will therefore develop different conceptions of his personality.[6] I take my cue from this definition and proceed accordingly.

If one observes a given subject over a certain period of time, one automatically comes to think of him in a certain way and to expect certain actions from him. Rigorously speaking, one integrates his various behaviors into a coherent whole in a distinctive manner by performing two operations:

1. One establishes a functional nexus between his several modes of behavior by formulating a unique conceptual scheme (referring to that individual), to be labelled his "personality." This conceptual scheme accounts—in theory at least— for all peculiarities of behavior displayed by the subject. Roughly speaking, one seeks to explain that individual's behavior in a unified manner.

2. One tests the validity of this conceptual scheme by predicting chronoholistically the future behavior of that individual; i.e., one examines the conceptual scheme "personality" and seeks to deduct from it logically the further properties of the system "individual *X*" not yet disclosed by actual observation.

Summing up, I view personality as a conceptual scheme, i.e., as a unified explanation and as a means of prediction.

6. I have shown elsewhere (*16*) that this differential reaction—the counter-transference—of the observer is the fundamental datum of the behavioral sciences. This statement goes much further than the concept defined by Mark A. May.

This definition suffices for present purposes. Nothing would be changed, as far as results are concerned, if one took a position regarding the independent reality or subjectivity of "personality." It is, of course, implicit in my methodological position that one may formulate several conceptual schemes of this kind, all accounting equally well for the occurrence of a given behavior and predicting future behavior equally accurately. None of these "explanations" and/or predictions is complete, however, nor is it necessary to assume that they overlap fully, either as regards the segments of behavior to which they refer, or as regards the concepts constituting the several schemes in question. It is important to bear this always in mind. (Complementarity.)

I am now prepared to correct a deliberate misstatement, or, rather, an illegitimate oversimplification, made above.

I have spoken of the conceptual scheme "personality" as an explanation. In fact, a conceptual scheme is not, and cannot be, an explanation in the sense in which Meyerson (*34*) uses this word. A conceptual scheme is not a "phenomenon" to which another phenomenon is reduced, nor is it, per se, such a process of reduction. However, it can serve as a frame of reference within which explanations can be made or within which explanations become possible. Hence, it is, loosely speaking, a means of explanation, but not an explanation per se. This distinction is of some importance.

Another grave logical error is the assumption that personality can be explained or reduced to other phenomena, which may be viewed as factors or determinants of personality, which I defined above as a conceptual scheme. It is impossible to explain a conceptual scheme in Meyerson's sense. The causes of this confusion are obvious. They result from the recurrent failure to distinguish between a logical class and the members of that class. Even a class having only one member is not identical with that member (*37*).

In short, only a phenomenon, or a set of phenomena, can be explained in Meyerson's sense. A conceptual scheme can merely be first constructed and then analyzed. Concretely, behavior can be explained. Personality can only be first constructed and then analyzed.

I will attempt to tackle this problem on the practical level, in order to avoid the complexities of a formal presentation of the subject.

I distinguish between two types of concepts. There are, first of all, inductive generalizations, exemplified by the concept "the solids." Next, there are analytic variables, exemplified by the concept "solid" (adjective) or "solidity." Epistemologically, the concept of solid bodies is prior to the concept of solidity. The latter was derived precisely from the study of solid bodies.

Somewhat anticipating the course of my analysis, explanations of behavior tend to be formulated in terms of inductive generalizations, whereas the conceptual scheme "personality" tends to be constructed out of analytic variables. This appears to be a rule of thumb statement rather than a dogmatic one (in the philosophical sense).

I now propose to inquire into the epistemological "genealogy" of these concepts.

Inductive generalizations (and, hence, also analytic variables) result from the study of sets of phenomena, studied *both jointly and severally*. This last specification refers to Russell's (*37*) distinction between "all" and "every."[7]

I naturally assume that no set actually studied is complete, but nonetheless assume that it is a representative sample of the complete set (i.e., no human biologist ever studied all men who ever lived).

Now, it is of crucial importance that two such sample sets may have the same members, i.e., that their memberships overlap more or less completely. However, even where the membership of both classes is rigorously the same, or when the larger of the two memberships comprises all members of the smaller category, the two sets or classes are not *logically*

7. The applicability to the behavioral sciences of the distinction between "a" and "any" is proven by my analysis of the social structure of a group of schizophrenics in a psychiatric hospital environment (*9*).

identical, i.e., all members of a sample group made up only of Mohave Indians (and of no one else) may also be members of a suitably constructed sample set of *Homo sapiens.* Yet, even in that case, "Mohave" and "*Homo sapiens*" are logically distinct types.

For the sake of simplicity, I will consider only this concrete instance. It is possible to evolve a set of propositions which will refer only to the Mohave Indians under study (i.e., I can write a *Mohave* ethnography). Likewise, it is possible to evolve a set of propositions which will apply specifically to the other sample group, e.g., the one composed of specimens of *Homo sapiens* who, in this instance, *could all* be Mohave Indians; i.e., I can write a book on human biology. Now, even though both these works would be conceptual schemes in the same sense, the Mohave ethnography will be a conceptual scheme of one kind, and the human biology a conceptual scheme of a different kind.

At this juncture concrete individuals can be handled in two different ways:

1. One can refer the behavior of a given individual (temporal ensemble) to the behavior of a spatial set of individuals (i.e., Mohave or *Homo sapiens*), or, more rigorously, one can refer it to certain inductive generalizations. These inductive generalizations may be considered as factors or as determinants of individual behavior and are derived from the study of a spatial ensemble. They can be used as "explanations" of the concrete behavior of my subject, in the strictly Meyersonian sense of the word. Naturally, it is assumed that one shall avoid the logical fallacies discussed by Russell (*38, 41*) in connection with such statements as: "*A* is a typical Frenchman" and "Napoleon had all the qualities that make a great general." This type of explanation is what C. Kluckhohn and Mowrer (*27*) may have had in mind, though they have certainly not made clear their views on this matter.

2. One can also analyze the conceptual scheme "personality," or, more specifically, "personality of *X*," by tracing

the epistemological genealogy of the concepts constituting that conceptual scheme. This does not constitute an "explanation," in Meyerson's sense. It does, however, provide one—loosely speaking—with a frame of reference for the explanation of behavior—*but not of personality*. (Obviously, this does not mean that I am now considering personality as a phenomenon sui generis, since I nowhere assert that conceptual schemes have *existence*.)

The distinction between the explanation of behavior and the analysis of the conceptual scheme "personality" is logically important, precisely because both types of (complementary) approaches yield identical results in terms of the *degree*—but not the *kind*—of understanding and prediction of concrete behavior (see Ch. 5).

If that be the case, those impatient of logical discussions may inquire why so much space has been devoted to the abstract problem of the analysis of the conceptual scheme "personality." In justification of this procedure it may be stated that the problem, thus formulated, at once removes the *substance* of debates of the nature versus nurture type in respect to human behavior and reduces them to purely formal distinctions. The question is no longer "Does biology or society determine human behavior?" but "Are biological or sociological concepts being used in the formulation of a given explanation or in the construction of a particular conceptual scheme?"

Let us suppose that we have formulated a conceptual scheme "personality" which is both unique and, within the limits of possibility, also exhaustive. But such a scheme, even if constructed seemingly on the basis of biological, sociological and other concepts (which are mostly analytic variables) will nonetheless be uniquely a psychological scheme (see Ch. 5). This is admittedly an ideal case, but one which has the advantage of not providing material for a controversy, for the simple numerical tabulation of the biological, sociological and other concepts utilized in this scheme is not likely to give offense to anyone.

It is probable, however, that this "ideal"—if it be one, which I venture to doubt—has not yet been reached, so that behavioral scientists continue to use not one, but several conceptual schemes of personality. One such conceptual scheme may be made up of biopsychological concepts, another one of sociological concepts, etc. Hence, the question is no longer "Where does human nature end and culture begin?" but "At what stage of the inquiry should one, for reasons of parsimony, *switch* from one conceptual scheme or frame of reference to another conceptual scheme or frame of reference?" Since this is purely a technical problem, only considerations of expediency (*commodité*) will determine the *moment* when one must cease, by means of laborious hairsplittings, to extract a few additional drops of comprehension from a scheme from which one has already extracted all it can conveniently produce and can pass to the exploitation of another scheme, whose yield, from that point onward, is greater. (See The Argument.)

It suffices to mention such technical issues in a logical analysis, but it is not necessary to expatiate unduly on them.

There exists, however, another problem of quite a different type, which also derives from the fact that the membership of certain sample sets tends to overlap either partially or completely. It is a problem connected with the theory of the "modal personality," i.e., with a conceptual scheme so abused by some that they sometimes actually presume to use it as an "explanation" (!) of the concrete behavior of individuals.

Logically, this problem too is so complex that it seems more expedient to deal with it in terms of concrete examples.

Can the personality of John Doe, a native of New York, be more completely understood by assigning him to the total American socio-cultural complex or by stressing chiefly his urban habitat and treating him, therefore, primarily as a city dweller, on a par with any inhabitant of Paris and Calcutta? Whatever one may decide, one must take into account, on the one hand, that the very possibility of there existing great metropolitan areas is a part of the American socio-cultural complex and, on the other hand, that New York differs in many respects from Paris and Calcutta, precisely because it is an *American* city.

Shall I, moreover, explain John Doe's behavior in terms of the prevailing American norms and practices, or in terms of the prevailing urban norms and practices? Shall the conceptual scheme "personality of John Doe" contain principally socio-cultural or urbanistic concepts? Shall I treat the socio-cultural frame of reference on a par with the urbanistic frame of reference? In brief, is John Doe a typical American or a typical urban man? Is his modal personality American or urban?

This problem cannot be solved in rigorously logical terms without starting with a discussion of the meaning of "modal personality." Unfortunately, if one does this, one is immediately in the midst of Russell's aforementioned discussion regarding statements of the type "*A* is a typical Frenchman" and "Napoleon had all the qualities of a great general." This, in turn, leads to the problem of mathematical types, which it is almost impossible to explain in nontechnical language.

Perhaps the nearest one can come to a simple explanation of this problem, as it refers to this topic, is to quote Russell: "How shall I define a 'typical Frenchman'? We may define him as one 'possessing all qualities that are possessed by most Frenchmen'. But unless we confine 'all qualities' to such as do not involve a reference to any *totality* [my italics] of qualities, we shall have to observe that most Frenchmen are *not* typical in the above sense, and therefore the definition shows that to be not typical is essential to a typical Frenchman.[8] This is not a logical contradiction, since there

8. I note in this connection that it is an actual fact that "not being a typical Frenchman" is precisely one of the most salient traits of the members of that nation of individualists. It goes without saying that this fact has no logical import in this context; it can at most explain why Russell (unconsciously) chose an example involving Frenchmen.

is no reason why there should be any typical Frenchman;
but it illustrates the need of separating off qualities that involve reference to a totality of qualities from those that do
not." Again, with reference to Napoleon and his qualities,
Russell observes "I must define 'qualities' in such a way that
it will not include what I am now saying, *i.e.*, 'having all the
qualities that make a great general' must not be itself a
quality in the sense supposed" (*38*, p. 189).

I now assert something that is completely obvious in terms
of Russell's theory of types (just quoted in the form of a
concrete example of direct interest to the student of culture
and personality). It is entirely illegitimate to consider modal
personality as a quality logically on a par with such other
quality or qualities as constitute modal personality or exist
outside of it, as idiosyncratic qualities, for example.

Indeed, modal personality is a *totality* of qualities. This is
crucial for my whole approach. When I say that John Doe
is a typical American or urban man, I assert—if I disregard
this warning—that he possesses all the qualities possessed
by most Americans or by most urban men, including the
quality (and therein lies the error) of having the *totality* (i.e.,
modal personality) of the qualities in question. This, of
course, is a vicious circle.[9]

The purpose of the above discussion is to clarify an aspect
of the meaning of modal personality not specifically elaborated by others and to define clearly the manner in which
this conceptual scheme is used in the following discussion.

The conceptual scheme "modal personality" (and the
special technique of construction and of investigation connected therewith) is a far more powerful tool than has been
suspected hitherto. There are, in fact, several modal person-

9. In elaborating his concept of "status personality," Linton (*29*) seems to
have avoided the "Napoleon" type of vicious circle. But, contrary to what
I thought (with some reservations) in 1940 (*7*), I now hold that Kardiner
failed to avoid this vicious circle in the construction of his scheme of the
"basic personality" (*24, 25*)—hence, my preference for the term "modal
personality."

alities, all cut logically on the same pattern, although not cut on the same pattern psychologically, i.e., as regards content. The basic finding which served as a point of departure for this conceptual scheme is well known. The Mohave resemble each other in a distinctive way, which differs radically from the equally distinctive way in which the Sedang resemble each other. Hence, one can speak of a Mohave modal personality and of a Sedang modal personality. This is, indeed, *a* modal personality, though not necessarily the *only* one, and perhaps not even the most fundamental one. All depends on the way in which the term "fundamental" (i.e., useful in a given context) is used in one's discourse.

In fact, one may *be* typically American, typically urban, typically middle-class, etc., simultaneously, strictly in Russell's sense of the, correctly used, word "typical"—*though this does not imply the possibility of being understood simultaneously and with the same precision* within the framework of each of these criteria of typicality (see Ch. 6). And it is precisely this finding which places the problem of a person's multiple "status personalities" within the scope of Russell's (*37*) analysis of the paradoxes of Epimenides and of the barber[10] which I discussed elsewhere (*16*).

But, one is typically human, before one is anything else. I am indebted to Géza Róheim for the suggestion that the most basic of all modal personalities is the one which is a consequence of all of us being human. This category of "the

---

10. Epimenides the Cretan says: "All Cretans are liars." If this is true, then he, too, lies; hence, what he says is untrue. But, in that case, the Cretans do not *always* lie; his statement *could* therefore be true; hence, being a Cretan, he *does* lie, etc., ad infinitum. *Solution:* A statement about all statements *does not apply to itself.* In saying what he does say, Epimenides does not speak qua Cretan, but qua self-ethnographer—as an observer of Cretan customs. *The barber:* In a village in which everyone is clean-shaven there is only one barber. This barber shaves all those—and only those— who do not shave themselves. *Question:* How does the barber manage to be clean-shaven? *Answer:* When he shaves himself he does not do so qua barber, but qua inhabitant of the village. *Theoretical model:* The class of classes not members of themselves.

fundamentally human" corresponds more or less to the
Kluckhohn-Mowrer (27) category "universal," except in
one respect. These authors stress—though less rigorously
than I do—that one's self-ascribed and socially recognized
status as a human being is part of the complex of being
"typically human." I cannot, however, accept their assertion that one may legitimately exclude from this category,
as it is used in culture and personality studies, such deviants
as idiots. My objection can even be proven empirically. The
Spartans did not think it necessary to institute exposure for
feeble newborn *animals*. The Romans destroyed monstrous
young *animals* in a way which differentiated them from monstrous *children* (Titus Livius, 31.12.8, 35.9.4, 36.37.1, etc.).
The Nazis loudly denied human status to Jews (see Ch. 6),
yet they treated them *differently* (worse) from the way they
treated animals. The Sedang Moi of Indochina (5) may have
devised means whereby a human being can renounce his
human (= social) status and "become a wild boar,"[11] and
yet reacted differently to real wild boars than to nominal
wild boars. Unlike game birds, the *vogelfrei* (etymology uncertain) German outcast of yore or the "gallows bird," was
not protected by poaching laws. On the other hand, *unless*
his *vogelfrei* status was *known*, he had the same social
stimulus value as any other human being. Conversely, the
Mohave may insist that dogs are "persons" (*ipā*) and yet
not treat dogs the way they treat human beings. Nor do
students of culture and personality ascribe to Rover—be it a
Mohave Rover—the kind of personality which they ascribe
to human beings, idiots included.

This modal personality is, thus, a conceptual scheme,
formulated in a distinctive manner and composed of biopsychological concepts and of concepts connected with
self-ascribed and socially recognized human status. In
other terms, the distinctive modes of behavior that are
relevant here may be explained most efficiently in terms of

11. Compare the Greek symbolic equation: fugitive exile = wolf.

biopsychological processes and of human status.

It is possible to deal more briefly with all other modal personalities: tribal versus national, urban versus rural, Gemeinschaft versus Gesellschaft, status, etc. (*8*). All of these types of modal personalities may be constructed by means of the same techniques. The formulation of the problem and the *type* of understanding desired, as well as the efficiency and the parsimoniousness of the means employed, will decide whether, in a given context, one chooses to emphasize the American, the urban, the leisure class (*40*), the occupational status, etc., modal personality of a given concrete individual.

The fact that the special technique in question, and the conceptual scheme "modal personality," apparently have a far broader application that was originally believed, greatly enhances their importance.

Thus, it is now known that, in simple societies—such as those from the study of which this conceptual scheme and this technique were evolved—the diverse modal personalities, though theoretically distinct, tend to overlap to a very considerable extent.

The same is not true, however, of polysegmented societies. I have stressed (*19*, Ch. 9) that the formulation of the American complex as a whole is far more abstract and hence far less useful in practice than is the formulation of the Mohave complex, for example. The same may be said of the relative abstractness and practical usefulness of such formulations as the "typical American" and the "typical Mohave" (*7*).

In polysegmented societies, the strictly classical type of modal personality tends to be very abstract and, therefore, technically relatively unproductive. This is also true, to a large extent, of societies which are disorganized or in a state of flux, as these terms were defined earlier in this paper. In polysegmented societies in general, and in disorganized and fluid societies in particular, the various statuses which, by definition, are necessarily reciprocal (e.g., husband and wife, employer and employee), are poorly articulated.

Hence, the corresponding modes of behavior (or, conceptually, the corresponding modal status personalities) tend to overlap to a negligible extent. Thus, as long as the peasant and the feudal lord both recognized the God-given nature and necessity of their relationship, and as long as there occurred at least symbolically equivalent "mutual prestations," in Marcel Mauss' sense, one could perhaps speak with some justification of a *technically useful* "medieval personality." Today, when the divine rights of manufacturers are not generally recognized by their employees, a similar generalization would be technically less useful. The validity of my statement is best proven by Kardiner's own analysis of the results of a shift in Betsileo economy from dry to wet rice farming (*32, 7*).

Hence, in situations of this type, it suffices to postulate, on a purely theoretical level, a modal personality of the classical type and to deal, in practice, principally with other types of modal personalities, e.g., urban, status, etc.

It is, however, necessary, both theoretically and practically, to make a distinction between, e.g., American modal personality (urban variety) and urban modal personality (American variety)—or to decide, in our day and age, whether one deals with an Indian (of the pauper type) or with a pauper (of the Indian type) (*10*). I am unable to discuss here whether these two formulations belong to one and the same, or to two different, logical types. Tentatively, as a target to shoot at, I am inclined to believe that they belong to the same logical type. This appears to be in accord with my initial assumption that there are (in terms of content, but not in terms of type) several kinds of modal personalities. (It should be noted that mere numerical differences in the membership of two classes do not imply differences in their degree of abstractness.) Suffice it to say that complex modal personalities, of the kind just mentioned, appear to be both useful and logically legitimate devices in concrete research.

I can now turn to the final logical problem of culture and

personality studies: the nexus between modal personality and the personality of a concrete individual.

Consider, first of all, the general problem of uniqueness, or of the idiosyncratic. Epistemologically, the concrete individual is obviously prior to any generalization. Yet, sometimes it is technically expedient to view the individual as the locus where several abstract classes overlap. In other words, it is technically possible to define the concrete individual as the *sole* member which several abstract classes have in common (see Ch. 6). It is even conceivable that the area (locus) where these classes overlap is, in itself, a kind of class containing one member only. I hold that this insight, including the enumeration of the classes it concerns, is, in fact, an explanation of the concrete in terms of the abstract, though it is not, strictly speaking, a Meyersonian type of explanation.

If, now, I succeed in establishing a logical nexus between these various classes, *other than* the fact that they have one member in common, I am actually constructing a conceptual scheme. I now state, as a (first) hypothesis, that a set of classes may overlap in *several places*, each area of overlapping being confined to a single individual member. I further state, as a (second) hypothesis, that the logical nexus established between these various classes, *at the point where* they have member A in common, *may be* distinct from the logical nexus which I may establish between them *at the point where* they have member B in common, etc. Each such distinct logical nexus may be considered as a configuration, which may be defined *also* as the *structure* of *a* conceptual scheme. In this manner I define individuals A, B, etc., as unique and idiosyncratic. At the same time, I specifically recognize that they *all* are the several members which a set of overlapping classes have in common. The several configurations pertaining to A, B, etc., as loci where these classes overlap, define concrete and unique personalities. The similarities between *these* configurations give a logical meaning to the modal personality.

I have carried this analysis in abstract terms sufficiently far to enable those interested in developing its implications to do so at their leisure. I, for my part, must turn at this juncture to more practical things.

Though each of these constructs, *A*, *B*, etc., is unique, this obviously does not mean that it occurred accidentally. It only means that it is unprofitable, *in the study of configurations, in terms of the frame of reference "configuration,"* to pursue in detail every causal chain, etc., to its remotest origins. In other words, I cannot understand the process whereby genes got together to form *this* John Doe, *in terms of John Doe's personality*. I can understand it only *in purely biological terms*. What is of interest is the specific logical nexus between the various classes, and *this* nexus is accidental only in terms of each class considered separately. In concrete terms, the configuration, which is idiosyncratic in terms of biology or physics, etc., is not accidental, though unique, in terms of the frame of reference "configurations." To be once more rigorous, the conceptual scheme "personality of John Doe" has a meaningful structure.

On the other hand, it is inadmissible to view the *"personality* of John Doe" as the locus where such classes, *and* certain modal personalities overlap. This is self-evident in terms of Russell's strictures on the (illegitimate) meaning of expressions such as "a typical Frenchman" and "Napoleon, the typical great general."

It must also be clearly understood that *"the* personality of John Doe" is epistemologically prior to *"the* modal personality." Both are conceptual schemes, but of different types; the latter is also more abstract than the former. It should be noted, furthermore—and this is an important point—that the modal personality is not idiosyncratic in terms of the frame of reference "personality," in the sense in which personality is idiosyncratic in terms of biology, physics, sociology, etc.

Hence, one must never view modal personalities as components of a unique personality, nor use them as explanations of the latter. If one is careful to use not merely the conceptual scheme "modal personality" but also the proper technique of constructing it—which many scholars fail to do—one can entirely avoid erroneous procedures, which inevitably lead to the more or less disguised vicious circles that one encounters all too often in the writings of Kardiner (*17*), though almost never in those of Linton.

In practice, it is very easy to distinguish efficiently, by a rule-of-thumb method, between personality and modal personality. Consider a policeman. It suffices to distinguish between expectations regarding the behavior of *any* policeman and expectations regarding the behavior of *a* policeman whom I know well. In the first instance, the set of expectations was formulated in terms of the fact that *any* policeman, be he known to me or not, will define a given situation in the same way. In the second instance, the set of expectations was formulated in terms of what this well-known person, who happens to be a policeman, will do in *any* situation, thereby manifesting the continuity of his personality in time (*13, 15, 18*). Substitute for "policeman," "Frenchman," "great general," or any other meaningful term, and the rule-of-thumb method can be used as an adequate test of whether one is talking about a modal personality or a unique and concrete personality.

In logical terms, in the first instance I consider a spatial ensemble and consider the reactions of modal personality to a constant situation. In the second instance, I consider a temporal ensemble and the reactions of a unique personality to a series of highly variable situations (*9*).

Sooner or later, it is roughly in this manner that the dividing line between psychology and sociology will be drawn. Psychology, in the strictest sense, wishes to know all that John Doe does qua "unique person." Sociology, in the strictest sense, wishes to know what (*each* and *any*) John Doe does qua "social animal" in general.

Culture and personality, as an autonomous discipline, is somewhat more specific than is sociology and wishes to know what *this* John Doe does qua American, or qua urban man, or qua judge, etc.

Consider the human species as a whole. Sociologists study men jointly, in groups. Psychologists study the same men severally (cf. the distinction between "all" and "every"). The former deal with a class of individuals, as a class. The latter, on the other hand, deal with a class of classes (each of the subclasses containing one member). The fact that both of these broad classes overlap completely as regards membership does not mean that they are the same. This is self-evident in class calculus.

I cannot do more than mention one final problem which I consider in detail in Chapter 5: the problem of the exact nature of the nexus between the psychological and the sociological understanding of human behavior. The problem is the following: is this nexus the same as the one between the mechanical description of the movements of individual gas molecules versus the statistical description of the volume of gas under study, or is there a complementarity relationship in Bohr's (*4*) sense between the psychological and the sociological understanding of human behavior? This crucially important problem of all sciences of Man must be solved if these sciences are to progress and are to be made useful to men and to mankind alike—and it actually is solved elsewhere (see Ch. 5).

[*Postscript:* The first version of this chapter, read before the New York Academy of Sciences, elicited profitable comments on the part of Professor C. G. Hempel. If the criticisms contained in the published version of his comments (*23*) did not seem applicable even to the first (1945) published version of this study, it is because, gratefully accepting the majority of his suggestions and criticisms, I had modified my text in the sense indicated by his comments. The present —and definitive—version also benefited by the development of my own thinking since 1945. Last, but not least, though my own point of view differs radically from that of G. W. Allport (*1*), his manner of differentiating the "idiographic" from the "nomothetic" served as a trigger for various fruitful reflections on my part.]

Bibliography

(1) Allport, G. W.: *The Use of Personal Documents in Psychological Science* (Social Science Research Council), New York, 1942.

(2) Bidney, David: On Theory and Practice, *University of Toronto Quarterly*, 7:113-125, 1937.

(3) Idem: On the Concept of Culture and Some Cultural Fallacies, *American Anthropologist*, 46:30-44, 1944.

(4) Bohr, Niels: Causality and Complementarity, *Philosophy of Science*, 4:289-298, 1937.

(5) Devereux, George: Functioning Units in Hä(rhn)de:a(ng) Society, *Primitive Man*, 10:1-7, 1937.

(6) Idem: Mohave Culture and Personality, *Character and Personality*, 8:91-109, 1939.

(7) Idem: Review of Kardiner and Linton, *Character and Personality*, 8:253-256, 1940 (cf. *24*).

(8) Idem: *Human Relations and the Social Structure* (M.S.). (A series of lectures on Culture and Personality, Department of Anthropology, Columbia University, New York), Winter 1944.

(9) Idem: The Social Structure of a Schizophrenia Ward and Its Therapeutic Fitness, *Journal of Clinical Psychopathology*, 6:231-265, 1944.

(10) Idem: *Reality and Dream: The Psychotherapy of a Plains Indian*, New York, 1951 (2nd augm. ed., 1969).

(11) Idem: *Therapeutic Education*, New York, 1956.

(12) Idem: Obsessive Doubt, *Bulletin of the Philadelphia Association for Psychoanalysis*, 10:50-55, 1960.

(13) Idem:*Mohave Ethnopsychiatry*, Washington, D.C., 1961 (2nd augm. ed., 1969).

(14) Idem: La Psychanalyse et l'Histoire: Une Application à l'Histoire de Sparte, *Annales: Economies, Sociétés, Civilisations*, 20:18-44, 1965.

(15) Idem: Transference, Screen Memory and the Temporal Ego, *Journal of Nervous and Mental Disease*, 143:318-323, 1966.

(16) Idem: *From Anxiety to Method in the Behavioral Sciences,* Paris and The Hague, 1967.

(17) Idem: Notes sur une "Introduction à l'Ethnologie," *Ethnologia Europaea*, 1:232-237, 1967.

(18) Idem: La Renonciation à l'Identité: Défense Contre l'Anéantissement, *Revue Française de Psychanalyse*, 31:101-142, 1967.

(19) Idem: *Essais d'Ethnopsychiatrie Générale*, Paris, 1970, 1972, 1977.

(20) Durkheim, Emile: *Les Règles de la Méthode Sociologique*, Paris, 1894.

(21) Idem: *De la Division du Travail Social*, 2nd ed., Paris, 1902.

(22) Hallowell, A. I.: Sociopsychological Aspects of Acculturation (in)

Linton, R. (ed.), *The Science of Man in the World Crisis*, New York, 1945, pp. 171-200.

(*23*) Hempel, C. G.: Discussion (of this chapter), *Transactions of the New York Academy of Sciences*, Series II, 7:128-130, 1945.

(*24*) Kardiner, Abram, and Linton, Ralph: *The Individual and His Society*, New York, 1939.

(*25*) Kardiner, Abram et al.: *The Psychological Frontiers of Society*, New York, 1945.

(*26*) Kluckhohn, Clyde, and Kelly, W. H.: The Concept of Culture (in) Linton, Ralph (ed.), *The Science of Man in the World Crisis*, New York, 1945.

(*27*) Kluckhohn, Clyde, and Mowrer, O. H.: Culture and Personality: A Conceptual Scheme, *American Anthropologist*, 46:1-29, 1944.

(*28*) Kluckhohn, Florence: *A Consideration of Method in the Social Sciences* (mimeographed), Cambridge, Mass., n.d.

(*29*) Linton, Ralph: *The Study of Man*, New York, 1936.

(*30*) Idem: *The Cultural Background of Personality*, New York, 1945.

(*31*) Idem (ed.): *The Science of Man in the World Crisis*, New York, 1945. (Contains *22* and *26*.)

(*32*) Idem (in) Kardiner, Abram and Linton, Ralph: *The Individual and His Society*, New York, 1940.

(*33*) May, M. A.: A Comprehensive Plan for Measuring Personality, *Proceedings and Papers of the Ninth International Congress of Psychology*, Princeton, 1930, pp. 298-300.

(*34*) Meyerson, Emile: *De l'Explication dans les Sciences*, Paris, 1921.

(*35*) Poincaré, Henri: *Electricité et Optique*, Paris, 1901.

(*36*) Idem: *The Foundations of Science, Lancaster*, Paris, 1913.

(*37*) Russell, Bertrand: *Principles of Mathematics*, Cambridge, Eng., 1903 (2nd ed., New York, 1938).

(*38*) Idem: *Introduction to Mathematical Philosophy*, London, 1919.

(*39*) Simmons, L. W.: *Sun Chief*, New Haven, 1942.

(*40*) Veblen, Thorstein: *The Theory of the Leisure Class*, (new ed.) New York, 1912.

(*41*) Whitehead, A. N. and Russell, Bertrand: *Principia Mathematica*, I, 2nd ed., Cambridge, Eng., 1925.

5

Two Types of Modal Personality Models (1961)

I T IS one of the hallmarks of a maturing science that each empirical problem which it solves raises new questions concerning the nature of the science itself. This chapter re-appraises the view that the basic construct of culture and personality studies—the socio-psychological conception of the personality—represents a true synthesis of the data and frames of reference of both psychology and social science. This new conceptual model is usually supposed to be a homogeneous, structurally integrated and coherent whole, equally relevant, *in the same way*, for the social scientist and for the psychologist. Logical qualities supposedly charac-terize all personality models of this type, regardless of varia-tions in their actual form, content or theoretical orientation. Thus, regardless of whether a given (psychoanalytic, Hul-lian, Tolmanian, etc.) model represents the modal person-ality of Mohave Indians, of males, of shamans, or of old persons, or the much more concrete and specific modal personality of old Mohave male shamans, it is usually sup-posed to possess all the above mentioned criteria of homo-geneity, coherence and dual relevance. Finally, it has been claimed that all such personality models are identical types of logical constructs and belong to the same universe of dis-course, in the broad sense in which triangles, squares,

pentagons and circles are all polygons belonging to the
domain of plane geometry.

This chapter seeks to disprove the belief that all modal
personality constructs used in culture and personality
studies are, in fact, specimens of one and the same category
of logical constructs. It will be demonstrated that there are
actually at least two ways in which current models of modal
personalities have been constructed and that each of these
two procedures produces a distinctive, sui generis model of
the modal personality. These two models do not differ from
each other in form and content only, the way the model of
the Mohave male differs from the conjugate model of the
Mohave female, or from the non-conjugate model of the
Hottentot female. Actually these models belong to wholly
different conceptual species, having different relevances and
demanding to be used in wholly different ways. It is unfortunate that there should—inevitably—exist two logically
distinct types of models of the modal personality. It is infinitely worse that this distinction is systematically ignored,
that the two models are treated as interchangeable. Yet,
because social scientists and psychologists ask entirely different questions, they must, of necessity, construct different
models of the modal personality if they are to find meaningful answers within their own frames of reference.

Those social scientists who are not exponents of the extreme "culturological" position and take cognizance of the
existence of real people, seek to develop the kind of model of
modal personality which will explain the type of cooperative, or conjugate, or parallel action on the part of many
individuals, which permits the unfolding of social and cultural processes. The question such social scientists ask, with
various degrees of sophistication, is: "Given all the known
facts about society and culture, what characteristics must I
impute to real people to make their actualization of social
and cultural processes understandable?" A typical modal
personality model evolved in order to answer this question
is the "economic man," whom no one ever met in the flesh,

for the good and sufficient reason that he does not exist (see Ch. 4). The logical construction process which culminates in the model of the economic man is fundamentally the same as the one which culminated in certain learning theorists' model of the "stat. rat" (statistical rat) which, even though it does not exist, is a construct or "thought token" enabling one to build one type of logically coherent pattern out of disparate facts related to learning.

The psychologist who is not too biologically oriented, nor too individual-centered, to ignore society and culture is faced with one of two tasks:

1. Whenever he observes certain biologically inexplicable congruences (which are nearly always "justified" by an appeal to some "values") between the behavior of two or more individuals, he seeks to develop the *kind* of model of society and culture which renders these congruences understandable. In so doing he may develop models of society and culture which are quite as esoteric and quite as unsociologistic and unculturalistic as the social scientist's concept of economic man is unpsychologistic. He may then, by circular reasoning, explain these inter-individual uniformities of observed behavior in terms of a psychologistic model of society and culture, exactly as the naïve social scientist circularly explains socio-cultural uniformities in terms of a sociologistic model of man.

2. The more sophisticated psychologist, aware of society and culture, will construct a modal personality which, by social and cultural means, can be *made* to fit the prevailing socio-cultural setting and to operate in a manner which implements social and cultural processes. The key characteristic ascribed to this model is socio-cultural teachability, reinforced by a postulated primary orientation to society and culture.

This model of man is definitely psychologistic, though its systematic use tends to produce, in the long run, a habitual lack of concern with the non-socio-cultural aspects of the personality. Where the "stat. rat" of at least some extreme

learning theorists has practically no sensorium and is made
up almost entirely of an imaginary sort of "inner motor,"
which has only the remotest connection with the real neurophysiology of living rats, the "stat. human" of the culture-
and-personality extremist seems to be all sensorium and no
"inner works" or backbone: he is only a puppet whose
strings are pulled by "society." At this point the extremist,
though remaining a psychologist, comes singularly close to
the exponent of superorganic or culturalistic extremism.[1]
The extreme culturological position in culture and personality studies is held by the neo-Freudians. Probably because
they can do so only by fleeing everything reminding them of
the non-socio-cultural segment of Man's personality, they
have managed to be accepted by certain anthropologists and
sociologists hostile to all authentic psychology as more
"modern" and more "realistic" than Freud.

At this point it seems expedient to turn to a set of carefully documented facts, obtained in America from a group
of some seventy recent (1956) Hungarian refugees by a
multidisciplinary team which included me.

The Relationship Between Psychological
and Social Analyses of Actual Behavior

The type of motivation in terms of which certain historians
and political scientists (6) tried to explain the participation
of *actual* persons in the 1956 Hungarian Revolution proved,
on careful depth-*psychological* scrutiny, to have played an
almost negligible subjective role in the case of those studied
individuals who actively participated in that struggle. Whenever such a discrepancy between the explanations of two
types of behavioral scientists occurs, it is a methodological

1.   It is probably more than a coincidence that the most extreme current
exponent of the culturological position took his master's degree in psychology at a time when the most primitive sort of behaviorism dominated all
learning theory and most of American psychology as well.

error—especially at first—to tackle the problem primarily in terms of concrete facts. It seems best to account for such discrepancies by determining the actual relationship between the divergent frames of reference with which the contending disciplines operate.

In such cases one deals essentially with the vexing problem of the real relationship between psychological-psychiatric (individual-subjective) and socio-cultural-historical-economic-political (collective) explanations of human phenomena. These two sets of disciplines study radically different phenomena. The basic difference between the two subject matters can be clarified most easily by means of an analogy from physical science, already outlined in *The Argument* and in Chapter 1.

1. The behavior of the individual, when seen as an *individual*, and not in terms of his membership in human society, is understandable only in a specifically psychological frame of reference and in terms of psychological laws sui generis. In the same sense, the behavior of the *individual molecule* in a given gas model must be understood in terms of classical ("celestial") mechanics, dealing with *reversible* phenomena.

2. The behavior of a group, seen *as a group*, and not primarily as an aggregate of discrete individuals, is understandable only in terms of a specific sociologistic frame of reference and in terms of socio-cultural laws sui generis. Similarly, the behavior of the gas model as a whole must be understood in terms of statistical mechanics pertaining to *irreversible* phenomena.

I recall, however, that classical and statistical mechanics are not complementary.

Somewhere between these two extremes lies a borderline, or transitional (*4*), set of phenomena, whose usual "locus geometricus" is the small group. I define as "small" any group in which the overall interaction pattern is about equally determined by, or equally understandable in terms of, the psychological makeup of the individuals composing it *and* in terms of the fact that these discrete individuals constitute a group. In such cases it is sometimes possible to explain even certain group events equally satisfactorily in exclusively social-collective *and* in exclusively psychological-individual terms (cf. *The Argument*). The extent to which this is possible depends primarily on the number of members. As their number increases, exclusively psychological-individual explanations account for increasingly smaller, and more and more peripheral, portions of the *total* group behavior, causing the explanations to become increasingly vague. A good physical analogy is the fact that the behavior of two bodies in relative motion to each other can be fully and precisely accounted for in terms of classical mechanics. By contrast, the behavior of three or more such bodies can be described only approximately in terms of classical mechanics because "the problem of three bodies" has never been solved in general terms. Moreover, such approximations become less and less accurate as the number of bodies in relative motion to each other increases. Hence, at the point where the number of bodies to be studied becomes unmanageably large, it becomes more efficient, economical and accurate to ignore the individual particles and to study instead the system, or aggregate itself, in terms of statistical mechanics. In so doing, one not only shifts one's frame of reference, but even seeks to obtain new and different kinds of results. The relevance of this analogy for an understanding of the difference between the psychological and the social is obvious (see Chs. 1 and 4; *1, 2*).

Thus, in abstract terms, the question is never "At what point do individuals and individual phenomena become irrelevant and society and social phenomena all important?"—nor vice versa, of course. The real question is simply this: "At what point is it more parsimonious to use the sociological, rather than the psychological approach?" The same is true, mutatis mutandis, in regard to the nature-nurture controversy (see Ch. 4).

Where only individuals, and relatively small groups, are concerned, the actual outcome of a given process can be equally effectively predicted and equally fully explained either sociologically or psychologically. Thus, it was possible to show (*3*) that the self-incited (provoked) murder (i.e., vicarious suicide) of a Mohave lesbian witch was as absolutely inevitable in terms of Mohave cultural mandates as in terms of that witch's distinctive and unique personality makeup (see *The Argument*). Moreover, in this case, and in numerous others as well, there is an almost incredibly coherent, perfect and subtle dovetailing of individual and socio-cultural processes: each intrapsychic development mobilizes certain reinforcing cultural mandates, and each cultural response mobilizes reinforcing subjective motives and processes. The real objective is not to determine whether the phenomenon is "ultimately" a psychological or a socio-cultural one, but to analyze, as precisely as possible, the dovetailing, interplay and mutual reinforcement (most often through a feedback) of the psychological and socio-cultural factors involved, but always in the form of a (complementaristic) "double discourse."

The possibility of adequately predicting and understanding an event in terms of a particular frame of reference, such as psychology, does not mean in the least that the phenomenon is *primarily* a psychological one and that equally satisfactory explanations and predictions concerning it could not have been formulated in socio-cultural terms. Indeed, even though any frame of reference necessarily uses —and operates in terms of—*partial* abstractions, it can, nonetheless, provide an *operationally* satisfactory and "complete" explanation and prediction of a given phenomenon. A failure to grasp this point is largely responsible for Kroeber's (*5*) recurrent objections to (alleged) attempts to "reduce" anthropology to psychology.

Even more important perhaps is the fact that there appears to obtain a genuine *complementarity* relationship between the individual (psychological) and the socio-cultural (collective) *understanding* of a given phenomenon (see Ch. 4; *2*). Thus, the *more fully* I understand John Doe's anger over the arrival of his mother-in-law in socio-cultural terms (autonomy of the occidental nuclear family, the traditional stereotype of the mother-in-law, etc.), the less I can understand it *simultaneously* in psychological terms (John Doe's irritability, his wife's infantile dependence on her mother, the mother-in-law's meddlesomeness, etc.)—and vice versa, of course. It is *logically impossible* to think *simultaneously* in terms of two different frames of reference, especially if, in terms of one of these, the key explanation is: "All mothers-in-law are defined by our culture as nuisances," while in the other system the key explanation is: "Mrs. Roe systematically interferes with her daughter's marriage." Needless to say, the same complementarity relationship also obtains between the sociological and the psychological understanding of phenomena involving large groups and nations. This accounts for many of the exquisite complexities of problems involving ethnic personality (see Ch. 6) and of many problems in so-called social psychology as well. The difficulty is simply that *systematic and consistent* thinking in terms of, for instance, the psychological frame of reference makes it impossible to think, *at the same moment*, also in systematically and consistently sociocultural terms.

The social scientist is thus literally forced to develop an individual "psychology" to fit *his* data. In order to understand how a large-scale phenomenon can be produced by an inherently heterogeneous collection of individuals, he must assume that these individuals function in accordance with a series of pseudo-psychological specifications. This "as if" approach is quite legitimate, but only in regard to *that* particular set of phenomena,[2] and only as long as one knows that one is dealing with "thought tokens" and "thought

2. In order to grasp the significance of this specification, it suffices to imagine what would happen were an economist to decide to fill in existing gaps in the present model of economic man by writing a study on "The Sexual and Love Life of Economic Man." His essay would be too weird even for a science fiction magazine.

experiments." What is *not* legitimate—though it is done day after day—is to go one step further and ascribe or impute to the real and living individual members of that group the specific characteristics ascribed to a construct: to the *explanatory model of man*, even though the two must never be confused. The radical difference between a real person and a modal personality model is crucial for my argument. A procedure which disregards this, is as scurrilous as would be, in statistical mechanics, the statement: "Since certain gas molecules go from the denser segments of the gas model to the less dense portions thereof, they obviously wish to escape crowding." This is strange reasoning indeed. Yet, it is precisely the type of reasoning used by some historians and political scientists, who assume that everyone who rebels and fights against an economically unfair and politically oppressive system has been *personally* underpaid and oppressed. No matter how sophisticated the manner in which such a statement is made, it is still factually incorrect and logically fallacious.

The reverse process—psychologistic sociologizing—is equally illegitimate. Since Man is, both actually and by definition, a "social" being—though in a very special sense (see *The Argument* and Ch. 1)—even the student of the individual must learn to view him as part of a society and as the product of a culture. For example, if one is a Freudian, one must explore and clarify the nexus between the Superego, the Ego Ideal and the patterning of Ego functions on the one hand, and the structure of the socio-cultural matrix on the other hand (see Ch. 4). This is both necessary and legitimate. What is by no means legitimate is the *transposition* of conceptual models pertaining to the individual to the socio-cultural system as a whole, and the interpretation of the socio-cultural structure and process *purely* in terms of the psychology of the individual, *even if* he does happen to belong to the society whose structure and processes one (mis-)interprets in this manner. Specifically, and in simplest terms, the Constitution of the United States *is* not and can never *be* the Superego or the Ego Ideal of American society. Moreover, a Constitution can never *function* in that capacity: as a Superego or as an Ego Ideal within that—or any other—society, for the good and sufficient reason that society does not have a Superego or an Ego Ideal, any more than the psyche of an individual has a Constitution or a Supreme Court. What can and does happen is that a particular individual may *incorporate* into his psyche—but only in the form of *psychological materials* —certain aspects of his society and culture and then *assign* these incorporated (internalized) psychic representations of outer socio-cultural "realities" to the sphere of his Superego or of his Ego Ideal. A jurist may *subjectively* adapt his Superego to the Constitution, while a pious Catholic may adapt his to the Creed of the Apostles. Conversely, in times of stress, society may change its formal tenets to fit the average Superego and Ego Ideal needs of the citizen. All this does not make the Constitution a social Superego, nor the Superego a psychic Constitution.

The social scientist must view *his conception of modal man* as a model valid only in the study of social phenomena, just as the psychologist must view *his conception of society and culture* as valid only in the study of individual phenomena. In the individual-psychological universe of discourse, society and culture are simply means for the implementation of subjective needs and psychic mechanisms, just as in the collective-sociological universe of discourse individual needs, psychic structures and processes are simply means for the implementation of the collective needs and mechanisms of the socio-cultural system.

A summary analysis of facts and fancies regarding the actual motivation of individual Hungarians—as distinct from the "motivation" of the Hungarian people—who revolted against the system under which brute force on the part of their enemies and timid tergiversation on the part of their friends obliged them to live—will demonstrate with striking clarity the points just made.

Motivation of the Hungarian Freedom Fighter

An inventory of the conscious motivations of individual Hungarian freedom fighters revealed that many of them had no genuinely personal experiences with cynical exploitation and brute oppression. In fact, quite a few of them were in relatively privileged positions and, externally at least, better off than they might have been under the Horthy regime. Hence, some political scientists concluded that those fighters who had no *private* grievances of a tangible and personal kind—and may even have had much to lose by participating in the revolution—were effectively and *subjectively* actuated by their indignation about the inherent viciousness of the system and the brazenness of alien rule, or else by national pride and the like (6). In so interpreting the motivation of these *individuals*, these political scientists actually ascribed to individuals certain characteristics of a sociologistic modal personality construct, developed strictly in order to account for collective participation in mass movements and social processes.

It is true, of course, that some of those who had no real personal grievances against the regime did, themselves, interpret their conduct in terms of sociologistic and socially respectable motives, such as patriotism, love of freedom and the like. It would, indeed, be quite fallacious to deny that they were in part actuated by such (internalized) social motives, which are essentially components of the (sociologistically conceived) motivational structure of the sociologist's construct of the modal personality.

Unfortunately, this explanation of the active fighting in which these persons had voluntarily engaged raises more questions than it answers. It leaves unexplained at least the following challenging facts:

1. Those fighters who did have private and personal grievances and did (in depth psychological interviews) cite these grievances in explanation of their participation in combat did not, in general, explain their own conduct *also*

in terms of patriotism and the like, or at least did not explain it *primarily and convincingly* in those terms. This raises the question whether admittedly gallant fighters, who did have personal grievances, were simply unpatriotic and unidealistic individuals, seeking to exact an eye for an eye and a tooth for a tooth. A supplementary question is whether those who, despite unpleasant personal experiences with the Communist system, did *not* fight, were unidealistic, unpatriotic, or cowardly, or else simply inhibited pious people, who refused to kill and left vengeance to the Lord.

2. The theoretically more relevant question is whether it has not become customary to cite sociologistically conceived "collective" motives *only* where *no information* about the individual's subjective motivation is available. In practice, it is precisely this criterion which is used in U.S. courts of law to determine the legitimacy of a plea of "not guilty by reason of insanity." A careful scrutiny of what actually happens when such a plea is made, shows that the plea is accepted only if the judge and the jury do *not* seem able to understand what could cause a person to commit *such* a crime. The accused is held to be "not guilty by reason of insanity" if his judges cannot *empathize* with his *deed*, as distinct from his motivation. Once the court feels that the *deed* itself is understandable in terms of the layman's conception of common sense (i.e., sociologistically defined) motives, the plea of insanity is nearly always rejected. Hardly ever is there an attempt to inquire into the accused's *real*, instead of *imputed*, motivation. Yet, only an understanding of the accused's real (personal) motives enables one to determine in a valid manner whether or not his seemingly understandable deed *actually* had the "sane" motivation *imputed* to it by judge and jury.

The fact is that if the list of non-subjective reasons for the individual fighter's participation in the revolution is supplemented by certain psychiatric insights, derived from data provided by the same informants to the interviewing psychiatrist (F. Kane, M.D.) and to myself, one suddenly realizes that these apparently socio-culturally motivated individuals were *also* motivated in a highly subjective manner, though their personal motivation may not have been entirely conscious to them, and may have had no direct relation to the social issues of the 1956 Revolution.

The simple fact is that, as a Roman common-sense "psychologist" pointed out long ago, "*Si bis faciunt idem, non est idem*" (if two people do the same thing, it is not the same thing.) Where one man revolts because he has been exploited, another because, twelve years earlier, the Russians raped his wife, another because he hates all authority, still another may revolt because he wishes to impress his girlfriend with his patriotism and valor and so on. All these men may fight with equal ardor, kill an equal number of secret political police (A.V.O.) and Russians, and therefore achieve militarily and socially identical results. Psychologically, however, the results may not be the same. Thus, the one who thought that he fought from idealism may, in the long run, experience fewer guilt feelings than will the one who sought to destroy a hated father imago by killing a secret political police captain or the one who, at great personal risk and with conspicuous courage, blew up a Soviet tank to impress his girlfriend or to reaffirm his membership in a nation noted for its valor.

An interesting case is that of a gentle, well-behaved and well-brought-up teenage Jewish girl, who, at the risk of her life, carried hand grenades to the active fighters. Except for the routine nationalization of her father's luxury goods store, this girl's family had not been particularly persecuted *by the Communists*. On the other hand, while she was still quite small, this girl and her family had been cruelly persecuted *by the Nazis*, and had twice escaped execution at the very last moment. Speaking in terms of so-called common-sense (sociologistic) psychology, the last person on earth who had real and obvious personal reasons to risk her life in the revolutionary fighting was this girl. Moreover, given her gentle disposition, she was the last person one would have expected—using a common-sense conception of the personality—to engage in violence, be it but to the extent of carrying hand grenades to the fighters.

On closer scrutiny, however, it became obvious that this girl, who had been a helpless child during the Nazi regime, was abreacting, twelve years later, her hatred of oppression and of oppressors. The most telling proof of this is the fact that she merely *carried* grenades to the fighters, but—unlike some other teenage girls—*did not lob* them personally at the foe, though, in so doing, she would have incurred little additional risk. In other words, she functioned in the revolution simply as a gallant *child*, doing what even a child can do : bring ammunition to adult fighters, as did countless children raised on the American frontier during the conquest of the West.

Many other examples of unconscious motivations of an authentically subjective nature, hiding behind a conscious façade of sociologistic motivation, could be given. This, however, would represent only a laboring of the obvious.

The real point to be stressed is that both organized and spontaneous social movements and processes are possible not because all individuals participating in them are identically (and sociologistically) motivated, but because a variety of authentically subjective motives may seek and find an Ego-syntonic outlet in the same type of collective activity. This is equally true of spontaneous revolutionary movements and of extreme conformity. Indeed, there are few groups so rent by internecine squabbles as revolutionary cells and hyper-conformist organizations. Moreover, just as a revolutionary may fight because he hates father figures, or because he has personal grievances, or else because he wishes to impress his girlfriend, so a man may be a hyper-conformist from sheer opportunism, from a fear of his own spontaneity, or else because emotionally he still needs his mother's approval.

The way in which the diversified subjective motivations of basically different individuals find an outlet in the same type of activity, be it revolutionary or conventional, is rather uniform, as far as social effects are concerned. Individual differences in personal motivation find a behavioral expression only in differences in the specific details of one's fighting pattern or conformity. Yet, though socially often unimportant, these individual motivational differences may determine intense subjective psychological reactions to the deed which one has performed as a member of a collectivity. Just as the conscious idealist among revolutionaries will, in the long run, probably experience fewer guilt feelings and self punitive urges than the one who killed an anonymous oppressor *instead of* killing his tyrannical father, so the conformist actuated by a real loyalty to the existing system will feel less shame in an hour of lonely self-appraisal than will the cowardly opportunist.

The real theoretical import of the finding that many, highly divergent, types of conscious and unconscious subjective motives can impel people to seek gratification through participation in a given social process is that it simplifies rather than complicates the possibility of obtaining a *psychological* understanding of the motivational structure of participation. Indeed—taking the Hungarian Revolution of 1956 as one's paradigm—were one to assume that all freedom fighters were identically "motivated" (in the sociologistic sense of that term), one would have "solved" the problem of motivation only to be confronted with an even more complex problem. One would have to explain the mystery of a sudden and synchronous mass intensification of one (social) type of motivation or need at a given point in history. At the same time, one would also have to account for its prolonged latency and non-exacerbation from 1944 to 1956. Figuratively speaking, one would have to imagine a single, massive, but subterranean torrent erupting suddenly and inexplicably from the ground, in a single huge explosion. By contrast, if one uses the model of multiple psychologistic motivations, each of which can derive a certain amount of gratification from a given collective act, one has to imagine only a very commonplace river, fed by a variety of tiny tributaries coming from various directions.

Hence, it is sufficient to postulate that a large number of differently motivated persons may perceive a given historical moment or event as *suitable* for the gratification of their various subjective, and hitherto unsatisfied, needs. In the psychological frame of reference, this position enables one to see the Hungarian Revolution of October 1956 as a sudden opportunity and means for the actualization and gratification of a variety of private needs, which had been present all along. Moreover, one can visualize various items of (social) motivation formulated by some sound sociologists, historians and political scientists—nationalism, class struggle, resistance to oppression, humanism, etc.—as (psychologically) *instrumental* motives, which render Ego-syntonic, and not *only* socially acceptable, the acting out of certain needs. Were these needs acted out privately, they would not only be unratified socially, but would also be highly anxiety arousing and productive of intense guilt feelings. Conversely, in the sociologistic frame of reference, this position permits one to view the variety of (*psychologically* pre-existing) highly individualized needs and motives as the means which permit a social process, spontaneous or traditional, to crystallize, just as a variety of fuels, simultaneously thrown in the same furnace, can heat the same boiler.

These considerations do not imply that one must discard, as useless and senseless, the sociologistic motivational structure of a given model of the modal personality. Indeed, a variety of differently and highly subjectively motivated individuals may find that one and the same (often revolutionary) process in society at large can provide certain long-desired gratifications and outlets. If they gratify their needs by participation in this social process, they may be able to render the necessary gratifying acts more Ego-syntonic than if they perform these acts privately. Thus, people go to church for many subjective reasons: to seem respectable; because of piety, and all that piety implies in the unconscious; to show off a new Easter bonnet—and so on. All derive some gratification from this act, even though they are not actuated by a homogeneous set of personal motives, nor by one massive social motive. Their actual personal motives, when juxtaposed, form nothing more than a conglomerate, which can be studied, in psychology, only as a conglomerate and not as a homogeneous motivational torrent, since each qualitatively different motivational unit present in that conglomerate will be gratified by the collective act in a different way, and to a different extent.

The differences in the degree of gratification obtainable in this manner are of some importance. One young Hungarian freedom fighter, who fought with real courage and efficiency, would certainly have been a great deal happier had he been able to fight from the deck of a battleship flying the banner of the Holy Virgin, "*Patrona Hungariae,*" not because he was an expert sailor or a Catholic traditionalist, but for purely subjective reasons. He could think of nothing more glorious than naval service (Horthy was an admiral!), except perhaps a saintly and virginal woman. Yet, this naïve worshipper of the Navy and of virgins fought as well as another, almost delinquent, young worker, who simply hated father representatives, or as well as still another worker, angered by Rákosi's betrayal of the idealistic-socialistic "essence" of communism, or another who had actually suffered persecution. The Russians and the members of the secret political police which these men killed were, moreover, equally dead.

In concrete terms, for the psychologist, society and culture provide, by means of something resembling feedback mechanisms, supplementary (instrumental) motivations, which do not modify the initial operant motivation of real persons, but reinforce, trigger and channel it, by making its implementation Ego-syntonic and by providing the occasion, and often also the means, for its actualization and gratification. This explains why a single exasperated but decent (real) man may not be able to force himself to shoot

down secretly a Nazi Gestapo, a Russian K.G.B. or a Hungarian A.V.O. man representing a hated father figure,
though he is able to do this if society provides him with
ready-made means of *defining* his act as an ethical and
patriotic one. Psychologically, this way of defining the situation may be a simple rationalization, facilitating, qua instrumental motive, the performance of acts leading to
subjective gratifications. Sociologically however, this (socio-
cultural) definition (ratification) of the act causes it to function as a bone fide sociological operant motive—particularly
insofar as the execution of an (also subjectively desired) act
is concerned. In the sociological framework, the real
person's subjective aggressiveness simply permits (qua instrumental motive) the actualization of social mandates
playing the role of operant motives. This is proven by a
traditional Hungarian battle cry: "Smite and slash him; he
is *not* your father!" By thinking it necessary to negate the
role of Oedipal hatreds in combat—which is a social event
—it indicates that Oedipal hatreds play the role of an instrumental motive in combat behavior.

The findings, so far, can be generalized, but only if one
does not confuse statements about real persons with statements about modal personality models and carefully differentiates also between statements concerning psychological
models and those concerning sociological models. If the
latter distinction is not kept in mind constantly, one ends up
either with sociological or with psychological reductionism,
both of which are inadmissible (infra). It is also necessary
to stress that even though epistemologically the *individual*
—qua source of sense data—is prior to *society*, which is a
construct (see Ch. 1), the psychological *model* is not prior
to the sociological *model* of the modal personality, since
both types of models are mutually independent constructs,
in regard to which the words "anterior" and "posterior"
have no operational meaning.

In the psychologistic model, the operant motivation is,
and must be, subjective. Hence, the motivational structure

of the psychological modal personality model of a given group must be made up of motives and needs which are systematically stimulated—either through constant and expectable gratification or through systematic frustration—*in that society*. In the sociologistic model, the operant motivation is, and must be, collective. Hence, the motivational structure of the sociological modal personality model of a given group must be made up of the type of common-sense motives (derived from social mandates) which the sociologist must *impute* to all members of a given group in order to be able to explain their participation in group activities: co-operativeness, patriotism, traditional conformism and the like.

I must now turn from these broad theoretical considerations to actual interpretation methods in the specific domain of culture-and-personality studies only. Though such studies were, in fact, originated by anthropologists, culture-and-personality studies belong primarily to the domain of psychology, since the object which that discipline studies is the individual (in his socio-cultural setting). This implies that in that discipline it is the psychological model's motivation which will be considered as operant, and the sociological model's motivation as instrumental. These two sets of motivations will be brought into play only consecutively (and in that order), because the complementarity principle makes it impossible to think of the same phenomenon simultaneously in terms of the psychologistic and of the sociologistic models of the modal personality. The common denominator—if any—of subjective motivations which are statistically frequent in a given society will, in culture-and-personality interpretations, be defined as the "true" mainspring—as the operant motive—of collective activities. The sociologistic model's operant motivations (i.e., social mandates, both positive and negative, treated as motives in that model), which are closely related to that society/culture's value system will, in culture and personality studies, be *defined* as instrumental motivations (means) for the actualization and gratification of statistically frequent subjective needs or motives.

Leaving aside now methods of interpretation specific to culture-and-personality studies, and returning to general theory, it is clear that nothing in the theoretical scheme offered above—and, a fortiori, nothing in culture-and-personality interpretative methods—can invalidate the sociologistic definition and analysis of social processes or of the individual citizens participating in them. Indeed, in such analyses, subjective motives play the role of instrumental motives only. Through something resembling feedback mechanisms, they make possible the actualization of sociologistic operant motives: of social mandates.

Since I am dealing here with a difficult matter, I must mention also another aspect of the problem. In the psychologistic model, social mandates (sociologistic operant motives) may simply play the role of rationalizations, which seem to ratify, in a particular context, the *actualization* of subjective (psychological) operant motives. Thus, the 1956 Hungarian Revolution ratified, so to speak, the killing of oppressors who, subjectively, were father surrogates. But this finding does not abolish the fact that, sociologistically, it is the hatred of the oppressor which is the operant motive. In short, as stated in *The Argument*, what is an operant motive in psychology is an instrumental motive in sociology —and vice versa, of course. Since one manifestly deals here with a complementaristic situation, any attempt at either a psychological or a sociological reductionism is, a priori, exluded as impossible and, indeed, absurd.

I note, in fine, one more point. In psychology the operant motive is, at times, unconscious and may—as in the already cited Hungarian battle cry—be specifically negated, while the instrumental motive (patriotism, love of freedom) is always conscious. By contrast, in the sociological interpretation of motivation, it is the instrumental motive that is at times "unconscious." But I hasten to add that this is only a manner of speaking, since the sociologistic model of the modal personality has, *by definition*, no "unconscious" segment or layer. Only in strictly culture-and-personality interpretation can one assert—as a manner of speaking—that the sociologistic model's instrumental motives (the parricidal impulse negated, but also revealed, by the aforementioned Hungarian battle cry) is "unconscious."

In short, the psychologizing sociologist studying what are, for him, instrumental motives, must know that, for the psychologist, he studies operant motives. Conversely, the sociologizing psychologist, also studying what are, for him, instrumental motives, must know that, for the sociologist, he studies operant motives.

Conclusion

Any explanation of behavior which uses not real persons' personalities but the conceptual structures known as models of modal personality must consist of a series of steps:

1. The first, psychologistic, step is the listing of the personal motives of the actual participants in a given collective activity. These motives may be discovered through interviewing techniques, psychological tests, psychoanalytic procedures and other psychological means.

2. This list serves as a basis for the construction of a psychologistic model of the modal personality, whose need-and-motivation structure is limited to those needs which are statistically prevalent in, and often appear to be closely linked to, the structure of a particular society and culture.

3. Next, it must be specified that the needs-and-motives ascribed to the model of this *modal* personality can be, jointly and severally, gratified in various social or cultural subcontexts, such as participation in rituals, in political parties, in revolutions, in counter-revolutions, in the acceptance of certain mandates of culture, in certain attitudes, and so forth.

4. Next, a sociologistic model of the modal personality must be constructed, to which are *ascribed* needs-and-

motives that explain sociologically—in terms of a socio-
cultural common-sense psychology related to value systems
—the actual participation of individuals in a given social
process. This list may include terms like "patriotism,"
"piety," "class consciousness," and "conformism."

5. This list of sociologically meaningful "motives"
ascribed to the modal personality model is then "psycholo-
gized," by being redefined as psychologically "instrumental." So redefined, these motives serve to ratify actual
individual maneuvers seeking to gratify subjective and
psychologically genuinely "operant" needs-and-motives;
they are also means for the actualization of subjectively
gratification-seeking behavior.

Of these five steps only the fifth and last permits the
formulation of statements genuinely pertaining to, and
relevant in terms of, the culture-and-personality frame of
reference.

Only the procedure just outlined permits one to construct,
on the logically most rigorous level, a genuinely valid
(double) model of the modal personality. However, on the
level of routine research, one can operate in a simpler
manner—but only on condition of never forgetting that a
technical procedure, however useful it may be, can never
play the role of a fundamental logical analysis; even less can
it obliterate or replace it.

This being said, on the level of concrete research and explanation one must undertake a *double*—but *never simultaneous*—analysis of the facts. This must be done in a
manner which highlights well the *complementarity*, *stricto
sensu*, of the two explanations, one of which is psychologistic
and the other sociologistic.

Indeed, it was shown that, within the framework of practical explanations, that which the social scientist treats as
an operant motivation, the psychologist will treat as an
instrumental motivation. Conversely, what the social scientist treats as an instrumental motivation, the psychologist
will treat as an operant motivation. Only recourse to this

kind of *double but non-simultaneous* explanation insures, on the one hand, a real understanding of facts and, on the other, a non-spurious autonomy of psychology quite as much as of social science. Last but not least, it is only by proceeding in this manner that one can avoid both the sociologistic pitfall, which makes of Man a marionette "activated" exclusively by society and culture, which (as indicated in Chapter 1) is only an explanatory construct, and the psychologistic lure which, when carried to the end, leads to a sociological or perhaps even biological conception of human nature and behavior. (See *The Argument.*) This, in turn, leads to so extensive a "concretization," that the "concrete" acquires all the characteristics not only of the conjectural and the abstract, but even of the fictitious— of the imaginary, pure and simple—in short, of the Platonic Ideal Type.

Bibliography

(*1*) Devereux, George: *A Study of Abortion in Primitive Societies*, New York, 1955 (2nd augm. ed., 1976).

(*2*) Idem: The Anthropological Roots of Psychoanalysis (in) Masserman, J. H. (ed.), *Science and Psychoanalysis, I: Integrative Studies*, New York, 1958, pp. 73-84, 171-173.

(*3*) Idem: *Mohave Ethnopsychiatry*, Washington, D.C., 1961 (2nd augm. ed., 1969).

(*4*) Idem: *From Anxiety to Method in the Behavioral Sciences*, Paris and The Hague, 1967.

(*5*) Kroeber, A. L.: *Anthropology*, new, rev. ed., New York, 1948.

(*6*) Society for the Investigation of Human Ecology: *Second Seminar on the Hungarian Revolution of October 1956*, Forest Hills, L.I., N.Y., Society for the Investigation of Human Ecology, Inc., 1958 (mimeographed). (See papers by Hinkle and by Stephenson and discussion by Devereux.)

6

Ethnic Identity:

Its Logical Foundations and Its Dysfunctions (1970)

IT IS proposed to analyze mainly the dissociative-differentiating and dysfunctional aspects of ethnic identity, whose associative-dedifferentiating and functional aspects are not denied. In fact, it is precisely the analysis of the former which permits one to grasp more fully the latter—as the study of neurosis helps one to understand better the meaning of normality.

I specify from the start that, throughout this study, the term "class" is always used in its logico-mathematical sense only. It is never used in the sense of "social class." As to the term "Spartan," it denotes only the truly "free" upper crust of that city-state—the "Equals" (*homoioi*) (*18*).

The Double Meaning of Identity

When one speaks of ethnic identity, it is relatively clear what *kind* of identity one has in mind. But I propose to show that this *kind* of identity (and the operations by means of which it is determined) can be usefully contrasted with another type of identity (and the operations by which it is determined). A discussion of this contrast is not a gratuitous display of logical virtuosity. It lays the foundations for a rigorous analysis of the dysfunctional-dissociative aspects of ethnic identity.

I. *Identity* = *the absolute uniqueness of individual* A; his *non*-identity with any other individual *B*, *C*, etc., as determined by at least one *very precise* operation which shows *A* to be the sole member of a class. The result of such an operation can often be expressed by means either of a cardinal or of an ordinal number.

A. A cardinal number expresses *A*'s unique weight in *x* millionths of a milligram. Nothing else has the same weight (except the aggregate of weights used to weigh him on a scale).

B. An ordinal number (masquerading as a cardinal number), such as a social security number, can also uniquely identify *A*.[1]

This kind of identity, this type of identifying operation, is of little immediate interest to the student of ethnic identity. I nonetheless note that *A*'s uniqueness—his *total distinguishability* in space and time (*24*), the latter implemented by means of what I call the temporal Ego (*8, 11*)—is of great importance. For, in order to have an ethnic identity, one must be human to begin with. And humanness implies precisely a capacity to be *highly* unique, *highly* different from others, for individuation is more characteristic of Man than of the amoeba. But the uniqueness of *A* is a direct consequence of the exceptional *range* of his potential behavioral repertoire, which is at the root of his extreme *plasticity*. This quality of *A* is relevant for the student of ethnic identity in two ways:

1. It permits *A* to *assume* an ethnic identity and to *maintain* it operationally under highly variable conditions.

2. It permits *A* to *change* his ethnic identity, when necessary.

1. Practices such as primogeniture and ultimogeniture prove this type of identification to be culture-historically ancient (*13*). But it is meaningful and *unambiguous* only if the class contains more than one member. Indeed, if a couple has one child only, that child will, in a primogeniture system, inherit as the "first born," and in an ultimogeniture system as the "last born."

Other problems arising out of the relationship between the exceptionally high degree of the individual's uniqueness and his ethnic (collective) identity will be analyzed below.

II. *Identity = absolute uniqueness defined by an unduplicable accumulation of imprecise determinations.* Each of these operations denies A's uniqueness in one respect, to a sufficient extent to permit him to be assigned, in that respect, to a particular class, which has at least one other member. Such an assigning to a particular class involves a deliberate imprecision which, in principle, is of a specifiable degree. (See Ch. 4.)

Case 1: Some women athletes have a female anatomy, are heterosexual, etc., but are *genetically* "less female" than other women. Their genetic anomaly is disregarded in nearly all sociological operations. Yet, I understand that athletic authorities increasingly question their right to compete with "real" women, for their anomalous genetic makeup appears to give them an "unfair" advantage in sports.

Case 2: Maria Theresa, quasi-absolute Queen of Hungary; Elizabeth II, constitutional Queen of England; Anne of Austria, the Queen of Louis XIII: all can be assigned to the class "queens," but only by operations of considerable imprecision, i.e., by leaving the concept "queen" very flexible.

The assigning of A to class X by means of a specifiable degree of imprecision in one respect—i.e., by means of the affirmation that, in that respect, A is not different from B— neither affirms nor denies A's total uniqueness in some other respect, such as weight, or the fact that only he discovered the theory of relativity.

I note, for the moment only in passing, that A's identity can be unambiguously determined, without enumerating *all* classes to which, within specifiable degrees of imprecision, he may be assigned. Broadly speaking, the more highly differentiated A is, the fewer of his class memberships need be enumerated in order to identify him uniquely.

Case 3: One can uniquely identify Freud by saying merely that he is:

a) A member of the class (having two members: Freud and Breuer) whose researches made the discovery of psychoanalysis possible; and

b) One member of (the more numerous) class of persons who actually laid the foundations of the science of psychoanalysis. This class includes Freud, Ferenczi, Abraham, etc., but excludes Breuer, who took fright and dropped out of the race.

Certain conventions tend to "hierarchize," in terms of "relevance," the various classes to which *A* belongs.

Case 4: Euripides was both a member of the class of all playwrights and of the class of all persons having facial warts, but the former class membership is usually held to be more relevant than the latter—for example, because more persons will be able to name the author of the *Bakchai*, than the person who had *x* facial warts.

In times of crisis this hierarchy of classes tends to become scrambled.

Case 5: Before Hitler, Einstein's most relevant class membership was "physicist." Under Hitler, at least in Germany, it was "Jew" and Einstein had to take this into account.

In times of crisis it can also happen that only one, or a very few, class memberships of *A* are considered relevant.

Case 6: Under Hitler, the most relevant class memberships were being a "pure" Aryan and being militarily useful. At the start of the war the Nazi regime did not fully realize the military usefulness of physicists; this led to the flight of many potentially useful Jewish physicists. By contrast, the military usefulness of generals was recognized: Göring himself declared the half-Jewish general Milch an "Aryan"; as to Germany's warlike Japanese allies, they were held to be "honorary Aryans."

These findings give us a first glimpse of the dysfunctional-

dissociative aspects of ethnic identity—and of other group
identities—though their detailed discussion must be postponed for the moment, in order to contrast "ethnic personality" with "ethnic identity."

Ethnic Personality vs. Ethnic Identity

Though in practice ethnic personality and ethnic identity
overlap in many ways, no satisfactory analysis of ethnic
identity is possible unless the two concepts are *first* sharply
defined and carefully contrasted.

I. *Ethnic personality* is, operationally, a conceptual
scheme, derived by means of inductive generalizations from
concrete data, which, in practice, are of two epistemologically not very distinct types:

A. Directly observed behavior which, as one's data become more numerous, appear to be—or may be viewed as
—prevalent in, typical of and distinctive for a particular
group. Such behavior is recognized as not being *simply*
"human" behavior, although it admittedly implements
some elements of the total possible human repertoire in a
distinctive way.

B. Directly observed verbal behavior of a particular kind:
generalizations enunciated about the ethnic personality by
informants acting as "self-ethnographers" (*9*). Only if such
statements are viewed as observable behavior can one lend
credence to the Cretan self-ethnographer Epimenides' affirmation that "All Cretans are liars." Bertrand Russell (*38*)
has shown that even though Epimenides was a Cretan, and
even though (by his own account) all Cretans are liars, it is
possible to accept Epimenides' self-ethnographic generalization as true, for it is a statement about all (Cretan) statements and therefore does not apply to itself (*9*). In the
ethnic personality perspective, the key word in Epimenides'
statement is "liars." The statement cannot be turned around
and expressed in the form "All liars are Cretans," even if it
could be shown that *only* Cretans lie, primarily because this

latter formulation—even if it were true—would pertain not to the ethnic personality but to a (bastard) ethnic identity model. I also note that, in Epimenides' statement, the term "Cretan" *could* be defined without reference to ethnic identity—for example, in purely geographical terms. As to the ethnic personality of Cretans, one predicates about it only the trait "liar." This very probably does not suffice to render Cretan ethnic personality distinct from all other ethnic personalities, since it is possible that one could correctly say also: "All *X*'s are liars," where *X* denotes an ethnic group *not identical* with the Cretans.

Now, in principle, there could exist an *ethnos* which does *not* enunciate anything whatever about its members' ethnic personality. There could, also in principle, exist an *ethnos* which does enunciate generalizations about its members' ethnic personality, but views them as a formulation of human personality (as distinct from animal behavior) *only*. This could happen in an imaginary tribe so completely cut off from other tribes for so long that it had lost any knowledge of the existence of "other" people.[2] Only an outside observer would realize that his informant enunciated the *ethnic* personality of that group's members.

At times, the generalizations enunciated by informants fit poorly the findings of the competent observer. In practice, such poor fits are often due to attempts to represent the ethnic personality—that which *is*—as congruent with the ethnic identity, treated, in *such* cases, as a *should be*: as an ideal model of conduct, which, logically, it is not, or is not primarily. In many such instances the traits ascribed to the ethnic personality, and believed to be part of the ethnic

2. As I understand it, the Cape York Eskimo formerly somewhat approximated this condition. The fact that some tribes call themselves simply "The People" is also suggestive in this context. But I note the occurrence of an inverse type of "misapprehension." In one instance, the Sedang Moi viewed as a *typically* Sedang (cleverly legalistic) *manipulation* of Sedang customs, a universally female act of ingratiation performed by a captive Annamese girl, who certainly had no knowledge whatever of Sedang law and custom.

identity, tend to have the quality of a value judgment.

Case 7: When a missionary told the Arunta about "original sin," the Arunta indignantly replied: "All Arunta are good!"—and this even though they occasionally expelled or punished for their "badness" persons whom they recognized to be Aruntas and who misbehaved in an Arunta manner.

Case 8: There are probably few ethnic personality self-models which do not include the self-ascription of "courage," though manifestly not every *ethnos* is equally warlike.

I will show further on that the treating of ethnic identity as an ideal self-model, composed of predicative statements of a psychological type, is, in terms of strict logic, an adulterated ethnic identity, i.e., one already contaminated by the ethnic personality self-model.

It is also significant that the logical construct "ethnic personality" presupposes the existence of sets of conjugate and well-articulated ethnic *sub*personalities.

Case 9: A Spartan man's ethnic personality differed significantly from that of a Spartan woman, though neither could have existed without the other. The Spartan woman, too, was laconic, dour, etc., but she did not fight in battles; she only encouraged her men to fight, mocked inadequate fighters and bore stoically the deaths of her men on the battlefield. But one notes that not even one of the 27 cases cited in Ploutarchos' essay *On the Bravery of Women* (*37*) concerns a Spartan woman.

One can supposedly exhibit the ethnic personality either in a good or a bad way. One may, in connection with the latter, think of Linton's (*25*) "patterns of misconduct."

Case 10: I understand that, according to the Israeli sabras, there is a "good" (sabra) and a "bad" (ghetto Jew) Jewish ethnic personality. The reverse valuation is ascribed to these patterns by the Chassidic Jews of Israel.

Case 11: The "black is beautiful" and the "Uncle Tom" Afro-American ethnic personality models contrast in similar ways.

   This leads to a more general finding: it is inherent in the notion of ethnic personality that various members of the *ethnos* possess and display that ethnic personality both in *various ways* and to a *different degree*. This finding leads to the logical problem of "ethnic typicality," so admirably analyzed by Bertrand Russell (*38*, cf. *46*) that it deserves being quoted a second time: "How shall I define a 'typical Frenchman'? We may define him as one 'possessing all qualities that are possessed by most Frenchmen.' But unless we confine 'all qualities' to such as do not involve a reference to any *totality* [my italics] of qualities, we shall have to observe that most Frenchmen are *not* typical in the above sense, and therefore the definition shows that to be not typical is essential to a typical Frenchmen. This is not a logical contradiction, since there it no reason why there should be any typical Frenchman; but it illustrates the need of separating off 'qualities' that involve reference to a totality of qualities from those that do not." Again, with reference to Napoleon and his qualities, Russell observes: "I must define 'qualities' in such a way that it will not include what I am now saying, *i.e.*, 'having all the qualities that make a great general' must not be itself a quality in the sense supposed."

   A distinction must also be made between the "actualization" and the "exhibition" of ethnic personality in behavior. Much ethnic-personality determined behavior is actualized (manifested) unwittingly and at times without an awareness that the behavior manifests the ethnic personality. Roughly speaking, such behavior is actualized because, owing to conditioning and habit formation, it follows the line of least resistance and involves the smallest amount of effort, at least for the one who performs it.

   Case 12: Though it is "easy" for a Cuban to display super-masculine *machismo*, a Hopi observer may view it as singularly strenuous behavior.

   When the ethnic personality is *consciously* implemented in behavior, it tends to be experienced also as an implementation of the *kind* of ethnic identity model which is *logically* already contaminated by the ethnic personality model.

In many cases, an unwitting, "spontaneous" actualization of some aspect of ethnic personality is less easily identifiable as such than is an act which intentionally "exhibits" it. An analogy may help to show what I mean.

Case 13 : Consider two sets of photographs. One set shows the faces of persons *genuinely* experiencing extreme grief, pain or stress; the other set shows the faces of good actors *mimicking* extreme grief, pain or stress. Psychologists have found that subjects misidentify the expression of a *genuinely* experienced state more often than a *mimicked* one. Actual laughter may, for example, be identified as "crying," while the facial expression of a "laughing" *actor* is generally correctly identified.

One last and extremely important characteristic of the formulation of the ethnic personality must now be noted. The generalization "ethnic personality" consists of a set of (usually hierarchized) sets of positive (= Ego-Ideal) predicative statements: "A Spartan is brave, dour, frugal, laconic, etc." Viewed synchronically, all such adjectives are attributes, even when they are negatively (= Superego) (5) worded: "A Spartan is *not* loquacious." One often encounters such *seemingly* negative statements in functionally diachronic formulations of the ethnic personality: "The Spartan is *not* loquacious (like the Athenian, whom he does not wish to resemble); he is *not* alcoholic (like the Helot, whom he despises)." I will show further on that such negative formulations often reflect historical processes; they highlight the dissociative-differentiating *origins* of many ethnic personality traits.

II. *Ethnic Identity*, in the strictly logical sense, is far more difficult to define than is ethnic personality, because, in practice, it is so often—and so abusively—contaminated by the latter. I must consider ethnic identity first in a rigorously logical manner, even though I concede from the start that this logically simon-pure view of ethnic identity has almost no direct practical applicability. It nonetheless needs to be defined in order to render more understandable both the way in which it becomes *contaminated* by the ethnic personality and how it functions *after* being so contaminated.

Ethnic identity is neither logically nor operationally an inductive generalization from data. In the narrowest and strictest sense, it is not even an ideal model. It is simply a sorting or labelling device. It has, *in principle*, nothing to do with modes of *behavior*, be they directly observed by the fieldworker or actually enunciated by the informant. But ethnic identity must be enunciable and be enunciated by the self-ethnographer. Let us consider once more Epimenides' statement: "All Cretans are liars." We saw that in the framework of the ethnic *personality*, the key word is "liars." But in the framework of ethnic *identity*, the key word is "Cretans," whose existence this statement postulates axiomatically. In the *present* frame of reference "Cretans are those who inhabit Crete" is practically the equivalent of "Cretans are liars," for we can consider here *only* the postulation of the *existence* of "Cretans"—*independently* of any quality we may attribute to them.

Exactly as in the case of the ethnic personality, we can also imagine an *ethnos* whose ethnic identity is—because of its unawareness of the existence of other people—identical with its notion of human identity (as distinct from being an animal). But I will show further on that even "pure" ethnic identity can develop only out of a confrontation with, and a differentiation from, others, to whom, *for whatever reasons*, a different ethnic identity is ascribed.

In logic, the ascription of an ethnic identity to someone need not presuppose any performance or predisposition. Where such an enlarged ascription *is* made, the concept is already "impure."

Case 14: A baby born to Spartan parents—an event which, for the newborn, was *not* a performance but a passive experience—was *labelled* a "Spartan." He had a Spartan ethnic *identity*. But it was recognized from the start that he would have to *acquire* a Spartan ethnic *personality*, through an extremely rigorous training, which all ancient studies of Sparta discuss at great length (*30*, *35*, *47*, etc.). By contrast, a Mohave baby was held to have a Mohave predisposition already in the womb. In cases of obstetrical difficulties, the shaman could appeal to the unborn child's Mohave personality to persuade him to be born (*4*). This belief made even birth a *performance* of the infant and, moreover, a characteristically *Mohave* performance.

The ethnic identity, being simply a label or sorting device, does not presuppose, at least in theory, the existence of ethnic subidentities. A Spartan man, woman, child, etc., were all equally Spartan as regards their ethnic *identity* and, moreover, Spartans *in the same sense*.

This implies that, within the framework of "pure" ethnic identity, one could not be more or less Spartan, nor Spartan in good or bad, male or female ways. One either was a Spartan or one was not. Ethnic identity is an all-or-nothing proposition, to such an extent that the very concept of "typicality" simply does not intervene at any point of the discourse concerning it.[3]

In this framework, then, ethnic identity is:

1. Operationally, a label, grid or sorting device, both for oneself and for others.

2. Sociologically, a label which can be attributed or withheld only *totally*.

Hence, it matters not at all, in *this* frame of reference and at *this* stage of the analysis, whether *A* asserts: "I am a Spartan" (with *B* concurring or dissenting), or whether *B* asserts: "*A* is a Spartan" (with *A* concurring or dissenting).

In practice, of course, such things do matter.

Case 15: Brasidas asserted that he was a Spartan, and the Athenians concurred.

Case 16: Róheim asserted that he was a Hungarian, but,

---

3. Similarly, any finite integer is either an even or an odd number: 2 is neither more nor less an even number than 6 or 20, nor more typical of the set of all even integers than any other even integer.

under Nazi influence, many Hungarians dissented and drove him into exile.

Case 17: The Hungarians asserted that, though Hungarian-born, Herzl was a Jew, and Herzl concurred.

Case 18: The Nazi-influenced Hungarians asserted: "Róheim is a Jew." Róheim, the exile, dissented so strongly that he arranged to have his coffin covered with a Hungarian flag when he was buried in New York.

With these findings we pass from purely logical considerations to actual operations involving ethnic identity.

The moment *anything* is predicated about ethnic identity, *other than* "*A* is, while *B* is not, an *X*" (Spartan, Hungarian, Mohave), ethnic identity begins to *function* as an ideal model, akin, at its worst, to a kind of Superego—which is but the residue of childhood traumata which were not mastered when they were endured (5)—and, at its best, to a kind of Ego-Ideal. Like them, the ideal model can be implemented to various extents and by various behavioral means; it may even be (quite illegitimately) argued that the concept "typical" *can* intervene in discussions of ethnic identity.

But, underneath it all, the all-or-nothing concept persists. A good example is the difference regularly made between the concepts "spy" and "traitor." I cite a curious example of the latter:

Case 19: When post-1918 Rumania was still a kingdom, its laws recognized the right of a Rumanian to acquire another nationality—and even another ethnic identity. Hence, unlike what could happen in certain countries, when a foreign-naturalized ex-Rumanian returned to Rumania on a visit, he was not held to be still sufficiently Rumanian to be forcibly inducted into military service. But there was *one* limitation: he could be penalized, even after his naturalization elsewhere, for service in the army of his country of adoption, if that army was fighting against the Rumanian army. Thus, had a (hypothetical) Transylvanian Hungarian who, in 1919, became through conquest a Rumanian citizen but who then moved to Hungary and resumed his Hungarian citizenship, been taken prisoner by the Rumanians *while* serving in the Hungarian armed forces, he could have been penalized for fighting, as a Hungarian citizen, against his (alleged) country of birth. But this is admittedly a highly unusual situation.

This all-or-nothing element continues to exist even where there are attempts to postulate partial or hyphenated ethnic identities.

Case 20: The WASP (White Anglo-Saxon Protestant) usually claims to have a more genuine American ethnic identity than, let us say, an Italian-American, who also claims an American ethnic identity. But, for the sociologist, what matters is that the WASP's (American) WASP-ness is *meaningful* only because there exist *also* non-WASPs. It is an important characteristic of "American ethnic identity" that both WASPs and non-WASPs can, and do, claim it, for this flexibility is inherent in the ideal American ethnic identity, and does not modify—at least for the logician—its all-or-nothing character.

The moment one begins to predicate *anything* about ethnic identity, one is faced with the *seemingly* paradoxical finding that one can instance one's ethnic identity by turning *traitor* (as distinct from *spy*), as far as other members of the *ethnos* are concerned, and even that one can instance one's ethnic identity by *not* instancing it *in a certain way*.

Case 21: During the eighteenth and nineteenth centuries, there existed a class of Catholic Hungarian aristocrats, whose claimed ethnic identity—conceded also by their opponents—was Hungarian, but whose entire *behavior* was un-Hungarian. Many of them spoke no Hungarian, lived in Vienna, were "aulic" (i.e., close to the Hapsburg court), and aimed at a total Austrianization of Hungary as being in the best interests of Hungary and of themselves, qua Hungarian aristocrats. It may even be said that they instanced their Hungarian ethnic identity in a way which differed from the manner in which aulic Bohemian (Czech) aristocrats, of similar outlook, instanced their Bohemian-ness, for similar reasons.

It is also necessary to specify that even though a particular conduct may be felt by the observer to instance both *A*'s ethnic personality and his ethnic identity (as an ideal model), it instances ethnic *identity* from the point of view *of the subject* only if the performance is intended, or is retrospectively felt, to instance it. Training usually made a Spartan "spontaneously" laconic (ethnic *personality*). But if he made a *show* of his laconicity, especially in his contacts with an outsider, so as to exhibit his ethnic *identity*, his performance was logically inseparable from *role playing*. I cite in this connection a curious observation.

Case 22: Hundreds of "typical" Spartan sayings have come down to us. Ploutarchos alone assembled about two hundred of them (*33, 35, 36*). Several observations can be made about these sayings:

a) All, or nearly all, of them are so "typical"—or ritualistic—that after one has read twenty or thirty of them, one feels that one has read them all. Allowances must, of course, be made for Ploutarchos' *selection* of these sayings. Nonetheless, I note a curious fact. Though we possess also a number of pithy sayings by such Athenians as Themistokles, Aristeides, Perikles, etc., their sayings are not only not monotonous, but are not even cited as specimens of "typical" Athenian wit. They are cited to shed light upon the *individual personalities* of these great Athenians, who were typically Athenian precisely by being so very different —for being highly individualistic was part of the Athenian ethnic personality and ethnic identity *model*.

b) At the same time, it is very striking that many of these Spartan sayings were addressed to non-Spartans, or concern non-Spartans, or concern Spartans *in their relations with foreigners*. I concede that, since the Spartans themselves were, for hundreds of years, intellectually unproductive, and since most accounts of Sparta were written by non-Spartans, this finding can be partly explained by considering that foreigners would hear—and report—mainly remarks *addressed to them by* Spartans, or *made about them between* Spartans.

But even when allowances are made for both these factors, it still would seem that Spartans were *more* laconic in connection with non-Spartans than in daily relations among themselves. I hold, for example, that the extreme and "typical" laconicity of these sayings was, to a large extent, due to role playing—to an "exhibiting" of Spartan ethnic identity. (See *Case 24*, below.)

I must, for clarity's sake, repeat here something I already mentioned in connection with the ethnic personality. Consider an activity which, from the viewpoint of the *performer*, seems "easy and natural" because it is a "consequence" (manifestation) of his ethnic personality. If the *observer* views it as an actualization of that person's ethnic identity, he does *more* than view it as role playing. He (rightly or wrongly) assumes also that it involves (intentionally) *more* effort than would the act which he, himself, would "naturally" execute under the "same" circumstances and for the "same" purpose. The observer may even hold that it entails more effort than an ideally parsimonious act, which seeks to achieve the "same" objective, would entail. I place the word "same" in quotes, since, owing to culture-specific evaluations, e.g., an acquisitive activity does not have the same meaning for the Mohave and the Yurok.

This brings me to the key findings of this paper:

I. Since the ethnic personality is an inductive generalization from behavioral data and may, in principle, be held to describe accurately some basic aspects of the personality of *any X* (Athenian, Spartan, etc.) in the form of a model, a particular activity which can be predicted from a knowledge of that ethnic personality, or explained in terms of it, must be viewed as a "natural" manifestation or actualization of that ethnic personality which it instances. Though the conceptual model of the Spartan ethnic personality was originally *constructed out of* the observation of certain modes of behavior current in Sparta, once that model was constructed, those modes of behavior were derivable from it. Thus, Brasidas was brave because, his ethnic personality being Spartan, he could not help being brave; in the framework of ethnic *personality* he did *not* act bravely *in order to instance* his Spartan ethnic personality.

II. Since the ethnic identity is, in strict logic, *not* an inductive generalization from behavioral data, it cannot be held to describe accurately any basic aspect of the personality of *any X* (Mohave, Spartan, etc.) in the form of a model. No particular activity can be predicted from a knowledge of the "pure" ethnic identity (label) or explained in terms of it. No activity can be viewed as a "natural" manifestation or actualization of that "pure" ethnic identity, nor can it be held to instance it, since, in strict logic, nothing is predicated about ethnic identity except that it exists—or rather, is claimed by and/or imputed to *A*. Only when (in a logically abusive manner) something is predicated about ethnic identity, does it become a model—more or less congruent in its *contents* with the ethnic personality, but quite distinct from it in terms of its *logical status*. Once one operates, as one must in practice, with the logically "impure" ethnic identity model, one can assert that Brasidas was brave also *in order to instance* his Spartan ethnic identity. I note in passing that a number of Spartan sayings, which I cannot cite here, do tend to represent the bravery of some particular Spartan, *A*, as something which *voluntarily instances* his Spartan ethnic *identity*, rather than as something which *automatically derives* from his Spartan ethnic *personality*.

I hold that the explanation which views Brasidas' bravery as an inevitable manifestation of his Spartan personality and the explanation which views it as an intentional instancing of his Spartan ethnic identity stand in a relationship of (N. Bohr type) complementarity to each other.[4] Speaking somewhat loosely—for lack of space does not permit me to be more rigorous—the analysis of Brasidas' bravery in

4. The nature and social/psychological importance of complementary explanations cannot be discussed here; they have been analyzed in a series of earlier publications (see Chs. 4, 5; cf. also 9).

terms of his ethnic *personality* is primarily a *psychological* one; its analysis in terms of his ethnic *identity* is primarily a *sociological* one.

I repeat that the preceding paragraphs are the core of this essay's argument.

This being said, I now pass from the (in practice not very useful) concept of "pure" ethnic identity, to the logically "impure" concept of the ethnic identity model, about which many predicative statements will be made. But the reader must bear in mind constantly that, from this point onward, "ethnic identity" denotes *not* the "pure" *concept* (label) but the "impure" ethnic identity *model*, which is more or less congruent, in terms of what is predicated about it, with the inductively formulated "ethnic personality."

I conclude this section by citing three types of observations which help one to distinguish fairly easily between behavior *voluntarily* instancing ethnic identity and behavior which manifests almost *automatically* the ethnic personality as it really is.

Ethnic-identity instancing behavior often disappears as soon as *A* ceases to be under the eyes of other members of his *ethnos*.

Case 23: An old oracle predicted that "Sparta would perish through greed." Spartans were therefore forbidden to own precious metals, and their houses could be searched for it (*47*, 7.6). Nonetheless, as soon as a Spartan went abroad—for example, as governor (*harmostes*) of a subject city—he notoriously displayed greed and corruptibility (*34*, p. 220F ff.). This suggests that impulses incompatible with the ethnic identity (functioning as a Superego) were inhibited, but were nonetheless part of the ethnic personality. (Compare also the striking Mohave belief that every ghost, even that of a very generous man, is highly acquisitive and possessive [*11*]).

Ethnic identity instancing behavior also tends to disappear when a strong upheaval brings about a state of affairs incompatible with the ethnic identity model.

Case 24: As soon as the previously invincible Spartan army was decisively beaten *on land* by a foreign power (the Thebans)—a state of affairs which not only destroyed forever Sparta's military paramountcy in Greece, but was also totally unimaginable in terms of Spartan self-definition— the Spartan negotiators for peace displayed such prolixity of speech that the victors mockingly remarked that they had put an end to Spartan laconicity (*33*, p. 193D, etc.).

There is often a tendency to exaggerate, with respect to foreigners, an ethnic-identity instancing trait, *less* obvious in intraethnic relations. Spartan laconicity in contacts with aliens exemplifies this (see *Case 22*, above). A variant of this behavior is the exaggeration of the tokens of one's ethnic identity during exile (see *Case 18*, above).

The Formation and Manifestation of Ethnic Identity

Logically, ethnic identity presupposes two symmetrical specifications:

1. A is an X (Brasidas is a Spartan);
2. A is not a non-X (Brasidas is not an Athenian).

I have already indicated that an absolutely isolated hypothetical tribe's ethnic identity model is totally congruent with its human identity model. It can cease to overlap with the latter only after the group enters into contact with another group and establishes its *difference* from the latter.

In the analysis—and perhaps also in the historical development—of the sense of ethnic identity, the statement "A is not a non-X ('they')" is prior to the statement "A is an X ('we')."

In short, specifications as to *what* constitutes ethnic identity develop only after the Xs recognize the existence of non-Xs. At the start, these specifications may conceivably include *only* certain real (racial, cultural, personality) traits of the Xs. But it is almost inevitable that these distinguishing traits will eventually acquire also valuative (good or bad) connotations.

Case 25: The Moi tribes have no generic name for themselves. They differentiate themselves from the non-Moi by referring to themselves both non-valuatively and accurately as "those who eat from wooden platters." In addition, they can also differentiate themselves by attributing to themselves a "good" trait said *not* to be characteristic of the non-Moi. One such (formerly correct) trait was "courage in war." Lastly, they also differentiate themselves by the admission that they lack some "good" traits of others: "We don't know how to talk to the buffaloes and therefore cannot yoke them." They even have a myth explaining why they are illiterate.

At times, a trait which the *X*s possess and value, they do *not* attribute to themselves on certain occasions, in order to differentiate themselves from others.

Case 26: A Spartan unable to grasp the speech of a Spartan orator would have deemed himself stupid and would have been called stupid by others. Yet, leading Spartans repeatedly—and contemptuously—professed not to understand the eloquent speeches of non-Spartan envoys (*43*, 1.86; *34*, pp. 223D, 232E).

I note in this context an unusual fact.

Case 27: Owing, no doubt, to Hungary's linguistic isolation in Europe, the Hungarian word "to explain" actually means "to Hungarianize," to put into Hungarian (*magyarázni*).

I will now cite some routine items internal to the race and/or culture, which, originally, had probably *no* relationship with ethnic identity, but acquired that quality when they began to be used as a means of differentiation: of being *X* by being non-*Y*.

1. *Physical traits:*

Case 28: The realism of Bushman wall paintings makes easy the identification of the animal species they depict. By contrast, the representations of human beings remained quite schematic until after the country of the Bushmen (who are small and yellowish) was invaded by the Bantu (who are tall and black) (D. F. Bleek). Nonetheless, paintings showing battles between the two races do not accentuate the *penis rectus (39)* of the Bushmen (castration anxiety?).[5]

A formerly *not* exploited racial *potential* may acquire the quality of a component of ethnic identity and may be arbitrarily held to be ancient.

Case 29: The "Afro" hair-do style seems to me Melanesian rather than African. It does not appear to be traditional in those parts of Africa where Afro-Americans originated. It seems to reflect a reaction to the former (assimilative) use of hair straighteners. But there may be more to it than that. The excessive use of inferior hair straighteners sometimes causes a considerable, if temporary, loss of hair. What little fuzz remains somewhat resembles a scanty Afro hair-do (9). Also, the Afro hair-do is something most other races cannot duplicate or imitate except artificially. It is therefore "Afro" only in the sense that it is *not imitable* by non-Africans (and non-Melanesians).

II. *Internal Cultural Traits* at times acquire the value of ethnic identity tokens, differentiating the *X*s from the non-*X*s, especially under conditions of stress.

Case 30: The ancient nomadic Hebrews probably had no pigs because pig breeding was inconvenient for nomads living in a semi-desert. They may therefore be presumed not to have *eaten* pork simply because they had no pigs. However, after they settled in Canaan, i.e., in the midst of nations who not only ate pork, but ate it at times *ritually*, and in whose myths (Adonis, etc.) wild boars played a significant

5. I am not altogether certain of the second half of this statement. One fairly reliable novel and one not altogether reliable informant affirmed that these battle scenes *did* emphasize the *penis rectus*. A specialist, consulted by mail, did not know the answer. My own examination of reproductions in the Rhodes Library, Oxford, yielded negative results, but the books I consulted were published in an age where "obscene" details were unscrupulously obliterated even in some scientific works.

role, the non-eating of pork became a token of Hebrew ethnic-religious identity. The custom remained the same all along, but acquired a new meaning by becoming related to the implementation of (dissociative) ethnic identity.[6]

Case 31: In the ninth and tenth centuries, the "pagan" Hungarians drank fermented mare's milk routinely, for it was their only alcoholic beverage. But they also drank with pleasure the beer and wine they found in sacked Western cities. However, beginning with Hungary's Christianization and Westernization, the Western priests decided to treat kymyss-drinking as a pagan practice (9)—as missionaries in Kenya treated Kikuyu clitoridectomy as a pagan practice, though nothing in the Bible forbids either of the two.[7] As a result, certain Hungarians, who wished to resist both Christianization and Westernization, defiantly began to drink kymyss in a new and different spirit: as a token of their old-fashioned, "pagan Hungarian" ethnic identity. Much the same may be said of certain educated Kikuyus' obstinate advocacy of clitoridectomy in response to missionary interference (21).

This brings me to what I believe to be an overlooked fact.

Case 32: Marie Bonaparte (1) divides mankind as a whole into "friends of the clitoris"[8] and "enemies of the clitoris." Now, in some areas of Africa, girls are, in fact, deprived of their clitoris and much of their labia (1, 2). But in certain other African tribes, girls are encouraged to manipulate and to tug at their external genitals, so as to increase their length and bulk (2). To my knowledge, neither of these symmetrical practices has been *correlated* with the fact that

6.   I note in passing that, even though the Hebrew dietary laws did *not* enunciate the taboo *in that form*, they tabooed *in effect* the flesh of all *polymastic* animals, perhaps because their neighbors had a polymastic female deity: the Artemis of the Ephesians. To my knowledge, this point has not previously been made.

7.   I note that Strabon (42, 16.4.9) erroneously (?) asserted that Jewish girls were "circumcised."

8.   I have discussed elsewhere the psychological roots of male interest in convex external female genitals (6).

Khoisan women naturally have very long labia: the "Hottentot apron" (*39*). Since the Khoisans formerly lived far
to the north of their present habitat (*39*), the Hottentot
apron of their women may *perhaps* have inspired both the
differentiating (Kikuyu, etc.) practice of female circum-
cision and the *assimilative* practice of the artificial lengthen-
ing of the labia (in certain other African cultures).

Tokens of ethnic identity can result either from *autoplastic* or from *alloplastic* activities.

A. *Autoplastic Activities* involve a deliberate modification of one's own culture. Some of the most striking tokens
of the dissociative nature of ethnic identity models are *new*
culture traits evolved in the form of an "antagonistic acculturation"—a process defined and analyzed by E. M. Loeb
and myself (see Ch. 8). I can enumerate only a few striking
maneuvers of this kind.

1. *Total Imitation in Reverse*, while not common, does
exist.

Case 33: Adult Spartans forced the despised Helots—a
subject population "neither slave nor free," as an ancient
authority puts it—to get drunk and then exhibited them to
young Spartans as *negative models* (*30*, 28.4-5): young
Spartans were expected to learn sobriety by observing
drunken Helot behavior. I note in passing that this did *not*
suffice to teach King Kleomenes I to be sober, for *he* had
learned to drink undiluted wine from (non-despised)
Skythian ambassadors (*19*, 6.84, etc.).

2. *Partially Deviative Imitation* consists in evolving practices which, though not always *totally* in opposition to traits
held to be part of the ethnic identity of Others, deliberately
deviate from them and become components of one's own
ethnic identity.

Case 34: The Bible repeatedly admonishes the Jews in
Canaan not to be "like unto" the people surrounding them.

Case 35: G. Vajda (*45*) has shown that, after Mohammed
lost hope of converting the "People of the Book" (Jews and
Christians), he devised a whole series of behavior patterns

for Mohammedans, whose main purpose was to *differentiate* them from the "unbelievers."

B. *Alloplastic Activities* involve changing the culture of others, who are either forbidden certain distinctive culture traits or forced to adopt them. The dominant group then treats both as tokens of the ethnic identity of the dominated. The yellow Star of David, which the Nazis forced the Jews to wear, is an obvious case. But it is striking that the forbidden trait can be smuggled into the culture of the oppressed *in disguise* and accepted as a token of ethnic identity; invidiously imposed culture elements can also turn into such tokens.

Case 36: Some Arab states forbade the Jews to ride camels. According to an informant, certain Jewish sects compensated for this by rocking themselves like camel riders while praying. But this explanation may well be only folklore.

Case 37: The Manchus imposed the pigtail on the Chinese, for whom it soon became a token of ethnic identity.

Case 38: The Chassidim consider certain garments necessary tokens of Jewish ethnic identity, even though they had been invidiously forced upon them by their former Polish overlords.

Case 39: Between 1926 and 1932, I never once saw a French Jewish boy or girl wear the Star of David as a necklace pendant. In 1946, after the Nazi occupation, I saw many French Jewish girls, and even boys, wear such pendants, but have seen none since my return to France in 1963. At present (1977) they seem to be worn again.

I note in passing that antagonistic acculturation often involves the borrowing of the other's means, the better to defeat his ends and to protect one's own ethnic identity. This sometimes takes the form of what Kroeber called "stimulus diffusion" (*23*).

Case 40: Sequoya invented the Cherokee alphabet in competition with (and as a result of stimulus diffusion from) the English alphabet.

A particularly interesting example of the implementation of ethnic identity is the acceptance of "ethnic" *psychological* traits invidiously attributed to certain oppressed groups.

Case 41: Many formerly warlike groups, forced to become despised mérchants and then accused of shrewd practices, tend to take pride in being "shrewd" and deem it a token of their ethnic identity. This is as true of medieval Jews as of Armenians in Mohammedan lands, of Levantine Greeks, etc. In the Homeric poems, only Odysseus—a great hero—is, in some respects, a Levantine Greek; he becomes almost caricaturally Levantine in certain Greek tragedies (*17, 40, 41*). Yet, only one scene of the *Iliad* (*20,* 6.234 ff.) depicts a profitable deal pulled off in a Levantine manner: Glaukos exchanges his golden armor, worth a hundred oxen, for Diomedes' bronze armor, worth only nine—a naïveté which the poet himself highlights and ridicules.

Case 42: In addition to dire necessity, the extreme military prowess of the Israelis is partly a reaction to their millenary intimidation, and partly also a conscious return to the (contaminated) ethnic identity model of the pre-Diaspora Jews, whose great military prowess was recognized even by their Hellenistic and Roman conquerors.

In note, in fine, that a change in one's ethnic self-definition is, at times, made possible by an undeviating adherence to *one* ethnic identity trait.

Case 43: A French Jewish acquaintance, who had fought in the Free French army and had deemed military prowess an important component of his French ethnic identity, began to feel that he had (also) a Jewish ethnic identity only *after* the Israelis displayed extreme military valor in 1948, 1956 and 1967.[9]

Several other and very important aspects of the implementation of ethnic identity may also be mentioned.

9. I suspect, however, that *part* of this shift in his ethnic identity was due to the 1940 French military disaster and to the antisemitic measures of the Pétain regime.

Behavior instancing ethnic identity tends to be more ritualistic and monotonous than behavior triggered by the ethnic personality (see *Case 22*, above). One cannot but think, in this connection, of a remark Dodds (*14*) made in another context: "History no doubt repeats itself: but it is only ritual that repeats itself *exactly*." This ethnic identity ritualism may even become exaggerated in times of decline: the Spartans under Roman domination seem to have *played at* being Spartans more consistently than they did at the peak of Spartan power,[10] and this despite the likelihood that, e.g., earlier Spartan sayings probably lost nothing of their "typicality" in the telling. In some cases such ethnic role playing leads to excesses comparable only to the absurdity of eighteenth-century castrati singing passionately sensual operatic roles.

Ethnic identity is sometimes maximally implemented by those who, by ordinary standards, would not be expected to possess it.

Case 44: The greatest Hungarian poet—a patriot who died a hero's death as a volunteer in the revolutionary army of 1848–1849—was of Serbian extraction and had Magyarized his name, Petrovics, to its Hungarian equivalent: Petőfi (Peterson).

Case 45: European public opinion forced the Emperor of Austria to dismiss in disgrace the half-demented Austrian general Haynau, notorious for his brutal repressions in Hungary after the 1848 Revolution. Haynau thereupon purchased an estate in Hungary, affected the Hungarian national costume, and went about proclaiming: "We Hungarians will not allow ourselves to be robbed of our national liberties." It won him no recognition as a possessor of Hungarian ethnic identity.[11]

---

10.   In the same sense, only a modern-day millionaire can have a 100 percent Louis XIV salon, for the salons of dukes in Louis XIV's time assuredly contained also Henri IV or Louis XIII heirlooms and portraits of ancestors.
11.   Compare also the exiled Athenian Alkibiades playing at being super-Spartan in Sparta.

The *intellectual* awareness that a trait previously felt to be an implementation of one's ethnic identity is actually *alien* does not necessarily destroy its capacity to be still experienced as ethnic.

Case 46: Until Bartók showed that gypsy music was *not* Hungarian, it was thought to be, and—despite Bartók—continues to be experienced as Hungarian. What little I preserve of a "Hungarian ethnic identity" is more easily aroused by a gypsy *csárdás* than by a pentatonic peasant song. /

Last, but not least, there are very few one-dimensional ethnic identities.

Case 47: I remind the reader once again that in the following discussion the term "Spartan" denotes *only* the "full" Spartans, the "Equals."

a) They claimed a Hellenic ethnic identity (as contrasted with that of the Barbarians).

b) At times they claimed a (racial) Dorian identity, as did King Anaxandridas, who called the eldest son of his favorite wife Dorieus (the Dorian). But at other times they claimed to be "successors" of the Achaian Atreids, as did the ephor Chilon and the son of his kinswoman (by Anaxandridas), King Kleomenes (*19*, 5.72). They validated the latter claim by "discovering" abroad and reburying in Sparta the bones of an Achaian, Orestes, son of Agamemnon and nephew, son-in-law and heir of Menelaos (*19*, 1.67). Thus, Spartan expansionism could be justified either by claiming Dorian (conqueror) identity or else Achaian (legal successor) identity.

c) The Spartans also claimed a Spartan identity:

(α) as contrasted, e.g., with the Athenians;

(β) as contrasted with their Helot serfs; and

(γ) as contrasted with Sparta's satellites, via the equation: Spartan = soldier, for only the Spartan was not permitted to be anything but a soldier.

Case 48: At a gathering of the armies of Sparta and of its allies, the latter protested that Sparta had contributed too

few soldiers. In response, the Spartan leader asked that all
the potters, smiths, carpenters, etc., of the assembled armies
stand up in turn. Eventually all the allied warriors stood up.
Finally, he asked that the (professional) soldiers stand up:
only the men of the Spartan contingent rose, for they alone
were *professional* soldiers *only*. This was supposed to prove
that Sparta had contributed more soldiers than anyone else
(*34*, p. 214A).

A last aspect of ethnic identity must now be considered.

C. *Ethnic Identity and Areal Climax*. In certain cases the
claim to incarnate the areal climax, in Kroeber's sense (*22*),
is part of the ethnic identity of more than one *ethnos*. At
least two Greek city-states professed to incarnate the essence
of Greece.

Case 49:

a) *Athens* was called the "school of Hellas" by Perikles;
a poet hailed it as the "Hellas of Hellas." It deemed itself
typical of Greece—in the sense in which the *finest* race horse
may be said to typify all of horsedom. How *different* Athens
was from other Greek states is shown by the characteriza-
tions of Athens by the Korinthian, Spartan and Athenian
orators at a gathering of Sparta and its allies, which had to
decide on peace or war with Athens (*43*, 1.68 ff.). In addition, Athens claimed to be the *most* Greek of all Greek cities
because only *its* people were truly "autochthonous," having
always lived in Attike (*19*, 1.56; 7.161). This, needless to say,
also made them very *different* from other Greek cities, in
which the pre-Greek (Pelasgian) racial element was minimal, and many of which, at the end of the Achaian period,
had been overthrown by the invading Dorians. Yet,
even dour Sparta acknowledged at least Athens' eminence,
if not *pre*-eminence, in Hellas. When Athens lost the Peloponnesian War, one Theban envoy urged that it be dealt
with as Athens had dealt with Melos: the city was to be
razed, the men slaughtered, the women and children en-
slaved. At that point, an envoy from Phokis, one of Athens'
enemies, rose and sang a choral ode from Euripides'

Elektra, and a dour Spartan envoy declared that Sparta was unwilling to destroy the city that had saved Greece during the Persian wars, some eighty years earlier (*30*, 15). At that moment, Athens' ethnic identity, as implemented by its past, became for it a capital reserve.

b) *Sparta*—so outlandish by ordinary Greek cultural standards—was also deemed by some to be "ideal Greece," on very different, and possibly even less valid, grounds. The "real" Spartans were Doric invaders (*18*), while much of Greece was *not* Dorian. No Greek state differed more—in qualitative ways—from the rest of Greek states than did Sparta. Athens differed from the others mainly *quantitatively*: it had *more* good poets, artists, philosophers, craftsmen, sailors, etc.[12]

III. *Mystique:* Unlike ethnic personality, ethnic identity nearly always has both a "self" mystique and an "ascribed" mystique. I propose to examine a most peculiar specimen of such a twofold mystique, which was, in significant respects, produced by outsiders.

Case 50: Several aspects of the mystique of Spartan ethnic identity must be considered.

a) The self mystique and the ascribed mystique converged in some respects: the Spartans deemed themselves invincible on land, and the Athenians—their enemies—concurred. At the outbreak of the Peloponnesian War, Perikles advised Athens to fight *only* at sea (*43*, 1.142 ff.).

b) The two mystiques may diverge, at least in their evaluations. The Spartan deemed absolute rectitude a token of his ethnic identity. The Athenians held the Spartan to be

---

12. I note the curious fact that even though it is generally recognized that the Roman conquerors preserved Sparta as a kind of "reservation for antiquarians," it is less well known that they *also* preserved Athens as a kind of "reservation for students," as a university town. It is even ironic that Sparta became a super-tough reservation when it *ceased* to be a military power, and Athens an intellectual reservation when it *ceased* to produce first-class minds.

totally dishonest, *especially* when he pretended to be righteous. It suffices to cite here Euripides' characterization of Menelaos, King of Sparta, in his *Andromache* (*16*), a characterization based not upon the image of the Achaian Menelaos of the *Iliad*, but upon the Athenian's image of the fifth-century-B.C. Spartan.

c) Even where the facts prove both the (convergent) self mystique and ascribed mystique to be false, they often continue to be accepted by both in-group and out-group. The myth of Spartan invincibility *on land* survived their severe defeat by the Athenians at Sphakteria. Ploutarchos wrote almost 500 years after his own city, Thebes, had forever broken Spartan pre-eminence at Leuktra; yet he too preserved the mystique of the Spartan's military superiority to the Theban hoplite—he attributed Sparta's defeat to the genius of a single Theban: Epameinondas (*34*, 214C ff.).

d) At times an *ethnos* can have a *double* ethnic-identity self mystique. Thus, Sparta's double (Dorian and Achaian) ethnic identity and mystique led only to alternations in the choice of foes; Sparta remained expansionist. As shown in *Case 47*, above:

(i) The Dorian ethnic mystique justified aggression by a Dorian superiority in arms, and

(ii) The Achaian mystique sought to give a mythico-legal basis to Spartan expansionism.

e) In the case of Sparta, much of the mystique of its ethnic identity was manufactured by outsiders, though the Spartans gladly went along with it.

As regards the mystique of superiority, the Spartans did originate what Ollier (*28*) calls the "romance of Sparta" regarding the antiquity and stability of its aristocratic constitution. But the "romance of Sparta" was *fully* elaborated only by pro-Spartan outsiders, the Spartans themselves being too brutishly uneducated to do it themselves. The real "romance of Sparta" was written by three Athenians, all of them disciples of Sokrates: the ghastly oligarch and traitor Kritias, the bright but naïve Xenophon, and Platon, who valued systems more than men and deemed abstractions more real than reality.

I must add that much of the mystique of Spartan ethnic identity rested on a misconception assiduously fostered by Sparta. Its "Lykourgan" constitution was almost certainly less ancient than claimed. But it may well have been the first "revolutionary" constitution of Greece, because Sparta had earlier and greater inner troubles than the other Greek city-states (*18*). Also, the stability of its institutions—on which the ethnic identity of the "real" Spartans largely depended —was achieved at the appalling cost of turning every free Spartan into a military slave of the state, for Sparta was sitting on a volcano (*7*). Other states refused to pay so high a price for stability, especially since the continuity of *their* ethnic identity did not depend on it. They, too, assuredly had occasional civil disorders, but it pitted, e.g., the Athenian aristocrats against the Athenians demos only. Whoever won, it was an Athenian who won. By contrast, in Sparta the overthrow of the "free" Spartans by the Helots would in the last resort have impaired and changed Spartan ethnic identity and destroyed the city-state. Solon's laws could afford to disenfranchise an Athenian who did not take sides in civil strife (*31*, 20)—the laws of Lykourgos could not afford this.

The Functionality and Dysfunctionality of Group Identities

Marcel Mauss (*27*) has shown that even though every person is aware of his own identity—of his "selfhood"—many primitive societies *do not implement* his distinctiveness socially. Sometimes the individual is, in some respects, functionally interchangeable with other individuals, and he may freely acknowledge this fact.

Case 51: A Sedang man had married two cousins, who were also best friends and therefore called each other by the same (invented) name. One day I asked one of them if she was jealous when her husband cohabited with her co-wife and cousin. She replied: "Why should I be? She is the same person as I" (in *this* respect). At the same time, this woman *knew* that she was a unique and strong personality, who knowingly repudiated many Sedang attitudes and beliefs.

It is convenient to approach the social implementation of individuality from the vantage point of types of relationships. Parsons has outlined three such types (*29*):

a) *The functionally specific* (e.g., buyer and seller). All that is not explicitly included is excluded. The *demand* must be justified. This type of relationship is highly segmental and predominates in complex societies.

b) *The functionally diffuse* (e.g., husband and wife). All that is not explicitly excluded from it is deemed to be included. Not the demand, but the *refusal* must be justified.

c) *The functionally cumulative* (e.g., employer-and-lover versus secretary-and-mistress). Such relations tend to cause conflict (*12*, Ch. 9).

But Parsons' scheme omits what I consider to be the type relationship in primitive societies:

d) *The functionally multiple.* Abraham was tribal chief, general, priest, pater familias, etc., and could not have been any one of these without being all the others as well.

But the predominance of functionally multiple relationships in some primitive societies does not necessarily represent the extensive social implementation of a person's uniqueness, for one may accede to many a status in which one's relations are functionally multiple, though having very few attributes only. In sororal polygyny, it suffices to be a married woman's sister in order to become a co-wife, though in that capacity the woman's social relations will certainly be functionally multiple: sexual partner, mother, cook, etc. In order to become king, one need only be a king's oldest son. The proclamation "Le Roi est mort, vive le Roi!" affirms the functional interchangeability (*3*) of the defunct king and his successor.

It is a striking fact that it is precisely at the top and bottom of the social scale that people are, on the one hand, functionally most interchangeable and, at the same time, possess—at least in principle—the highest degree of freedom in the selection of the segments of the total potential range of behavior they choose to actualize at any moment. The law of ancient Persia was that the king was not subject to the law (*19*, 3.31). Under the Ancien Régime, the law was, in theory, the king's untrammelled will: "Le Roi le veut"; "Car tel est Notre bon plaisir." Even more relevant is Dollard's (*15*) observation that the Southern police often overlooked a black's misconduct, though they would have arrested a white for similar behavior.

It seems evident that the *social* recognition and implementation of personal identity resulted from the disintegration of functionally multiple relationships into their components. This appears to have gone hand in hand with what Durkheim called "social polysegmentation," which permitted, for example, a woman to become *A*'s wife, *B*'s mistress, *C*'s cook, etc. Historically, the *socially implemented* individual identity of *A* emerged apparently from the recognition that a person could have *simultaneously* plural class identities with respect to *B*, and even that each of his class identities (memberships) could be relevant only with regard to a *different* person and/or in *different* contexts. Also, the number of conditions a person had to satisfy in order to be assigned to any particular class tended to increase. Though King Louis XIV was, in principle, still Commander-in-Chief, in war his armies were commanded by his generals.

One also observes that in many instances *A*'s membership in class *X* gains added dimensions by:

1. his belonging *also* to classes *Y*, *Z*, etc.: his status as a (Bourbon) Serene Highness greatly increased Condé's authority as a brilliant general; and

2. his *not* belonging to classes *M*, *N*, etc.: a ruined French nobleman of Normandy, wishing to restore his fortune by

engaging in commerce, could temporarily place his nobility "in escrow" with the parliament of his province.

But the social recognition of *A*'s *multiple* class memberships can entail also the recognition that he belongs to some class cutting across ethnic lines: a Mohave of gens Hipā would commit incest if he married a Yuma woman also belonging to the Hipā gens. It can also lead to the formation of outlooks or character traits cutting across ethnic barriers: both some Plains Indian songs and *Fragment 10* of the Spartan poet Tyrtaios (*44*) affirm that the corpse of a *young* man fallen in battle is a beautiful and inspiring sight.

Case 52: A Spartan's Spartanness compelled him to implement intensively *and exclusively* the segment of behavior related to military prowess. Sparta seems to have produced no intellectuals between the time of Alkman and Tyrtaios (seventh century B.C.) and the unimportant Hellenistic savant Sosibios (third century B.C.). The law prohibiting gainful occupations also caused Sparta to enter the Peloponnesian War with only a negligible amount in the treasury (*43*, 1.130, etc.). In short, the Spartan's Spartanness tended to exclude *entirely* the implementation of many of his potentialities and to subordinate to his Spartanness even those of his potentialities which were deemed compatible with his being a Spartan: he had the right to be a husband and father, but his family life was reduced to a minimum, to give him more time to be a Spartan. By contrast, the Athenian's Athenianness *also* demanded that he implement valor, but he was free—and, indeed, expected— to implement other behavioral segments as well. Sophokles was a manufacturer, general and statesman, as well as a dramatic poet; he was, moreover, entitled to a *genuine* private life and to a meaningful—at once social and strictly personal—identity. The flexibility of the Athenian's ethnic identity was probably due to the early establishment of a true unity and equality of all the inhabitants of Attike. Attic "synoikismos" contrasts greatly with the basic disunity of the Spartan state, inhabited by "true" Spartans, Perioikians (dwellers about) and Helots—not to speak of a variety of intermediate layers: Partheniai, Neodamodeis, etc.—all with very unequal rights. The constant conflicts of these groups were both Sparta's raison d'être and curse (*7*).

It is conceded that in selecting, and in being *made* to select, for implementation only certain segments of his total repertoire, Man theoretically impoverishes and constricts himself—at least in principle. But, in practice, this "loss" (in certain areas) is *more* than compensated for by a greater and more satisfying expertness in segments selected for implementation (*12*, Ch. 2). Moreover, this selectiveness also has valuable psychological and social consequences. Linton (*26*) hinted long ago that the flexibility of Man's instincts is so great that they are unable to *organize effectively* and to render predictable his behavior and personality to a sufficient extent to make life in society possible. In order to organize his personality and render it predictable, Man needs to provide himself with a stabilizing skeleton of habits and customs.

I now specify that what, in one perspective, is a (necessarily) selective "custom" (or habit) is, in another perspective, the selection, for consistent implementation, of certain segments of Man's total potential repertoire. In still another perspective, the selection of certain of these segments for a consistent behavioral implementation entails the assigning of *A* to a whole series of class memberships: the ascription to him of a series of *class identities*, one of which is his ethnic identity.

But, if one bears in mind what was said at the beginning of this study—that *A*'s individuality can be made *totally unique* by enumerating all his class identities (by assembling an *unduplicable accumulation*, structured or not, of [specifiably imprecise] informations about him)—it becomes evident that this selectiveness as to the segments of the repertoire which *A* implements in his behavior makes him wholly unique, and also exceptionally creative and spontaneous. In short, *A* becomes, and is made to appear, unique and differentiated from all others by his distinctive and *unduplicated* selection for special implementation of certain segments of his total potential repertoire. Since the selection of certain of these segments can, in another perspective, be viewed as the self-ascription of a *series* of class memberships (class identities), *A*'s unique identity can be determined by an enumeration of all his class identities—or at least of a sufficient number of his class identities to make it impossible for any other person *B* also to belong to all these classes.

When an individual has a sufficient number of sufficiently varied class identities, each of them becomes a "tool" and their totality becomes a kind of "toolbox," which both actualizes and implements socially his unique *pattern* of personality.

But when one of *A*'s class identities becomes hypercathected to the point of severely conflicting with, or else totally subordinating to it, all the rest of *A*'s class identities, singularly dysfunctional manifestations of class identity begin to appear.

One conflict can arise when what is deemed to be the principal class identity is actually less effective in certain circumstances than are other class identities.

Case 53: The Marseillaise appeals to all "enfants" *only* of "la Patrie"; a Marxist slogan urges *only* "the *workers* of (*all*) the world" to unite. Yet, in order to encourage the Soviet armies to resist the Nazi armies to the utmost, Stalin had to appeal to *ethnic* identity and represent the struggle as taking place between Russians and Germans.

Turning specifically to ethnic identity, when a *hypercathected* ethnic identity overrides all other class identities, it ceases to be a tool—let alone a toolbox—and becomes, as was shown for Sparta (see *Case 52*, above), a straightjacket. Indeed, the achievement of a *collective distinctiveness*, by means of a hypercathected and overimplemented ethnic identity can, as a simple example will show, lead to an obliteration of *individual distinctiveness*.

Case 54: The Spartan hoplite wore a red cloak, which *distinguished* him from all other heavily armed infantrymen. But the redness of his cloak had another function as well: it *obliterated* the hoplite's *individual state* in one respect; if he was wounded, the blood he shed did not show up on the red cloak (*35,* 24; *47,* 2.3). Hence the *wounded* Spartan individual's special condition could neither encourage the foe nor elicit his compassion.[13]

In short, in implementing one's hypercathected ethnic identity, one increasingly minimizes and even negates one's individual identity. Yet, Man's *functionally relevant* dissimilarity from all others is what makes him human, similar to others precisely through his high degree of differentiation. It is this which permits him to claim a human identity, and therefore also a personal identity.

A hypercathected ethnic identity's implementation can also become onerous to the point of becoming dysfunctional.

Case 55: A Roman magistrate was sometimes compelled by his (Roman) ethnic identity to sentence his own son to death—and to do so with a stiff upper lip. By contrast, Perikles could afford to plead in tears with the Athenian assembly to secure the acquittal of his mistress, Aspasia (*32,* 32).

Case 56: The cost at which the Jews preserved their ethno-religious identity need hardly be recalled. Under Antiochos Epiphanes, they circumcised their sons at the risk of their lives.

In short, it may be argued that a hypercathecting of the ethnic identity leads, in effect, to a reduction of the subject's *relevant* class identities to one only—and thus to the annihilation of the individual's real identity. The same occurs when only one of a person's class identities is deemed

13. Compare Homeros, *Iliad* 12.390 ff.: Glaukos, wounded, withdraws from the battle so that his (wounded) state would not encourage the foe (*20*).

relevant. Under the Nazis, the Jews were gradually stripped of all their *relevant* class identities, save only their Jewish identity—and, in the process, were denied a personal identity.

It is dysfunctional—and indeed catastrophic—when one reduces someone else to such one-dimensionality. But the contemporary scene abounds in examples of persons stripping *themselves* of all their potentially meaningful class identities, ceasing to be *anything but X*s, where *X* denotes a real or spurious *ethnos*. This process is more impoverishing than ever today, when one's ethnic identity can structure only increasingly limited segments of one's total potential repertoire. Hence, the moment *A* insists on being *only*—and *ostentatiously*—an *X*, twenty-four hours a day, large segments of his behavior, which cannot, by hook or by crook, be correlated with his ethnic identity, are deprived of any organizing and stabilizing "skeleton." His behavior therefore tends to become increasingly chaotic, particularly when he operates as a member of an actual group.

As a result, there tends to appear, side by side with what little structuring of Man's behavior his ethnic identity ("being an *X*") provides—even when it is asserted mainly dissociatively ("not being a *Y*")—a logically untenable and operationally fraudulent *incorporation* into the ethnic identity of ideologies based on principles which are, in essence, not only *non*-ethnic, but downright *anti*-ethnic. It is, and must be, possible to be an American without being a capitalist, a Russian without being a communist and a Jew without being orthodox. In this latter connection, I note a paradox. For all practical purposes Israeli law holds that a Gentile can become a Jew only by becoming a convert to *orthodox* Judaism. But a person born of a Jewish (and possibly *non*-orthodox) mother is a Jew even if he is an atheist.

Viewing things from another angle, ethnic identity can be functional *only* if it is both substantially expanded as to scope and appreciably decathected. It must not be permitted to engulf—or to become parasitical upon—one's other class identities, whose unduplicable accumulation is, as pointed out earlier, the very basis of an authentic identity.

I now come to a crucial point—crucial logically as well as in practice. Even though ethnic identity (and practically every other class identity) is both logically and historically the product of the assertion "*A* is an *X because* he is not a *Y*," and of the differentiating implementation of this distinctiveness, it is truly functional *only* if it involves the *uninvidious* appreciation of "*B* is a *Y by* being a non-*X*." To take a currently fashionable slogan, "black is beautiful" can be true and functional *only* if it subsumes that "white is also beautiful"—albeit in a different way. The reverse is, needless to say, also true (*9*).

Any *ethnos* incapable of recognizing this elementary fact condemns itself dissociatively to a slow drift, as a "closed system," toward total meaninglessness, and thereby brings itself—and mankind—to a standstill and gradually annihilates the individual claiming exclusively such a *purely dissociative* ethnic identity by reducing him to one-dimensionality.

I was not quite twenty years old, and had not, as yet, become interested in the human sciences when, in an open letter to a famous German regional periodical, the now extinct *Böttcherstrasse*, I asserted that human civilization depended on the diversity of cultures and ethnic identities. I reached this conclusion solely on the basis of my early studies in theoretical physics, for the second law of thermodynamics teaches that a totally homogeneous closed system soon ceases to produce externally perceptible work (entropy). As Bertrand Russell expressed this law—the law of entropy—in one of his more popular books: "Things left to themselves tend to get into a mess." That mess mankind cannot afford.

I therefore hold than an insistent and even obsessive stressing of and clinging to one's ethnic (or any other "class") identity reveals a flaw or a lacuna in one's self-conception as an *induplicably multidimensional* entity. The

Nazi SS who pleaded that in performing atrocities he only
obeyed commands, implicitly affirmed that his SS status
took precedence over all his other group identities—including his membership in the human estate. Sane and mature
persons do not hypercathect their ethnic identity *or any
other class identity*. An excessive stressing of *one* of one's
several class identities, such as ethnic identity, simply seeks
to shore up a flawed self and an uncertain and shaky awareness of one's identity as a person. The current tendency to
stress one's ethnic or class identity—its use as a crutch—is
prima facie evidence of the impending collapse of the only
valid sense of identity: one's differentness, which is replaced
by the most archaic pseudo-identity imaginable. I do not
think that the so-called "identity crisis" of our age can be
resolved by recourse to the artificial props of collective
identities: of ethnic, class, religious, occupational or any
other "assistant identity." I have said elsewhere that this
can lead only to a renunciation of identity, in order to fend
off what is apprehended as a danger of total annihilation
(*10*). I consider the evolving and assuming of any massive
and dominant class identity whatever as a first step toward
such a "protective" renunciation of true identity. If one is
nothing but a Spartan, a capitalist, a proletarian, or a Budd-
hist, one is next door to being nothing and therefore even to
not being at all.

Bibliography

(*1*)   Bonaparte, Marie: Notes on Excision (in) Róheim, G. (ed.), *Psycho-
        analysis and the Social Sciences*, 2:67–83, 1950.
(*2*)   Bryk, Felix: *Dark Rapture*, New York, 1939.
(*3*)   Devereux, George: Social Structure and the Economy of Affective
        Bonds, *Psychoanalytic Review* 29:303–314, 1942.
(*4*)   Idem: Mohave Indian Obstetrics, *American Imago*, 5:95–138, 1948.
(*5*)   Idem: *Therapeutic Education,* New York, 1956.
(*6*)   Idem: The Significance of the External Female Genitalia and of
        Female Orgasm for the Male, *Journal of the American Psychoanalytic
        Association*, 6:278–286, 1958.
(*7*)   Idem: La Psychanalyse et l'Histoire: Une Application à l'Histoire de

Sparte, *Annales: Economies, Sociétés, Civilisations* 20:18–44, 1965.

(8) Idem: Transference, Screen Memory and the Temporal Ego, *Journal of Nervous and Mental Disease*, 143:318–323, 1966.

(9) Idem: *From Anxiety to Method in the Behavioral Sciences*, Paris and The Hague, 1967.

(10) Idem: La Renonciation à l'Identité: Défense Contre l'Anéantissement, *Revue Française de Psychanalyse*, 31:101–142, 1967.

(11) Idem: *Mohave Ethnopsychiatry*, 1961 (2nd. augm. ed., Washington, D.C., 1969).

(12) Idem: *Essais d'Ethnopsychiatrie Générale*, Paris, 1970, 1972, 1977.

(13) Idem: Quelques Traces de la Succession par Ultimogéniture en Scythie, *Inter-Nord*, 12:262–270, 1972.

(14) Dodds, E. R.: (Introduction to) *Euripides: Bacchae*, 2nd ed., Oxford, 1960.

(15) Dollard, John: *Caste and Class in a Southern Town*, New Haven, 1937.

(16) Euripides: *Andromache*.

(17) Idem: *Hekabe*.

(18) Forrest, W. G.: *A History of Sparta*, London, 1968.

(19) Herodotos: *The Histories*.

(20) Homeros: *The Iliad*.

(21) Kenyatta, Jomo: *Facing Mount Kenya*, London, 1938.

(22) Kroeber, A. L.: Cultural Intensity and Climax (in) *The Nature of Culture*, Chicago, 1952, pp. 337–343.

(23) Idem: Stimulus Diffusion (in) *The Nature of Culture*, Chicago, 1952, pp. 344–357.

(24) Lenzen, V. E.: Individuality in Atomism (in) *The Problem of the Individual*, *University of California Publications in Philosophy*, 20:31–52, 1937.

(25) Linton, Ralph: *The Study of Man*, New York, 1936.

(26) Idem: Culture, Society and the Individual, *Journal of Abnormal and Social Psychology*, 33:425–436, 1938.

(27) Mauss, Marcel: Une Catégorie de l'Esprit Humain: La Notion de Personne, Celle de "Moi" (in) *Sociologie et Anthropologie*, Paris, 1950, pp. 333–362.

(28) Ollier, François: *Le Mirage Spartiate*, 2 vols., Paris, 1933, 1943.

(29) Parsons, Talcott: The Professions and Social Structure, *Social Forces* 17:457–467, 1939.

(30) Ploutarchos: *The Life of Lykourgos*.

(31) Idem: *The Life of Solonos*.

(32) Idem: *The Life of Perikles*.

(33) Idem: *The Sayings of Kings and Commanders*.

(34) Idem: *The Sayings of Spartans*.

(35) Idem: *The Institutions of the Lakonians*.

(36) Idem: *The Sayings of Spartan Women*.

(37) Idem: *On the Bravery of Women*.

(38) Russell, Bertrand: *Introduction to Mathematical Philosophy*, London, 1919.

(*39*) Schapera, I.: *The Khoisan Peoples of South Africa*, London, 1930.
(*40*) Sophokles: *Aias*.
(*41*) Idem: *Philoktetes*.
(*42*) Strabon: *Geography*.
(*43*) Thoukydides: *The Peloponnesian War*.
(*44*) Tyrtaios: *Fragment 10* (Edmunds ed.).
(*45*) Vajda, Georges: Juifs et Musulmans Selon le Ḥadît, *Journal Asiatique*, 229:57–127, 1937.
(*46*) Whitehead, A. N. and Russell, Bertrand: *Principia Mathematica*, I, 2nd. ed., Cambridge, Eng., 1925.
(*47*) Xenophon: *The Constitution of the Lakedaimonians*.

7

Ethnopsychoanalytic Reflections
on the Notion of Kinship (1965)

THE present study seeks to elucidate the origin of the
notion of kinship and the nature of the needs which it
satisfies. The general phenomenon of the "circulation of
women" is far from being able to explain it, and it seems
evident to me that only a most unusual aspect of this
phenomenon—an aspect neglected hitherto by the specialists of kinship as well as by psychoanalysts[1]—can explain it.

And yet, Freud had inaugurated this line of inquiry since,
as Lévi-Strauss stresses (55), *Totem and Taboo* (40) is devoted chiefly to the problem of kinship. It is thus striking
that not even one of the few specialists of psychoanalytic
anthropology followed Freud's example. The cause of this
state of affairs is, no doubt, the extreme difficulty of this
kind of study but, even more probably, also the relative
failure of Freud's attempts, who, as Lévi-Strauss rightly
noted, erred in not having applied his own method consequently, to the very end. This criticism, which is perfectly
warranted, enables me to specify—and thereby to justify—

---

1.   My criticism is not directed only at my colleagues. Though in my book
on abortion in primitive societies (26), I tried to show to what extent the
decision to abort or to continue the pregnancy is directly determined by the
kinship system, I failed to raise the problem of the very existence of the
notion of kinship.

the method I intend to use in this study, which seeks to be psychoanalytically consequent to the very end. Lévi-Strauss writes: "These boldnesses . . . and the hesitations which accompany them, are revealing: they show a social science such as psychoanalysis . . . still vacillating between the tradition of a historical sociology seeking . . . in a remote past the 'raison d'être' of a present situation, and a more modern and scientifically more solid attitude, which expects the analysis of the present to provide a knowledge of its future and of its past. That is assuredly the practitioner's point of view; but one can never sufficiently stress that in studying in depth the structure of the conflicts whose theater the patient happens to be—in order to retrace his history and to reach by these means the initial situation around which all subsequent developments had organized themselves—the practitioner uses an approach which is the opposite of that of the theory presented in *Totem and Taboo*. In one case he proceeds from the experience to the myth and from the myth to the structure; in the other he invents a myth in order to explain the facts: in short, instead of interpreting the myth, he operates like the patient" (*55*, p. 611).

I begin by recalling two basic postulates, which I enunciated as far back as 1955 (*26*; cf. Ch. 3):

1. Each man is a complete specimen of Man and, if one studies him on all levels, his total behavior is a complete repertoire of human behavior.

2. Each society is a complete specimen of society and its behavior, too, is a complete repertoire of social behavior.

I speak here of repertoire and not of structure. Now, contrary to structure, a repertoire does not and may not distinguish between real behavior and a repressed fantasy, nor between an explicit and positive custom and a taboo or criminal act. Thus, for example, it does not distinguish between the sacred and obligatory marriage of a Pharaoh with his sister and the taboo on such a marriage in other societies; in both of these cases the basic notion is that of a "marriage with a sister." In the same way, Greek tyranny

(*3*) and the Athenian system, whose rabid republicanism was meant to be a prophylaxis against possible tyrants (*15*), both pertain equally and for the same reason to the idea of tyranny. Last but not least, each "extremist" social attitude, each "emphatic" custom, always indicates the presence, sometimes on another level, of the opposite custom or attitude (*31*, Ch. 16).[2]

This principle also permits one to assert from the start— even if one lacks supporting data—that if one tribe holds a certain action to be criminal, another tribe will consider the selfsame action to be legitimate—and vice versa.[3]

I will cite first the data which provided a point of departure for this study: on the one hand, information furnished by my patients; on the other hand, the customs of various peoples, both contemporary and historical; and finally, certain general psychological and cultural facts. Then, proceeding "from experience to myth and from myth to structure," as Lévi-Strauss put it, I will seek to highlight the reverse and hitherto neglected aspect of the problem of reciprocity—i.e., precisely that aspect which, in *Les Structures Elémentaires de la Parenté* (*55*), manifests itself through the "circulation of women."

My hypothesis does not challenge the central thesis of Lévi-Strauss, who links the exchange of women with the general problem of reciprocity. As a matter of fact, I wrote already in 1939 the following passage which, be it noted, Lévi-Strauss himself quotes: "An incestuous couple as well as a stingy family automatically detaches itself from the

2. Among the Mohave, one finds, side by side with an ideology and with customs which tend to overvalue twins, another ideology and other customs which depreciate them. Both these ideologies presuppose—and reflect— the usual ambivalence toward privileged but also unusual beings (*18*).
3. Thus, having encountered the belief that the violation of certain taboos causes a spontaneous and involuntary miscarriage, I concluded that there had to exist, somewhere on this Earth, at least one tribe whose women, when they wished to abort, would deliberately violate a taboo of this kind. It was only while I was reading the proofs of my book on that subject that I located a text mentioning this practice among the Maori (*26*).

give-and-take pattern of tribal existence; it is a foreign body
—or at least an inactive one—in the body social" (*17*). It is
evident that I owe my conception of incest, which is a concrete obstacle to exchange—whatever that exchange may
be—to the theory of *prestations mutuelles*, which my re-
gretted teacher Marcel Mauss set forth in his "*Essai sur le
Don*" (*59*).

The Oedipus Complex

Having stated the principles of my method, it would be
logical for me to proceed here and now to a summary presentation of my thesis. However, that thesis would seem so
singular, were it presented before I cite the facts which
literally forced it upon me, that one would take it for a
fantasy born from a psychoanalyst's imagination. This supposition seems the more certain, as I myself postponed its
enunciation, for several years, even though it seemed to me
unavoidable from the start and to be clearly implicit in my
clinical data.[4]

I state at once that the Oedipus complex is inseparable
from the notion of kinship and that the notion of incest pre-

4.   The basic material was obtained in 1960 and jotted down the same day.
This material seemed to me at first to be a very interesting clinical finding,
and I began to write a strictly clinical article, without getting even a glimpse
of its ethnological or sociological import. It was only when I was trying to
draft that article that I began to feel a certain uneasiness. Though I was
convinced that I had fully grasped the clinical meaning of my data, I dimly
felt that their real import escaped me. I felt a kind of "malaise" produced
by the feeling that I was on the threshold of a new domain which, I must
admit, I did not really wish to cross. Hence, the partly drafted article was
left gathering dust in my files for five years. I have described this state of
affairs in detail, so as to warn the reader against his own foreseeable
resistances to my conclusion. I, myself, postponed for years the enunciation
of a thesis which the facts themselves forced upon me. These hesitations
and evasions on the part of someone who is himself a psychoanalyst
fully confirm what I stated in a book entirely devoted to the problem of
anxiety and countertransference elicited by research in the field of human
sciences (*29*).

supposes it. Indeed, as Lowie (*57*) noted, the animal is unable to *commit* incest—and I add that it is, for the same reason, unable to refrain from committing it—simply because it is unable to entertain the notion of incest and, consequently, that of kinship. Lowie added that even if zoologists were able to prove that the gorilla has, or has not, sexual relations with his daughter or mother, this fact, though important for them, would be of no interest whatever to the sociologist.

Now, even though the Oedipus complex is first and foremost a psycho-social phenomenon, one must not lose sight of its physiological dimension. I specify at once that I do not intend to lapse here into the kind of "biological paleopsychology" to which far too many psychoanalysts are addicted and which I call "pseudobiologia phantastica"—for this "dimension" pertains to a capital difference between Man and other mammals; to a difference which I repeatedly discussed—without ever managing to get a hearing—in the course of the last twenty years (*27, 28*). Although I stress this difference in connection with the Oedipus complex, I have no intention of asserting the priority of either. Were I forced to take a position on this point, I would call the human psyche and culture co-emergents, in the evolutionist sense of the term (*31*, Ch. 15). The difference I just alluded to concerns a peculiarity of human female sexuality. Woman is sensual and maternal simultaneously and not cyclically, whereas, with the exception of certain periods of sexual inactivity, animal female sexuality alternates between phases of rutting and maternity. Human female sexuality preserved, however, an imprint of this phylogenetical periodicity; this is shown by a joint monograph of Benedek (a psychoanalyst) and Rubenstein (a gynecologist) (*11*).[5]

These authors have demonstrated that during the first half of the menstrual cycle, characterized by the predominance of estrogens, Woman dreams (on the latent level) chiefly of coitus, while during the second half, which is

5. Their findings are not accepted by all specialists.

characterized by the predominance of progesterone, Woman dreams of pregnancy and maternity. What makes this fact particularly interesting is that, contrary to what happens in female mammals in general, both pregnant and lactating women are not only able to make love, but also to desire it and enjoy it. Pregnant women may even be especially sensual.

Case 1: A young woman, in love with her husband, happy to be pregnant by him, and until then faithful to him, made a long journey during her pregnancy, solely in order to co-habit with a man whom she had never met, but whose charm and virility she had heard spoken of in praise.

I do not deny that the sensuality of a pregnant or lactating woman can also have causes which, in a way, are nonsexual: the pregnant woman need not take contraceptive measures; she may wish to make love to prove that despite pregnancy she continues to be desirable; etc. This being said, the fact remains that a pregnant or lactating woman can continue to be wife or lover, while a bitch or a cow, in the same state, is entirely mother. Moreover, this double state can elicit anxieties in certain women, for it represents for them a rending asunder.

Case 2: A young woman who was still nursing her baby said: "I feel as though I were sawn into two: my breasts and the upper half of my body belong to my baby, while my sexual organs and the lower half of my body belong to my husband, for we continue to make love."[6]

Case 3: A married woman, who had given birth several times, always without anesthesia, said: "For me, giving birth is simply an enormous orgasm of an unutterable intensity."

The conscious or unconscious motives of this kind of reaction are of no interest in this context. What does matter, is that the sexualization of maternity is at the root of the

---

6. I was unfortunately unable to find again the psychoanalytical article which mentions this case.

Oedipus complex, which is triggered by the unconscious seductiveness of the mother (*27*).

However, certain ethnological facts reveal a desynchronization and an intentional alternation of the two phases of female sexuality. Very many tribes forbid sexual relations during pregnancy and lactation: the woman must be wife or mother, but never both simultaneously.[7]

In primitive societies scruples are sometimes excessive: among the Mohave a man may not kiss the breasts of his partner, for this would make their coitus resemble incest (*17*). If a Chaga husband dreams of intercourse with his wife while she is pregnant, she must abort, for, even in dream, she may not be both mother and wife at the same time (*64*). The Chaga even forbid the mother to have sexual relations after her daughter becomes nubile. The mother's sexual life must cease the moment her daughter reaches puberty. Hence, those mothers who do not wish to give up marital relations so soon, use magical means for delaying the puberty of their daughters.

Case 4: A woman psychoanalyst, to whom I mentioned this custom, told me that one of her patients, a young woman under thirty-five, had a premature menopause as soon as her daughter reached puberty. Her analysis revealed that, exactly like Chaga women, she deemed it impossible that she and her daughter should be women simultaneously.

Certain other tribes encourage—or almost encourage—such a simultaneity. Thus, Kroeber (*53*) analyzed customs

7. I noted in a lecture given before the Philadelphia Association for Psychoanalysis (*32*) that certain customs seek to prevent any fusion whatever of the partial instincts. For example, the Sedang Moi separate oral drives from sexual ones by prohibiting the eating, even in a symbolical form, of a woman (or female buffalo) who has been the sexual partner of a man of their village. By these means they rigorously separate that which is "food" from that which is "sexual partner." They also separate—even more rigorously than does the Old Testament—milk from meat: the eating of the flesh of an animal whose milk one had drunk would symbolize the cannibalizing of the mother.

which permit a man to marry a woman and then to make his step-daughter her mother's co-wife. The reverse sequence occurs among the Mohave: fairly often a man, weary of his flighty and silly young wife, divorces her and then marries his ex-wife's mother, because older women are better house-keepers and take pains to please their young husbands (*22*).

Other examples involve not customs but individual pre-ferences: Justinus, in his *Epitome of the History of Trogus Pompeius* (*50*, 26.3.4 ff.) cites the case of Arsinoë, a Hellen-istic dowager queen, who seduced her daughter's husband. Before the First World War, ladies of the upper middle classes sometimes encouraged their lovers to marry their daughters. Freud mentions a case of this kind (*41*), and this situation is also the crux of a novel by Claude Farrère: *La Marche Funèbre* (*36*).

Among certain Naga, having an affair simultaneously with a woman and her daughter is a source of prestige (*42*). Polly Adler (*1*), the former owner of the most luxurious clandestine brothel of New York, mentions in her memoirs —which are a first-class sociological document—that her customers paid exorbitant prices for the privilege of co-habiting *simultaneously* with a young and pretty mother and the latter's daughter.

In isolated Swedish farms, if the mother is chronically ill, her oldest nubile daughter first takes over her mother's domestic functions and then often also her place in her father's bed (*65*). The Navaho, apparently in order to avoid all temptations of this kind, prohibit even the most super-ficial relations between a man and his mother-in-law (*8*).[8]

All these findings must be related to the fact that the Un-conscious tends to confuse—and even to fuse—different generations (grandparents, parents and children) on the one hand and affinal and consanguine relatives on the other hand.

8. Some ethnologists say that occasionally the future Navaho mother-in-law tests the sexual prowess of her daughter's husband-to-be, but I could not discover any trace of this custom in anthropological publications. It is also said that Catherine of Russia made the ladies of her court try out her prospective lovers.

The Unconscious Meaning
of the Exchange of Women

Case 5: The following details were obtained in the course of
the psychoanalytically oriented psychotherapy of a likable
and gifted young intellectual, born in a French-speaking
"exotic" country, who came to consult me because of his
impotency, which was sometimes partial, sometimes complete, but always strictly circumscribed. It occurred only
when he made love to his second cousin, with whom he was
in love and whom he wished to marry. (I note in passing that
the two branches of this family, that of the patient and that
of his girl cousin, hated each other.) This type of impotency,
which is linked with the Oedipus complex and is often
caused by a hysterical type of repression, is, in general,
fairly easy to cure. I saw the young man twice a week and he
was cured after two years of treatment. Incidentally, he
married his cousin soon after completing his first year of
psychotherapy. After some fifteen months of treatment, the
patient, already married at that time, narrated the following
dream:

"Jean, a young man who was my best friend in the lycée
and whose sister later on became my mistress, wishes to lie
down on my bed beside my wife and make love with her. He
tells me this frankly and specifies that he desires my wife
because he knows that she has a 'farting vagina.' I reply that
he is mistaken: it is not my wife, but my older married sister,
who has this peculiarity.[9] I was quite aware, even in dream,
that, in answering him this way, I was offering him my sister
—or almost offering her to him."

The patient then added: "Jean is at present in this city.
For several weeks he stayed with us in our tiny apartment,
where he had simply invited himself. He irritated us, both
by his presence and by his behavior. Me, I have become an
adult; he is still the perpetual adolescent. He lacks culture,

---

9. The patient was "fixated" both on his mother and on his older sister.

is extremely nervous and gesticulates too much. We felt relieved when he left."

It is to be noted that the patient did not permit himself to have this dream until some time after the departure of his former friend.

In reply to some simple and very neutral questions which I asked, the patient explained that he had not offered his sister in a simple and straightforward manner but, specifically, as a substitute for his wife who, as noted before, was also his cousin. He then added: "It seems to me that in dream, and in reality too, I feel that I owe to my friend a woman who, in one way or another, belongs to me—who is related to me. I feel that I am in his debt, because I had seduced his sister and then abandoned her when I became the lover of the woman whom I married. It is my duty to yield to him a woman belonging to me."[10]

Developing his thoughts further, the patient added: "The fact that a man has seduced someone else's sister does not mean that he will therefore accept the seduction of his own sister. My friend was abroad when his sister became my mistress. Had he been at home, he would certainly have asked me whether I meant to marry her or meant to treat this as a passing adventure. The fact is that I never thought of marrying this girl, even though she was very well behaved and not in the least promiscuous. Making love to her was, in the circumstances, injurious both to her and to her brother, who was my friend. In order to even the score, I owe him a woman belonging to me."

The concept which these data reflect most clearly is the law of talion, which requires a restitution: "an eye for an eye, a woman for a woman, your sister for mine." Coitus with a woman concerns also her brother. In short, up to this

10. In Euripides' tragedy *Hekabe*, the old queen, who had become Odysseus' captive, requires Agamemnon to help her take revenge on Polymestor. She claims that Agamemnon became her debtor when he made her captive daughter Kassandra his mistress (35, 824 ff.). Thus, the fact of sleeping with a woman, even if she is one's slave, makes one a debtor of her family, although her family did not consent to this concubinage.

point we are faced only with one of the many causes of the exchange of women.

At this point I asked my patient for his free associations related to the notion of the "farting vagina." He said at first that this detail seemed strange to him. I let him meditate aloud and after five minutes of efforts to "bracket his target" (as artillerymen put it) he said: "It is not the vagina that farts, it is the anus. The dream must therefore necessarily concern an anus." After a short silence, he spoke again, in a somewhat hesitant manner: "Without quite knowing why, I have the impression that it is not my wife's anus, nor that of my sister, nor even the anus of a woman—it is my anus. [Silence] I have the feeling that my having slept with the sister of my friend Jean gives him the right to take revenge: to have intercourse with me, so as to even the score. It seems to me that, in dream, I offer him my sister as a substitute, not only for my wife but even more for myself. In the last resort, it is I who specify that I give him access, not to my wife—whom my friend mistakenly believes to have a 'farting vagina'—but to a vagina which does actually fart: to that of my sister. It seems evident to me that he, quite as much as I, is not concerned with such-or-such a woman, believed to have a 'farting vagina.' We are concerned with something that farts, i.e., with the anus—with my anus. My maneuver is very complicated. I pretend to offer instead of my wife a seemingly better substitute. [One is struck by the implicit notion that a sister is to be preferred to a wife-cousin.] But the fact is that my wife herself is already a substitute: she is substituted for me. In seeming to divert my friend from my wife, by directing his desires at my sister, I make the talion completely symmetrical: I slept with his sister, he will sleep with mine."

The patient's mood became more somber; the spring of his associations seemed to have dried up. I took the initiative[11] of briefly summing up his remarks for him.

11. Note that this was a psychotherapy and not a classical psychoanalysis.

"Your proposed compromise has at least two meanings : on the one hand you accept that he should do unto your sister what you did unto his; this is the law of talion. The symmetry is thus perfect,[12] and, what is more, *you* oblige him not to make a mistake; you compel him to transfer his desire from your wife to your sister. On the other hand, you avoid by these means the homosexual anxiety which a sharing of your wife would elicit in you: to share a woman with another man represents a (symbolical) homosexual relationship with the rival, through the medium of the woman and under the guise of a heterosexual act."[13]

The patient then made some relatively incoherent remarks, which seemed to concern the overly abundant mucous secretions of certain women during coitus and used in this connection a slang word of his native country. This word interested me, because it concerned precisely the phenomenon of the "farting vagina" of which he had dreamed. However, the patient seemed, at least as far as his words were concerned, unaware of the connection between these vaginal noises and the overabundance of mucous secretions—and it goes without saying that I did not point it out to him. I note, however, at this juncture, that I first heard of the existence of such noises from the Mohave Indians, who find them very amusing (*20*). A gynecologist told me, moreover, that this phenomenon actually occurs in certain women, whose extremely moist vagina is very relaxed during and after coitus. According to the Reservation physician, the Mohave woman does, in fact, have a very large vagina of slight tonicity. As for myself, I would link this fact also with the characteristic tendency of Mohave

12.   Symmetry and equilibrium play an important role in the patient's profession.
13.   The notion that one can have vicarious "homosexual" relations with a man by sleeping with his wife or mistress is admirably confirmed in psychoanalytical publications. The same patient had, moreover, told me that whenever one of his uncles learned that one of his friends had made a new conquest, he was promptly inflamed by the desire to seduce his friend's new mistress.

women to "vaginalize" the mouth (*19*) and the anus (*23*) and, conversely, to "oralize" and to "analize" the vagina (*20*).

The conscious drift of his ideas having changed, the patient spoke to me once more of his Oedipal attachment to his mother. He reminded me of the fact that he had freed himself of that attachment and had recovered his virility as soon as he realized that his cousin symbolized his mother.[14] The manner in which he came back to this point revealed, in fact, that he had (for the moment) once more completely repressed a series of fantasies and neurotic ideas, though we had discussed them already on several occasions:

1. The psychological equivalence of the mother and the spouse.[15]

2. The feeling of triumph over the father during the Oedipal conflict, a feeling based upon the seductive behavior of his mother, who had made the patient the confidant of her long adultery with a friend of the family and had, moreover, sent the patient money which she had secretly taken from her husband.

3. The wholly conscious feeling that he owed his father a *heterosexual* compensation, because he had "robbed" him of his wife. This attitude explains why, though he detested his father, he was very fond of his mother's lover, even though the latter, much more than the former, was his real rival.[16] A series of dreams and fantasies reflected, moreover, the patient's deeply rooted conviction that he had to make a woman "belonging" to him—his sister, or his wife—available even to those whose wife, fiancée or mistress he had simply desired.

14. He had dreamed that, on the eve of his wedding, his mother gave back to him a fish (penis symbol) which belonged to him, but which she had chosen to hold in escrow for him until then.

15. This equivalence, already noted by Ferenczi (*37*), was admirably confirmed by one of Cora Du Bois' informants, who said to her: "At night, when half asleep, we sometimes call our wife 'Mother' " (*34*).

16. Thus, the patient differs from Hamlet, who, as Jones (*49*) has shown, hated his uncle precisely because the latter had dared to do what he, Hamlet, had never dared: he killed Hamlet's father and married his mother. One may think also of Orestes (*60*).

4. Conversely, the patient felt that his father owed him a *homosexual* revanche for having feminized and homosexually "attacked" him. This fantasy had some roots in reality. While still in the lycée, the patient had, in a short time, contracted gonorrhoea three or four times in a row and had been prescribed prostatic massages, which had been administered to him by his own father. The patient's wish to even the score manifested itself (during his psychotherapy) in a dream in which he subjected his father to the law of talion (*31*, Ch. 6). Although, in this case, the roots of this fantasy are quite unusual, I indicate elsewhere that a fantasied homosexual triumph over the father is a *sine qua non* stage in the resolution, or sublimation, of the boy's Oedipus complex (*25*).

When I pointed out to the patient this new repression of already elucidated ideas, he observed: "All this would then imply that my friend has the right to fuck me, since I have fucked his sister and my dream means that my friend seems to believe that, in fucking his sister, I fucked him." I replied: "And since it is not he but you who have dreamed this . . ." He smiled and, completing my sentence, said: "It means that I, too, feel that, in making love with the sister of my friend, I cohabited with him, with his sister as intermediary." This idea is in no way peculiar; one finds it already in Bakchylides [*Ep*. 5, Jebb or Snell] (*9*) who records Herakles' admiration of the beauty of Meleagros' shade, which he met in the course of his descent to Hades. The poet put the following words into Herakles' mouth: "Is there . . . in the palace of Oineus, dear to Ares, an unmarried daughter, whose beauty is similar to thine? I would gladly make such an one my gorgeous bride." And the shade of Meleagros replied: "I left at my home Deianeira, with the green of youth upon her sweet neck, unknowing still of the golden enchantress Kypris" (vv. 165-175). The situation is perfectly clear: Herakles, whose Dorian penchants for both sexes are known, being in love with the shade of Meleagros, tried to substitute to this handsome dead youth his living sister—which Meleagros' shade seems to have considered perfectly natural. Moreover, Herakles did subsequently marry Deianeira.[17]

The Role of the Brother and of the Husband in the Circulation of Women

In order to understand the unconscious significance of the circulation of women, this clinical material must be analyzed in accordance with the method outlined at the beginning of this study. Since all of its deep meanings do not pertain to the same level, its significance must be discovered by proceeding from one level to the next; in so doing one proceeds, as Lévi-Strauss indicates, from the experience to the myth and from the myth to the structure—here: psychical.

The analysis of the patient's dreams and associations fully confirms that, on the conscious level, what was at stake was exclusively the exchange of women: *do ut des*, I give you my sister so that you will give me yours.

On a less conscious level, the nuance changes. The barter, the reciprocal benevolent "prestation" (in Mauss' sense) becomes attack, hostility, "*bilanisme*"; that is to say, a jealous quest for symmetry—in short, the law of talion. And, hence, one cannot but refer here to obsessive-compulsive neurosis, with all that it involves in terms of anal aggressiveness and repressed homosexuality (*40*).

One must, however, not proceed by leaps and bounds. One notes, first of all, the change of nuance which becomes manifest as soon as one analyzes the exchange of sisters more rigorously. On the conscious level one says: "You

---

17. Since Greek literature had recorded several genuine homosexual love affairs, it would be interesting to locate cases in which a homosexual love affair was followed by a marriage with a sister or kinswomen of the beloved youth. According to certain traditions, Herakles made his nephew and ex-boy-love, Iolaos, marry his divorced wife Megara, as he made his son marry his mistress, Iole, whom his death left without husband or lover. I discuss elsewhere (*30*) the problem of such "slippages" in Greek homosexuality.

have offered me your sister in so friendly a manner that I take pleasure in offering you mine." On a less conscious level one says angrily: "I defiled you by sleeping with your sister; I must therefore bear your defiling me by sleeping with mine."

Thus, the woman is not the *only one* to be "defiled": her brother, her father, her husband, are, if possible, even more "soiled." The fact of being mounted soils the honor of the *woman*, but *even more* and perhaps *primarily*, that of the men of her family. "Even more" are the key words. They express the phantasm that to mount a woman is to mount her spouse, her father and her brother. It means degrading, castrating and feminizing them. These men can refurbish their honor only by proving that they have not been feminized, that they are even more virile than the man who seduced their wife, daughter or sister.[18] This is shown by the fact that they kill him and mutilate his corpse. So did Odysseus: he castrated the goatherd who was the accomplice of Penelope's noble suitors—men who corrupted his handmaidens, who were also Odysseus' sexual chattels, but were punished *only* by hanging. The goatherd's sexual organs, nose and ears were thrown to the dogs. His punishment was, thus, much more severe than that of the lewd handmaidens.[19]

I must cite here also another attitude toward the exchange of women. As Lévi-Strauss notes in the last two pages of his

18. Anal aggression against the seducer of a wife in Greece: Aristophanes (*5*, 1083 and the note of K. J. Dover *ad loc.*; *6*, 168); Xenophon (*73*, 2.1.5); in Rome: Catullus (*14*, 15.19); Horatius (*47*, 1.2.44); Valerius Maximus (*70*, 6.1.13); Appuleius (*4*, 12), etc.
19. Priamos (*45*, 22.75) is horrified by the notion that dogs may devour the privy parts of an old man. I cannot prevent myself from stressing here that Odysseus—and only he (*46*, 22.474 ff.)—commits the atrocities which rumor ascribed to the monstrous king of Epeiros, Echetos (*46*, 18.86 ff.; both deeds are described in the same [formulaic] manner). I conclude therefore that Echetos is only an *epiklesis* (double) of Odysseus. This might explain why archeologists found no trace of his palace in Ithake. One

book, Man finds it difficult to reconcile himself to barter: "To this day mankind dreams of grasping and perpetuating the fugitive moment, in which it was permitted to believe that one could circumvent the law of barter, win without loosing, enjoy without sharing... the delight, forever denied to social man, of a world in which one could live '*entre soi*' (within the nuclear family)" (*55*, p. 617). One easily recognizes in this the primary narcissistic position: that of the infant who receives without having to give anything in return.

Case 6: One of my patients, whose obsessiveness bordered on schizophrenia, said to me one day: "As a newborn, I would have wanted to be paid for taking the trouble to breathe."

All the forces of society struggle against this narcissism which wishes to receive insatiably without ever having to give anything in return. It is, thus, *socially* praiseworthy to participate in the exchange of women. But on the narcissistic level, the problem presents itself in another manner. Only the weak and the simpletons engage in barter. It is more glorious to seduce—or better still to rape—a woman than to obtain her by barter. I have shown elsewhere (*24*) that the Plains Indians, grim guardians of their sisters' and daughters' virginity, deem the seduction of the wives and daughters of others a glorious deed, comparable to the taking of a scalp. Similarly, Genghis Khan declared that mounting the wives and horses of the vanquished constituted the triumph of the victor (*43*). The history of a thousand massacres, pogroms, sieges, conquests, sackings of cities, abundantly highlights the glory of raping the wives of the foe; greater still is the glory of raping them *in the presence* of their fathers, brothers or husbands—though *not*

---

should perhaps look for it in Epeiros (Epirus). [*Addendum 1974:* see now for castration or else blinding for sexual misbehaviour: G. Devereux, The Self-Blinding of Oidipous in Sophokles' *Oidipous Tyrannos, Journal of Hellenic Studies*, 93:36–49, 1973.]

before their mothers or sisters. To barter one's wife against one's life goes back to the Stone Age. When a small band of Australian natives is attacked by a stronger band, the men seek to save their lives by offering their women to the aggressor: if the foes cohabit with them, they must spare the lives of the men. *(68)* [*Addendum 1975:* King Ninus threatened to blind Onnes if he did not yield up his wife, Semiramis, to him (Diodoros the Sicilian [*33*, 2.6.9 ff.])

Pseudo-Ploutarchos recorded a similar anecdote[20]: Smyrna, besieged by the army of Sardis, lost hope of being able to resist when the army of Sardis promised to raise the siege if the Smyrniots yielded up their wives to them. The Smyrniots were on the point of agreeing to do so when one of Philarchos' slave girls suggested a stratagem: she offered in her own name and in the name of other slave women to satisfy, disguised as free women, the sexual desires of the overly powerful warriors of Sardis.[21]

To make love with the wife of someone else seems to feminize or to kill him symbolically. This certainly calls for an explanation. Why is coitus without a counter-gift held to degrade, or to kill socially, the brothers, the father or the husband of the woman, *more even* than the woman herself?

I deem inacceptable the current notion that it is the woman herself who feels *primarily* humiliated by coitus and that the resentment of her kinsmen or of her husband is simply the consequence of her own feeling of humiliation. It seems evident to me that a normal woman does not feel humiliated when she makes love; in fact, strange as it may seem, in the last resort she does not feel humiliated even by

20.   In his *Greek and Roman Parallels* (*63*, 30, p. 312E), which must not be confused with the *Parallel Lives* of the genuine Ploutarchos.
21.   This story seems perfectly plausible to me. A reliable English news-paperman, Timperley (*69*), reports a similar story in his book on Japanese atrocities: During the sack of Shanghai, the Japanese demanded that the girl students of Gin-Ling College, who belonged to the upper classes, be made available to them. The female director of the college managed to save them by persuading the prostitutes of Shanghai to substitute themselves for these young ladies. I consider this account to be adequately documented.

rape.[22] Undeniably, the fear of penetration is as real in the case of men as in that of women[23]; but, as Marie Bonaparte (*12*) rightly notes, Woman's sexual life depends precisely on her capacity to turn penetration anxiety into pleasure.

Thus, in opposition to generally accepted ideas, I will interchange effect and cause: it is not the woman's humiliation through coitus which explains the shame of her kinsmen; on the contrary, it is the latter which explains the former—Woman humiliates *her* men through her behavior.[24]

The humiliation a man feels when one of "his" women is seduced by someone else can be analyzed on several levels, of which the most obvious is also the least important: the man who lets "his" woman be taken from him, without demanding one in return, reveals thereby his weakness— and this regardless of whether he is a peasant who lets his lord exercise the *ius primae noctis* or an Australian attacked by someone stronger than he is. Given the psychological equation virility = power,[25] a man who is unable to defend "his" woman, to take revenge or to exact a corresponding

22. I know of no better proof of this than the long, verbose and naïve discussion of the suicide of Lucretia—who had been raped by Sextus Tarquinius—found in the writings of that delightful moralist Diodoros the Sicilian (*33*, 10.21). He finds this suicide so admirable and at the same time so outlandish that he seems to wonder what kind of encomium would render it comprehensible to his readers.

23. I have seen young and perfectly healthy sailors faint when vaccinated by means of an injection; this fact is well known to physicians. I have never been able to persuade a single Sedang to let me give him an injection, even when, having been bitten by a snake, he believed himself doomed to die.

24. One of my papers (*31*, Ch. 8) shows the role of the desire to humiliate the parents in female juvenile sexual delinquency. A duchess who prostitutes herself so as to take revenge on her husband—such is the plot of a short story by Barbey d'Aurevilly (*10*).

25. When I participated in research on the effects of testosterone (male hormone) on schizophrenics, I noticed that one of the first effects of the injection was the tendency of the schizophrenic to overestimate his social position: a patient who, before the injection, admitted that he was a workingman, said afterwards that he belonged to the middle class.

counter-prestation, feels diminished on the social level and symbolically castrated and feminized as well.[26]

On a second level, on which causes seem to be somewhat more complex, the man who yields a woman to another man—and especially his sister or his daughter, who is sexually taboo to him—not only renounces for himself what Lévi-Strauss called "*la douceur de vivre entre soi*" but, above all, does so for the benefit of a stranger. Hence, he feels doubly robbed.

Although the definitive solution of the problem is still far away, it is indispensable, already at this stage, to draw certain conclusions from this fact. Society cannot afford the luxury of ignoring so violent an internal conflict, whose manifestations on the level of behavior would threaten the actual foundations of the social system. Society therefore has recourse:

1. on the one hand to reciprocal prestations—exchange of women, bride price, services rendered to the girl's parents, simulated abduction and pursuit, and

2. on the other hand to marriage rites, with all that such rites involve in the way of ceremonies, of the sacred (dangerous) and of the irrational, whose meaning and purpose is always to deny the hostility engendered by the cession of a woman and to disguise the outrage suffered by the "victim of theft" quite as much as the triumph of the "thief."[27]

In short, this denial highlights the very real feeling of theft and hostility which the "gift" of a woman elicits. The proverbial remark the middle-class son-in-law addresses to his bride's parents, "You are not losing a daughter, you are gaining a son," pretends to underscore the reciprocity of the

26. In his description of the horrors inflicted upon the wretched Witoto Indians, Hardenburg (*44*) mentions in particular that a woman was raped before the eyes of her castrated and fettered husband.

27. It suffices to think of how Napoleon rolled about voluptuously in the bed which he was to share on the morrow with his latest conquest, the Archduchess Marie-Louise von Habsburg-Lorraine.

prestation—but, precisely by denying them, inevitably underlines also the frustration and the loss. The essential purpose of the marriage rite is not the creation of a bond between *husband and wife*, nor even of an alliance between the *two families*; its function is to mask hostility by proclaiming the creation of an alliance, to affirm an understanding so as to avoid a brawl, to substitute peace for war. There are few examples of the latent hostility of the "givers of women" as striking as that found of the thirty-fourth chapter of Genesis, in which Shechem, after deflowering Dinah, falls in love with her and sends his father to ask for her hand. Verse 9 specifies: "And make your marriages with us and give your daughters unto us and take our daughters unto you." The crafty sons of Jacob pretend to agree, but demand that the men of Shechem's tribe should first be circumcised. Then, while the newly circumcised men are still too weak to defend themselves, Simon and Levi massacre them, so as to "avenge" their sister. In this particularly striking case the prenuptial symbolic castration makes possible the massacre of the fiancé (seducer) and his men by the woman's brothers. Admittedly Jacob curses the cruelty of this vengeance, *but there is no allusion whatever to Dinah's own feelings*—either during the coitus (to which she may or may not have consented) or after the vengeance.

The analysis of the marriage rites makes it seem complex and charged with multiple meanings, chiefly in societies where marriage implies the notion of the ownership—be it but in a limited sense, as among the Australians—of the very *person* of the woman.

Now, I have twice noted (*28*; *31*, Ch. 16) that a ritual over-elaboration reflects the need to justify that which, on the level of emotions and of phantasms, seems unjustifiable. The very complexity of the marriage rite proves that it seeks to mask a kind of witches' caldron of conflicting emotions. One must therefore examine how marriage is contracted in a society which has almost no rituals.

The classical example is that of Mohave marriage which,

as a rule, involves no ritual and is not preceded by any negotiation. If the woman has not been married before, the suitor sometimes seeks to obtain the favor of her family by providing free services. As to the marriage ritual proper, what is striking about it is its total absence: to get married means to go and live under the same roof, to divorce means to leave the conjugal domicile. This fact can be explained, first of all, through the instability of the Mohave family: quite a few Mohave children grow up with so many successive parents that familial fixations cannot attain a high degree of intensity. Everyone gets along with everybody; no one, with the exception of the old husbands of very young women, becomes neurotically attached to anyone (*22*, *28*). Thus, even though the familial complexes do exist, they are fairly feeble; hence, one "hypercathects" no one later in life.

Secondly, the Mohave, quite as much as the other Yuman tribes of the Colorado River, despise property, preach generosity, and never manage to accumulate any capital, for whatever they have not spent during their lifetime on helping all those who need it, is destroyed at their death (*51*, *52*). Thus, getting married involves no economic transactions: the lack of possessions[28] makes any financial transaction impossible, and the woman is, moreover, no one's possession—not even on the affective level. In fact, the Mohave say that one can count more on one's son than on one's daughter because girls are irresponsible (*21*).

The exception to this rule is one of my most conclusive data. There exists *one* kind of marriage, and *only one*, in which the young must wrest consent from the family, even though, ordinarily, the young couple consults no one before getting married. It is, moreover, the *only* kind of marriage which requires a rite which is at once complicated, expensive and endowed with multiple symbolic meanings. Finally, it is the *only* marriage for which society seeks to

28. Though the Mohave owned land individually, there was no lack of farm land; there was enough for everyone.

prohibit divorce. This marriage is that of cousins, and it amounts to incest in the strictest sense of the term (*17*). The primary significance of this rite is not the *creation* of a *conjugal* bond, but the dissolving of the bond of consanguine kinship between the young people. Here the contrast between kinship and marriage is perfectly clear. This dissolving of the bond of kinship is brought about through the fictitious death of the fiancé: he provides a horse which is killed and eaten. The death of the horse symbolizes the social death of the young man; in providing this horse himself he even seems to commit vicarious suicide, in that he authorizes others to kill him symbolically. Thus, exit the cousin of the bride; in his place there appears the groom deemed to be a "new boy"; as to the bride, her identity does not change.[29] The Mohave say, however, that this prophylactic ceremony is not very efficient, for this type of marriage, just like straightforward incest outside marriage, leads, sooner or later, to the extinction of the lineage. The indissolubility of such a marriage, when divorce is very common among the Mohave, is explained to the newlyweds as follows: "Since you wanted this incestuous marriage so much, it is forever forbidden to you to separate." In short, what is involved here is a punishment—and this punishment seems so natural that no means exist for preventing a subsequent divorce.[30] Nonetheless, I have no record of the separation of such a couple, except through the (psychosomatic?) death of one of the spouses.[31] As regards the "vicarious suicide" demanded from the fiancé, it can be compared to another type of behavior known to occur among the Mohave: to suicide disguised as murder. Kroeber recorded

29. Is this a remnant of matrilineal descent? I can only note the paradoxical fact that among the Mohave *only* the woman bears the name of her gens, though only the man can *transmit* that name to his daughters.

30. Incestuous loves are often both violent and lasting.

31. The number of such marriages is too small to make statistical conclusions possible. All that I was able to note myself or could hear reports of was that one of the spouses tends to die rather rapidly. This, for the Mohave, suffices to prove the tragic consequences of incestuous marriages.

that witches literally incite the kinsmen of those whom they have bewitched to murder them. They do this by taunting them, saying that their cowardice stops them from avenging a member of their in-group (*52*). My Mohave informants explained these vicarious suicides in the manner which I am about to describe, and their statements were confirmed by the confessions of a drunken witch who was not yet ready to get himself murdered. In general, the sorcerer bewitches only those whom he *loves*, sometimes incestuously. Subsequently he dreams of incestuous coitus with the shade of his victim—and those dreams are so exquisite that he begins to long for death so that, by becoming himself a shade, he can join his victim. But the witch cannot achieve this aim simply by killing himself or by dying of an illness. He must be assassinated. He therefore takes the necessary steps to be assassinated by the kindred of his victim, who are sometimes also his own kinsmen (*16, 28*).

In short, among the Mohave:

1. The only marriage which requires the assent of the families and therefore brings in its train wranglings, negotiations and complications; the only one which concerns the group, involves a rite and must be permanent, is marriage between cousins—that is, an illegal and immoral marriage, dangerous both for the spouses and for their lineages.

2. This kind of marriage is incestuous and is preceded by a symbolic suicide, which recalls the "suicide" (provoked murder) of incestuous witches.

3. Just like the marriage of a middle aged man and a girl much younger than he—and even more strikingly—it involves romantic love in the occidental sense of the term—and the Mohave consider romantic passion ridiculous (*20*).

4. Exactly like coitus with the shade of the dead, such marriages generally cause a premature death. Similarly, the disruption of a marriage between a man and his much younger wife is also disastrous, albeit to a lesser degree: it often triggers a temporary madness (*bouffée délirante*) in the abandoned husband (*28*). This is not at all surprising

since, according to the Mohave, a marriage between a grown man and a very young girl borders on incest (*17*).[32]

Hence, if one concedes that the only "real" Mohave marriage—that is, the only one which, being ritualized, resembles marriage in other societies—is an absolutely forbidden incestuous marriage, it seems necessary to conclude that the function of the marriage ritual is the legitimization of the illegitimate, the defense of the indefensible, and the substitution of a pretended benevolence to a real hostility.

Marriage is sacred, that is: dangerous, precisely because it permits what is forbidden; it consecrates a sacrilege.[33] Both clinical and cultural data seem to indicate that marriage is not primarily a transaction between a man and a woman, nor even, as many anthropologists think, an alliance between two families: it is first and foremost a transaction between men, involving women.

It is now possible to isolate several aspects of the marital bond which, as regards the individual, can be treated as successive stages of his psychological evolution with respect to marriage. In so doing, one does not postulate implicitly an authentic evolution whose successive stages would correspond either to a biological evolution of the species or to socio-cultural evolution.

Before undertaking their analysis, I must record a commonplace fact: the Unconscious is not a specialist of kinship

32.   Lévi-Strauss, who quotes my remarks (*55*, p. 605 f.), stresses the fact that "unequal" marriages are often assimilated to incest. This may seem paradoxical, though it is psychologically natural, the prototype of inequality being, precisely, the age difference between parents and children.
33.   I must call attention here to a quite peculiar aspect of Catholic marriage. According to St. Paul, celibacy is preferable to marriage. Hence, in principle, every girl should become the bride of Christ (nuns wear wedding rings). This means that women who give themselves to a man instead of marrying God commit a sacrilege which only the sacrament of marriage can justify; knowing that which is better they choose that which is worse. Yet, if a girl takes a lover, this does not represent a sacrilege of the same kind. Indeed, a reformed prostitute (*fille repentie*) may become a nun, which a married woman cannot, without special dispensation, do during the lifetime of her husband.

systems! For the Unconscious, kinship *qua concept* does not exist; all that is real is the attitude toward certain persons which provides the affective infrastructure of socially established bonds of kinship and of bonds whose existence society recognizes precisely by seeking to deny or to forbid them. As soon as matters are envisaged in this manner, the difference between the following two phenomena seems minimal.

1. In the Trobriand Islands biological paternity does not exist, in principle, on the social level (*58*). Nonetheless, as Róheim (*66*) has shown, the nescience of the Aranda is purely fictitious, and one could prove the same thing also as regards the Trobriand Islanders (*58*, pp. 156 f., 359) among whom, be it noted, the "paternal" sentiment often manifests itself at the expense of the official heir: the uterine nephew.

2. The desire of incest is violently denied in the majority of human societies. As a result, it transforms itself into the Oedipus complex or, in a broader sense, into a familial complex, and manifests itself in various ways: in the jealousy of the brother or of the father toward the fiancé of the sister or the daughter, and even in the husband's jealousy, which is, in part, a late manifestation of a disguised and repressed jealousy, whose original object was the mother and the sister and is later transposed to the wife and then to the daughter. I was even able to observe outbreaks of unexpected and transitory "matrimonial" jealousy in men whose sister or daughter had just married.[34]

Similarly, the Unconscious makes no distinction between consanguine and affinal kinship; it fuses and tangles the two; it confuses sister and wife; one can cite in this context a verse of the Song of Songs, in which the man calls his beloved "my sister," as well as the Trobriandese term which signifies both "cross-cousin" and "mistress" (*58*). The Unconscious can even confuse different generations, for example, grandchildren and grandparents. It suffices to think

34.   This can happen even among psychoanalysts; one of the best known among them, while showing to a friend his infant daughter in her cradle, exclaimed: "How I hate the bastard who will take her from me!"

in this context of many societies in which the grandson is identified with his grandfather, and this in accordance with social norms which echo the inversion of the generations in the Unconscious (*48*).

This being said, I must return to the analysis of the manner in which the circulation of women becomes established. The law of talion was already discussed sufficiently to require only a reminder of its importance: "You have the right to sleep with my sister, since I slept with yours." It is nonetheless strange to observe to what extent—even in societies in which this kind of barter is not institutionalized —everything that tends to suggest this kind of exchange acquires a special significance. Thus, in the occidental world, "double weddings" are sentimentally highly valued and are solemnized by a special and complicated ritual. It does not matter in this context whether an exchange of sisters or the marriage of two sisters to two brothers is involved, since the Unconscious does not distinguish between affinal and consanguine kin. The reason for this special solemnity seems to be that double marriages recall both barter and incest.

One can relate to the idea of barter, of talion, a number of customs: the deflowering of the bride by someone other than the groom, or the bouquet which the bride tosses to the bridesmaids—the one who catches it will be the first to get married. I am inclined to see manifestations of the spontaneous sentiment of talion even in the amorous adventures which come into being between the members of the wedding party. Things happen in a manner which suggests that the wedding night of the newly weds provides a "precedent" for the best man and the bridesmaid, and also for the other unmarried male and female guests, a precedent which gives the members of these two groups the right to "compensate" each other for some "loss" which they had sustained.

My interpretation epitomizes the explicit statements of a girl of jealous disposition whose best girlfriend had just married. She told her psychoanalyst that she had had a "one night stand" affair with a man belonging to the wedding party. I also quote elsewhere (*29*) a young female psychiatrist's dream, which revealed the bridesmaid's jealousy of the bride (who happened to be also her cousin). The 1944 advertising slogan of a cosmetics firm also tried to exploit this jealousy of the bridesmaid.

Similarly, it is in terms of the idea of barter, of talion and of everything that notion implies in terms of the "voyeurism" and Oedipality of every human being that one must explain one of the weirdest marriages in the history of mankind; the marriage of "the Siamese [actually Chinese] Twins" to two sisters belonging to the conventional and puritanical white middleclass. Racial prejudices, added to the contempt in which are held circus performers and, above all, freaks—giants, dwarfs, bearded women, etc.—should have made this marriage impossible. However, in a situation in which *one* ordinary Chinese would have failed, "the Siamese *Twins*" succeeded. Paradoxical as it may seem, this double marriage assuredly occurred precisely because it conjured up barter and the law of talion and not only skirted incest but also gratified voyeuristic and polygamous tendencies. These conjugal relations were exhibitionistic—but, since these twins were in fact inseparable, the exhibitionism was inevitable and, therefore, forgivable.

On the other hand, the circulation of women and, above all, their bartering, is linked through the law of talion with an obsessional tendency toward "*bilanisme*" (*61*)—otherwise expressed, with a compulsive quest for symmetry with all that this kind of obsession involves in terms of latent homosexuality, jealousy and desire for vengeance.

The most respectable aspect of this compromise "between men" is the bond which, in primitive societies, marriage creates not so much between *two persons* as between *two families*. Much the same happens in our own society: it suffices in this context to re-read the pages in which Saint-Simon (*67*) describes how he asked for the hand of the *daughter* of the Duke of Beauvillier, which is something

very different from the desire to marry *Mademoiselle* de
Beauvillier. The speeches he made to the Duke do not refer
at all to Mademoiselle de Beauvillier's own charm; the
decisive source of attraction is the Duke, whose the son-in-
law he sought to become. Now, even if one does not suspect
any latent homosexual attraction in Saint-Simon's case, one
easily slides from such a situation to the Australian man's
circumcising of his future son-in-law or to the Keraki custom which encourages a youth to marry a girl belonging to
the moiety of the men who played the active role in the, at
first ritual, homosexual experiences of his adolescence
(*72*).

Finally, in order to fulfil my promise to be psychoanalytical to the very end, I will mention in conclusion the
fantasy of a barter between father and son and will begin by
quoting a smutty story, viewed here as the reflection of the
Unconscious (*41*). A father upon learning that his son had
fornicated with his paternal grandmother, exclaims: "How
did you dare to cohabit with my mother?" The son replies:
"And you, how did you dare to cohabit with mine?"

This recourse to symmetry is discernible also in the case
of my patient who, thinking that he had deprived his father
of the love of his wife (i.e., of the patient's mother) fantasied
that he had to allow his father to take revenge not only by
cohabiting with his daughter-in-law (the patient's wife) but
directly with the patient himself in the guise of prostatic
massages, in connection with which the son dreamed of
sodomizing his father, as a compensation.

It is to be stressed that this treatment was made necessary
by this young man's *heterosexual* relations with prostitutes.
The sequence is, thus, the following:

1. Heterosexual coitus with prostitutes, which, as psychoanalysis shows, is directly linked with the Oedipus complex; the prostitute being the "polar opposite" of the
mother, she symbolizes the mother by her opposite.

2. The father "takes revenge" by performing prostatic
massages (*per anum*), which are painful to the son and also

anxiety arousing, since they represent for him a punitive homosexual assault.

3. The son therefore seeks to take revenge, in dream, by symbolically raping his father (*31*, Ch. 6).

Thus, in a very real sense, the patient's dream concerning his friend Jean is directly linked with this initial problem, on which it is patterned in many respects.

1. *Successive Stages of the Hypothesis:* The seduction of Jean's sister symbolizes for the patient a homosexual attack perpetrated against Jean. It is even possible that he had *chosen* Jean's sister from among ten other available girls because he was unconsciously attracted by—but also hostile to—Jean, though he flatly denies it; but, if so, why would he, on the level of fantasies, have interpreted the seduction of Jean's sister as harm done to Jean *and* also as a homosexual attack? The tone of his remarks is ambivalent: desire and hatred mingle in them. The homosexual act is disguised as a heterosexual act, which nonetheless betrays its homosexual sources: he had degraded, castrated, feminized the brother of the seduced girl. This was, of course, foreseeable, since the connections between the components of repressed homosexuality—love, hatred, jealousy, revenge—are self-evident in psychoanalysis and need no further proof; it suffices to refer here to Freud's well-known study (*40*).

2. *The Stages of Observation* must be enumerated in an order which is the opposite of the historical order, since analysis, starting from the Concious proceeds, via the Preconscious, to the Unconscious.

The sequence of identities is: the "farting vagina" of the patient's wife = that of the patient's sister = the patient's own anus = Jean's right of access to this anus, deriving from the fact that the patient, who had *in reality* cohabited with Jean's sister, had symbolically sodomized Jean.

The subjectively distressing aspect of these fantasies is somewhat attenuated if one imputes to Jean a desire to cohabit with the patient's sister. This explains why, in the dream, Jean—tacitly appealing to the law of talion—demands a combined homosexual *and* heterosexual compensation, both for the *real* crime (seduction of his sister) and for the *imaginary* crime (the desire to sodomize him). The double meaning of this retaliation is perfectly condensed in the image of the "farting vagina," which is at once vagina and anus.

This interpretation is not one of the fantasies one so readily imputes to psychoanalysts. Brantôme (*13*), a "spicy" writer but also a good sociologist, reports the following anecdote: A certain aristocrat, in love with his wife's lover, contrived to catch them in flagrante delicto. As a compensation, he demanded the right to sodomize the lover *while* the latter was cohabiting with that aristocrat's wife.

A smutty story, which circulated in Hungary some sixty years ago, has a similar pattern: During the great maneuvers a sergeant of the hussars was quartered in the house of a stupid peasant, very jealous of his young and pretty wife. The sergeant managed to convince the peasant that military regulations obliged him to sodomize his host. The horrified but credulous peasant implored the hussar to accept his wife as a substitute. The hussar made him beg for quite a while and granted him this favor only on condition that things happened in a manner compatible with the fictitious regulations: the husband, lying flat on his belly had to serve as a mattress for his wife and the hussar. Now, while the hussar was cohabiting with the wife, the peasant had such an erection that his penis pierced the mattress and became visible to his old mother, who was present during this scene. At that point the old woman exclaimed: "This hussar's penis is sure big! It went right through both my daughter-in-law and my son and there is enough left over of it to satisfy me as well." The intrusion of this incestuous element is not at all surprising, since all homosexual activity has an Oedipal component. A less crude and more symbolical version of this motif can be found in Appuleius (*4*, 12); some clinical findings provide comparable data.

Case 7: A patient, who was neither an ordinary nor a

compulsive liar, met a young woman on the beach and courted her. He assured me that she did not seem crazy in the least. The young woman required no urging and invited him to her house, adding, however, that her husband—a homosexual—insisted on watching his wife in the act and then on being sodomized by his wife's lover. The patient added that he was so shocked by this proposal that, to the great surprise of the lady, he took French leave.

These few data—to which many others could be added— show the close relationship between the barter of women and the latent homosexual urges of the men who exchange them. Now, it is precisely this barter which permits the *indirect manifestation* of homosexual urges. It is well known (1966) that certain rich and well educated inhabitants of the elegant and sophisticated suburbs of New York practice wife swapping, while condemning, it is said, *unilateral adultery*.

It is, of course, impossible and would moreover be fruitless to seek to make a sharp distinction, as regards the possession of a woman, between the hostile fantasy of causing injuries to her first "owner" (father, brothers, husband) on the one hand and a homosexual fantasy of coitus with the "owner" on the other hand. Such an undertaking would be a sterile quibble, simply because homosexuality—which is by definition ambivalent—inextricably mingles love and hate.

On the social level, it is, however, clear that marriage is chiefly a means of resolving conflicts between the "takers" and the "givers" of women. The giver's hatred manifests itself in a thousand ways, but always in conformity with the ethos of the society to which he belongs. In a strongly property-minded and avaricious society, a prohibitive price will be paid for the marriageable girl: among the Yurok, children born to a married woman who has not been bought or else has been bought cheaply, are considered to be bastards (52). Plains Indians deem it extremely honorable for the future husband to pay for his wife the greatest possible number of horses. A Kiowa woman boasted of the exorbitant price her husband had paid in order to marry her (*54*). This attitude is clearly connected with masochism and also with blackmail through an appeal to pity, which, as I have shown (*24*), is a salient trait of warlike societies.[35]

Thus, the *rite de passage* theory of marriage must be slightly modified. The incestuous Mohave marriage shows clearly enough that one has to emphasize the *first* part of the ritual, which seeks to detach the woman from her initial owner, since the second half, which seeks to attach the woman to her new family, is quite rudimentary.[36] The center of gravity and the real goal of the transaction is not the establishing of a conjugal bond, but the compensating of the family for the renunciation to which it has agreed, though, under the guise of a gift, it has, in fact, lost a woman.

All this seems to be linked with a fact which is very simple indeed—perhaps even too simple, since it has not attracted the attention of specialists. Indeed, the insistence that affinal kinship should be patterned upon consanguine kinship is not rooted in heterosexual but in homosexual drives. Now, the latter are directly linked with the Oedipus complex, without which homosexuality qua perversion would not exist.[37]

Let me now return to the essential *human* character of the Oedipus complex and of incest, to which I referred at the beginning of this study, by quoting Lowie—for men are only too prone to attribute their own reasoning to animals. A whole series of ancient authorities—Aristoteles (*7*, 9.40.7 f.); Ailianos (*2*, 4.7; cf. 3.47, which concerns a camel);

---

35. But I hasten to add that a Rhadé Moi sergeant (of the former native militia) boasted that his wife had to pay 80 piasters in order to marry him. In that matrilineal tribe, it is the woman who buys herself a husband.
36. The nuptial Mass comes to an end the moment the man and the woman are pronounced man and wife.
37. I am manifestly not speaking here of homosexuality due to deprivation such as one observes in prisons, in boarding schools, etc.

Varro (*71*, 2.7.9.); Plinius the Elder (*62*, 8.156)—mention
the suicide of a colt, who had been induced by trickery to
cover his own dam. The following case is even weirder:

Case 8: A small municipal zoological garden in America
had a pair of Alaskan sled dogs, whose puppies it sold to the
public. A psychoanalyst who had bought a female puppy
subsequently wanted to have her covered by a male of the
same race. Having tried in vain to find such a male in town,
he addressed himself to the zoological garden, asking to
have his bitch covered by her own sire. He was rebuffed by
the administrative secretary, who found the planned
"incest" absolutely scandalous.

It is quite normal that a certain type of behavior, which,
in Man, is determined by the notion of kinship, should be
discernible also among mammals, especially when the young
animal also needs to be protected and fed by its mother.
Similarly, animals too can display jealous "marital behavior": the stallion, the male deer, and (in most cases) the
baboon (*74*), etc., do not allow other males to take their
females. But they lack the notion of kinship and therefore
also the Oedipus complex and true homosexuality.[38]

Were the homosexual urge—and only that urge—at the
root of the notion of kinship and of the *rite de passage* which
marriage is, men, just like animals, could easily have dis-
pensed with both that notion and that rite. One could, of
course, object that in that case a good proportion of men
not strong enough to conquer a harem would, like weak
baboons, live almost without sexual relations.[39] But, if the
problem is formulated in this manner, it already implies the
idea of equity, equality and symmetry—notions which are
themselves the positive product, or, better still, the sublimation of compulsions and obsessions partly linked with latent

38.   I do not refer here to the homosexuality of animals denied all opportunity for normal coitus, nor to the "sexual presentation" of the weak
baboon (*74*).
39.   I disregard here the arguments of certain exponents of eugenics, for
whom such a situation would improve the human species.

homosexuality which, in turn, is derived from the Oedipus complex.

What society regulates is, thus, not the mere circulation of women; it is the *form* which it assumes and the *circumstances* and *conditions* in which it takes place: abduction, exchange, purchase, bride service, etc. Moreover, the principal regulations do not concern the relationship between men and women but the relations between the men themselves, since such transactions occur between men; women are simply their objects. The institution of marriage which stands with kinship, both consanguine and affinal, in a relationship of co-emergence has as its goal not the socially advantageous resolution of the heterosexual problem but the repelling of the threatening specter of latent homosexuality, product of the Oedipus complex.[40] My hesitating five years to present this theory explicitly shows sufficiently that I am aware of its importance and reach. If I publish it at last, it is because, on the psychological level, it seemed impossible to me to propose a different one.

In order to deepen one's understanding of problems concerning matrimonial exchange and in seeking to apprehend more clearly the infrastructure of kinship systems, it is necessary to change one's frame of reference and to pass from the sociological discourse to the psychoanalytic discourse. This is exactly what the present study attempts to do.[41]

It is unnecessary to add that my analysis is perfectly compatible with Lévi-Strauss' structural analysis, as well as with

40. A homosexuality which is often incomplete and sometimes only approximated for nonerotic purposes plays an important role in the regulation of social relationships among certain monkeys. When a weak male's food is about to be taken from him by a strong one he assumes the she-monkeys "sexual presentation" position. This protects him against attack as efficiently as does, among dogs and wolves, the vanquished's baring his throat to the victor (56).

41. I discuss elsewhere the methodological principles governing such changes of frames of reference as soon as the first, having been fully exploited, ceases to be sufficiently productive (see Ch. 4).

the whole of his conclusions regarding the total *sociological* meaning of kinship. The relationship between our respective analyses of the same phenomenon is a *typical* complementarity relationship. Hence, those who might try to oppose his theory of kinship to mine, or inversely, will labor in vain.

Appendix

Nine years after the first publication of this paper, Professor Melford E. Spiro cited the following facts in a lecture entitled "Some Psychodynamic Determinants of Household Composition in Village Burma," given at the panel discussion on "Psychoanalysis and Anthropology," held during the 1974 Annual Meeting of the American Anthropological Association. It is quoted here with his permission.

In Burma there exists "a stereotypic, culturally expected tension, allegedly motivated by the brother's resentment of his sister's (especially his younger sister's) husband. 'Until her marriage' as one villager put it 'she has been his. Hence, he is jealous if she shows affection to anyone else' let alone marries him. His (putative) feeling is reflected in the proverb 'When the younger sister takes a husband, her brother develops a pain in his anus' (*huama lin nei/maun pin cein*). The expression 'pain in the anus' is intended as a *double entendre*, i.e., it pains the brother to lose her, and it arouses pangs of sexual longing for her."

The confirmatory value of this evidence hardly requires comment.

Bibliography

(1) Adler, Polly: *A House Is Not a Home*, New York, 1953.
(2) Ailianos: *On the Characteristics of Animals*.
(3) Andrewes, A.: *The Greek Tyrants*, London, 1958.
(4) Appuleius, Lucius: *Metamorphoses* (i.e.: *The Golden Ass*).
(5) Aristophanes: *Clouds*, Dover, K. J. (ed.), Oxford, 1968.
(6) Idem: *Ploutos*.

(7)   Aristotle: *History of Animals*.

(8)   Bailey, F. L.: Some Sex Beliefs and Practices in a Navaho Community, *Papers of the Peabody Museum of American Archaeology and Ethnology*, 40: no. 2, 1950.

(9)   Bakchylides: *Fifth Epinikion* (Jebb or Snell).

(10) Barbey d'Aurevilly, Jules: *Les Diaboliques*, Paris, 1874.

(11) Benedek, Therese and Rubenstein, B. B.: The Sexual Cycle in Women, *Psychosomatic Medicine Monographs*, 3: Nos. 1–2, 1942.

(12) Bonaparte, Marie: *De la Sexualité de la Femme*, Paris, 1951.

(13) Brantôme, Pierre de Bourdeilles, Seigneur de: *Les Dames Galantes*, Rat, Maurice (ed.), Paris, 1955.

(14) Catullus: *Poetic Works*.

(15) Crahay, Roland: *La Littérature Oraculaire chez Hérodote*, Paris and Liège, 1956.

(16) Devereux, George: L'Envoûtement chez les Indiens Mohave, *Journal de la Société des Américanistes de Paris*, n.s., 29:405–412, 1937.

(17) Idem: The Social and Cultural Implications of Incest Among the Mohave Indians, *Psychoanalytic Quarterly*, 8:510–533, 1939.

(18) Idem: Mohave Beliefs Concerning Twins, *American Anthropologist*, n.s., 43:573–592, 1941.

(19) Idem: Mohave Orality: An Analysis of Nursing and Weaning Customs, *Psychoanalytic Quarterly*, 16:519–546, 1947.

(20) Idem: Heterosexual Behavior of the Mohave Indians (in) Róheim, G. (ed.), *Psychoanalysis and the Social Sciences*, v. 2, New York, 1950.

(21) Idem: Status, Socialization and Interpersonal Relations of Mohave Children, *Psychiatry*, 13:489–502, 1950.

(22) Idem: Atypical and Deviant Mohave Marriages, *Samīkṣā, Journal of the Indian Psycho-Analytical Society*, 4:200–215, 1951.

(23) Idem: Cultural and Characterological Traits of the Mohave Related to the Anal Stage of Psychosexual Development, *Psychoanalytic Quarterly*, 20:398–422, 1951.

(24) Idem: *Reality and Dream: The Psychotherapy of a Plains Indian*, New York, 1951 (2nd augm. ed., 1969).

(25) Idem: Why Oedipus Killed Laius: A Note on the Complementary Oedipus Complex in Greek Drama, *International Journal of Psychoanalysis*, 34:132–141, 1953.

(26) Idem: *A Study of Abortion in Primitive Societies*, New York, 1955 (2nd augm. ed., 1976).

(27) Idem: *Therapeutic Education*, New York, 1956.

(28) Idem: *Mohave Ethnopsychiatry*, Washington D.C., 1961 (2nd augm. ed., 1969).

(29) Idem: *From Anxiety to Method in the Behavioral Sciences*, Paris and The Hague, 1967.

(30) Idem: Greek Pseudo-Homosexuality, *Symbolae Osloenses*, 42:69–92, 1967.

(31) Idem: *Essais d'Ethnopsychiatrie Générale*, Paris, 1970, 1972, 1977.

(32) Idem: *The Cultural Implementation of Defense Mechanisms*, Lecture held before the Philadelphia Association for Psychoanalysis (MS).

(33) Diodoros the Sicilian: *Historical Library*.

(34) Du Bois, Cora: *The People of Alor*, Minneapolis, 1944.

(35) Euripides: *Hekabe*.

(36) Farrère, Claude: *La Marche Funèbre*, Paris, 1929.

(37) Ferenczi, Sándor: Psycho-Analysis of Sexual Habits (in) *Further Contributions to the Theory and Technique of Psycho-Analysis*, London, 1926.

(38) Freud, Sigmund: *Jokes and Their Relations to the Unconscious, Standard Edition*, vol. 8, London, 1960.

(39) Idem: *Totem and Tabu, Standard Edition*, vol. 13, London 1955.

(40) Idem: Some Neurotic Mechanisms in Jealousy, Paranoia and Homosexuality, *Standard Edition*, vol. 18, London, 1955.

(41) Idem: Psycho-Analysis and Telepathy, *Standard Edition*, vol. 18, London, 1955.

(42) Fürer-Haimendorf, Christoph von: *The Naked Nagas*, Calcutta, 1946.

(43) Grousset, Reneé: *L'Empire Mongol* (First Part), Paris, 1941.

(44) Hardenburg, W. E.: *The Putumayo: The Devil's Paradise*, London, 1912.

(45) Homeros: *The Iliad*.

(46) Homeros: *The Odyssey*.

(47) Horatius (Q. . . . Flaccus): *Satirae*.

(48) Jones, Ernest: The Phantasy of the Reversal of Generations, *Papers on Psycho-Analysis*, 3rd ed., London, 1925.

(49) Idem: *Hamlet and Oedipus*, New York, 1949.

(50) Justinus: *Epitome of the History of Trogus Pompeius*.

(51) Kelly, W. H.: Cocopa Attitudes and Practices with Respect to Death, *Southwestern Journal of Anthropology* 5:151-164, 1949.

(52) Kroeber, A. L.: Handbook of the Indians of California, *Bureau of American Ethnology, Bulletin 78*, Washington, D.C., 1925.

(53) Idem: Stepdaughter Marriage, *American Anthropologist*, 42:562-570, 1940.

(54) La Barre, Weston: Personal communication.

(55) Lévi-Strauss, Claude: *Les Structures Elémentaires de la Parenté*, Paris, 1949 (2nd ed., Paris and The Hague, 1967).

(56) Lorenz, Konrad: *Man Meets Dog*, London, 1954.

(57) Lowie, R. H.: The Family as a Social Unit, *Papers of the Michigan Academy of Science, Arts and Letters*, 18:53-69, 1933.

(58) Malinowski, Bronislaw: *The Sexual Life of Savages in North-Western Melanesia*, 3rd ed., London, 1932.

(59) Mauss, Marcel: Essai sur le Don (in) *Sociologie et Anthropologie*, Paris, 1950.

(60) Murray, Gilbert: *The Classical Tradition in Poetry*, New York, 1968.

(61) Odier, Charles: Le Bilanisme et l'Horreur du Discontinu, *L'Evolution Psychiatrique*, No. 2:35-80, 1939.

(*62*) Plinius the Elder: *Historia Naturalis*.
(*63*) Pseudo-Ploutarchos: *Greek and Roman Parallels* (in) Ploutarchos: *Moralia*.
(*64*) Raum, O. F.: *Chaga Childhood*, Oxford, 1940.
(*65*) Riemer, Svend: A Research Note on Incest, *American Journal of Sociology*, 45:566–575, 1940.
(*66*) Róheim, Géza: The Nescience of the Aranda, *British Journal of Medical Psychology*, 17:343–360, 1937.
(*67*) Saint-Simon, Louis de Rouvroy, duc de: *Mémoires*, Paris, 1829–1830.
(*68*) Spencer, Sir Baldwin and Gillen, F. J.: *The Arunta*, 2 vols., London, 1927.
(*69*) Timperley, H. J.: *Japanese Terror in China*, Freeport, N.Y., 1938.
(*70*) Valerius Maximus: *Memorable Doings and Sayings*.
(*71*) Varro, M. T.: *Rural Matters*.
(*72*) Williams, F. E.: *Papuans of the Trans-Fly*, Oxford, 1936.
(*73*) Xenophon: *Memorabilia*.
(*74*) Zuckerman, Sir Solly: *The Social Life of Monkeys and Apes*, London, 1932.

8

Antagonistic Acculturation (1943)

(in collaboration with EDWIN M. LOEB)

THE process of "antagonistic acculturation" does not seem so far to have been given explicit recognition either in sociological or in anthropological theory, even though it is one of the most interesting and characteristic processes of the contemporary social scene. We propose to describe and define it and to analyze it both in psychoanalytical terms and in terms of the means-end schema.

The failure to recognize antagonistic acculturation as one of the basic processes of social change is due to:

1. a somewhat narrow preoccupation with mere diffusion, and

2. the fact that antagonistic acculturation, at least in its "dissociative" phase, seems almost the reverse of diffusion proper, even if the term "diffusion" is broadened to include Kroeber's "stimulus diffusion" (24).

A subcommittee of the Social Science Research Council (composed of Redfield, Linton and Herskovits) defines acculturation as follows:

"Acculturation comprehends those phenomena which result when groups of individuals having different cultures come into continuous first hand contact, with subsequent changes in the original culture patterns of either or both groups. Under this definition, acculturation is to be distinguished from culture-change, of which it is but one aspect, and assimilation, which is at times a phase of acculturation. It is also to be differentiated from diffusion, which, while occurring in all instances of acculturation, is not only a phenomenon which frequently takes place without the occurrence of the types of contact between peoples specified in the definition given above, but also constitutes only one aspect of the process of acculturation" (*22*, p. 10).

In a later study (*28*) Linton makes several significant additions to this definition.

"Culture change normally involves not only the addition of a new element or elements to the culture, but also the elimination of certain previously existing elements, and the modification and reorganization of others" (p. 469). "No society as long as it exists as a distinct entity, will take over even the purely objective aspects of an alien culture in toto" (p. 487). "If one group admires another it will take a great deal of trouble to be like them. If it despises them to be unlike them" (p. 488). "Overt hostility, that is actual warfare, seems to impose very little bar to cultural borrowing. Each of the hostile groups may recognize in the other a foeman worthy of its steel, and one from whom elements of culture can be taken with gain rather than a loss in prestige" (p. 498).

Linton then proceeds to point out the significance of the borrowing of military techniques and also stresses the fact that some traits of the culture of the vanquished tend to become incorporated into the culture of the victor, by means of the slave economy and concubinage resulting from the exploitation of the vanquished.

Linton's work always excepted, the preoccupations of students of acculturation may be defined as primarily quantitative, in that they seek to assign the phenomena which they study to one of the following categories: 1) *Sterile contact*; 2) *Partial borrowing*; 3) *Partial lending*; 4) *Wholesale borrowing* (passive); 5) *Wholesale lending* (active).

Resistances

Only in relatively recent times did students of acculturation give theoretical as well as descriptive recognition to the resistances to diffusion and acculturation. Our reference to resistances does not concern, of course, such obvious phenomena as mere traditionalism. Sumner (*53*) rightly stresses that men tend to regard the ways of their ancestors as sacred and to believe that these time-hallowed procedures are watched over by the spirit of their forefathers. In this mentality any change, regardless of the advantages or disadvantages which may accrue therefrom, is always regarded as a bad change. Lowie says: "But man is not built so as to do the reasonable thing just because it is reasonable. It is far easier for him to do an irrational thing because it has always been done" (*33*, p. 68). This phenomenon is, however, cultural *inertia* rather than *resistance*.

We cannot, however, stop here. The task of our analysis is outlined for us by Lowie's warning that "man is not a total abstainer from common-sense even if he indulges with fanatical moderation" (*33*, p. 60). Hence, we first undertake a structural analysis of the phenomenon of resistance, which, in the last resort, forms the foundation of the process of antagonistic acculturation.

An analysis of resistance must take into consideration several modes of classifying phenomena and use several frames of reference. Two major frames of reference will, however, suffice in this context, since our study is not primarily devoted to resistance as such:

1. The distinction between resistance to borrowing and resistance to lending.

2. The distinction between resistance to the borrowing or lending of specific cultural items as such, and resistance to, or antagonism toward, the prospective lender or borrower.

Analytically the two frames of references are distinct, though in concrete cases a complete analysis cannot be achieved without using both frames of reference.

I. *Resistance to Borrowing:*

  A. *Due to Resistance to the Cultural Item:*

    1. The Mentawei Islanders refused to borrow the art of rice cultivation from the neighboring Malay, even though the cultivation of rice would have raised their standard of living. Rice cultivation demands, however, continuous work, which cannot be reconciled with the demands of Mentawei religion that all work cease for months at a time. Hence the staple crop of the Mentawei Islands is taro rather than rice (*31*, p. 163).

    2. The Zafimaniry Tanala of Madagascar borrowed from their neighbors the technique of wet-rice culture, which is more profitable than their own dry-rice technique. Eventually they found it desirable to revert once more to the relatively unprofitable dry-rice technique, because the wet-rice technique tended to undermine their existing social structure (*29*, p. 284).

  B. *Due to Resistance to the Lender:*

    1. The Scriptures constantly admonished the Hebrews not to be like unto the Midianites or other neighbors, who were at the same time their enemies.

    2. Colonizing "Nordics" tend to reject many of the successful techniques of adjustment of the subject races to the tropical environments, and to ostracise those of their fellows who "go native."

II. *Resistance to Lending:*

  A. *Due to the Cultural Item:*

    1. The knowledge of certain segments of cult and belief tends in most cultures to be limited to the initiates, and is jealously guarded from women and children (*30*, p. 250 ff.). Even visiting anthropologists, who cannot in any sense be considered as prospective borrowers, often experience considerable difficulties in their attempts to record all phases of esoteric cults and beliefs (*41*).

    2. Patents, though seldom secret, are protected by law against being used by all. (The Treaty of Versailles compelled Germany to surrender to the allies all of its chemical patents.)

B. *Due to Antagonism Toward the Borrower:*

1. Shamans more consistently conceal their knowledge from their competitors, the missionaries, than from the neutral visiting anthropologist.

2. Military secrets are exceptionally well guarded from the spies of other nations. During the Second World War, United States Air Force bombardiers were under oath to protect a certain highly secret bomb-sight with their very lives.

Psychologically, resistance to the culture trait differs from resistances due to group antagonism, but the two processes are highly similar in their actual operation.

Developing further our analysis of resistance to lending, we find an important distinction between resistance to in-group diffusion and resistance to out-group diffusion. The former prevents the homogenization of the group and the disappearance of caste and class barriers, while the latter aims to prevent the homogenization of culturally and ethnically distinct groups.

Each group has a jealous regard for its own ethnic distinctiveness and cultural autonomy, which is clearly reflected in resistance to borrowing, and, even more conspicuously, in resistance to lending. This pride stands in the way of acculturation and assimilation in the socio-cultural sphere, and in the way of miscegenation in the biological realm. Distinctive racial characteristics may even be amplified in works of art. Thus, the Bushman rock paintings often exaggerate the steatopygia of their women.

In its operations, the resistance to lending closely resembles the function of patents.

I. *Resistance to Internal Lending* is exemplified in:

1. Certain old Italian laws forbidding the education of the poor.

2. Sumptuary laws.

3. Dollard's proof (*15*) that Southern whites deliberately kept the blacks improvident, immoral and infantile, i.e., outside the sphere of the "Protestant Ethnic" (*59*), in order

to rule them and in order to justify their rule. The Spartans behaved in a similar way toward the Helots (*12*).

4. Poll taxes and property tests for franchise.

5. The disenfranchisement of women.

6. An African practice which forbids the common people of a certain tribe to own fertile cows. This property restriction prevents intermarriage between nobles and commoners, since a noble bride must be paid for in fertile cows (*37*, p. 130).

7. Patents and monopolies.

II. *Resistance to External Lending* is exemplified in:

1. Former Brazilian laws against the exportation of the rubber tree (*Hevea brasiliensis*).

2. Deliberate monopolistic maneuvers on the part of the trading Venetians directed against the competing Genoese, which consisted in inciting the Mohammedans against the latter.

3. The secrecy surrounding Portuguese charts showing the route to the East Indies via the Cape of Good Hope.

4. A deliberate exaggeration of the dangers of the Silk Road, on the part of those who habitually travelled that route and held the monopoly of the silk trade.

5. Secret diplomacy of all types.

6. Former Dutch colonial laws, discouraging and even preventing the learning of the Dutch tongue by the Malay subjects (*55*, p. 200).

Cause and Function of Resistance

Negative reactions to acculturation and diffusion can be better understood when one notes that diffusion and acculturation both represent a particular type of socio-cultural group adjustment, necessitated by the crisis situation of a bilateral challenge resulting from new contacts. One can define "crisis-situation" in terms of three criteria:

1. Vested interests are in jeopardy.

2. Existing modes of adjustment to existing problem

situations fail, because they cannot be applied to the new problems arising from the bilateral challenge of contact between groups by means of what the psychologists call "transfer of learning" (*9, 10*).

3. [*Addendum 1971*] A vicious circle comes into being: every measure taken in order to solve the problem only creates new difficulties (*13*, Ch. 1).

Because of what Bain (*3*) calls "organic cultural interaction," the adoption of a new trait, regardless of its magnitude, invariably challenges the adopting culture, insofar as the new trait has to be geared to, and articulated with, the remainder of the culture. Three cases are possible:

1. Sometimes the new trait modifies one segment, or the whole, of the social structure. A conspicuous instance of this is the effect of the introduction of the horse into the Great Plains (*61*).

2. Sometimes the new trait undermines, or threatens to undermine, the social structure, and is therefore rejected after a brief trial period. An instance of this is the Tanala crisis, which resulted from the temporary adoption of wet-rice culture (supra).

3. Very rarely, the more or less unassimilable trait becomes "encysted" or remains "free-floating." In other words, it fails to become articulated with the rest of the culture, or with parts thereof, and remains a foreign body in the social structure. Sometimes, as in the case of the Sermon on the Mount, it becomes part of the covert culture, but not of the overt culture,[1] i.e., of the content and pattern of culture, but not of behavior or of "culture in action." In other instances, e.g., premarital sex relations in America before 1941, the trait is incorporated into overt culture but not into covert culture, and sometimes its very existence is denied.

We are now prepared to discuss some psychological resistance to acculturation.

1.   The distinction is Linton's. The term "covert" replaced his earlier term "essential." (Cf. *27*, p. 299.)

1. We have so far described the desire for ethnic distinctiveness and cultural autonomy simply as facts, without inquiring into the psychological motivation which has created them. Psychoanalysts have provided us with excellent devices for an understanding of this motivational structure. Freud (*19*) has carefully analyzed the meaning of the narcissism of small differences, already known to Diodoros the Sicilian (*14*, 1.89.6), and the psychological function of the sense of the "uniqueness of the self" is one of the cornerstones of psychoanalytic psychology. These interpretations can readily be connected with Pareto's residue of the "integrity of the individual" (*39*, pp. 727-806). The need to be distinct from one's fellows seems a significant component of Man's sense of his own integrity and explains resistance to, and ambivalence toward, regimentation or even conformity. It is this ambivalence which has served as a point of departure for Fromm's (*20*) analysis. On a broader social plane, the individual's desire for integrity (which includes distinctiveness) is expressed in the form of a desire for ethnic distinctiveness (see Ch. 6) and cultural autonomy.[2]

We need not be puzzled by the strength of this desire for uniqueness, either on the psychological or on the social level. Genetic psychoanalysis has shown the difficulty which the child experiences in becoming aware of the distinction between the self and the environment (*51*), and culture-history shows a similarly arduous struggle for cultural autonomy in the face of constant, though tempting, dangers of encroachments. By "reaction formation," these strenuously achieved techniques of becoming and remaining distinct are clung to with great intensity.

The practical implication of this finding is equally obvious: it always seems desirable to prolong indefinitely the usefulness of existing patterns of adjustment, which might fail were one's culture modified or were the balance of strength between one's own group and the out-group

2. The best definition of "autonomy" is that of Angyal (*1*, pp. 20-35).

(radically upset through indiscriminate processes of one-sided or cross-fertilization; for acculturation invariably creates new challenges and problems for lender and borrower alike.[3]

2. The problem of resistance must also be connected with the general psychological problem of the "in-group" and the "out-group." The logical nexus is the following:

Ferenczi's (*16*) studies show that in early childhood the dominant mechanisms of social adjustment in the individual are "identification" and "introjection." Whosoever and whatsoever enter the life-space of the child, while identification is the dominant psychological process, automatically becomes part of the in-group, respectively of the "culture of the in-group," and is considered good and just. This is clearly implied in Kimball Young's statement: "From [his in-group's behavior] pattern the child constructs his own role and status" (*62*, p. 630). Gradually, however, identification, as the *major* technique of adjustment, recedes and yields its dominant place to the mechanism known as projection. Individual personality comes into being at this stage, and the "system" becomes "closed." New persons and objects are therefore automatically assigned to the out-group and its culture, and are often automatically labelled "evil" and "wrong." Thus, MacCrone (*34*, pp. 233–257) rightly stresses that in race prejudice one projects into the out-group one's own repressed and rejected wishes and therefore characterizes the out-group in terms of these repudiated impulses. The physiological equivalent of the

3. This analysis, while sufficient for present purposes, does not profess to be exhaustive. It becomes subsequently necessary to consider the very elusive psychological and sociological implications of the problem of uniqueness as regards both the individual and the culture. This phase of the problem acquires altogether different dimensions, when one tackles it in terms of the "definition of the situation" (W. I. Thomas), of the concept of "orientation" of Devereux (*13*, Ch. 9) and, more generally, in terms of the problems connected with "social visibility" (as defined by R. E. Park) and of the substitution of social status regalia for "expressive behavior" (which, according to psychologists, is both equivocal and misleading in Man).

"closing" process might be myelination (in certain nerve fibers) whose socio-cultural significance was somewhat overstressed by Kardiner (*23*, pp. 33–34).

In summary,

1. There is resistance to borrowing because of a resistance to identification with the out-group which represents one's repressed impulses (rejection of affiliation).

2. There is a resistance to lending because lending would force the borrower into the closed circle of the lender's in-group (rejection of adoption).

It would be tempting here to pursue further our analysis of the implications of this scheme, which forms the basis of the theory of antagonistic acculturation. For reasons of expository convenience we must, however, next consider Kroeber's theory of "stimulus diffusion," because it forms the logical bridge between the psychological analysis of resistances to acculturation, and an analysis, in terms of the means-end schema, of antagonistic acculturation.

Suffice it to say, at this stage, that the mere contact of culturally different groups is always a challenge to both and a cause of social and cultural change which can take three major forms:

1. Purposive isolation, exemplified in barriers, "silent barter," etc.

2. Borrowing and lending

3. Purposive dissociative change, i.e., *negative* acculturation

Stimulus Diffusion

Kroeber (*24*, p. 344) defined a hitherto neglected type of diffusion. "It occurs in situations where a system or pattern as such encounters no resistance to its spread but there are difficulties in regard to the transmission of the concrete content of the system. In this case, it is the idea of the complex or system which is accepted, but it remains for the receiving culture to develop a new content. This somewhat special process might therefore be called 'idea diffusion' or 'stimulus diffusion'." The process is clearly reflected in one of Kroeber's examples. Europeans in the early eighteenth century deliberately attempted to discover the technique of manufacturing Chinese porcelain, since transportation risks and costs made Chinese porcelain extremely expensive. In this instance, the *idea* of porcelain was borrowed from the Chinese, whereas the technique of manufacturing it was rediscovered independently.

While Kroeber's study deals with significant and hitherto neglected phenomena, it does so unfortunately only on a descriptive, and not on a theoretical level. (Definition and analysis are not the same thing.)

Kroeber's terminology is, moreover, not acceptable, since his use of the word "stimulus" is at variance with the standardized psychological connotations of this term. What Kroeber denotes by the term "stimulus" is, properly speaking, merely a segment of what Linton (*27*) originally called "essential" culture, and which he subsequently designated by the more neutral and hence more appropriate term: "covert culture." Above all, Kroeber's "idea" or "stimulus" is merely a *segment* of covert culture, since, in the case of the porcelain culture complex, the covert culture complex would include also a mental blueprint of the (hypothetical) manufacturing processes.

This terminological difficulty can be overcome by a blending of the concepts "covert" and "overt" culture with Parsons' (*41*) "means-end" schema. In terms of this schema one may define what Kroeber calls "idea" or "stimulus" as the end segment of a covert culture complex. For example, the Chinese idea of porcelain and its use is, in the last resort, nothing more than a part of the end segment of the covert culture complex "porcelain," whose means segment includes, among other things, techniques of manufacturing the object in question.

Kroeber's study of stimulus diffusion has certain important broader implications for societies undergoing what is more or less "contactless" culture change. Two types may be considered:

I. *Ersatz*, which may be defined as the deliberate reproduction, by different techniques, of objects which are lacking, or the deliberate production of different objects having the same function.

A. *Reproduction by Different Technique:* The most famous example is perhaps the Haber nitrogen-fixation process, which enabled Germany, in 1914–1918, to wage a long war, even though it was cut off from Chilean nitrates.

B. *Production of Functionally Similar Objects:*

1. The Polynesians seem to have possessed pottery in their original habitat. When they migrated to islands without potter's clay, they imitated clay containers in wood and stone;

2. Expensive goods are often imitated with cheap raw materials, e.g., imitation leather.

II. *Form Persistence:* In many instances there is a tendency to retain the external appearance of an object about to be replaced by a more useful one, by adding functionless external details to the latter. This is exemplified by the tendency of early automobile builders to make their vehicles resemble broughams or victorias.

In each and all of these instances there is a persistence of the idea or stimulus, or, more properly, a persistence of the end segment of covert culture complexes, accompanied by a substitution of means. This phenomenon took on extremely broad proportions during the early Renaissance, where the borrowing of Greco-Roman classical "ends" led to a wholesale restructuring of medieval society. Ersatz products and form persistences occur when society becomes aware of cultural lacunae. This awareness is, however, very often a result of interaction between groups. Sequoya, the nearly illiterate inventor of the Cherokee system of writing, became aware of a deficiency of his tribal culture only because contact with Americans, who knew how to write, created in his tribe a need for a similar efficiency in communication and recording. Kroeber rightly stresses that

when the idea is a borrowed one, the act of borrowing itself
indicates a lack of resistance to the cultural item. Affectively,
end or goal diffusion implies at least benevolent neutrality,
or else competitive admiration for the group whose culture
is being imitated.

We are now prepared to gather together our threads and
undertake an analysis of antagonistic acculturation per se.

Antagonistic Acculturation

Antagonistic acculturation is the diffusion of the means
segment of a covert culture (or overt culture) complex of
traits. We distinguish between three types:

1. Defensive isolation
2. The adoption of new means in order to support existing ends
3. Dissociative negative acculturation, or the evolving of
culture complexes deliberately at variance with, or the opposite of, the culture of the out-group

We now propose to analyze these three types of antagonistic acculturation, to study their motivational structure
as "social actions," and, finally, to establish their significance for the study of the social process.

I. *Defensive Isolation.* The bilateral challenge of culture
contact can be met, among other ways, by defensive isolation. History is replete with accounts of forbidden lands
(e.g., Mecca, Thibet, etc.). Defensive isolation may be either
partial or complete. Logical analysis enables us to distinguish between two types of isolation.

A. *The Suppression of Social Contact* is exemplified in
"silent barter" between alien or hostile groups.

The Sakai of Malaya leave near a tree certain forest products, such as wax, rattan, etc., and then retire out of sight.
In due time, a Malay will collect these goods and leave
manufactured products in their place. This type of relationship is frequent between pygmies and full-size natives; it is
reported from Africa, Malaya and the Philippines. It is also

noteworthy that in the Malay language "Sakai" means "dependents," "retainers" or "subjects" (*60*, p. 219), although the relationship between Malay and Sakai is often decidedly reciprocal and mutually beneficial.

Cases which constitute a transition between the suppression of relationships and obstacles to the spread of selected cultural items are by no means lacking.

1. The Sedang Moi of Indochina tended to kill foreigners in general, and Annamites in particular, as soon as they entered their tribal territory. An exception to this rule were Annamite salt traders, who were not only not molested, but were actually protected by the tribe as a whole.

2. During the First World War, belligerent countries sold large quantities of war material to neutral countries, pretending not to be aware of the fact that these goods were promptly resold to their enemies. Napoleon excluded coffee from Europe when he blockaded England, but, being himself a heavy coffee drinker, never inquired where his own coffee came from.

B. *The Suppression of Cultural Items* can be of three types, and each of these types may be total or partial:

1. Tariff barriers, exclusion and boycott
2. Embargo on exports and blockade
3. A combination of the two

Examples of the suppression of cultural items have been given above in connection with our discussion of resistance to diffusion. One interesting case does, however, merit mention. Since the very handy Arabic numeral system was a creation of the "infidels," Florentine merchants were forbidden to use it and had to use the clumsy Roman numerals instead (*6*, p. 121).

The trend toward autarky, so obvious in prewar Nazi Germany, also illustrates this process, which can be readily linked with the theory of stimulus diffusion. The suppression of cultural items and their replacement is particularly frequent in times of war. In many other instances it is due to a lack of purchasing power.

II. *The Adoption of New Means* without a corresponding adoption of the relevant goals is a common process in socio-cultural change. The new means are adopted in order to support existing goals, sometimes even for the specific purpose of resisting the compulsory adoption of the goals of the lending group. Theoretically the issue is clear: means are adopted and the goals pertaining to them are rejected. However, because of what Bain (*3*) calls "organic cultural interaction," the adoption of means is often accompanied for a certain length of time by what we may term a "pseudo-diffusion of goals." Hence, in order to justify our position that in the cases under study only means are genuinely diffused, we now propose to examine an instance of pseudo-diffusion of goals.

A. *The Pseudo-Diffusion of Goals* is conspicuously illustrated by the recent history of Japan, during the so-called Meiji era. This process is often an automatic and more or less unconscious one, but in the case of Japan it was more or less deliberate.

Subsequent to the opening up of Japan, there arose in certain Japanese circles a movement, whose purpose was the wholesale Westernization of the country by means of an assimilation of Japan's means-end system to the Western social structure. Japanese intellectuals spoke of adopting not only the British parliamentary system, but also the U.S. type of republican government. Ancient Japanese ways fell into disrepute. Jiujitsu, Japanese archery and other folkways were frowned upon as barbarous and were preserved only in outlying rural districts. Many "enlightened" Westerners, deceived by these phenomena, believed that Japan had forsaken its traditional goals in order to replace them by Western ones. Japan's victory over imperial Russia was hailed by many as a triumph of democracy over the forces of darkness. Though a few sentimentalists deplored the passing of "quaint" traditional ways of life, the majority of Westerners welcomed Japan into the family of civilized nations.

Strangely enough, the process of Westernization was welcomed even by some Japanese diehards; though despising the Westernized among their compatriots, they used them for the purpose of persuading Western powers of Japan's complete Westernization. The confusion was complete. Not until Pearl Harbor did Western diplomacy and the Western "man in the street" awaken to the realization that the *pseudo*-adoption of Western goals on the part of Japan was, as far as the country as a whole was concerned, nothing more than protective coloring. It did, however, enable Japan, with the help, or at least with the complicity, of Western powers, to achieve the degree of industrialization and militarization which, in 1941, enabled it to make a bid for world domination, in accordance with traditional Japanese political philosophy.

The case of Japan proves conclusively that the borrowing of means is frequently undertaken only for the ultimate purpose of turning the tables on the lender.[4]

The same process is also manifest in the exploitive industrialization of cheap labor areas, e.g., the colonies and the U.S. Deep South. We disagree with those optimists who believe that the industrialization of the Deep South will truly modernize its spirit. Rather do we feel that the rising economic power of the Deep South, within the economic structure of the United States, is likely to bring about a state of affairs in which the industrialized South will make a bid for an *ideological* domination of the United States as a whole. In simpler terms, the industrialization of the Deep South is likely to undermine the "American Way of Life," unless constructive efforts are made to reconstruct the ideology of the South first, and to industrialize it afterwards (*15*).[5] All these conclusions appear to be confirmed by the example of Japan, quite as much as by the occidentalization of pre-1945 Germany, which was ideologically sterile

4. See also Wagatsuma's excellent article (*57*).
5. These lines were written in 1942 and are applicable also to other countries.

because it was almost entirely confined to the sphere of performances.

B. We may now give a few examples of the *adoption of means without either real or apparent adoption of goals*:

1. *Signalling:* The Apache of Geronimo substituted for the tribe's traditional system of smoke signals, the heliographic method of signalling, which they borrowed from the United States Army, i.e., from the foe whom they wished to defeat (*32*).

2. *Kingship:* The Hebrews (I Samuel, chs. 8 and 10) asked the prophet to give them a king so that they would be like other nations. In support of this demand, they made it clear that they wished to have a king so that he would go before them in battle against the self-same nations whose kingship pattern they wished to borrow.

3. *Skirmishing and Deployment:* During the French and Indian Wars the British troops were compelled to adopt the guerrilla tactics of their opponents and to create the American Rifles. After the American Revolution this body of fighters was replaced by the Rifle Brigade, and men trained in these tactics by Sir John Moore played an important role in the Peninsular war against Napoleon. After the Boer War —chiefly under the impetus of Churchill—new skirmishing and deployment tactics were introduced into the British Expeditionary Force of the First World War.

4. *The tank* was invented by the British, whose initial use of the tank was, however, injudicious. The theory of tank warfare was developed by Colonel J. F. C. Fuller, R.A., and the theory of the blitzkrieg by General de Gaulle. The German Army borrowed first the tank, then tank tactics and, finally, the strategic theory of the blitzkrieg, in order to turn the tables on the inventors of these devices and techniques.

5. *Army Structure:* In order to defeat the German Army, the United States Army was reorganized in 1942 along German lines. Two phases of this reorganization may be considered:

a) *The Triangular Division*, composed of three rather than of four regiments, was originated in Germany during the twenties, when the *Reichswehr* was organized as a cadre or skeleton army, rather than as a field force. In simpler terms, the triangular division is not the product of profound military philosophy, but of lack of manpower during the early days of the *Reichswehr*.

b) *The Ratio Between Tanks and Other Types of Ordnance.* During the Second World War, certain American military strategists asserted that the Germans had discovered the ideal ratio between various types of ordnance in general, and between tanks, aircraft and guns in particular. The plain fact was that the Germans equipped their combat units with as many tanks as their industrial plants could furnish— neither more, nor less. The "ideal" Nazi ratio between tanks and other types of ordnance was, once more, not a product of the Nazi's military philosophy, but of their industrial capacity. As regards the *use* of tanks, the Germans set a pattern which was, again, not "ideal," but determined by the nature of the terrain. Thus, in 1941, the British command in Burma had tanks enough, but they were of no particular use in the jungle, where they were constantly outflanked by Japanese jungle troops.

We have mainly quoted military examples, because they provide conspicuously clear examples of the adoption of means without an adoption of goals. It may be objected, of course, that no adoption of goals was necessary, because the goals of the opponents were identical to begin with: i.e., victory. This statement is nonsense when examined in the light of the theory of goals combined with MacIver's theory of interests (*35*, pp. 18–58). That the goals in such a case are not identical, and that victory is but an intermediate goal or "intervening opportunity" (*52*), is well expressed by von Clausewitz' famous dictum: "War is the continuation of policies by other means" (*7*). Since war was brought about by a clash of policies, the allegation of an identity of goals is necessarily fallacious.

We must, however, attempt a closer analysis of this problem in terms of MacIver's work, in view of the fact that alarmist circles in America have asserted (1942) that, because in time of war America was borrowing certain Nazi means of coping with problems, it was inevitably doomed to adopt the *whole* of Nazi philosophy. Some viewers-with-alarm actually saw the shadow of the proverbial man on the White Horse fall across the pages of rationing booklets. This regulation of consumption was held to be in fundamental opposition to the "American Way of Life" (ethos). It goes without saying that the fears of these good people could be dismissed as nonsense, since it is obvious that, whereas the Nazis gloried in regimentation, the Americans merely endured it temporarily for the purpose of not having to endure it forever (1942).

Theoretically the issue is broader:

1. Victory is a "like interest." Like interests or goals are attained by competition, and only by establishing *exclusive* possession of the goal can a contender feel entirely satisfied (e.g., armies fighting).

2. Policies (mentioned by Clausewitz) are cultural goals, i.e., "common interests," which can—in principle—be attained by cooperation and whose satisfaction does not imply *exclusive* possession. (E.g., Ishi, the last Yahi Indian [*46*, p. 168; *25*] could speak no language other than his own and no one could speak his. As long as this state of affairs lasted, the goal of his language behavior—communication —remained unattainable.)

It is, hence, our thesis that the borrowing of even intermediate goals of the like interests type (e.g., victory or desire for rule by presidential decrees) must still be treated in this scheme as a diffusion of means, and be kept distinct from the diffusion of genuine goals and particularly of goals of the common interests type.

Since this statement stands in need of concrete proof, we now propose to examine historical instances supporting this interpretation.

According to Henri Pirenne (*43*) the "Roman Way of Life," which he calls "Romania" for short, did not disappear until the time of Mohammed and Charlemagne; it certainly did not founder at the time of the barbarian invasions. In support of this assertion, he rightly stresses that when, e.g., the Vandals conquered North Africa, and when the Visigoths conquered Spain, they took over the Roman administrative system and became more or less Romanized themselves. Related phenomena are the Persianization of the Arabs, the Indianization of the Moguls and the absorption of the Mongols and of the Manchus by the Chinese. In our view, the invading barbarians borrowed merely the intermediate goals and probably, in most cases, borrowed merely the means of the Roman (or other) social structure. The very fact that "Romania" did eventually disappear under the combined impact of Germanic feudal-tribal organization, as represented by Charlemagne, and of Islam, suggests that the true spirit of "Romania" (i.e., the goal structure) had foundered imperceptibly already during the barbarian invasions. We similarly hold that the Arabism and Mohammedanism of the post-Persianization period is unlike "primitive" Mohammedanism, and that China modified some of its goal structure, as a result of Kublai Khan's rule.

The relevance of these comments for our own time is obvious. There is no denying that if the Nazis had conquered the Western nations they eventually would have succumbed to the pleasures of Western democracy, as Hannibal's army succumbed to Capuan delights. After all, Napoleon, on the eve of the Russian campaign, complained that his marshals, now wealthy and comfortable in their new castles, displayed little enthusiasm for months in the saddle and in camp (*18*). This does not mean, however, that the Capuanized Nazi conqueror would have adopted more than the means structure and some of the intermediate goals of the conquered democracies. Post-Napoleonic France was unlike the France of Louis XVI. For a proper analysis, the problem must be subdivided into two parts.

1. It is correct to say that, despite the repeated triumph of barbarians over civilized nations, civilization never disappeared because the barbarian conquerors preserved the means structure of the vanquished group.

2. It is, on the other hand, a gross overstatement to assert that the conquering barbarians adopted also the basic goal structure of the conquered. It is one of the gravest shortcomings of European culture-history—manifest, in an attenuated form, even in the works of Pirenne—that the contributions of the barbarian tribal social structure to the social structure of our contemporary civilization are consistently soft-pedalled, in contrast with the exaggerated emphasis put on the heritage of Greece, Rome and Israel. The tendency in question is partly explained by the availability of documents bearing on the culture of our civilized ancestors, but much of it is also due to vanity.

Summing up, we may say that whereas means, and even intermediate goals, of the like interests type, diffuse readily enough, the ultimate goals of the common interests type seldom spread. This explains perhaps why, in practice, Christianity has so seldom gone beyond the stage of ritualism and lip service. The process as a whole is readily understandable in terms of Merton's analysis of anomie (*36*). The adoption of means, and of intermediate goals, and the rejection of ultimate goals, is but a variant of Merton's "Ritualism." In a sense, ritualism involves a misuse of means, i.e., the use of a surgeon's scalpel for murder. On a "plane clearly different" we find resemblances with Merton's "Class V: Rebellion," which he defines as a "transitional response which seeks to *institutionalize* new procedures oriented toward revamped cultural goals." This process is manifest in the adjustment of the barbarian conqueror to the vanquished high civilization, to whose goals he now pays lip service. This process may explain, in part, the fluctuations of cultural mentalities discussed by Sorokin (*50*, vol. 1, pp. 153-191 and passim).

The question now arises: Why is the borrowing of means, and possibly of intermediate goals, *without* a concomitant borrowing also of the ultimate goals, generally destructive? Why does the resulting situation seldom fail to give one an impression of "misuse," in the sense that the drug addict's use of pharmacological substances, such as morphine, strikes us as an antisocial misuse of cultural values?

The answer lies in the inherent basic unity of the means-end schema. The diverting of means *a* from the corresponding goal *A* to the service of some other goal *B* must strike those steeped in the habit of considering means *a* and goal *A* as a unit, as little short of sacrilege. We insist on the specification "those steeped in the habit, etc.," since we cannot assert on any other grounds the existence of a logically necessary nexus between any means and end. One concrete illustration should suffice to prove the rightness of this thesis. The use of gunpowder for military purposes would have struck the Chinese of yore as revolting, for they seem to have invented it for pyrotechnical displays. Yet no Frenchman felt scandalized when Stovarsol, intended by its inventor, Professor Fournier, as a preventive of syphilis, was, in the end, used exclusively in the treatment of dysentery. On the other hand, not a few civilized men will deplore the fact that the airplane, heralded as a means of improving relations between nations, is now being used for destructive purposes. Comparing the attitude toward the "misuse" of the airplane to the attitude toward the "misuse" of Stovarsol, we must conclude that the logical nexus between cultural means and ends is usually conceived of in ethical rather than in mechanical terms. This nexus should therefore be understood in terms of Sorokin's concept of "logico-meaningful" relationships (*50*, vol. 1, pp. 18–21; vol. 4, pp. 21–22). The adoption of means, without the concomitant adoption of ends, is culturally destructive, simply because it disturbs a logico-meaningful relationship of a type which forms the basis of the social structure.

III. *Dissociative Negative Acculturation.* The realization

that the borrowing of means without the borrowing of the goals pertaining to them results in social crisis, bridges the conceptual gap between the diffusion of means pure and simple and dissociative, i.e., antagonistic, acculturation.

Dissociative acculturation may be defined as the creation by group *A* of new cultural items of the means type, which are purposively at variance with, or the reverse of, the life techniques of the group *B*, from which group *A* wishes to dissociate itself. As in the case of the diffusion of means, so in the case of dissociative acculturation, the purpose of this act of cultural creation is ultimately the preservation of existing goals. Although this process is an extremely common one, it is seldom interpreted in this way (*13*, Ch. 3). Hence it is necessary to give several examples in support of our views.

1. *Apache vs. Navaho vs. Hopi.* A curious case of what may possibly be antagonistic acculturation of the dissociative type may be reported from the Southwest. Among the Hopi, a man turned to his father's sister's daughter (real or classificatory) for his first love affair "since he could not be expected to marry her" (*49*, p. 55). Among the neighboring Navaho, cross-cousins were very companionable, and there were few restrictions on their relationship, except that they could not marry legitimately (*47*, p. 87). Among the Western Apache, whose contact with the Navaho was rather intimate, though not always friendly, the native term for "cross-cousin" was synonymous with "sweetheart." Goodwin (*21*, p. 302) believes that in aboriginal times interclan cross-cousin marriages (i.e., marriage into the father's sister's clan) were frequent. On the other hand, the neighboring Chiricahua Apache were so austere in their conception of incest, that even the remotest familiarity with blood or affinal kin was frowned upon. Hence, cousins of the opposite sex were prone to hide behind trees when meeting accidentally. The Chiricahua rationalize this by saying that "cousins love each other very much and wish to show their respect" (*38*, p. 61).

2. *Yuma vs. Pueblo.* E. C. Parsons (*40*, vol. 2, p. 1096) has shown that the medicine societies of the Hopi and of the Zuni might well have developed as a result of resistance toward the individualistic dream-shamanism of the Pima-Papago and Yuman tribes of Southwestern Arizona (see Ch. 9). Though the Hopi and the Zuni also felt the need for curing, dream-shamanism would have disrupted their socially overorganized communities. Hence they developed medicine societies, which worked by routine rather than by inspiration. Thus, we have here an instance of dissociative acculturation, which produced an end result quite unique and different in technique, although its general purpose was the same as that of its "anti-type," which had negatively inspired its creation.

3. *Israel vs. Its Neighbors.* The Old Testament is replete with admonitions to the Jews not to be like unto their neighbors and foes, be they Canaanites, Midianites or Philistines. In this section we propose to examine specifically the sources of the sex morality of the Old Testament. According to Wallis (*58*, Introduction, p. xxx), the religion of the Prophets was the result of contact between the cults of the primitive Semitic nomads and the cults of the city dwellers of Canaan. In Wallis' words, we meet here with a "cross-fertilization of cultures." The historic steps seem to be as follows.

Upon entering Canaan, the Israelites found the Ishtar cult flourishing among the settled and civilized agriculturalists of that area. Barton (*5*, p. 83) notes that "The Ishtar cult is coextensive with the Semitic people, traces of it appearing in Assyria, Babylonia, North and South Arabia, Ethiopia, Nabathea, Moab, Palestine, Phoenicia, Cyprus, Malta, Sicily and Carthage. The goddess in all these countries was a mother goddess, and a patroness of unmarried love. In Babylonia, Arabia and Cyprus virgins must sacrifice to her their chastity by an act of free love; at Byblos it might be commuted to a sacrifice of hair; and at Carthage and elsewhere her feasts were attended by impure ceremonies, in which sexual excesses formed a prominent feature.[6] The Israelites found this cult among the Canaanites and adopted, as many scholars hold, many features of its ritual."

This view is substantiated by Badé (*2*, pp. 197–198), who points out that "both male and female temple prostitutes, known as the 'holy ones', were anciently attached to sanctuaries of Jahveh." Amos and Hosea denounce this form of "impurity" as they observed it at Israel's sanctuaries (Amos 2:7, Hosea 4:14; cf. I Samuel 2:22), and the Deuteronomists expressly provide that "there shall be among Israelitish girls and boys none who becomes a temple prostitute." Evidently the proceeds of this traffic passed into the treasury of the sanctuary, for the Deuteronomists, scornful of such profits, sought to expel the custom from Jahvism (Deuteronomy 23:18).

In brief, while it may be conjectured that the nomadic Hebrews were acquainted with, and condoned at first, homosexuality, these passages would suggest that they became acquainted with *commercialized* religious homosexuality and prostitution only upon their entrance into Canaan. The Hebrew prophets, who desired to keep the Jahve-cult apart from the Canaanite cults, therefore condemned the homosexuality and prostitution which had crept into Hebrew religion through contact with the Canaanite cults. This rejection of these cult techniques eventually led to the formulation of Hebrew-Christian sex morality, which is completely alien to the sex morality of Greece and Rome. The very violence of the Hebrew-Christian sex-morality complex seems to indicate that it was originally a reaction formation, in the strictly Freudian sense of the term.

6. [*Postscript 1966* (G. Devereux): Though the substance of Barton's statements is correct, its formulation is deplorably tendentious. Instead of "unmarried love" one should read: "socially approved, non-patrilineal and non-durable sexual relations." As to the obligatory sacrifice of virginity, it represents "free love" as little as does the obligatory promiscuousness of young girls among the Muria and the Trobrianders. On this last point, see G. Devereux (*11*, pp. 151–157).]

4. *Arabs vs. Jews and Christians.* The dissociative acculturation of the Arabs with respect to both Jews and Christians is set forth with admirable clarity by Vajda (*54*): "La
tradition musulmane condamne certains gestes, comme
propres aux Juifs (ou aux Chrétiens)" (p. 83). The Jews
were aware of this antagonism and resented it, saying of
Mohammed "Cet homme ne veut laisser aucune de nos doc-
trines sans opposition" (p. 68, quoted from *Muslim Ṣaḥīḥ*,
Cairo 1329–1333). Vajda hence justly concludes: "Le
premier principe qui régit l'attitude correcte du Musulman
envers les gens du Livre [i.e., Jews and Christians] est la
réaction contre toutes les pratiques qui leur sont propres,
même si elles ne touchent ni à la foi, ni aux moeurs. Nous
avons fait remarquer le parallélisme qui existe sur ce point
entre le Judaïsme et l'Islam" (p. 123). We wish to draw attention to the fact that Vajda constantly uses the term *tout*, i.e.,
"all." In other words, we find here a *complete* attempt at
dissociative acculturation. This view, and our psychological
explanation in terms of reaction formation, is reinforced by
the fact that Vajda is simply a learned Orientalist, and not
in the least a psychologist looking for Freudian mechanisms. Yet, the situation is obvious enough to enable him to
note that in reality the *Ḥadīt* condemns Mohammedan
abuses by asserting that they belong to the customs of Jews
and Christians (p. 124). The basic ambivalence present in all
reaction formations is made completely clear by the fact
that "une tradition eschatologique . . . fait dire au prophète
qu'avant le jugement dernier les Musulmans suivront pas à
pas la manière d'agir de leurs prédécesseurs. On lui de-
manda: 'parles-tu des Juifs et des Chrétiens?' 'De qui donc
parlerai-je?' " he replied. (Abû Huraïra's version of this inci-
dent speaks of the Persians and Romans, instead of the Jews
and Christians, as the ultimate model of Mohammedan
deportment [p. 84].) The above data speak for themselves.

5. *Naziism vs. the democracies.* Nazi Germany made
deliberate attempts to differentiate itself from "Jewish-
Marxist-pluto-democracy." In doing so it frequently cut
off its nose to spite its face:

a) By getting rid of desirable culture traits and individuals (the expulsion of Jewish physicists, sorely needed later on for the German war effort [see Ch. 6]).

b) By violating its own codes and rules of logic, e.g., by declaring the Japanese and certain sorely needed Jews "honorary Aryans" (cf. Göring's famous dictum, a propos of the half-Jewish General Milch: "I am the one to decide who is Aryan and who is not!").

During the Second World War, America similarly dissociated itself from the customs of the Nazis, e.g., by giving the eight famous saboteurs a more than fair trial and by explicitly justifying this as a proof that Americans are not like the Germans.

The above examples suffice to prove that we are speaking of very genuine phenomena indeed. Dissociative acculturation can be accomplished by means of three distinctive techniques: regression, differentiation and negation.

A. *Regression:* This is the most common technique and consists in reverting to the conduct pattern obtaining before the contact took place, e.g., the human sacrifice perpetrated by the Athenians at Salamis (*44*, 13.2; *45*, 9.2) or Gandhi's spinning-wheel and *dhoti*. A variation of this technique is the creation of an imaginary "super-past," in which Germans were super-Germanic, or Indians super-Indian (*10*, 2nd ed. p. 97). It is interesting to note that this ideal past state of affairs is brought back—or an attempt is made to bring it back—by means of techniques borrowed from, or influenced by, the culture whose very influence this process purports to negate.

A conspicuous example of this is the Ghost Dance religion, replete with culture traits and ideas borrowed from Christianity (*26*) and used as a *means* to a native Plains-Indian cultural end. The psychological infrastructure of this movement has been ably analyzed by Barber (*4*). We might also note that, according to Shimkin (*48*), the Wind-River Shoshoni of Wyoming did not revert to the "old time religion" (i.e., to the *very modern Ghost Dance*) until the economic advantages of their early alliance with the whites had waned.

B. *Differentiation:* This technique is essentially an adaptation of the means segment of "overt culture," but not of "covert culture." It involves the creation of differential, but not negative, forms of conduct, under the stimulus of external contacts. The British "Oxford accent" is also of this type, since it differentiates the upper classes from the lower classes.

C. *Negation* involves the creation of customs which are the opposite of the customs of the neighbor. This is clearly manifest in the Semitic examples and in the Arab instances referred to above.[7] We are now prepared to attempt a psychological analysis of this type of acculturation, whose significance, despite its neglect by social scientists, is very great for an understanding of the historical process in general, and of socio-cultural change in particular.

Perhaps the most obvious aspect of the problem is the element of ostentatious differentiation, or of "conspicuousness," in a strictly Veblenian sense of the word (*56*). The factor of ostentatious differentiation is closely linked with invidious comparisons with the ostentatiously *not* imitated group. The customs created by negative suggestion are ostentatious "counter-mores," i.e., the outcome of what psychologists call "negative suggestibility." Hence, the "vices" or "patterns of misconduct" (*27*, p. 433) or "latent culture patterns" of one group are often the "virtues" of their neighbors or of more remote people. Greek funeral cremation horrified the Kallatiai; the funeral cannibalism of the latter horrified the Greeks (Herodotos 3.38).

The existence of negative suggestibility need not puzzle us, in view of what has been said above concerning the relationship between diffusion resistances, on the one hand,

7. On the general problem of "social negativism," compare *13*, Ch. 3.

and reaction formation, on the other, particularly in connection with the projection of the "repressed" into the out-
group.

Society *A* is negatively suggestible to society *B*, because it
defines the mores and customs of society *B* in terms of its
own culturally repressed materials (*supra*). The same mechanism is met with also in criminal and other "socially negativistic" groups (*13*, Ch. 3).

Briefly stated, the process is as follows:

1. psychic and social stress;
2. introjection of norms, and in-group feeling in opposition to the already identified Others;
3. projection of the repressed, and formation of out-group
concepts;
4. reaction formation;
5. defining the out-group as the polar counter-type (*Gegentypus*);
6. intentional dissociation from the out-group's mores
and the formation of "counter-mores," which express social
negativism in a *pseudo*-sublimated form, i.e., as an even
further developed reaction formation. In naïve terms, "in
order to be *good* one has to do the opposite of evil, evil being
represented by the ways of the alien." Thus, in America,
socially rejected views and modes of behavior are branded
as "un-American," and among the Hopi, as *ka-Hopi* (un-
Hopi) (*49*, p. 88; *8*).

Acculturation of all types, and in particular antagonistic
acculturation, is the outcome of a bilateral challenge resulting from socio-cultural contact. This challenge is frequently
responded to autoplastically,[8] even where autoplastic be-

8.   The contrast between autoplastic and alloplastic adjustment is fundamental in biology. In autoplastic adjustment the organism adapts itself to
the environment by modifying itself. In alloplastic adaptation the organism
modifies the environment in order to fit it to its needs. The process of autoplastic adjustment is best defined in terms of Le Chatelier's principle, as
formulated by Enrico Fermi (*17*, p. 111): "If the external conditions of a . . .
system are altered, the equilibrium of the system will tend to move in such a
direction as to oppose the change in the external conditions." For a
justification of this conception of a social process, compare Chapter 1.

havior involves such *superficially* alloplastic behavior as active proselytizing, or such apparently neutral behavior as isolation. The autoplastic process is conspicuous even in the primarily alloplastic one of lending, or the passive one of borrowing, because of the change in the balance of power which lending involves and because of the incorporation and elaboration process which borrowing necessitates.

It is the importance of the autoplastic factor which enables us to conceive of resistances, means-diffusion and dissociative acculturation as aspects of the single broad phenomenon of antagonistic acculturation, which has perhaps received its most perfect formulation in the famous tongue twister in the Koran (said to be used also as a test for intoxication):

Surah CIX Al Kâfirûn (The Disbelievers). "In the name of Allah, the beneficent, the merciful. 1. Say: O disbelievers! 2. I worship not that which ye worship; 3. Nor worship ye that which I worship. 4. And I shall not worship that which ye worship. 5. Nor will ye worship that which I worship. 6. Unto you your religion, and unto me my religion" (Revealed at Mecca) (*42*, p. 673).

Whether automatic or purposive—if indeed this distinction is a genuine one, which we doubt—the process of autoplastic socio-cultural change is one of the basic social trends. To lose sight of it means to lose sight of all that truly matters in dynamic sociology and to relapse into the platitudes of mere diffusionist theology. Diffusionists, at their worst, are the modern counterparts of the chronicle writers, i.e., they are the bookkeepers of the great surges and ebbs of socio-cultural life. Our article is itself an instance of antagonistic acculturation to the theories of the diffusionists.

Summary

Human societies are sometimes negatively influenced by their neighbors. They resist the adoption of the neighbor's goals through isolation and/or through adoption of the neighbor's means and techniques, the better to resist the adoption of his goals, and also by evolving customs deliberately at variance with, or the opposite of, the neighbor's ways. Thus, while response to the out-group's means and techniques may seem positive, response to its goals and ends is frequently negative. The problem was analyzed both sociologically and psychologically.

Bibliography

(*1*)   Angyal, András: *Foundations for a Science of Personality*, New York, 1941.
(*2*)   Badé, W. F.: *The Old Testament in the Light of Today*, New York, 1915.
(*3*)   Bain, Read: Sociology and the Other Sciences, *Scientific Monthly*, 53:444–453, 1941.
(*4*)   Barber, Bernard: Acculturation and Messianic Movements, *American Sociological Review*, 6:662–667, 1941.
(*5*)   Barton, G. A.: *A Sketch of Semitic Origins, Social and Religious*, New York, 1902.
(*6*)   Cajori, Florian: *A History of Mathematics*, New York, 1924.
(*7*)   Clausewitz, Karl von: *Vom Kriege*, vol. I, 1932 (cited s.v.: "War" in Mencken, H. L.: *A New Dictionary of Quotations*, New York, 1942).
(*8*)   Devereux, George: *Hopi Field Notes* (M.S.), 1932.
(*9*)   Idem: The Mental Hygiene of the American Indian, *Mental Hygiene*, 26:71–84, 1942.
(*10*) Idem: *Reality and Dream: The Psychotherapy of a Plains Indian*, 1951, New York (2nd augm. ed., 1969).
(*11*) Idem: *A Study of Abortion in Primitive Societies*, New York, 1955, 2nd augm. ed. 1976.
(*12*) Idem: La Psychanalyse et l'Histoire: Une Application à l'Histoire de Sparte, *Annales: Economies, Sociétés, Civilisations*, 20:18–44, 1965.
(*13*) Idem: *Essais d'Ethnopsychiatrie Générale*, Paris, 1970, 1972, 1977.
(*14*) Diodoros the Sicilian: *Historical Library*.
(*15*) Dollard, John: *Caste and Class in a Southern Town*, New Haven, 1937.
(*16*) Ferenczi, Sándor: Stages in the Development of the Sense of Reality (in) *Sex in Psychoanalysis*, New York, 1950.
(*17*) Fermi, Enrico: *Thermodynamics*, New York, 1937.
(*18*) François, H. K. B. von: *Napoleon I*, Berlin, 1929.
(*19*) Freud, Sigmund: *Group Psychology and the Analysis of the Ego*, Standard Ed., vol. 18, London, 1957.
(*20*) Fromm, Erich: *Escape from Freedom*, New York, 1941.

(*21*) Goodwin, G.: *The Social Organization of the Western Apache*, Chicago, 1942.

(*22*) Herskovits, M. J.: *Acculturation: The Study of Culture Contacts*, New York, 1939.

(*23*) Kardiner, Abram and Linton, Ralph: *The Individual and His Society*, New York, 1939.

(*24*) Kroeber, A. L.: Stimulus Diffusion (in) *The Nature of Culture*, Chicago, 1952, pp. 344–357.

(*25*) Kroeber, Theodora: *Ishi in Two Worlds*, Berkeley, California, 1965.

(*26*) La Barre, Weston: *The Ghost Dance*, New York, 1970.

(*27*) Linton, Ralph: *The Study of Man*, New York, 1936.

(*28*) Idem (ed.): *Acculturation in Seven American Indian Tribes*, New York, 1940.

(*29*) Idem: *The Tanala of Madagascar* (in: *23*).

(*30*) Loeb, E. M.: Tribal Initiations and Secret Societies, *University of California Publications in American Archaeology and Ethnology*, vol. 25, No. 3, Berkeley, Calif., 1929.

(*31*) Idem: *Sumatra, Its History and People*, Vienna, 1935.

(*32*) Idem: *Apache Field Notes* (M.S.).

(*33*) Lowie, R. H.: *Are We Civilized?* New York, 1929.

(*34*) MacCrone, I. D.: *Race Attitudes in South Africa*, New York, 1937.

(*35*) MacIver, R. M.: *Society*, New York, 1937.

(*36*) Merton, R. K.: Social Structure and Anomie (in) *Social Theory and Social Structure*, Glencoe, Ill., 1949.

(*37*) Oberg, Kalervo: The Kingdom of Ankole in Uganda (in) Fortes, Meyer and Evans-Pritchard, E. E. (eds.), *African Political Systems*, London, 1940.

(*38*) Opler, M. E.: *An Apache Life-Way*, Chicago, 1941.

(*39*) Pareto, Vilfredo: *The Mind and Society*, 4 vols., New York, 1935.

(*40*) Parsons, E. C.: *Pueblo Indian Religion*, 2 vols., Chicago, 1927.

(*41*) Parsons, Talcott: *The Structure of Social Action*, New York, 1937.

(*42*) Pickthal, Marmaduke: *The Glorious Koran*, New York, 1930.

(*43*) Pirenne, Henri: *Mohammed and Charlemagne*, New York, 1939.

(*44*) Plutarchos: *Life of Themistokles*.

(*45*) Plutarchos: *Life of Aristeides*.

(*46*) Pope, T. S.: The Medical History of Ishi, *University of California Publications in American Archaeology and Ethnology*, vol. 13, No. 5, 1920.

(*47*) Reichard, Gladys: *Social Life of the Navajo Indians*, New York, 1928.

(*48*) Shimkin, D. B.: Dynamics of Recent Wind River Shoshone History, *American Anthropologist*, n.s., 44:451–462, 1942.

(*49*) Simmons, L. W.: *Sun Chief*, New Haven, 1942.

(*50*) Sorokin, P. A.: *Social and Cultural Dynamics*, 4 vols., New York, 1937–1941.

(*51*) Spitz, R. A.: *No and Yes, On the Genesis of Human Communication*, New York, 1957.

(*52*) Stouffer, Samuel: 'Intervening Opportunities: A Theory Relating

Mobility and Distance, *American Sociological Review*, 5:845–867, 1940.

(*53*) Sumner, W. G.: *Folkways*, Boston, 1906.

(*54*) Vajda, Georges: Juifs et Musulmans Selon le Ḥadît, *Journal Asiatique*, 229:57–127, 1937.

(*55*) Vandenbosch, A.: *The Dutch East Indies*, Berkeley, Calif., 1941.

(*56*) Veblen, Thorstein: *The Theory of the Leisure Class*, new ed., New York, 1912.

(*57*) Wagatsuma, Hiroshi: *Problems of Cultural Identity in Modern Japan*, (in) De Vos, G. and Romanucci-Ross, L. (eds.), *Ethnic Identity*, Palo Alto, Calif., 1975.

(*58*) Wallis, L.: *Sociological Study of the Bible*, Chicago, 1927.

(*59*) Weber, Max: *The Protestant Ethic and the Spirit of Capitalism*, London, 1930.

(*60*) Wilkinson, R. J.: *An Abridged Malay-English Dictionary*, Singapore, 1919.

(*61*) Wissler, Clark: The Influence of the Horse in the Development of Plains Culture, *American Anthropologist*, n.s., 16:1–25, 1914.

(*62*) Young, Kimball: *Personality and Problems of Maladjustment*, New York, 1940.

9

Dream Learning and Individual Ritual Differences in Mohave Shamanism (1957)

> Every shaman tells a different story of the creation. One may hear it told in several ways. All stories relate to the same event, but the way of telling it is different, as though different witnesses related it, remembering or forgetting different details. It is as though an Indian, a Black and a Frenchman would tell it, or as though I, my husband, Hivsû Tupōma (Burnt Raw) or you were describing a car accident we witnessed.
>
> HAMĀ UTCĒ, Mohave informant

IN Mohave culture, magical powers and the knowledge of the myths, skills and songs pertaining to them are supposed to be acquired in dream (*17, 24, 12*). Given the fundamental similarities between the beliefs and curing rites of various shamans, and between the songs sung by various singers who "learned" a given song cycle in dream, not only anthropologists but even some Mohave informants reached the conclusion that actual learning in a waking state is responsible for the acquisition of the knowledge and of skills related to some specialty, but that this knowledge remains barren, i.e., ineffective, unless it is also "dreamed." Thus, after allowing me to record and to learn his ritual curing songs, a shaman explained that this would not enable me to cure people by singing these songs, because I had not "potentiated" them by learning them also in dream.

Since it is quite certain that no one could possibly dream the full text of a long song cycle or myth of the type recorded by Kroeber (*17*, *18*), it is evident that if these myths—though structurally similar to dreams (*18*)—are dreamed at all, they must be dreamed in a condensed or allusive form.

Before I examine this problem more closely, it should be stressed that, in those primitive societies which emphasize dream life and encourage the recall of dreams and their narration, dreams tend to be quite long and elaborate and may therefore confront the psychotherapist with real difficulties in interpretation (*8*).[1] It must also be recognized that a book read, a story heard, or a play seen during the day may provide most of the raw material ("the day residue") from which the following night's dream is constructed (*15*). Thus, it is quite probable that an affectively unstable youth who has just attended a curing ritual may, in the course of the following night, have one or more dreams pertaining to and derived from this (non-logical) experience. In addition, given the cultural importance of dreams in Mohave society (*17*, *24*, *11*), it is likely that this dream will preoccupy him during the following day, especially since, because of his temperamental behavior, he is likely to have heard repeatedly that he is bound ultimately to become a shaman (*4*). This preoccupation will lead to a "secondary elaboration" of the dream, which will probably consist in the expansion and rearrangement of the actually dreamed material by the addition of information about myths, songs and rituals acquired in a waking state.

These observations and inferences suggest that what is dreamed and what is juxtaposed and coordinated with the dream the following day are inseparable—the more so since

1. Patients in psychoanalysis, or in "expressive psychoanalytically oriented therapy," sometimes resist treatment by producing so many and such complex dreams in a single night that, by the time they are narrated to the therapist, the therapeutic session is ended and no time is left for their interpretation. This represents "mock compliance" and a manifest reductio ad absurdum of the therapist's interest in dreams.

a good many primitives do not differentiate too sharply between what was dreamed and what was thought or experienced. Kroeber (*20*) had specifically stressed that the growth of civilization is in the general direction of greater realism and of a more systematic differentiation of dream experience from real experience. I have, for my part, expressed certain reservations concerning this matter (*13*, Ch. 10). This being said, what remains to be considered is the problem of what the incipient shaman may actually dream and the manner in which he reaches the conclusion that his dream is the actual equivalent of the *entire* myth and ritual.

My basic hypothesis is that no matter how lengthy the actual dream may be and no matter how greatly cultural training and expectation may facilitate its total recall, the Mohave shaman or singer is not likely to dream, either in a single night or in installments, the entire text of a myth or song cycle. It must therefore be a highly condensed and possibly allusive dream version of a long myth which both the dreamer and his society define as an actual dreaming of the myth. This inference is materially strengthened by the fact that Mohave culture provides a model for equating an allusive "catch phrase" with a set of mythical meanings.

In 1932 it was possible to record Ahma Humāre's (Quail Young) and Harav Hēya's (Whiskey Mouth) sets of songs for treating the *hiwey lak* (anus pain) group of illnesses. Ahma Humāre's four songs—each consisting of only two words—could be translated, according to Ahma Humāre himself, in three different ways, or on three different levels:

The first (semantic) level of translation: Some fifteen years after the songs were collected, an excellent linguistic informant, Pulyīk—who was not a shaman but a singer—translated them verbatim, giving the English equivalent of the core meaning of each word as used in daily speech. Although he provided a rigorously accurate translation, he did not deny that the two words which form one song have a broader set of meanings, not only for the shaman but also for the patient and the audience, all of whom have a fairly

accurate idea of the broader range of information these
words are supposed to convey. I shall call this additional
information the "halo meaning" of these words, with the
understanding that it is present only when these words are
used in a ritual context. A simple analogy may clarify this.
In ordinary conversation the words "pathologically jealous
husband" mean just that and nothing more. In a discussion
about Shakespeare, the same three words evoke the entire
plot and atmosphere of the tragedy of Othello. In a similar
way, the two words of Ahma Humāre's first song, which in
ordinary conversation mean simply "Heaven right-down-
here,"[2] mean "They are in heaven as we are on earth." Fully
explained, however, these words convey the idea that heaven
is beautiful and full of life, as is the earth; that people too
were meant to be healthy and full of life, and that, as the
shaman sings, the illness, which is incompatible with this
ideal pattern, will depart.

The second (meta-semantic) level of translation was suggested by Ahma Humāre to the expert interpreter Hamā
Utcē (Testicles Charcoal). As stated above, this was "They
are in heaven as we are on earth." In this instance one may
simply speak of an expanded significance: the word *hamayvi*
means not only "heaven" but also the heavenly beings; the
word *konō(h)yi* means not only "down here" but the earth
and all that is on it.

The third (exegetic) level of translation brings into play
the similarity between heaven and earth and also the contrast between what is ideal and what is accidental and system
alien. Technically, this type of translation is no longer a mere
translation but an actual exegesis and, moreover, an exegesis provided by Ahma Humāre himself.

These three translations—the semantic, the meta-semantic and the exegetic—form a kind of inverted pyramid, pre-
cariously standing on the point represented by the two catch
words, crammed full of meanings and surrounded by an

2.   I ignore in this context the distortion of words in songs, which is so
characteristic both of Mohave singing (*17*) and of Greek tragic diction (*3*).

extensive halo of implicit meanings which can be "decoded" only if one knows Mohave culture and mythology well.

A similar type of inverted pyramid is familiar to psycho-analysts, who knows that a very short dream, such as "I raised my hat to a man," can have extremely complex meanings. The bare narration of the dream is in a sense a narrow, semantic, quasi-translation, which conveys only that single meaning to any audience which does not know that this is a dream and not an account of an actual happening. However, in investigating this dream, the psychoanalyst will first learn its meta-semantic meaning. He may discover that "hat" also symbolizes other items of clothing, containers, and so forth, and that "to raise" (the hat) also has a large variety of supplementary meanings. On the exegetic level, the patient may say, "In dream I greet a man first. I am of no account and must therefore be polite to everyone. The man reminds me of my father, who insisted that his children show him great respect." In brief, when analyzing this dream, comparable in its terseness to one of Ahma Humāre's songs, one finds that it actually reveals a major segment of the dreamer's personality and problems. Thus, this simple dream, like Ahma Humāre's catch phrase, is really a con-ventional signal which opens broad horizons of meaning, just as the signal "pathologically jealous husband" opens many vistas to the student of Shakespeare.

My second working hypothesis is that the prospective shaman's dream may stand in the same relationship to the full-length myth and ritual as his sung catch phrases do. The power-giving and knowledge-imparting dream may be nothing more than an extreme condensation of and allusion to the myth, which, in the ritual, is recondensed into the catch phrase and simple rite. In other words, the actual dream may be more similar to the simple ritual songs than to the lengthy myth to which both the dream and the rite are theoretically reducible. It is not suggested that the culturally pre-existing and standardized ritual is actually what the prospective shaman dreams; what he *did* dream, before he elaborated his dream and made it congruent with a pre-existing myth, presumably cannot be inferred either from the songs or from the ritual. I specifically do *not* postulate an extensive similarity between the content of the initial dream and the actual rite. I do postulate that, from the cultural point of view, both may be defined as condensations of the myth; that psychologically they stand in an identical relationship to the myth, at least in terms of the present-day situation. Whether originally the rite preceded the myth and a dream preceded the ritual, or vice versa, is a problem which does not arise in the present context.

It is postulated that:

1. The aspiring shaman, presumably stimulated by witnessing curing rites and hearing songs and myths, has one or more relatively brief dream, whose day residue (raw material) is derived from these stimuli.

2. Incited by the social evaluation of his misbehavior as an indication of his nascent shamanistic powers, such a youth views his dreams as allusions to the relevant myth, partly because some of their day residue pertains to the ritual and/or to the songs and myths related to the ritual. Psychoanalytically speaking, he uses the long myth he learned in a waking state as an "association" to his brief dreams.

3. The rite and the songs pertaining to it are, in turn, traditionally defined as condensations of, and allusions to, the broad mythical model and text.

4. The cultural tenet that the singing of a brief song is the functional equivalent of the narration of the entire myth motivates the dreamer to view also his brief dream as a *complete* equivalent of the entire myth, and permits him to assert subsequently that he dreamed the myth, the song cycle and the therapeutic rite.

5. Dreaming a condensation of, or allusion to, the myth, rite or song imparts supernatural effectiveness to one's recitation of the myth, performance of the rite and singing of the songs, whose actual text is learned in a waking state.

I have so far taken no account of the cultural tenet that the songs are taught and learned in dream. The mechanism underlying this belief was described by Pulyīk, who brought up this matter spontaneously in a discussion concerning a different topic:

"My father and my brother both sang the *Tumānp'à Utàūt* song cycle (*17, 5*). I paid no attention to it and did not learn it. After my father died, my brother took up the singing of this cycle. Fifteen or twenty-five years later he, too, died. I was in my teens during the last years of my brother's life. I was in a row [quarrel]. I think I am doing well. I asked my brother to sing this cycle and I listened. I slept during the day and listened at night. Then I asked him to tell me the story [the myth, i.e., the prose exegesis] that went with his songs. I sang it and I was doing well. I missed once and my brother corrected me. I worked at it for two weeks, learning it. [G. D.: You did not dream it at this time?] No, not yet. I will tell you [later]. I sing for a year. [Later] I start thinking about my boys and about what the Mohave do to [with?] children and the family. I sing all night to keep awake and prepare for a funeral [where songs are sung]. I sing all the time. Then, for one year, I dream at night. In dream I thought that some good singers of the *Tumānp'à Utàūt*, who had died, come close to me and sing. I could not hear the words [of their song] plainly. Then I said to them: "This is how the song goes," and then I sing to them.[3] They sing a little differently. I sang the way my brother taught me to sing. Then we had a sort of fight. They *deliberately* sang differently. A week later these [dream] singers name every place where that [mythical] couple stopped on the Colorado River.[4] So, it took two nights to dream all that. After that, it is always in my head, even when I work hard."

At this point the interpreter, Hamā Utcē, signified her acceptance of this experience as a genuine dream by saying

3. A Plains Indian in psychotherapy repeatedly dreamed that he showed other people how to do something (*8*).
4. Place names play a major role in Mohave epics and myths (*17, 18, 19*).

to me: "This is just like the dream you had last night."[5]

The preceding account shows that Pulyĭk's interest in this song cycle postdates his father's death and that he was taught both the text of the songs and their prose exegesis by his older brother, before he also learned it in dream, *after* becoming a father himself. However, the most important aspect of this account is the fact that the long-dead dream teachers "deliberately" sang a somewhat different version of the cycle and that there was a fight between the student-dreamer and his dream teachers. This dream struggle parallels the prospective Siberian shaman's dream fight with a great shaman, from which, although he is the underdog, he must emerge victorious or at least unhurt (*23*).

It is a basic feature of Mohave supernaturalism that a shaman specializing in the cure of an ailment such as *hiwey lak* (anus pain) may become enraged and resort to retributive witchcraft if another *hiwey lak* specialist tells the myth pertaining to this illness differently, or sings different songs. It is therefore my next task to account both for the existence of such differences and for the shaman's anger over any deviation from his particular version.

I propose to show that the existence of multiple versions of the same myth, song cycle, curing song or ritual is directly related to the fact that the songs and rites are condensations of and allusions to the full-length myth. Let me return to the Shakespearean example. The tragedy of Othello may be called to the Shakespearean student's mind not only by the phrase "pathologically jealous husband" but also by "unjustly suspected wife." Similarly, in psychoanalysis, dreams differently worded, or having different manifest contents, may pertain to the same broad conflict (*8*). The two phrases allude to the same tragedy from different, though conjugate, points of view; the personality of the speaker will determine whether he chooses to stress Othello or Desdemona. This view is fully compatible with the thesis (*9*) that all versions

5. I often told my dreams to my Mohave friends, so as to induce them to tell me theirs.

of a given myth implicitly tell the same story, albeit from different psychological points of view.[6]

The multiple versions of myths and of rituals represent an acute problem for the Mohave. As stated above, it is a standard belief that if one shaman's account differs from that of another, be it simply in the order of events, this will give offence, and the one who considers that his account has been challenged will retaliate by bewitching the "heretic" or "dissident." Shamans discussing their powers repeatedly voice the fear that they may be bewitched by another shaman who clings to his own phrasing of a justificatory myth, theory, song or ritual.

Objective differences between the theories, justificatory myths and curing songs of various specialists do exist. They are explicitly recognized by shamans, who fear that other specialists may punish them magically for these discrepancies; they are also recognized by laymen, who, like Hamā Utcē, may state that Harav Hēya's account of the *hiwey lak* group of diseases "goes deeper" than that of Ahma Humāre. Depending on whether the curing powers are derived from the Ancient Ones or from the gods, the right or the left hand may be the curing hand. The curing songs, too, may be quite different. For instance, Ahma Humāre's first song contained only two words; that of Harav Hēya contained three; and the two songs had only one word-root in common—*amay*, which means "sky." The strict (semantic) translation of Ahma Humāre's first song is: "Heaven put down lower and lower." Its meta-semantic translation may be given as: "They are in heaven as we are on earth." Its exegetic translation describes the fullness of life in heaven, which should be matched by a similarly rich life on earth, and affirms that shamanistic singing will cause illness to depart and to be replaced by this ideal state. Harav Hēya's first song is semantically translated as: "Face toward

6. That the structure, as distinct from the content, of the variants of a given myth is invariant was shown two years later by Lévi-Strauss (*21*, Ch. 11).

heaven and you will see"; a meta-semantic translation could not be obtained; the exegesis states that the three words of that song refer to pathogenic dreams about the (now destroyed) homestead of the dreamer's youth.[7]

When ritual songs are forgotten because the last practitioner of a given specialty died before he could transmit the songs to a younger person, future healers of that illness will use for therapeutic purposes the more or less complete prose text of the myth, with equal effectiveness. Such shamans voice the socially acceptable opinion that the power of the allusive songs is not a result of the "correct" singing of a firmly established "lyric"; unlike strongly ritualistic groups, the Mohave do not seem to feel that verbal magic is effective only if it is letter perfect. Psychologically stated, Mohave ritual is singularly devoid of obsessive liturgical features. In fact, as I have stressed elsewhere (7), Mohave ritual itself provides a model for its simplification and ultimate obsolescence: the menstrual rite is a greatly simplified version of the puberty rite, and therefore provides a living model for stripping a rite down to its essentials.

When someone receives the power to cure a certain illness whose last healer died long ago, he will not know the lost songs but will recite the myth instead, since the curing power is derived from the myth rather than from the song which is a condensation of the myth. The power of the song does not lie in its actual wording but in the fact that it "stands for" the myth. This was explicitly stated by several competent informants, including one who actually cured by means of the prose version of the myth. This finding has important implications for the understanding of the equivalence of myth and ritual in Mohave culture. It is a Mohave axiom that the shaman's power can be externalized either by singing or by narrating a myth, even without additional ritual actions; Hamā Utcē felt convinced that she became ill because she had listened to and interpreted for me Harav

7.   The Mohave house is burned down when any of its inhabitants dies— even a child, provided he has stopped sleeping in a cradle.

Hēya's account of his powers and his curing songs. This finding contradicts Kluckhohn's (*16*) inference that some Mohave myths may be unrelated to ritual, since the preceding data show that the very act of reproducing a (dreamed) myth in any manner whatsoever externalizes power and is therefore an oral ritual, even in the strictest Durkheimian and Maussian sense of that term.

On a superficial level, one might say that Harav Hēya's songs differed from those of Ahma Humāre only because they were learned from different teachers. This view would seem to imply that, like Maori genealogists, each of these two sang, practically letter perfect, the songs he learned from his particular teacher. This supposition is contradicted by Pulyīk's account of the way he acquired his knowledge of *Tumānp'a Utaūt*. In this society, which does not value letter-perfect singing, it is almost certain that both Harav Hēya and Ahma Humāre modified somewhat the texts of their respective teachers or models.

Several psychological factors are responsible for such deviations from the model. The most significant point is the immense affective importance attached to the "rightness" of one's own songs and accounts, coupled with the desire to harm those whose version differs from one's own and with the fear that the other, on his part, may attack one by magical means.

One is dealing here with an attitude already known to Diodoros the Sicilian (*14*), and which Freud has called "the narcissism of small differences"—a tendency to attach great subjective importance to the differences between one's own version and that of a competitor.[8] Small as such technical differences may be, they tend to assume a great importance in esoteric contexts; a familiar example is the celebrated Byzantine religious controversy over the problem of whether Christ was consubstantial with, or merely similar

8. By contrast, a shaman specializing in disease X does not view a shaman specializing in disease Y as his competitor, and may even refer patients to him.

in substance to, God the Father. This controversy is some-times referred to as the "battle of the iota," since in Greek the words *homoousios* (ὁμοούσιος) (consubstantial) and *homoiousios* (ὁμοιούσιος) (of similar substance) differ from each other only by one letter, the iota.

I am therefore led to conclude that trifling divergences are emotionally overvalued and explosively laden with affect and significance, because they gratify the shaman's idio-syncratic neuroticism. One may recall in this context that the useful clinical-psychological Babcock test consists in narrating a brief story to the subject and then noting the differences between the standard narrative and the sub-ject's reproduction of it. The study of the diffusion and ex-pansion of rumors involving race prejudice (*1*) also reveals the psycho-diagnostic and cultural significance of the meta-morphoses which rumor undergoes in spreading from one person to another.

I postulate that the (inferred) differences between the songs of Ahma Humāre and those of his teacher—or of who-ever else served as his model—are a direct result of Ahma Humāre's distinctive personality makeup and, more speci-fically, of the areas of tension in his own personality. This inference is supported by data: Ahma Humāre was at first only a healer of the *hiwey lak* diseases. Subsequently, his wife died in childbirth while he stood by, unable to help her or the baby which could be seen moving in its mother's body. Soon afterward he acquired in dream the power to function also as an obstetrician (*6*).

The shaman's narcissistic overvaluation of the details in which his account differs from that of another, and his—culturally reinforced—neurotic fear that another specialist may magically penalize him for these deviations, result from the fact that his particular version satisfies him precisely because these minor differences express and gratify his private, internal needs and tensions. From the viewpoint of a disturbed youngster, the broad pattern of shamanism is a socially tendered and culturally prepatterned general bromide for his "subjective headache" (*13*, Ch. 1). From the socio-cultural point of view, it is a "type solution" for his conflicts, which are the "type conflicts" of his society.[9] From the psychological point of view, the shamanistic pattern is, for the individual, a socially tendered defense against his internal tensions (*13*, Ch. 1).

These minor innovations and changes result from the individualization—the "customizing"—of the generalized shamanistic defense, which only fits the ordinary, broadly typical needs of certain tense and neurotic youngsters. It is the customization of this broadly effective psychic remedy which provides specific relief, and is therefore valued and defended against all comers.

An additional and important factor is that the neurotic is so constituted that his self-soothing symptoms *must* be at variance with the social norm. Neurosis is, by definition, "socially negativistic" (*13*, Ch. 3; *10*) and, to an appreciable extent, finds relief in a given symptomatic defense only to the extent to which this defense is *at variance with* the norm —including the norm represented by the beliefs of other shamans. All *hiwey lak* specialists have an equally autistic, though culturally patterned, general conception of their powers and of the cause and treatment of *hiwey lak*, and differ only on technical details. Psychologically stated, they adapt cultural material to their private needs, so as to be able to use it symptomatically. This is a further clear-cut proof of the thesis (*13*, Ch. 1) that any adjustment which utilizes cultural material for neurotic ends is psychopathological. The symptomatic nature of the singer's attachment to his own version and his paranoid conviction that there is something intentionally provocative about another singer's obdurate adherence to another version, are shown by Pulyīk's dream fight with long-dead singers who "deliberately" sang a different version of the *Tumānp'à Utàūt*

9. I elaborated the theory of type conflicts and type solutions and of atypical conflicts and atypical solutions already in 1934 and communicated it to Linton in 1937.

cycle, and this *uniquely* (he felt) in order to provoke him.
Given his definition of the situation, a dream fight with these
obdurate deviationists—who pursue heresy for its own sake
—was inevitable.[10]

The existence of liturgical differences between two
shamans, the intensity of each shaman's attachment to his
own version, his feeling that the deviations of another
shaman are deliberate and provocative, his urge to retaliate
by bewitching the "heretic," and his concomitant fear of
being bewitched in turn, as well as the "fight" which Pulyĭk
had in dream with those who sang differently, support the
thesis that the broad shamanistic pattern is a social solution
made available to youngsters who experience certain type
conflicts which are characteristic of their society and related
in substance to the unconscious segment of the group's
ethnic personality (*13*, Ch. 1). This socially prepatterned
solution or symptomatic defense is then customized by
means of certain modifications, which adapt it to the idiosyncratic component of the subject's personality and conflicts. These minor modifications are overvalued (hypercathected) both because they are "all one's own" and because they serve to express social negativism, which those
who made different changes in the broad pattern view as
provocative. These psychological factors make understandable, at least on the psychological level, the "contest of
shamans" motif, found not only in Siberia and in North
America but also in ancient Greece (*2*, 6.2 ff.). These data
greatly strengthen the thesis (*20*, *22*; *13*, Ch. 1) that the
shaman is a fundamentally neurotic person who is fortunate
enough to be able to cope with his problems by means of

10.   Differences of opinion also satisfy Man's critical urge. *Time* (Vol. 69,
No. 17, p. 79, April 29, 1957) states that "one frustrated critic left a Casals
concert complaining that there was nothing to say." The guild humor of
musicians echoes the same attitude: Two highbrow School of Music students hear Heifetz play Beethoven's Violin Concerto. After the performance
one of the students says haughtily: "If you happen to like great music
perfectly performed, I guess it was all right."

socially sanctioned symptomatic defenses, instead of having to improvise, like the psychotic of our society, his own (socially penalized) symptoms and defenses.

Conclusions

1. Although Mohave shamans and singers are supposed to acquire their esoteric knowledge and/or their curing songs in dream, they actually learn it in waking life and then have dreams which condense or allude to this body of knowledge. Society accepts these condensations or allusions as equivalents of the myth's full text in the same sense in which a song, consisting of a telegraphically worded catch phrase, is accepted as the ritual equivalent of the full-length myth. The power of the songs is not inherent in their letter-perfect wording and reproduction; it is due to the fact that they are accepted as condensed equivalents of the myth. Hence, whenever the songs are forgotten, the prose version of the myth is used therapeutically. Power dreams and the songs which actualize power are both condensations of the myth, which does not mean that the two condensations are necessarily the same, although differences between two versions of a set of songs may be due to the actual dreams dreamed by the singers.

2. Each shaman overvalues his specific version of the myth or song and feels that those who sing different versions are deliberately provocative and obdurate. The differences are overvalued because they satisfy the neurotic shaman's key idiosyncratic needs. They also implement his social negativism and therefore arouse a fear of retaliation from those who sing a different version.

3. So-called borderline psychotics in our own society acquire what *only they* believe to be magical powers by means of subjective psychological processes which are in effect identical with those by means of which the shaman acquires his socially sanctioned and accepted powers (*10, 12*).

Bibliography

(1) Allport, G. W. and Postman, L. J.: The Basic Psychology of Rumor, *Transactions of the New York Academy of Sciences,* Series II, 8:61–81, 1945.

(2) Apollodoros: *The Library.*

(3) Aristoteles: *Poetics.*

(4) Devereux, George: L'Envoûtement chez les Indiens Mohave, *Journal de la Société des Américanistes de Paris,* n.s., 29:405–412, 1937.

(5) Idem: The Social and Cultural Implications of Incest Among the Mohave Indians, *Psychoanalytic Quarterly,* 8:510–533, 1939.

(6) Idem: Mohave Indian Obstetrics, *American Imago,* 5:95–139, 1948.

(7) Idem: The Psychology of Feminine Genital Bleeding: An Analysis of Mohave Indian Puberty and Menstrual Rites, *International Journal of Psycho-Analysis,* 31:239–257, 1950.

(8) Idem: *Reality and Dream: The Psychotherapy of a Plains Indian,* New York, 1951 (2nd augm. ed., 1969).

(9) Idem: Why Oedipus Killed Laius: A Note on the Complementary Oedipus Complex in Greek Drama, *International Journal of Psycho-Analysis,* 34:132–141, 1953.

(10) Idem: Belief, Superstition and Symptom, *Samīkṣā, Journal of the Indian Psycho-Analytical Society,* 8:210–215, 1954.

(11) Idem: Mohave Dreams of Omen and Power, *Tomorrow,* 4, No. 3:17–24, 1956.

(12) Idem: The Origin of Shamanistic Powers, as Reflected in a Neurosis, *Revue Internationale d'Ethnopsychologie Normale et Pathologique* 1:19–28, 1956.

(13) Idem: *Essais d'Ethnopsychiatrie Générale,* Paris, 1970, 1972, 1977.

(14) Diodoros the Sicilian: *Historical Library.*

(15) Freud, Sigmund: The Occurrence in Dreams of Material from Fairy *Standard Edition,* vol. 12, London, 1958.

(16) Kluckhohn, Clyde: Myths and Rituals: A General Theory, *Harvard Theological Review,* 35:45–79, 1942.

(17) Kroeber, A. L.: Handbook of the Indians of California, *Bureau of American Ethnology, Bulletin 78,* Washington, D.C., 1925.

(18) Idem: Seven Mohave Myths, *University of California Anthropological Records,* 11, No. 1, 1948.

(19) Idem: A Mohave Historical Epic, *University of California Anthropological Records,* 11, No. 2, 1951.

(20) Idem: *The Nature of Culture,* Chicago, 1952.

(21) Lévi-Strauss, Claude: *Anthropologie Structurale,* chap. 11, Paris, 1958.

(22) Linton, Ralph: *Culture and Mental Disorders,* Springfield, Ill., 1956.

(23) Róheim, Géza: Hungarian Shamanism, *Psychoanalysis and the Social Sciences,* vol. 3, New York, 1951.

(24) Wallace, W. J.: The Dream in Mohave Life, *Journal of American Folklore,* 60:252–258, 1947.

10

Cultural Thought Models in Primitive and Modern Psychiatric Theories (1958)

If the ox could paint a picture, his god would look like
an ox.   XENOPHANES, *Fragment* 15

THIS chapter will discuss the influence of nonscientific
and culturally determined thought models upon psychiatric theories, in order to make a contribution to the
sociology of knowledge, that is, to the science which investi-
gates the influence of social and cultural factors upon the
content and form of human knowledge in various cultural
settings and at various points in history. On the whole,
sociologists of knowledge have not, as yet, studied psychiatric theories in a systematic manner. It is true, of course,
that statements to the effect that Freud patterned his
theories upon nineteenth-century physics are, technically,
related to the sociology of knowledge. However, regardless
of their truth or falseness, these remarks can hardly be called
scientific statements, since they remain at best isolated
insights, and, at worst, mere barbed quips of no scientific
import (5, 19).

The sociology of knowledge predicates that each ethnic group and each historical period has its preferred thought models and therefore patterns most or all of its theories upon these models. Sorokin and others have shown that changes in the general orientation or mentality of a group cause significant fluctuations in its system of truths (*44*). Marbe has moreover shown that, within a given culture area, the possibilities of independent thinking are sufficiently limited to make possible a naturalistic explanation of mind reading, for he, whose mind one "professes" to read, has at his disposal only a limited number of thought models (*37, 38*).

The most common and most consistently ignored influence upon thought is the structure and vocabulary of one's language; this is being vigorously investigated by the metalinguists (*45*). A few, quite elementary, examples will help define the nature of their problems. Certain concepts are practically untranslatable into English and must be borrowed from foreign languages if their entire halo of meanings is to be preserved: for example, *logos, Realpolitik, Soviet* and *totem*. Some languages emphasize static states, while others stress process and change; some differentiate between masculine and feminine, others between animate and inanimate.

The structure of society is also a major thought model which, as Durkheim has shown, is often directly projected into and imposed upon the supernatural world (*24*). Thus, the Greeks projected Greek social structure upon the Olympian gods; it is Greek kingship that provided the actual model for Zeus' kingship, even though, in theory, Greek kings modeled their own royal status upon the divine kingship of Zeus (*4*).

In the Trobriand Islands a social thought model is foisted upon primitive zoological science: the inhabitants project their matrilineal social structure into the animal kingdom. Since they firmly believe that cohabitation is not the cause of pregnancy, they castrate all domestic boars, but indignantly repudiate the suggestion that their sows are impregnated by bush boars, which are tabooed as food (*36*).

Culturally prepatterned thought models may influence even advanced forms of scientific thought. One of the greatest mathematicians of all times, Henri Poincaré, pointed out that the practical-minded Anglo-Saxon physicists thought in terms of quasi-material, mechanical models, whereas the theoretical-minded French and German physicists thought in terms of conceptual schemes (*41*). When Freud called psychoanalytic metapsychology "our mythology"—a remark gloatingly quoted by his narrow-minded critics—he simply meant that he was thinking in terms of conceptual schemes and not of mechanical models. Yet, when psychoanalysis became popular in the Anglo-Saxon world, vigorous attempts were made to take Freud's metapsychological concepts, or "thought tokens," literally, almost to the point of trying to locate the Id in the endocrine glands or in the hypothalamus; the Ego in the forebrain; and so forth. Actually a concept such as the Ego is a purely abstract thought token, in the same sense in which Dirac once defined the electron simply as a differential equation.

Scientific thought models are, moreover, unstable and change in the course of time. Thus, E. T. Bell stressed that even though Henri Poincaré had at his fingertips all the knowledge needed for devising the theory of relativity, he could do no more than approximate it, because he had been conditioned to think along radically different—Newtonian —lines (*2*). The rapid changing of the dominant thought models of modern physics is often cited in explanation of the fact that nowadays most physicists make their principal discoveries before they are thirty, apparently because, as they grow older, they are unable to change over to newer thought models.

An "incorrect" thought model may be a basically scientific one, whereas a "correct" thought model may not be scientific (*20*). For example, the phlogiston theory of heat was manifestly incorrect and was easily disproved by

Lavoisier. However, unlike the alchemists' mythological thought models, it was a scientifically oriented theory, as was the now-obsolete first model of the atom, which was patterned upon the structure of the solar system. By contrast, a wholly "correct" Mohave Indian theory of hystero-epileptic convulsions (*20*) is not a truly scientific theory, since it is derived from a thought model which seeks to explain primarily the nature and origins of shamanistic powers.

Historians of psychiatry sometimes "discover" that an early author "anticipated" some of the insights of modern dynamic psychiatry. In many instances these alleged anticipations are entirely spurious, for one or more of three reasons:

1. At best, such anticipations represent isolated insights, which do not form part of an equally sensible and coherent scheme. One is therefore not entitled to view them as truly scientific insights. They are either the equivalents of a blind hen finding an occasional grain of wheat, or else direct empathic illuminations, not secondarily elaborated by logic, and not correlated logically with other sound insights. This view necessarily implies that science does not consist in the discovery of isolated bits of truth, but in an intellectual position which demands that disparate bits of truth should be coherently correlated with each other.

2. Quite often these insights are manifestly patterned upon nonscientific thought models. In some instances these cultural thought models *happen* to be applicable to the data. In other instances they are not, but are nonetheless resorted to in every possible situation by means of what I have called "artificial (or forced) compendences (connexities, linkages)" (*22*, Ch. 16). It is, of course, easier to differentiate between cultural and scientific thought models in non-psychiatric than in psychiatric theories. Greek atomic theories were obviously the products of mathematico-philosophical speculations rather than of scientific research, since the Greeks had no laboratories (*25, 43*) and were often not even aware of those characteristics of some physical

phenomenon—such as fire—whose complete explanation requires the atomic hypothesis. By contrast, even primitive men possess the two principal tools of psychiatric research: an unconscious which can empathize with neurotics and psychotics, and logical faculties capable of organizing insights so obtained into a body of theory. Hence, one can never be certain that the primitive "psychiatrist's" data are not genuine scientific insights—that they are merely fantasies derived from a cultural thought model. It is, therefore, best to disregard the problem of the inherent validity of primitive psychiatric data and to demonstrate only that they are organized into a body of theory sometimes successfully patterned on cultural thought models.

3. In still more numerous cases, what an ancient psychiatric writer really meant may simply be misunderstood to the point where one imputes to his statement a meaning which is the product of a later type of thinking about the same problem. Thus, even though Shakespeare did speak of "method in madness," his statement certainly reflects no awareness of the logic of the unconscious. Indeed, his remark—although objectively correct—is manifestly informed by a much more primitive thought model: it echoes the belief that the madman voices oracular truths or inspired insights in the form of poetical riddles. Thus, the utterances of King Lear are clearly mere riddles, in the sense in which a sane man defines riddles (*1*).

Some Cultural Aspects
of Primitive Psychiatry

It is now proposed to discuss some actual psychiatric theories which reveal the influence of cultural thought models upon theoretical formulations. Since it is not easy to accept the fact that some of one's most cherished theories —which sometimes can even be true—are not purely scientific and wholly objective, I will first subject some primitive psychiatric theories to a critical scrutiny. Then, perhaps, it may be easier to discern also the readiness of modern scientists to accept as science certain notions clearly patterned upon cultural thought models.

THE THEORY OF NERVE CONDUCTIVITY

The Sedang Moi, a jungle tribe of Indochina, believe that the sensations of the various sense organs are conveyed to the seat of the intelligence, which is the ear, by means of certain threads which crisscross the whole body. Did this primitive tribe make an inspired leap across several millennia and intuitively anticipate the theory of nerve conductivity? The answer, needless to say, is a categorical No. Hence, the real problem is to discover precisely what cultural thought model underlies this pseudo-correct theory.

Just before the rice harvest, one sees along the jungle paths creepers slung on miniature "telegraph poles," which are definitely not modeled upon modern telegraph poles. These creepers are the "road of the rice spirits," along which they proceed from the rice fields to the village, thereby increasing the "rice soul" of the villagers and, consequently, also the "quantity"—or, rather, the ability to satiate—of the rice stored in the granaries. A similar movement of supernatural substances—or souls—occurs when the medicine man transfers from his hands to those of the patient a portion of his own soul powers so as to strengthen the flagging soul of the sick person. A related procedure is the one whereby the seller of a valuable commodity—such as a slave, or a big gong—transfers to the buyer not only the actual sold commodity, but also that portion of his own "property soul" which consists of, or corresponds to, the soul of the slave or gong.

In brief, the Sedang theory of nerve conductivity is not an anticipation of modern neurophysiology. It is a theory of sensations based upon a strictly primitive and animistic thought model. Not sensations or electric impulses are thought to travel along the nerves, but anthropomorphically conceived "things" or beings, of a purely supernatural order.

Actually, the situation is even more complicated, at least on the psychological level. Psychoanalysis has provided many examples of the projection of the body model upon the external world. Thus, Róheim (*42*) plausibly suggests that the "external world" of dream imagery is actually an extension of the dreamer's body image, while Lenzen (*33*) stresses that the physical concept of force is too anthropomorphic to be really satisfactory in physics.

However, in the Sedang instance just cited, there is—at least on the manifest level—an internalization of the external world and its imposition upon the body image, instead of a projection of the body image upon the external world. It can be argued, of course, that, in the history of culture as well as from the point of view of depth psychology, the idea of a "spirit road" and of "transferable souls" was originally modeled upon body sensations and upon the image of the body. True or false as this statement may be, it has no direct bearing upon the present problem.

The relevant problem is simply the nature of the actual model from which the official Sedang Moi "scientific" concept was derived. The question is not from what model they originally derived their notion of soul transfer and their idea of building a road for the rice spirits. Even if it could ever be shown that the latter idea was derived from bodily sensations, this would still explain only the *technological item* "spirit road" qua projection of bodily sensations and not the pseudo-theory of nerve conductivity, which is derived not from bodily sensations but from the spirit road, and its halo of supernaturalistic meanings. This device was then reinternalized through a *nonexperiential conception* of the body, that is, in a manner which led to an *objective*—quasi-scientific—conception of the body and its sensations, rather than to a *subjectively experienced image* of the body.

While this process is clearly circular, it does involve a logical progress, which utilizes reality as the means whereby the primary-process type of *experience* of bodily sensations is eventually translated into a more or less secondary-process type of *conception* of bodily sensations. One cannot but suspect that similar circular processes also led to a great many other theories in the biological and psychological sciences. The exploration of these processes would be a rewarding undertaking, not only for the historian of science, but perhaps even more for the theoretician who seeks to reappraise the objective validity of his principal conceptual devices and procedures.

SEDUCTIVENESS OF THE PSYCHOTIC

Another Sedang psychiatric theory holds that certain spirits are the ghosts of persons who died insane. Such a spirit can deliberately cause a living person to become insane by putting his arm around the shoulders of his intended victim and "making relatives" with him—that is, adopting him. It could thus be alleged that the Sedang discovered the indefinable seductiveness of the insane, whose uninhibited release of his unconscious impulses tempts others to do likewise. Actually, however, even though the Sedang may have obtained this insight unconsciously and unscientifically, their etiological theory of psychosis is nonetheless not truly a theory of psychic contamination. It is simply part and parcel—a corollary—of their mythology, one of whose themes is the adoption of human beings by spirits, which is one of the cornerstones of their religion (*30*).

The preceding considerations do not seek to intimate that the primitive is chronically addicted to mysticism. Thus, it is almost certain that the Sedang discovered the circulation of the blood—although not the hydrodynamics of that circulation. Indeed, even though they do cite in support of this theory the bubbling of blood from wounds and the phenomenon of bleeding to death, they compare the movement of the blood through the blood vessels to the manner in which sloping bamboo pipes bring water into the village *by gravitation*. Their idea of the causes of the circulation of the blood does not include the concept of the heart as a hydraulic pump, since they possess bellows, but not hydraulic pumps.

It is not denied that primitives are capable of scientific theorizing, or, more correctly, of evolving theories which the Western world would call "scientific." For example, once I literally blundered upon the realization that the Sedang had an idea of the infinite divisibility of matter. They said: "If you had a knife sharp enough, you could keep on halving a stick indefinitely." Then, in reply to a direct— but not leading—question, they also assured me that, if one but had words for it, one could count forever; which indicates that, in a way, they were aware of infinity.

In brief, it is not denied that the Sedang might well, if properly tutored, become scientists (*8*). However, they are not scientists *now*. They are only inclined to speculation, but their insights remain sterile, because they are never placed in a scientific context and are not coordinated with other insights, but only with mythology.

CONVULSIONS

The Mohave Indians of California and Arizona have evolved a theory which appears to be very similar to some modern psychoanalytic views concerning the damming-up and massive discharge of the Libido. They believe that the convulsive patient's sexual urge is so intense that he cannot abreact it either by coitus or by masturbation—only by convulsions. Let me seemingly argue against my central thesis for a moment and stress not only the reasonableness of this native theory, but also the possibility that it came into being exactly the way the corresponding psychoanalytic theory did—by noticing the *arc de cercle* both in convulsions and in orgasm, and by realizing that there is a kind of "absence" during both.

Let me carry even further my false hypothesis and imagine that the Mohave became preconsciously or unconsciously aware of the epileptic's basic inability to establish intensive human relations and to abreact affect through an orgasm, and that this awareness is revealed also by their repeated references, in connection with convulsions, to masturbation, to which no adult Mohave has to resort for lack of normal sexual opportunities (*10*). It is also quite certain that the Mohave understand the difference between psychological orgastic potency, as defined by analysts, and the ejaculation mechanism, which is a purely organic phenomenon (*9*). I propose to show that even if one supposes all this—and it is a lot—the Mohave still cannot be held to have developed a truly *naturalistic* theory of convulsions.

Indeed, the notion of a damming-up also occurs in other Mohave beliefs. Thus, they hold that a budding shaman who refuses to make use of his gifts goes insane. His power, denied an external outlet, turns against him and works within and upon him, driving him insane. It could even interview such a person, who had actually been confined to a state hospital with the—perhaps questionable—diagnosis of manic-depressive psychosis.

What matters here is that the Mohave theory of convulsions is neither naturalistic nor scientific; it is patterned upon theories of shamanistic powers, which are wholly non-naturalistic. What is more, the very idea of a psychic "flooding" of the organism may have been inspired by the agriculturally important (Nile-like) periodic floods of the Colorado River. Needless to say, this suggested explanation does not represent a return to outmoded eighteenth- and nineteenth-century rationalistic speculations about the "meaning" of myths. What I wish to stress here is exclusively the objective fact that major experiences—which may be labeled type experiences—provide Man with cognitive, affective and attitudinal models, such as one observes day after day in transference phenomena. This argument is especially valid in the case of the Mohave, whose creation myth supposedly provides a precedent or prototype for every single possible human practice or experience (*31, 20*).

One may, of course, object that Mohave theories about

convulsions contain no direct reference to the budding shaman's refusal to become a practicing shaman. It can, however, be demonstrated that the two phenomena are related to each other, even though only implicitly. The Mohave apparently characterize the convulsive as a psychologically impotent, although physically (ejaculatorily) potent, person, who remains unsatisfied because he is not psychologically and emotionally involved in his sex acts. It is important in this context that the Mohave explicitly define coitus as a psychosomatic activity: "Persons who cohabit, do so on two levels: their bodies cohabit with each other and their souls cohabit with each other" (9). This is a very big claim and also a very mature one, but seems to be validated by the basic characteristics of Mohave sexuality. The final clue is the reference to the masturbation of convulsives; the average adult Mohave simply does not masturbate, because he has no need for it—no actual need and no psychological need. A psychologically impotent, although ejaculatorily potent, person is incapable of discharging affect in coitus. He is therefore actually very much like a person who received shamanistic powers but refuses to put them to use.

The preceding data suggest that the Mohave theory of the dynamics of convulsions is correct, but not scientific. It was probably derived, by analogy, from theories accounting for the insanity of shamans, who refuse to "give"—to use and to externalize their powers for the benefit of others. This means that the Mohave theory of convulsions is not the end product of series of observations, inductions, and intuitive generalizations. Hence, even though it is correct, it is not science, and therefore cannot be a first step toward a scientific psychiatry, any more than Platon's fantasies about bisexuality could have led, in fourth-century Athens, to the corresponding theories of Freud. Hence, Platon's fantasies, like the theories of the Mohave, remained scientifically sterile. There are also many other examples of primitive psychiatric ideas which, while essentially correct, are not truly scientific. For instance:

1. The Mohave have an amazing insight into early sibling rivalry, but only because the adult, who is constantly under pressure to be overly generous, projects or attributes his resentment upon the infant who is being weaned because its mother is pregnant once more (7).

2. The Mohave have a singularly modern-sounding theory of depression, mourning and funeral suicide, which is, however, formulated in purely eschatological terms, derived from beliefs about seductive ghosts (20).

3. They are able to identify and to describe a special form of agitated depression afflicting old husbands deserted by young wives, because marriages of that type have a specific, although atypical, social and psychological function in that tribe (20).

4. Mohave shamanistic psychotherapists inquire into the patient's dreams and demand that their narration should fit the Mohave equivalent of the basic rule of psychoanalysis (20). However, the shaman is interested in dreams chiefly because they enable him to identify the supernatural agency —or the witch—responsible for the illness.

The point which such examples illustrate is a relatively simple one: the primitive psychiatrist is never more completely the culture-bound empiricist than when he seems to assume the guise of a sophisticated theoretician, or meta-psychologist.

Cultural Aspects of Modern Psychiatric Theories

It seems desirable to discuss three modern psychiatric theories derived from three different schools of thought: First, the theory that the criterion of adjustment is the gauge of sanity; this theory is derived from descriptive psychiatry. Second, the view that all mental disorders have an organic basis, although sometimes the exact nature of their organic causation is not known; this represents the laboratory-oriented psychiatric position. Third, the theory of the *primary* death instinct, which is held by many to be a cornerstone of classical psychoanalytic theory.

I readily admit that I have chosen to discuss these three theories because I find them unacceptable. This only means, however, that my rejection of these theories helps me to grasp more easily their essentially culture-bound patterning. Moreover, I must state once more that the demonstration that a theory is patterned upon a cultural thought model does not prove that it is false. I wish to deal simply with the *genesis* of these theories, and not with their inherent validity.

ADJUSTMENT

I already challenged elsewhere (*6*; *22*, Ch. 1) the value of this concept, which is often confused with the concept of reality acceptance and therefore treated as a decisive criterion of sanity. I therefore postulate here only that not *adjustment*, which is be definition static, but the capacity for creative *readjustment* is the real criterion of sanity. Were it otherwise then, as Richard L. Jenkins rightly points out (*22*, Ch. 1), the hospital-adjusted mentally ill patient would, because of his adjustment, have to be called normal. The real question is why adjustment, in its most superficially motor and verbal sense, came to occupy so *important* a position in psychiatric diagnosis. The emphasis here is precisely on the word "important." It is this emphasis that creates problems; for the view that a completely unadjusted person is abnormal is certainly acceptable.

The word "adjustment" plays a tremendous role in America, both in psychiatry and in daily speech, although usually mere outward conformity rather than an inward acceptance of norms is meant. In fact, it is even possible that self-revelation is so highly penalized in American society precisely because it tends to unmask an underlying emotional nonconformity, carefully hidden behind the façade of outward conformity.

The origins of American society may provide one clue to the manner in which outward adjustment and conformity came to play so great a role in American psychiatry—and even in the psychiatric theories evolved or adopted by immigrant psychiatrists and psychoanalysts.

When America was still underpopulated, great efforts were made to attract to this country immigrants of working age, in order to man the rapidly expanding industries, farms and mines. Persons from a variety of cultures were imported by droves and had then to be fitted into the economic and local scene. This was far from easy, since economic conditions in Europe were at that time such that a goodly proportion of the immigrants came from non-Anglo-Saxon countries. They were usually adults, who had already been indoctrinated in terms of their respective cultures.[1] Hence, even though most of these people may have been abused at home and may have been rebels at heart, they nonetheless brought with them a fully internalized cultural heritage.

The first task of those who wished to put immigrants to work was to make them accept, at least superficially, the practically relevant behavioral patterns of Americans. Thus, the men were expected to learn some English, so as to understand orders, and to abandon flowing peasant garments, which were easily caught by machines. By contrast, little or no effort was made to indoctrinate them with the deeper significance of the "American way of life" (*17*). Outer adjustment was all that was aimed at—and, more especially, adjustment related to economic performance. The basic European patterns were permitted to—and did in fact— remain largely undisturbed; witness the culture conflict between first- and second-generation Americans. Hence, there are few other countries in which the term "maladjustment" so definitely means "strange"—that is, ultimately, "alien," "out-group," or even "outlaw" or "outcast."

The American people's great geographical mobility also required the evolving of a concept of adjustment which permitted a Kansas farmer to become a "real" cowboy, simply by donning the appropriate costume, while status mobility

1.   For reasons explained elsewhere (*17*) the word "indoctrinated" is used here in its most rigorous sense.

led to a nonpsychological definition of class-linked adjustment, formulated in terms of possessions and of outward manners rather than in terms of a "class mentality." Thus, just as the immigrant's Americanization was defined in terms of clothing, manners and accent, any rise in social or class status was also defined in terms of certain externals. In a sense, conformism, or Americanization, came to imply primarily an increasingly successful adaptation to higher living standards, while maladjustment, in the sense of strangeness and non-American alienness, came to be identified with low economic status, because so many poor people were recent immigrants.

At present [1958] it is, of course, fashionable for commencement speakers to rail against the tame conformism of the younger generation and its quest for secure employment. However, the very persons who vehemently condemn the younger generation's timid cult of adjustment offer no constructive program of creative dissent. In fact, they advocate nothing more spectacular or novel than a return to the swashbuckling age of robber barons, which originated the cult of purely external adjustment in the first place, because it had no *mystique* worth mentioning. In brief, commencement philosophers of individualism offer nothing more than a Greenwich Village hippie type of obsessive nonconformism, transposed to Main Street and Suburbia, which represents but another form of uncreative dedifferentiation, this time [1976] animated [as predicted in 1958] by a special form of "social negativism" (*22*, Ch. 3) which is almost indistinguishable from a compulsive reverse adjustment to what Linton aptly called "patterns of misconduct" (*34*).

There is no trace of real humanization—that is, of differentiation and individualization—on the subjective level, and no functional and creative ethos on the socio-cultural level, in all this pseudo-nonconformism, and if there were, commencement orators would not dare to advocate it.

Now, it is extremely interesting that the emphasis on

adjustment in psychiatric diagnosis was actively fostered by some immigrant psychiatrists, for example by Karen Horney (*29*) and certain other self-styled—but actually mis-styled—"culturalists." These immigrant psychiatrists, who had remained fundamentally alien and European, soon realized that they were unable to appraise empathically their American patients' degree of *internal* adjustment to the American way of life. They therefore tried to construct a purely logical, intellectually understandable, criterion of adjustment, or of conformity. Actually, the realistic, cul-ture-oriented diagnostician must appraise not the patient's degree of behavioral conformity, but the manner in which he handles culture as a unique type of experience (*22*, Chs. 2 and 15).

Relatively homogeneous cultures do not seem obsessed with external conformity, either in psychiatry or in daily life. Thus, adjustment seems to occupy less space in French or German textbooks of psychiatry than it does in American ones, because in France and in Germany behavioral devia-tions are less readily defined as signs of maladjustment and alienness. Above all, in France certain seemingly deviant behavioral types are more likely to be viewed as the "*French* Bohemian group," or as "characters straight out of a *French* romance of chivalry." There are few such persons who will, in the American manner, be considered as non-French—as deculturated—or transculturated—deviants. Most of these "deviants" are thought of simply as variations on a funda-mentally French theme: as idiosyncratic, regional or his-torical phrasings of the French ethos—which they often are.

Nothing said so far can—or is meant to—prove that the appraisal of conformity should not be the crucial diagnostic test, even though I happen to doubt the diagnostic value of this criterion (*22*, Ch. 1). I simply sought to clarify some of the social, cultural and historical processes which caused the concept of adjustment to assume so preponderant a role in American psychiatric thought. In short, valid or invalid though it may be, the criterion of adjustment is not the

product of scientific inquiry, but of a social myth or cultural
type-casting process. Even if it should happen to be correct,
it has yet to be shown that it is scientific.

ORGANICITY

No mention will be made here of the more grotesque extremes of organic mindedness; I shall consider only wholly
"respectable" and "conservative" theories of the organic
causation of certain mental disorders, which equally respectable functional psychiatrists believe to be primarily
psychogenic. In brief, the problem is the subjective impulse
of many deservedly respected psychiatrists to turn first to
the laboratory, instead of to their own unconscious, for
valid insights into the causation of mental disease (*21*). It
will be shown that—regardless of how sound and legitimate
this procedure may be—it is derived from two clearly cultural thought models.

1. *Social Status Aspirations:* Each profession has both a
self-definition and an awareness of its social definition by
outsiders. The physician defines himself traditionally as a
biological scientist or engineer; and the social—or popular
—definition of the "ideal" physician dovetails extensively,
although often naïvely and grotesquely, with this professional self-definition. The layman's naïve prototype of
the physician is usually Dr. Kildare—that gallant hero of
the movies—rushing into the breach. At other times it is the
good gray country doctor sitting up with a sick child on a
lonely farm, or a Pasteur—who was *not* a physician—
creating new miracle vaccines or drugs in his laboratory.
This latter stereotype even forms the basis of certain hostile
caricatures of the medical profession: of the diabolical
medical genius.

By contrast, the "collective representation" of the psychiatrist is—both in terms of medical self-definitions and in
terms of social stereotypes—somewhat outside the classical
medical tradition. The medical psychotherapist is just beginning to appear as a hero in detective stories and in serious

literature. Thus, in one of his earliest appearances on the literary scene, in Poe's *The System of Dr. Tarr and Professor Fether*, the psychiatrist is actually not even present in person, but is deceitfully, though convincingly, impersonated by patients. While jokes about psychiatrists, as distinct from jokes about village morons and lunatics, abound at present, they still circulate chiefly among "sophisticates." Last, but not least, all psychiatrists have felt the sting of the barbs which their colleagues in the other branches of medicine direct at them. As regards the struggle of psychoanalysis for recognition and the cowardly compromises it thought it had to accept in America in order to be acknowledged as a therapeutic discipline, it is still so recent that it need be mentioned only in passing (*11*).

Now, it is a fact that psychiatrists, too, are human beings and therefore necessarily feel threatened by a challenge to their self-definition as biological scientists. They are no more immune to accusations of being "witch doctors" or "head-shrinkers" than were their early forebears in scientific organic medicine, whom the Inquisition anathematized as heretical witches, and Molière ridiculed. It would be unfair to expect physicians practicing psychiatry not to seek to establish once and for all that they, too, are within the medico-biological tradition. Hence, even if no mental disease whatsoever were definitely known to have an organic basis, or were susceptible of being influenced (though not cured) by electric shock therapy or by chemotherapy, some psychiatrists would—quite understandably and forgivably —feel nonetheless impelled to look to the laboratory for insights into the etiology of—and to the pharmacy and the surgery for means of treating—psychic illness. How much more understandable is it, then, that they *do* turn to the laboratory and to the pharmacy when—within limits—the very concept of the "organism as a whole" makes such undertakings legitimate? It seems certain that the psychiatrist has something definite to look for in the laboratory and in the pharmacy. It is simply suggested that *one* of his reasons for doing so is his desire to validate his self-definition as a physician and biological scientist.

2. *Scientism:* The scientists of democracies rightly ridicule Nazi and Communist sciolism, which disdainfully contrasts "effete" Jewish or "bourgeois" science with "red-blooded" Nazi or Communist science. Yet, foolish and self-satisfied as such verbiage is, it does reflect a minimum of insight into the influence of socio-cultural ideologies upon scientific thought. By contrast, Western scientists are inclined to ignore the influence of their culture upon their own science and therefore profess to practice not democratic science or Euro-American science, but absolute science. In this respect they are deceiving themselves (*21*), even though science in a democracy is, in fact, more naturalistic and closer to being absolute science than is either Nazi or Communist science. This is due in part to the fact that absolute science is a bona fide cultural theme of democratic society. It is, nonetheless, desirable to become aware of this cultural bias of Occidental science, because it enables one to approximate more closely the ideal of absolute science.

I do not feel obliged to make a profession of faith in exact science before being permitted to discuss its cultural roots. I shall therefore enter directly into a discussion of the fact that the cultural prestige of exact science—as distinct from its *objective validity*—is so great today that only academic tradition prevents the inventors of the atom bomb from earning a great deal of money by endorsing vaginal deodorants or even candidates for public offices. Indeed, physical science is today presented as a model for all sciences. As a result, a good many students of Man agonize over the fact that they are not "real," true-blue scientists and, in their attempt to remedy this "sad" situation, often write papers and books filled with pseudo-mathematics, and otherwise parade in the borrowed mantle of the exact sciences (*18, 21*).

The point to be stressed is that physics has become the social stereotype of science per se. Its specific methodology, which is heavily influenced by its subject-matter-bound techniques, is therefore systematically confused with logic and scientific method in the more general sense. Hence, the fact that physics is quite genuinely way ahead of the other sciences is ascribed to its "perfect" (but also specific) methodology, instead of to two much more simple, realistic and obvious reasons:

   1. Physical phenomena are *simpler* by far than are biological, psychological or social ones.

   2. The study of physics is less hampered by the subjective anxieties of the scientists on the one hand and by self-appointed saviors of mankind and metaphysicians on the other hand, than is the study of phenomena related to the more sensitive spots of Man and society (*21*).

The result of this situation is quite simple: behavioral scientists investigating complex universes of discourse are dazzled by the success of physicists in dealing with simple ones and therefore seek to apply to the study of complex universes a physicalistic *methodology* which is heavily tainted by physical *techniques*. Yet, competent physicists know that this is not possible, precisely because they themselves occasionally have to effect a shift in their own methodology. Thus, physicists deal with two particles in terms of classical mechanics, but formulate the laws governing the behavior of many particles, forming a system, in terms of statistical mechanics, which is rooted in a wholly different methodology (see *The Argument*).

The mathematician of space—the geometrician—likewise differentiates between the special geometry of limited or finite space—Euclidean geometry—and the geometry of, roughly speaking, infinite space—Riemannian geometry. Now, it is extremely important to realize that it is finite Euclidean geometry which is the so-called limiting case, or special case, of Riemannian geometry—not vice versa. The same is true in cosmology. Newtonian physics, applicable to finite systems, is the special or limiting case of Einsteinian physics, and not vice versa. Euclid (Eukleides) can be deduced from Riemann, as Newton can be deduced from Einstein, but not vice versa. A. Meyer, who understood this state of affairs, instead of advocating a physicalization of biology, asserted that physical laws are deducible from biological ones, but not vice versa (40). Without expressing an opinion about the objective validity of this view, I would agree that, in empirical science, the simple is often a special case of the complex. If, however, one accepts the above thesis, one might go even further and say that the most general laws are those derived from the study of that which is most complex—that is, from the study of the human-organisms-as-a-whole-in-society—and that the complementary sets of laws so obtained become, when gradually restricted and simplified, the laws of sociology and psychology, of physiology and biology, of biochemistry, chemistry and physics. I deliberately represent here, in a schematical form, a problem already considered elsewhere (21; cf. Chs. 1 and 3).

The asymmetrical nature of this logical sequence is amply clear to many first-rate exact scientists. However, the organicistic or quasi-extrapolatory approach in psychiatry often proceeds in the opposite direction and seeks to derive the laws of mentation from the laws of physiology, which is about as feasible as trying to derive the laws of statistical mechanics from those of classical mechanics, which they nonetheless presuppose. It simply cannot be done, and could not be done even if it were possible to prove that every single psychic disorder has an organic basis and cause. If quasi-extrapolation there must be, it must proceed in exactly the opposite direction—from the "organismal" to the "organic."

Now, it is a demonstrable fact that organicistic reasoning in psychiatry has, until now, proceeded in the opposite (i.e., wrong) direction, and has done so for culturally determined reasons. Preconsciously at least, its procedures have been inspired by the social prestige of physical science, rather than by the inherent accomplishments of physical science.

It is unnecessary to argue, for the moment, whether the physicalistic thought model is, or is not, applicable to psychiatric investigations. What has to be pointed out is that, applicable or not, it is, because of the prestige of exact science, *made* to *seem* applicable to psychiatric research. Hence, the harder psychiatrists try to adopt the limiting case as their thought model, even though their own subject matter is too complex to allow this prestige-laden model to be useful, the slower becomes their real progress toward a genuine science of the organism as a whole.

One example of a concrete, organicistic "method of demonstration," which claims that it constitutes a proof, and which is clearly patterned upon a nonscientific and archaic cultural thought model, is the view that the purely palliative results of surgical and chemotherapeutical approaches to the treatment of psychic illnesses are, somehow or other, evidences of the organic etiology of psychopathology. It should be stressed once more that one need not argue here that, in the last resort, they do not constitute a proof; it suffices to point out that these results are, *for cultural reasons*, believed to be a proof, thus demonstrating the cultural basis of a supposedly scientific reasoning.

It is known that the pharmacotherapy of mental derangement dates back to primitive and ancient societies, many of which believed psychosis to be due to possession by an intruding demon. When the administration of some (magical) drug was followed by an improvement, this was held to *prove* the etiological theory of demonic possession, it being said that the demon did not like the drug and took flight. The simple fact is that, to this very day, a good many psychiatric chemotherapies, including even some which are admittedly effective, are purely empirical; witness the infinity of proposed explanations of the effectiveness of insulin therapy, all of which prove only that insulin therapy in psychiatry is sometimes useful, and nothing more. It is, likewise, well to remember that, fundamentally, psychiatrists know little more about why *Rauwolfia serpentina* is apparently useful in the treatment of mental disorder than did the ancient Hindu who first used it. It would be preposterous indeed to argue on this basis against chemotherapy in the treatment of the psychoses, but it is equally preposterous to infer that their *partially* effective treatment by chemotherapy *proves* their organic causation. In brief, true or false though that theory may be, it is based upon a nonscientific cultural thought model, a point which a simple analogy will help to clarify.

Menomini Indian women who wished to abort ate the finely chopped tail hairs of the blacktailed deer (*Odocoileus columbianus*) (*28, 15*) mixed with bear fat. The hairs irritated the gastrointestinal system and therefore facilitated abortion exactly the way a strong cathartic does. Menomini medical theory holds, however, that these chopped hairs are magic arrows, which seek out and destroy the life in the womb. Now, were one to reason in the way some historians of psychiatry do, one might say that even though the pharmacodynamic explanations of the Menomini are wrong, one is entitled to claim that the Menomini discovered, or had an inkling of, the fact that some substances do gravitate toward and become fixed by preference in certain organs — as, for example, iodine gravitates toward the thyroid, or strontium toward the skeletal system. It is hardly necessary to say that such a proposition is nonsensical. All the Menomini knew was that these hairs sometimes caused abortion, but they did not know that they caused abortion because they irritated the intestines, causing abdominal spasms. Thus, Menomini abortionists were mere empiricists masquerading as theoreticians, who slavishly rephrased certain characteristic thought models of their culture.

It is desirable indeed that psychiatrists continue to improve and expand the chemotherapy of mental disorders, but let them not delude themselves into believing that they have a rationale even when they operate simply as empiricists, and, above all, let them not affirm that the demonstrable palliative successes of their medications can be cited in support of general theories of organic etiology. Indeed, even if the case for the organic causation of all psychoses should ever be proved, logically untenable theories will only delay the development of a sound biology of psychic diseases.

THE PRIMARY DEATH INSTINCT

Freud formulated this concept in response to the observation that the dreams of shellshocked First-World-War soldiers were characterized by a kind of repetition compulsion which *seemed* to contradict his view that dreams represented wish fulfillment in accordance with the pleasure principle. Freud felt that the most parsimonious solution was to hypothesize a death instinct, which seeks to restore the state of inorganicity preceding the advent of life upon earth (*27*). Thus, in order to salvage the wish-fulfillment component of his dream theory, Freud abandoned his initial frustration-aggression hypothesis and postulated that outward-directed aggression was derived from self-aggression and not vice versa. The fact that many classical analysts, such as Fenichel (*26*), rejected the theory of the (primary) death instinct shows that some alternative interpretations of the repetition compulsion were at least theoretically possible.

The theory of the primary death instinct appears to be patterned upon a whole series of cultural thought models.

1. *The Physicalistic Model* is the second law of thermodynamics, the law of increasing entropy being often cited in support of the theory of the death instinct (*3, 39*). Actually, it *may* be possible to cite this law in explanation of the *fact* of death—but never of a death *instinct*, as instinct is defined today. Instinct is, if I may use a physicalistic model, a force or vector which *impels* a given system in a certain direction. The movement of a system toward entropy is, however, something entirely different. It is not a purposive force which propels a system in a given direction; it is a *drift* within a

system, which results from the operations of the laws of chance, and from nothing else.

2. *The Biologistic Model* subtends Freud's attempt to solve the problem presented by the fact of the repetition compulsion, by postulating a second biological instinct, instead of by means of a minor revision of his first scheme of psychic functioning. Everything said previously about organicistic psychiatry is also applicable to this type of biologizing.

3. *The Mythological Model* is an ancient one indeed; it goes back to the concept of a struggle between two opposite principles in the universe and in the human microcosm. This model may antedate even its best known example, the Zoroastrian concept of a struggle between Ormuzd and Ahriman, since it is already present in many primitive mythologies, which ascribe the origin of death and evil to the malignant intervention of a trickster, spoiler or devil.

4. *The Ethical Model* is the threefold concept of original sin, predestination and the evilness of human nature, in its most rigid, puritanical and Old-Testament sense.

5. *The Specifically Culture-Historical Model* is the romanticism of the nineteenth century, which idealized the individual to such a point that even his death had to be viewed as self-willed—a grotesquely neat parallel of the Arunta belief that every death is due to witchcraft. A perfect expression of this form of megalomania is found in Henley's famous lines: "I am the master of my fate: I am the captain of my soul." Philosophically, this implies the erroneous view that Man is an endocentric, closed system. Ethically it postulates that "guilt is destiny"—although Greek tragedy, which allegedly first formulated this view, actually says something quite different (*13*).

6. *The Clinical Model* is perhaps the therapeutically most inconvenient and objectionable one, since the postulation of a death instinct has no direct applications in the analytic hour. Hence, what has invaded the analytic chamber in

some instances is an excessive emphasis upon the patient's sole responsibility for his misfortunes, usually in the guise of an (extremist) theory of moral masochism. As Loewenstein has pointed out, this can be grossly exaggerated, since, to put it crudely, it is but seldom that the patient's moral masochism causes him to walk past a house the very moment the wind blows off the roof a tile which then lands on his head. This example is admittedly grotesque, but no more so than the tendency to emphasize only the means employed by the Jews to invite aggression, while minimizing the patent hostilities of their environment—which is precisely the attitude so rightly criticized by Loewenstein (*35*). In brief, it is senseless to harp incessantly on the patient's moral masochism, while refusing to recognize the extent to which the patient, while still a helpless child, was subjected to outbursts of blind parental sadism. In fact, the psychotherapist's irresponsible refusal to recognize explicitly the sadism of a patient's parents deliberately weakens the patient's confidence in his capacity to test reality and strengthens his sadistic Superego. Furthermore, a constant and exclusive preoccupation with the patient's moral masochism is often little more than an at once cynical and slothful clinical trick: since the patient is on the couch, while the devouring mother, the harsh father or one of their many successors, *all* of whom even the most masochistic patient could not have deliberately chosen, are not, it is easiest to pick on the patient, whom one has at one's mercy.

This point need not be labored, since I stressed elsewhere (*13, 14*) that the Occidental, culturally determined conception of children led to an almost exclusive preoccupation with the Oedipus complex and to an almost total disregard, at least in theoretical formulations, of the role of counter-oedipal attitudes, which actually trigger off the Oedipal ones. It is in such contexts that seemingly clinical attitudes are most easily recognized as being patterned upon archaic theories of criminal justice, moral masochism being often defined in a manner which makes it, for all practical purposes, indistinguishable from criminal intent or guilt, regardless of neuroticism, inevitable accident and provocation.

This set of cultural models, which inspired the formulation of the death instinct, reappears in an almost undisguised form in certain marginal, but far from negligible, new developments in psychoanalytic thought. For example, it was stressed elsewhere (*12*) that the formulation of the death instinct marks a turning point in the psychoanalytic attitude toward the so-called occult phenomena. Thus, previous to the genesis of this theory, all clinical psychoanalytic papers dealing with seemingly telepathic phenomena were resolutely anti-occult. After the death instinct was formulated, three out of five analytic papers dealing with this subject, including Freud's own, began to take telepathy seriously. At the same time attempts were made to coordinate psychoanalytic thinking with Occidental forms of supernaturalistic thought. It is not necessary to argue against supernaturalism to realise that there exists a causal relationship between the formulation of the death instinct and the recent aligning of *some* psychoanalytic thinking on supernaturalism [and, by now (1976) also on naïve metaphysics]. The same causal—or temporal—connection also seems to underlie the replacement of early, psychoanalytically inspired, theories of pedagogical leniency by certain, historically far more recent, views favoring a return to punishment and anti-instinctuality, or even—what is worse—by a systematic refusal to provide the child with the support his fragile Ego so badly needs (*11*, *17*) [and by a spineless tolerance of chaos, 1976]. As regards theories of personal responsibility, I was shocked to read during the last great war a supposedly psychoanalytic paper on malingering, which represented an attitude toward combat fatigue subsequently made sadly famous by General Patton's slapping of a hospitalized enlisted man suffering from combat fatigue. The same moralistic attitude is echoed, albeit in a more restrained form, also by a good many other supposedly psychoanalytically oriented papers on war neuroses.

It can be objected, of course, that in each of the preceding cases it is possible to establish only a temporal, rather than a strictly causal sequence and that, therefore, the suggested connections must be thought of as being of the post hoc ergo propter hoc type. In rebuttal, it seems legitimate to stress that there are simply too many of these *psycho-analytically all-too-foreseeable* "coincidences" to make their noncausal and purely sequential explanation seem convincing, or even simply plausible. I therefore feel that the *invention* of the death instinct hypothesis marked the onset of the gradual *Gleichschaltung* of the previously iconoclastic and culturally neutral psychoanalytic point of view with some major tenets and thought models of Occidental culture.

Deculturalization and Reculturalization of Science

Many Hellenists and historians of science are puzzled by the seeming paradox that early Greek science was, at least in its intentions, truly scientific and objective in the age of the Milesian "philosophers," such as Thales, whereas later Greek science (Pythagoras, etc.) was heavily tainted with philosophical mythology. This development was probably due to the following culture-historical process. Much of the substantive content of early Greek science was directly—though *minus* its cultural halo meanings—borrowed from Egyptian and Mesopotamian temple science and technology. The Greeks were therefore in a position to practice pure—that is, *non*cultural—science. However, as soon as this pure science became respectable and so to say naturalized, it rapidly acquired specifically Greek cultural connotations and was transformed into a kind of Greek magical science. This evolution explains why E. R. Dodds calls Pythagoras and Empedokles "Greek shamans" (*23*). Pythagoras worked creatively in mathematics, but did so for non-mathematical reasons and in pursuit of mystical objectives. In brief, he was a mathematical genius who *preferred* to be a numerologist. The selfsame process was repeated when the Arabs took over Greek science *minus* its specifically Greek connotations; after practicing pure science for a while, they too began to surround it with a halo of meanings, which, in their case, were derived from Islamic mysticism. When the Christian Renaissance borrowed Graeco-Arabic science, it too was subjected to the same initial deculturalization, followed after a while by reculturalization. The Age of Reason once more deculturalized science. However, at this point in history science itself became an "idol of the marketplace," a nonobjective bit of cultural magic. Hence, this time it was not mysticism, but sciolism, disguised as scientificality, which began to invade science (*22*, Ch. 16).

The same deculturalization and reculturalization process manifests itself also in the history of psychoanalysis. Originally, psychoanalytic thought broke with culturally provided thought models and, despite certain wild fancies which characterize every nascent pioneer science, was, on the whole, quite tough minded and truly scientific in its orientation. However, when it finally became proper to "believe" in psychoanalysis, an attempt was made to reculturalize this formerly outlawed science and to make it respectable by providing it with a halo of cultural connotations. Thus, one meets with increasingly bold attempts to integrate psychoanalysis as a science with religious beliefs and with metaphysics. Also, as indicated above, the evolving of the death instinct concept automatically led to a change in psychoanalytic attitudes toward telepathy (*12*). Last, but not least, pseudo-psychoanalytic considerations are nowadays more and more often marshalled in support of the specific ideology of present-day Occidental culture or even, in a typically Occidental manner, *against* it (Fromm, Marcuse, etc.).

In this context, it is wholly irrelevant whether religion is true, whether telepathic phenomena are real, and whether

Occidental culture is or is not the best of all possible cultures. The real issue is simply that, by means of a *circular* reasoning, cultural connotations are—rightly or wrongly—assigned to psychoanalytic theories, which are then cited for nonanalytic purposes and in nonanalytic and nonscientific contexts. If this process continues, psychoanalysis will become one of the myths of the Occidental world, instead of remaining a science. In this context, the renewed prestige of the theories of Jung is something which should give the objectively scientific psychoanalyst much food for thought and also much cause for concern. It should also incite him to subject his own convictions to a critical scrutiny.

In other words, there is taking place at present a reculturalization of psychoanalysis, inevitably accompanied by a change in the analyst's status: by the transfer of psychoanalysts from Greenwich Village to Park Avenue or even to an equally fashionable *anti*-Park Avenue setting. Psychoanalysis may become too respectable in the end and turn into an "idol of the marketplace" in the same sense in which nuclear physics is an idol today—and may therefore cease to be an objective science. Real science is never respectable —it is an unwashed urchin perpetually in rebellion against meaningless shibboleths and forever questioning even the most firmly established scientific truths (*16, 32*).

Bibliography

(*1*)   Aristoteles: *Poetics*.

(*2*)   Bell, E. T.: *Men of Mathematics*, New York, 1937.

(*3*)   Bernfeld, Siegfried and Feitelberg, Sergei: The Principle of Entropy and the Death Instinct, *International Journal of Psycho-Analysis*, 12:61–81, 1931.

(*4*)   Chantepie de la Saussaye, P. D. (ed.): *Manuel d'Histoire des Religions*, Paris, 1921.

(*5*)   Colby, K. M.: *Energy and Structure in Psychoanalysis*, New York, 1955.

(*6*)   Devereux, George: Maladjustment and Social Neurosis, *American Sociological Review*, 4:844–851, 1939.

(*7*)   Idem: Mohave Orality: An Analysis of Nursing and Weaning Customs, *Psychoanalytic Quarterly*, 16:519–546, 1947.

(*8*) Idem: The Potential Contributions of the Moî to the Cultural Landscape of Indochina, *Far Eastern Quarterly*, 6:390–395, 1947.
(*9*) Idem: Heterosexual Behavior of the Mohave Indians (in) Róheim, Géza (ed.), *Psychoanalysis and the Social Sciences*, vol. 2, New York, 1950.
(*10*) Idem: Mohave Indian Autoerotic Behavior, *Psychoanalytic Review*, 37:201–220, 1950.
(*11*) Idem: *Reality and Dream: The Psychotherapy of a Plains Indian*, New York, 1951 (2nd augm. ed., 1969).
(*12*) Idem: *Psychoanalysis and the Occult*, New York, 1953, 1970.
(*13*) Idem: Why Oedipus Killed Laius: A Note on the Complementary Oedipus Complex in Greek Drama, *International Journal of Psycho-Analysis*, 34:132–141, 1953.
(*14*) Idem: A Counteroedipal Episode in Homer's *Iliad*, *Bulletin of the Philadelphia Association for Psychoanalysis*, 4:90–97, 1955.
(*15*) Idem: *A Study of Abortion in Primitive Societies*, New York, 1955. (2nd augm. ed., 1976).
(*16*) Idem: Notes on the Dynamics of Post-Traumatic Epileptic Seizures, *Bulletin of the Philadelphia Association for Psychoanalysis*, 5:61–73, 1955.
(*17*) Idem: *Therapeutic Education*, New York, 1956.
(*18*) Idem: The Criteria of Dual Competence in Psychiatric-Anthropological Studies, *Journal of the Hillside Hospital*, 6:87–90, 1957.
(*19*) Idem: The Anthropological Roots of Psychoanalysis (and) Reply to Kardiner (in) Masserman, J. H. (ed.), *Science and Psychoanalysis*, vol. 1, New York, 1958.
(*20*) Idem: *Mohave Ethnopsychiatry*, Washington, D.C., 1961 (2nd augm. ed., 1969).
(*21*) Idem: *From Anxiety to Method in the Behavioral Sciences*, Paris and The Hague, 1967.
(*22*) Idem: *Essais d'Ethnopsychiatrie Générale*, Paris, 1970, 1972, 1977.
(*23*) Dodds, E. R.: *The Greeks and the Irrational*, Berkeley, Calif., 1951.
(*24*) Durkheim, Emile: *Les Formes Elémentaires de la Vie Religieuse*, Paris, 1912.
(*25*) Farrington, Benjamin: *Greek Science*, 2 vols., Harmondsworth, Middlesex, 1949.
(*26*) Fenichel, Otto: A Critique of the Death Instinct (in) *The Collected Papers of O. F.*, First Series, New York, 1953.
(*27*) Freud, Sigmund: Beyond the Pleasure Principle, *Standard Edition*, vol. 18, London, 1955.
(*28*) Hoffman, W. J.: The Menomini Indians, *Bureau of American Ethnology, Annual Report*, 14, Washington, D.C., 1893.
(*29*) Horney, Karen: *The Neurotic Personality of Our Time*, New York, 1937.
(*30*) Kemlin, J. E.: Les Alliances chez les Reungao, *Bulletin de l'Ecole Française d'Extrême-Orient*, 17:1–119, 1917.
(*31*) Kroeber, A. L.: Handbook of the Indians of California, *Bureau of American Ethnology, Bulletin 78*, Washington, D.C., 1925.

(*32*) La Barre, Weston: *The Human Animal*, Chicago, 1954.

(*33*) Lenzen, V. F.: Physical Causality, *University of California Publications in Philosophy*, 15:69-96, 1932.

(*34*) Linton, Ralph: *The Study of Man*, New York, 1936.

(*35*) Loewenstein, R. M.: The Historical and Cultural Roots of Antisemitism (in) Róheim, Géza (ed.), *Psychoanalysis and the Social Sciences*, vol. 1, 1949.

(*36*) Malinowski, Bronislaw: *The Sexual Life of Savages in North-Western Melanesia* (3rd ed.), London, 1932.

(*37*) Marbe, Karl: Über das Gedankenlesen und die Gleichförmigkeit des psychischen Geschehens, *Zeitschrift für Psychologie*, 56:241-263, 1910.

(*38*) Idem: *Die Gleichförmigkeit der Welt*, 2 vols., München, 1916-1919.

(*39*) Menninger, K. A.: Psychological Aspects of the Organism under Stress, Part 1: The Homeostatic Regulatory Function of the Ego, *Journal of the American Psychoanalytic Association*, 2:67-106, 1954.

(*40*) Meyer, Adolf: Zwischen Scylla und Charybdis; Holistische Antikritik des Mechanismus und Vitalismus, *Acta Biotheoretica*, 1:203-217, 1935.

(*41*) Poincaré, Henri: *The Foundations of Science*, Lancaster, Pa., 1913.

(*42*) Róheim, Géza: *The Gates of the Dream*, New York, 1952.

(*43*) Sambursky, S.: *The Physical World of the Greeks*, New York, 1962.

(*44*) Sorokin, P. A.: *Social and Cultural Dynamics*, 4 vols., New York, 1937-1941.

(*45*) Whorf, B. L.: *Collected Papers on Metalinguistics*, Washington, D.C., 1952.

11

Time: History vs. Chronicle

Socialization as Cultural Pre-Experience
(1975)

Preamble

SINCE I feel unable to differentiate in an operationally meaningful manner between socialization and enculturation, the present study was so planned as to make a distinction between the two phenomena—assuming that they are two, rather than only one—unnecessary. The process of socialization/enculturation is, throughout this paper, represented by the symbol S/C.

As regards "cultural communication," it is defined as information which cannot be obtained through—or inferred from—direct observation (sense data); it must necessarily pass from one mind to another. This specification can be clarified by means of a simple distinction between two major types of communicated information.

1. *Nomothetic Information* (usually in the imperative mood): All single, nubile persons must be chaste ("That is our custom").

2. *Descriptive Information* (usually in the indicative mood): All—or nearly all, or most—single nubile persons are chaste ("That is our practice").

The descriptive information could be obtained through non-verbal research (by the accumulation of sense data only), and, on the basis of the data accumulated in this manner, one could formulate the generalization: "That is our (or their) practice." But, regardless of the amount of sense data *so* accumulated, one remains incapable of formulating the nomothetic statement, or even of evolving the notion of "custom." For it is an inherent quality of every statement in the imperative mood that it is (logically) *future directed*. This finding remains true even if a person, who has violated the custom in the past, is being punished for it here and now and, possibly, for some time to come.

These brief preliminary observations indicate that the principal objective of the present study is the articulation of S/C with the time dimension.

Terminology and Symbols: So as not to overload the text with repetitive specifications, the following symbols will be used:

S/C (as stated) denotes socialization/enculturation.

T/E denotes learning by trial and error.

H/N denotes here and now.

P/E denotes pre-experience.

Pre-experience is a symbolic anticipation of a "thing" or situation which, in the absence (H/N) of any part or direct emanation (scent, etc.) of the "thing" or situation, produces a subjective experience comparable to that which one would have were that "thing" or situation present H/N. This P/E subsequently enables the subject who has undergone it to cope efficiently with the "thing" or situation as, if and when —if *ever*—it *is* present H/N. I state at once that P/E, as here defined, appears to be a purely human experience, resulting from cultural communication. Thus:

1. A mother coyote can, on perceiving a human smell, "teach" her cubs to dread that (H/N) smell and—*as a serendipity*—to avoid subsequently anything smelling that way. But she can do this only as, if and when the scent *is* present, H/N.

2. A human mother can cause her city-bred child to avoid wolves or lions, simply by telling it about these animals, no constituent part or trace (smell) of which is present H/N. She can even make her child fear (inexistent) bogies, etc.

The human capacity to have P/Es appears to be directly

related to the human capacity for anticipation. Köhler's ape, finding that there was a banana which he could not reach, and observing that his cage contained a number of boxes, seemed to "reflect," exhibited what Köhler calls a "Eureka-reaction," piled the boxes on top of each other and thus managed to reach the banana (7). But, unlike Man, the ape cannot *anticipate* a problem and cannot figure out (plan) in *advance* how it would eventually pile up boxes in order to reach a banana hung just beyond his reach, if that situation ever arose.

Two further terms also have to be elucidated.

1. *Referral or Relevance:* Though I may learn H/N about the 1776 American Revolution, I must be able to *refer* this information, just acquired, to the past. I may learn H/N that there will be an eclipse of the moon *x* years hence, but must *refer* this information to the future. I may learn H/N of the existence of Mt. Everest, but must *refer* this information to "elsewhere" (Asia).

2. *Pertinence:* This term denotes the time and/or place at which the information acquired H/N will be useful—will lead to a "reward" or "positive reinforcement." Thus, when an alien is naturalized, he is asked questions about the American Revolution, i.e., about facts which are clearly to be referred to the *past*. But, in terms of the theory underlying naturalization procedures, this knowledge is held to have pertinence with regard to the *future*; it is supposed to make the former alien a better citizen.

Any study of the S/C process must sharply differentiate between relevance and pertinence.

Practically all S/C training is deemed to have future pertinence, even if it has past relevance (knowledge of the creation myth or of history) or does not refer to "here." (Hungarians are taught that they came from Turan, which is *still* located in Central Asia.) Now, since most S/C training concerns matters which are *not* "present" H/N and are, moreover, held to have pertinence largely for the future, it is evident that hardly any S/C learning can be strictly of the T/E type. For, in practically all T/E learning, the pertinence (positive reinforcement, reward) is part of a rather *short* temporal configuration. Thus, if one seeks to train a rat to press a lever *in order* to get a pellet of food, the pellet must become available a few seconds after the lever is pressed. If it does not materialize almost at once, the rat seems unable to connect his pressing of the lever with the appearance of the pellet of food. It will, of course, eat the pellet even in that case, but will not experience it as the result or goal (pertinence) of its previous lever-pressing activities; it will probably experience the pellet as a "chance (non-serendipity) find."

This interpretation acquires added significance in the light of the finding that most animal activities which have a remote (future) pertinence, are "instinctive." A certain female wasp paralyzes a caterpillar with her sting and then lays her egg in it. When her egg hatches, it will feed on the paralyzed caterpillar. But one cannot hold that the wasp "planned" this. For the *individual* wasp this happy outcome is not a reward; it is strictly a "species serendipity." Similarly, many spider species weave nets which, as it turns out, will subsequently be useful as traps for their prey. But, since it cannot be held that the *individual* spider intentionally wove a *hunting* net, the net's (future) *usefulness* is, for the *individual* spider, a serendipity. By contrast, if a man manufactures a hunting net, *intending* to use it in the hunt, his net's future usefulness is not a serendipity, but a genuine reward for an H/N effort which had future pertinence.

In Man, S/C training, which is, by definition, held to be future (and/or elsewhere) pertinent, tends to affect even the manner in which he learns (H/N) things that *do* exist H/N. Strange as it may seem, he learns them *as though* they did *not* exist H/N—but only partly because even *this* learning has largely future pertinence. A few examples will clarify this statement:

1. I am studying H/N a book on gravitation. Though gravitation keeps me firmly seated on my chair and prevents the book I am studying from floating off ceilingward, I am

not attending H/N to these H/N manifestations of gravitation. I would attend to them H/N only if there occurred a *perturbation* of the laws of gravitation I am just now reading about.

2. The situation would be exactly the same if I were just now studying a book about the functioning of the lungs. I would attend to the functioning of *my* lungs H/N only if, "inexplicably," I suddenly had an attack of dyspnea.

3. I am studying H/N a paper describing the process of learning through repetition. I would attend to *my* learning H/N about this process only if I realized that the *more* I reread that paper, the *less* I remembered its contents, which would be contrary to what the paper which I am studying describes.

One of the conclusions one may draw from the data just cited is that, unlike animals, "learning Man" is singularly estranged from the present, from here-and-now. I note in particular the extreme rareness of *situations* in which *true* T/E learning (promptly rewarded by an H/N pertinent success) occurs. I found myself in such a situation only once in the course of the last year: my standing lamp ceased to function on a weekend (i.e., at a time when no electrician could be summoned), just before nightfall (i.e., at an hour when a prompt repair of the lamp was imperative: the repair had H/N pertinence). I had to discover, by T/E, how to repair the lamp, *for* an H/N pertinent reward: *in order* not to spend *that* evening in the dark.

I deem it useful to analyse my performance on that occasion in some detail, for it permits me to highlight one special aspect of "intelligent" learning behavior, which I am provisionally inclined to connect with Man's high degree of estrangement from the present, as exemplified by the future pertinence of many of his activities.

In order to repair the lamp, I had to *disassemble* it first, though lamps obviously operate only when properly assembled. In other words, I was, for all practical purposes, obliged to move away from my goal (a once-more-functioning lamp), the better to attain it. An apparent moving away from the goal pursued—the better to attain it—is highly characteristic of many day-to-day human activities. If my front door opens inward, I must first *back away* from the doorway, pulling the door inward, so as to be able to pass easily through the doorway. Similarly, one of the best ways of obtaining certain greatly desired things is, proverbially, "to play hard to get."

Such situations demand the construction of a "social-cultural space" in which what, in Euclidean geometry, *must* be *represented* as a moving away from the objective, *can* be *represented* as a moving toward.

As I indicated twenty years ago (*4*), physics provides us with a model for the construction of such a special "geometry." In Euclidean geometry, the shortest distance between two points, *A* and *B*, is the straight line. But in reality, if *A* and *B* are separated by a mountain, proceeding from *A* to *B* in a straight line (shortest line) obliges one to dig a tunnel through the mountain; this involves a great expenditure of energy. Much less time and energy would be expended if one proceeded from *A* to *B* by walking *around* the mountain, following the valleys, though this may, at times, *increase* one's distance from the goal *B*. In such an "economy-of-effort" geometry, the "shortest" path from *A* to *B* is the one which involves the least expenditure of effort.

It is, I think, only by representing the socio-cultural "space" in a manner which so defines the shortest distance between *A* (situation to be coped with) and *B* (goal pursued by means of that coping) that a provisional and economical (Euclidean) moving away from the objective pursued *during the T/E (coping) period* could be *represented* as a constant decreasing of the distance between *A* and *B*. In fact, socio-cultural space/time can so be conceived that even past/future/elsewhere referable learning, *acquired H/N*, but having primarily a future/elsewhere pertinence, could be so *represented* on such a space/time map—or socio-cultural multidimensional space—that the H/N learning situation would be "situated" in the immediate "vicinity" of the (future/elsewhere) point/event at which that learning will become pertinent (useful). In simpler terms, it is possible to construct a socio-cultural space/time map in which my H/N past referable learning (e.g., that the eclipse of the moon on 27 August 413 B.C. was fatal to an Athenian army) will, in terms of its time axis, be located in the immediate vicinity of the point at which that information will actually be *pertinent* (an examination in ancient history, or my citing this example in the present paper).

Such "geometrically" contrived *temporal contiguities* as regards learning (H/N) something which is *not* H/N relevant (past/future/elsewhere) and will "normally" be pertinent (rewarding) only much later, are less artificial than they may seem. I am thinking here in particular of what is usually called the "timeless" aspect of dreams, but which could, more suitably, be called the "incessant H/N character" of all dream experiences, upon which a *sense* of duration or sequentiality is, in my opinion, *imposed* only during the secondary elaboration represented by the recalling of the dream. I view this matter as follows.

Consider an imaginary dream: *X* dreams that he is escaping from a bandit's lair and is heading for the safety of a friend's home. Let attention now be focused on a *moment* of this dream, during which the dreamer dreams of racing *toward* his friend's home and *away* from the bandit's lair. So stated, my formulation *imputes* to the running dreamer an awareness both of anteriority ("I was [recent past] in a bandit's lair and escaped") and of posteriority ("I am heading toward the [future] safety of a friend's house"). I hold that this formulation distorts the running dreamer's actual experience. The danger represented by the bandit's lair is, in dream, not "situated" in the past: it "exists" as an H/N *present* motivation (of the running). Likewise, at *that* moment of the dream, the prospect of reaching the safe haven of a friend's house is psychologically not situated in the future: it is experienced in dream as a *present* (H/N) striving toward a goal. In fact, though the dreamer dreams of running, *just then*, from the bandit's lair to a friend's house, in his dream experience the lair does not exist elsewhere: it exists as a (subsequently past referred) *present* image ("push"). Similarly, the house of the friend which the runner seeks to reach is *not* situated elsewhere: in dream it exists H/N as a motivating pre-experience (P/E "pull") *while* he dreams of running: it is only later on that it is retroactively future referred.

In fact, since one might just as well be hung for a sheep as for a lamb, I admit that I am not certain that my two cautious phrases—"subsequently past referred" and "subsequently future referred"—are more than somewhat timid attempts to temporize, to achieve some sort of compromise with the indubitable fact that, in the *remembering* of dreams, the events *seem* to be arranged in conformity with the traditional articulation of time into past, present and future. Logically it is very probable that all dream content is originally experienced purely H/N—the "past" perhaps in the form of an "away from" (push) (present) motivation and the "future" perhaps in the form of a "toward" (pull) (present) motivation.

I concede that this interpretation is very difficult to confirm directly. But it appears to shed some light upon the finding, known already to Aischylos (*1*), that long stories can be dreamed in a few minutes only. Also, there exists one phenomenon which may, perhaps, indirectly substantiate this view.

The crucial datum is the impossibility of causing an animal, particularly by means of an H/N experience, to *refer* that experience to the past: an animal can be taught neither history nor autobiography.

A puppy I once owned was in the habit of jumping on my lap and curling up on it. But by the age of about eighteen months, when he weighed 145 pounds, he discovered that he could no longer curl up on my lap. It would be crude anthropomorphization to assume:

1. either that my dog realized that he had grown from 20 pounds to 145 pounds.

2. or that he supposed that I had shrunk in the course of the first eighteen months of his life.

I concede, of course, that after covering the "outward-bound" itinerary *a, b, c, d, e, f,* a cat can "reverse" this sequence and follow an "inward-bound" itinerary *f, e, d, c, b, a.* I even concede that, on its return journey, the cat may take certain shortcuts (e.g., proceeding directly from *e* to *c,* without passing through *d* as it did on its "outward-bound" journey). But, just as in dream the bandit's lair and the friend's house do not seem to be *experienced* in the past or in the future, but have a strictly H/N "existence" even while the dreamer dreams of running *from* the bandit's lair *to* the friend's house, so the basket to which the cat seeks to return is (psychologically) *not* referred to the past; the effort made to reach it (soon, though still in the future) is, likewise, not future pertinent in the sense in which I define this term. Speaking in a deliberately speculative manner, I imagine that the basket to which the cat seeks to return is, *before* it actually gets there, experienced in a *manner* which is the exact reverse of a déjà vu. I realize that this hypothesis may, perhaps, be unprovable; I at least cannot think, for the time being, of an experiment which *could* prove it. But I hold nonetheless that the adoption of some such working hypothesis or thought token greatly simplifies the understanding of how mankind can H/N learn something that has a *sense* only if it is held to be relevant in terms of the past, of the future or of the elsewhere, and has, admittedly, only future pertinence. I recall that I am *not* rewarded H/N for learning H/N the date 1776, the predictions of futurologists or the fact that Mt. Everest "is" elsewhere (in Asia).

And, though I have indicated that one can construct a socio-cultural space/time frame of reference in which H/N learning (especially of a non-H/N relevant fact)—and the future pertinence thereof—can be represented as contiguous, it is nonetheless useful to be able to explain at least two commonplace phenomena (dreaming and the homing "instinct" of animals) *without* imputing to the dreamer or to the cat an authentic awareness of the past and of the future, and even less the capacity to perceive that his (its) H/N learning activities are clearly future pertinent.

These considerations bring me to a final difficulty. Though most S/C relevant teaching (communication) and learning occurs H/N, without real T/E, it is (as noted) strictly future (and elsewhere) pertinent *only*. Thus, one can teach the sixth commandment, forbidding adultery, to a six-year-old boy, though his learning *that* commandment H/N is not likely to be useful (or, indeed, meaningful) to him until several more years have gone by.

But even this is not the main problem. Nearly all S/C training concerns a hypothetical (if probable) future, rather than a *certain* one.

If I learn to swim H/N in fresh water, it is absolutely predictable that I will be able to swim even better if and when I have occasion to swim in salt water.

By contrast, in times of rapid change—especially if it is deliberately and masochistically of an anomic, driftlike type —nearly all S/C learning (acquired *in the belief* that it is future pertinent) ceases, when the "future" comes around at last, to have pertinence: the rules of the game will have changed or (in anomic situations) will have been abolished entirely. Hence, S/C type of knowledge learned (H/N) in the *expectation* that it will be rewarded twenty years hence, may, by that time, become a handicap or even be penalized. Persons trained to become (well-rewarded) model citizens of *one kind* of society may end up on the gallows of the *next* society. Even future pertinent inhibitions, learned H/N, may become severe handicaps. Percival was taught that proper gentlemen do not ask personal questions. But his failure to question the ailing Fisher-King about his illness prevented him from finding the Holy Grail on his first attempt; he found it only after he had learned to discard his gentlemanly discretion.

Another, particularly striking, example may also be cited:

1. Twenty years ago even non-virginal girls claimed to be virgins.

2. Nowadays some authentic virgins claim to be promiscuous.

Tempora mutantur et nos mutamur in illis.

Such observations oblige one to ask whether S/C training continues to be useful—or even possible—when it is likely to become counterproductive by the time the future, to which it *supposedly* pertained *when* it was learned, comes around—when the future, *for the sake of which* that S/C was acquired, proves to be unmanageable by means of the S/C tools one had acquired. Can one *really* persuade the young that saving one's money is worth one's while at a time when inflation destroys the purchasing power of one's savings? Can S/C *responsibly* condition people to be truthful, loving and considerate when what is manifestly more and more rewarded is lying, selfishness and brutality? One even wonders whether one can teach the worthwhileness of the effort to think rationally when, in many places, even psychoanalysis itself—the one science which studies the irrational rationally—is lapsing into a near-delusional rhetoric.

The finding that the rapid obsolescence and long-term counterproductivity of all or most S/C learned "socal reflexes" necessarily undermine also the sublimatory mechanisms does not revive but invalidates more than ever the traditional confusion of adjustment (a sociological concept) with sanity (a psychological concept) (6, Ch. 1); moreover, it does not violate the principle of complementarity. Indeed, it stands to reason that sanity (which includes sublimation) facilitates adjustment to a *sane* (i.e., person-centered, rather than society-centered) milieu and vice versa. Hence, the highlighting of the socio-culturally and personally deleterious effects of an overly rapid obsolescence of all or most S/C learned social reflexes does not constitute a plea for social stand-patism and for a personal refusal of maturation (6).

The crucial consideration is that many of the psycho-

logical processes that make future-pertinent S/C learning
possible—the renunciation of immediate and direct gratification, the acquisition of foresight and even of the sense
of historical time (*infra*), etc.—are, for all practical purposes, *also* processes that make *sublimation* (a uniquely
species-characteristic potentiality of Man) possible in the
first place. A situation in which all or most S/C learned social
reflexes become counterproductive necessarily undermines
also the capacity to sublimate, thereby dehumanizing Man.

S/C learned social reflexes (which include efficient ap-
praisals of situations) are admittedly acquired at a particular
moment and in a particular socio-cultural setting. This
means that they can be "good," "bad" or "indifferent,"
either in terms of a universal ideal ethic or in terms of a particular ethos at a given point in time. By contrast, sublimation—and the *capacity* to sublimate—are unconditionally
"good" and even indispensable in terms of any ethic, ethos
or point of view which presupposes that Man's humanity is
a sine qua non basis of society and culture on the one hand
and of personal self-actualization through maturation on
the other hand, simply because society/culture and the
human psyche are co-emergents (6).

No society—not even a commando or a group of trance-
dancers—can exist even during a short span of time without
a minimum of sublimation. Thus, were the aggressiveness
of the members of a commando totally uninhibited, the
slightest jostling would elicit an immediate murderous
reaction: aggression would not be redirected at the foe, i.e.,
postponed until the actual raid begins. But even this is not
the whole story, though—as I will show below—society dis-
integrates and anomie arises when all or most S/C learning,
acquired in the belief that it is future pertinent, ceases to be
rewarded and may even be penalized. For, beyond a
sociological concern for the preservation of society and a
psychological concern for the person made intolerably
anxious—and even destroyed—by his realization that he is
totally disoriented because his S/C acquired techniques of

reality testing (correct definition of the situation) turn out to be misleading and his social reflexes—acquired through (supposedly future pertinent) S/C learning—prove to be maladjustive, there must be a sociological concern for the steady improvement of society and a psychological concern for the expansion and stabilization of Man's humanity.

In short, all these decisive problems must be reconsidered in the light of the radical distinction I first made over forty years ago (in a seminar report) between sanity and adjustment—stressing subsequently that the main criterion of sanity is the capacity for a continuous *creative* readjustment (6), without a loss of one's sense of selfhood ("temporal Ego") (3, 5).

This finding leads me to consider in detail the problem of Time.

According to Leibniz, time is the order of events. But it must be specified at once that for Leibniz an "event" was not a mere "happening," because for him the term "order" had a meaning. And I hasten to add that *that* meaning is not abolished even by the most probabilitarian modern theories of causality.

Though I somewhat oversimplify matters, it suffices, in the first approximation, to differentiate here between two conceptions of Time: the conception of the chronicle writer, who simply lists—strings together—what he considers (in a way) as (random) happenings, and the conception of the historian, who elucidates objectively the *order* of events and the *nature* of that order which also gives a meaning to the events. And I note that, at present, the dominant historical perspective is radically false, and much of the rest little more than chronicle writing. But that is by the way.

What matters is that responsible and rewarding S/C teaching/learning is possible only within the framework of an authentic and valid *historical conception of time*. Where socio-cultural change is viewed as a random sequence of happenings, all S/C—which, as noted, *necessarily* passes from one mind to another—becomes inherently irrational.

If a situation arises in which the *concrete* knowledge and experience of the elders becomes—as Margaret Mead says (*8*)—irrelevant to the young, society is headed for the anomie of the pseudonymous Ik tribe of Africa (*11*), where, as among animals, nearly all learning seems to be of the T/E type and nearly all behavior appears improvised —irrelevant for both past and future and for elsewhere— devoid of all true future pertinence. In that tribe—and in similar situations—all "coping" is related to H/N situations only: to random happenings in the chronicler's unilinear, overmeticulous and *therefore* fractured time chaos. And one must firmly bear in mind that situations resembling that of the Ik tribe have existed throughout history—from the Athenian plague, as described by Thoukydides (*10*), to modern concentration camps—but nearly always only in the most marginal areas of society, or else during relatively brief and notoriously catastrophic periods of history.

The present generation of adults may not be able to transmit to the next one any particular *recipe* of the S/C type, learnable H/N, though rewarding only in the long run (future pertinent). But it *can* and *must* transmit to the next generation a *sense of*—or feeling for—the crucial socio-cultural *and individual* importance of a non-T/E type H/N learning that has a *genuine* future pertinence, *whatever* that H/N learning and that future may be. Unless my generation accomplishes this, the very concepts "society" and "culture"—and even the concept of "person"—will lose any meaning whatever, and the structures corresponding to them will cease to exist, as (for all practical purposes) they have ceased to exist in the Ik tribe, except for the sharing of a language and of a ghetto territory.

Thus, paradoxical as it may seem, it is *precisely* in times of excessively rapid and almost anomic socio-cultural change that the depositaries of a *human* future are not the young, but the adults: they alone have had—for however short a time, and however tragically—the *actual* experience of an S/C learning (H/N), which had a *real* future pertinence.

Deprived of this senior-mediated S/C *experience*, there is no alternative for the young but to cross the Ik desert and then to reconstitute slowly a generation capable of devising and experiencing a future-pertinent S/C teaching/learning and of mediating it (H/N) to the young. For the cornerstone of human existence is Time—history, if one prefers: an articulation of the H/N with the past, the future and the elsewhere. That historians *are* beginning to grapple with the basic notion of Time, is shown by a magnificent recent study of Alain Besançon (2), who is my friend and also—not by chance, as he himself stresses—one of my former students.

In my experience, the present crisis does not have at its root a refusal of the young to learn—but the refusal of some of their "disillusioned" seniors to teach and to assume their responsibilities. And, as one who has learned and still learns much from her writings, even if he often comes up with very different conclusions, I attest that Margaret Mead at least has never ceased teaching her juniors *in a future-pertinent manner*.

This is logically unquestionable: in terms of Bertrand Russell's (9) theory of mathematical types a teaching concerning the irrelevance of *all* teaching is not applicable to itself. Thus, without Margaret Mead's most recent teachings concerning the *irrelevance* of the teachings of the adults, this essay—whose greater part goes back to drafts written in the early 1930's—would not have crystallized into a paper written in honor of one whose teachings are and remain future pertinent.

For it is the role of adults to *mold* all that is otherwise only a socio-cultural drift, into history and then into tradition. This role Margaret Mead has fulfilled: like Herodotos' Persians, she taught her contemporaries and her juniors alike "to shoot straight and to speak the truth."

Bibliography

(*1*) Aischylos: *Agamemnon*, vs. 893 ff.

(*2*) Besançon, Alain: *Histoire et Expérience du Moi*, chap. 4, Paris, 1971.

(*3*) Devereux, George: *Reality and Dream: The Psychotherapy of a Plains Indian*, New York, 1951 (2nd augm. ed., 1969).

(*4*) Idem: *Therapeutic Education*, New York, 1956.

(*5*) Idem: Transference, Screen Memory and the Temporal Ego, *Journal of Nervous and Mental Disease*, 143:318–323, 1966.

(*6*) Idem: *Essais d'Ethnopsychiatrie Générale*, Paris, 1970, 1972, 1977.

(*7*) Köhler, Wolfgang: *The Mentality of Apes*, New York, 1927.

(*8*) Mead, Margaret: *Culture and Commitment, A Study of the Generation Gap*, New York, 1970.

(*9*) Russell, Bertrand: *Principles of Mathematics*, Cambridge, Eng., 1903.

(*10*) Thoukydides: *The Peloponnesian War*, II, 47 ff.

(*11*) Turnbull, Colin: *The Mountain People*, New York, 1972.

Permissions and
Bibliographic Indications

Chapter 1 fuses two of my articles: "Social Time: A Methodological and Functional Analysis," *American Journal of Sociology*, 43:967–969, 1938, and "A Conceptual Scheme of Society," *American Journal of Sociology*, 45:687–706, 1940. They are reprinted by permission of the University of Chicago Press, owner of that periodical.

Chapter 2 was published, in French, under the same title, in *Revue de Médicine Psychosomatique*, 8:101–113, 1966. It is republished here by permission of that periodical.

Chapter 3 constituted originally the fourth chapter of the second part of George Devereux: *A Study of Abortion in Primitive Societies*, New York, Julian Press, 1955 (2nd augm. ed., New York, International Universities Press, 1976). Copyright © 1955 and 1976, by George Devereux.

Chapter 4 was originally published under the same title in *Transactions of the New York Academy of Sciences*, Series 2, 7:110–130, 1945. It is republished here by permission of the New York Academy of Sciences from its *Transactions*.

Chapter 5 was first published under the same title in Kaplan, Bert (ed.): *Studying Personality Cross-Culturally*, Evenston, Ill., Row, Peterson & Co., 1961. Copyright © 1961. It is republished here by permission of Harper & Row Publishers, Inc. It was published also in Smelser, N. J., and Smelser, W. T. (eds.): *Personality and Social Systems*, New York, John Wiley & Sons, Inc., 1963, and, subsequently, in a second edition of that anthology.

Chapter 6 was written at the request of Professors George De Vos (University of California, Berkeley) and Theodore Schwartz (University of California, San Diego) for the symposium on *Ethnic Identity: Cultural*

314   *Ethnopsychoanalysis*

Continuity and Change, Burg Wartenstein (Austria), Symposium No. 51
(Sept. 5–13, 1970) of the Wenner-Gren Foundation for Anthropological
Research, New York. The original text was reproduced by offset for the
exclusive use of the members of that symposium by the Wenner-Gren
Foundation (New York, 1970). It is republished here by permission of
Professors George De Vos and Theodore Schwartz, both in their capacity
as organizers of that symposium and on behalf of the Wenner-Gren
Foundation under whose auspices that colloquium was held. That sym-
posium was published as a whole in G. De Vos and L. Romanucci-Ross
(eds.): *Ethnic Identity*, Stanford, Mayfield Publishing Co., 1975.

Chapter 7 was published, in French, under the title "Considérations Ethno-
psychanalytiques sur la Notion de Parenté," in *L'Homme*, 5:224–247,
1965, and is republished here by permission of Mr. Jean Pouillon, General
Secretary of *L'Homme*, acting on behalf of the editorial board of that
periodical.

Chapter 8, written in collaboration with the late Dr. E. M. Loeb, was first
published under the same title in the *American Sociological Review*, 7:133–
147, 1943. It is republished here by permission of the late Dr. E. M. Loeb
(co-author) and by permission of the American Sociological Association,
whose official organ that periodical is.

Chapter 9 was first published under the same title in the *American Anthropologist* (n.s.), 59:1036–1045, 1957. It is republished here by permission of
the American Anthropological Association, whose official organ that
periodical is.

Chapter 10 was published first under the same title in *Psychiatry*, 21:359–
374, 1958. Copyright © by the William A. White Psychiatric Foundation,
whose official organ that periodical is.

Chapter 11 is not included in the French, Spanish and Italian editions of
this book. It was first published in *Ethos*, as part of a special issue in honor
of Professor Margaret Mead. It is reprinted here by permission of the
editors and of the University of California Press.

I wish to thank all persons, periodicals, scientific societies, foundations
and publishers who permitted me to republish my articles. I reserve all
rights to the additions, changes and transpositions effected in the
present text.

Name Index

The name index includes persons as well as mythological and literary characters. Names of tribes and other groups of people are listed in the Index of Geographical Names and Peoples.

Abel, Niels Henrik, 67
Abraham (biblical character), 166
Abraham, Karl, 139
Abû Huraïra, 241
Adler, Polly, 184
Adonis, 155
Agamemnon, 161, 186n
Ahma Humāre, 251–253, 257, 259–260
Ahriman, 289
Ailianos, Klaudios, 209
Aischylos, 5n, 304
Alkibiades, 161n
Alkman, 168
Allport, G. W., 110
Amos (biblical character), 240
Anaxandridas, king of Sparta, 161
Angyal, András, 223n
Anne of Austria, queen of France, 138
Antiochus Epiphanes, king of Syria, 171
Appuleius, 192n, 207
Archimedes, 68
Aristeas of Prokonnesos, 80
Aristeides, 149
Aristophanes, 192n
Aristoteles, 209
Artemis, 156n
Aspasia, 171
Aspinwall, Judith, xi

Badé, W. F., 240
Bain, Read, 222, 230
Bakchylides, 190

Barber, Bernard, 242
Barbey, d'Aurevilly, Jules, 195n
Bartók, Béla, 161
Barton, G. A., 239, 240n
Bastian, Adolf, 74–75
Beauvillier, Marie-Louise de, 204–205
Beauvillier, Paul, Duke of, 204–205
Beethoven, Ludwig van, 262n
Bell, E. T., 267
Benedek, Therese, 181
Besançon, Alain, xi, 14, 311
Bidney, David, 88–89, 90
Bleek, D. F., 155
Blum, H. F., 25
Boas, Franz, 12n
Bohr, Niels, 18, 51; and complementarity, 9, 16–17, 24–25, 39, 110, 151; *Abtötungsprinzip* of, 16; and indeterminacy, 72.
Boltzmann, Ludwig, 28
Bólyai, Janos, 44
Bonaparte, Princess Marie, 156, 195
Bourbons, 43
Brantôme, Pierre de Bourdeilles, Seigneur de, 207
Brasidas, 146, 150–153
Braudel, Fernand, x
Breuer, Josef, 16–17, 139
Briand, Claude, xi
Brown, J. F., 21, 24, 38

Cannon, W. B., 30
Cantor, Georg, 67

Carrel, Alexis, 58
Casals, Pablo, 262n
Catherine II, empress of Russia, 184n
Catullus, Gaius Valerius, 192n
Charlemagne, 235
Chilon, 161
Chomsky, Noam, 3, 6n, 12
Churchill, Winston, 232
Clausewitz, Karl von, 233-234
Condé, Louis II de Bourbon, Prince de, 167-168
Cuvier, Georges, 26
Cyrano de Bergerac, Savinien de, 81

Davidson, Ronald, x
Day, Richard, x
Dedekind, Richard, 53, 61
Descartes, René, 41
Desdemona, 256
Diodoros the Sicilian, 194, 195n, 223, 259
Dirac, Paul, 267
Dodds, E. R., 160, 292
Dollard, John, 167, 220
Donnan, F. G., 25, 30, 32, 43, 46n, 50, 72
Dover, Sir K. J., 192n
Du Bois, Cora, 189n
Durkheim, Émile, 21, 31-32, 63, 66, 67, 70, 90, 94, 106, 167, 259, 266

Echetos, 192n
Ehrenberg, Rudolf, 25
Einstein, Albert, 41, 139, 284-285
Elizabeth II, queen of England, 138
Empedokles, 292
Epameinondas, 164
Epimenides, 16, 69n, 103, 140-141, 145
Euclid (Eukleides), 44, 284-285
Euripides: *Bakchai*, 139; *Elektra*, 163; *Andromache*, 164; *Hekabe*, 164n

Faraday, Michael, 36
Farrère, Claude: *La Marche Funèbre*, 184
Fechner, Gustav Theodor, 53
Feldman, S. S., 75
Fenichel, Otto, 288
Ferenczi, Sándor, 139, 189n, 224
Fermi, Enrico, 245n
Foucault, Michel, 13
Fournier, Professor, 237
Franklin, W. S., 29, 33

Freud, Sigmund, 5, 16, 63, 74, 139, 184, 206, 240, 241, 265, 275; *Standard Edition* of, 17; P. Jordan's comments on, 17-18; and the Superego, 49; and methodology, 66-67, 70; and modern culturalists, 116; the individual studied by, 121; *Totem and Taboo*, 177, 178; and the narcissism of small differences, 223, 259; and thought models, 267; and the primary death instinct, 288; and repetition compulsion dreams, 288-289; and telepathy, 291
Fromm, Erich, 223, 293
Fuller, J. F. C., 232

Gandhi, Mohandas K., 242
Gaulle, Charles de, 232
Gauss, K. F., ix
Gellius, Aulus, 80
Genghis Khan, 55, 193
Gibbs, Josiah Willard, 28, 32
Gobard, Henri, xi
Goldenweiser, Alexander, 73-74
Goodwin, Grenville, 238
Gorer, Geoffrey, 2n
Göring, Hermann Wilhelm, 139, 242
Guggenheim, E. A., 25, 72

Haber, Fritz, 227
Habsburg-Lorraine, the Archduchess Marie-Louise de, empress of the French, 196n
Hallowell, A. I., 88-89, 90, 91
Hamā Utcē, 249, 252, 255-259
Hamilton, Sir William Rowan, 29
Hamlet, 189n
Hannibal, 235
Harav Hēya, 251, 257-259
Hardenburg, W. E., 196n
Haynau, Baron Julius von (Austrian general), 160
Heifetz, Jascha, 262
Heisenberg, Werner, 9, 16-17, 39, 45, 72
Hempel, C. G., 110
Henderson, L. J., 30
Henley, William Ernest, 289
Herakles, 190-191
Herodotus, 311
Herskovits, M. J., 216
Herzl, Theodor, 147
Hess, René, xi

Hinkle, L. E., Jr., 59
Hitler, Adolf, 139
Homeros (Homer): *Iliad*, 159, 171n
Horatius (Horace), 192n
Horney, Karen, 280
Horthy, Nicholas (regent of Hungary), 123, 129
Hosea, 240
Hume, David, 27

Ishi, 234

Jacob (biblical character), 197
Jeans, Sir James, 25, 72
Jebb, Sir Richard C., 190
Jenkins, Richard L., 277
Jolas, Tina, xi
Jones, Ernest, 74, 80, 189n
Jordan, Camille, 35n, 49, 50, 53, 60, 61
Jordan, Pascual, 17–18, 25, 51, 72
Jung, Carl Gustav, 75, 294
Justinus: *Epitome of the History of Trogus Pompeius*, 184

Kane, F., 124
Kardiner, Abram, 94, 102n, 106, 109, 225
Kassandra, 186n
Kelly, W. H., 90
Kelvin, Lord William Thomson, 36
Kleomenes I, king of Sparta, 157, 161
Kluckhohn, Clyde, 90, 95, 98, 104, 259
Kluckhohn, Florence, 89
Köhler, Wolfgang, 298–299
Kritias, 165
Kroeber, Alfred Louis, 119, 158, 162, 183–184, 250, 251; on the Mohave, 199–200; on stimulus diffusion, 216, 225–228
Kubilai Khan, 235

Lagrange, Count Joseph Louis, 69n
Lavoisier, Antoine Laurent, 268
Le Bon, Gustave, 21
Le Chatelier, Henry, 245n
Lear, King, 269
Leibnitz, Freiherr Gottfried Wilhelm von, 23, 24, 33, 42, 309
Lenzen, V. F., 29, 46n, 271
Lévi-Strauss, Claude, xi, 12, 81, 177–179, 191–193, 196, 201n, 211
Lewin, Kurt, 21
Lewis, G. N., 25, 33

Linton, Ralph, 22, 64, 90, 102n, 109, 142, 216–217, 222n, 226, 261n, 279
Livius, Titus (Livy), 104
Lobachevski, Nikolai Ivanovitch, 44
Loeb, Edwin M., xi, 75, 157
Loeb, L. B., 46n
Loewenstein, R. M., 290
Louis XIV, king of France, 31, 160n, 167
Louis XVI, king of France, 235
Loukianos, Lucian, 81
Lowie, R. H., 181, 209, 218

MacCrone, I. D., 224
McDougall, William, 21
Mach, Ernst, 37, 40
MacIver, R. M., 233, 234
Marbe, Karl, 266
Marcuse, Herbert, 293
Maria Theresa, queen of Hungary, 138
Marx, Karl, 170, 241
Mauss, Marcel, 165, 191, 259; *Essai sur le Don*, 180
Maxwell, J. C., 23, 36, 40
May, Mark A., 95
Mead, Margaret, 310–311
Menelaos, 161, 164
Merton, R. K., 33, 35–36, 236
Meyer, Adolf, 285
Meyerson, Emile, 22, 96, 98, 99
Milch, Erhard, 139, 242
Milne, A. E., 35
Mohammed, 157, 241
Molière, Jean Baptiste Poquelin, 282
Montaigne, Michel de, 63
Moore, Sir John, 232
Mowrer, O. H., 95, 98, 104

Napoleon I, 98, 101, 102, 108, 143, 196n, 229, 232, 235
Neurath, Otto, 21
Newton, Sir Isaac, 26, 33, 267, 284–285
Ninus, king of Assyria, 194

Odysseus, 159, 186n, 192
Ollier, François, 164
Onnes (Assyrian general), 194
Orestes, 161, 189n
Ormuzd, 289
Othello, 252, 256

Pareto, Vilfredo, 30, 42, 223
Park, R. E., 224n

Parsons, E. C., 226, 239
Parsons, Talcott, 166
Pasteur, Louis, 281
Patton, George S., Jr., 291
Paul, Saint, 201n
Peirce, S. S., 36
Percival, 306
Perikles, 162, 163, 171
Pétain, Henri Philippe, 159n
Petőfi (Petrovics), Sándor, 160
Petzgold, Joseph, 26
Philarchos, 194
Pirenne, Henri, 235–236
Platon (Plato), 88, 135, 165, 275
Plinius the Elder (Pliny), 80, 210
Ploutarchos, 81, 149, 164; *On the Bravery of Women*, 142. *See also* Pseudo-Ploutarchos
Poe, Edgar Allan: *The Purloined Letter*, 71; *The System of Dr. Tarr and Professor Fether*, 282
Poincaré, Henri, 1, 21, 38, 44, 86, 267
Priamos, 192n
Pseudo-Ploutarchos, 194. *See also* Ploutarchos
Pulyīk, 251, 255, 256, 259, 261, 262
Pythagoras, 292

Rákosi, Mátyás, 129
Redfield, Robert, 216
Rhine, J. B., 27
Richmond, C. A., 33
Riemann, Georg Friedrich Bernhard, 44, 284–285
Róheim, Géza, 74, 103, 146–147, 202, 271
Rousseau, Jean Jacques, 41
Rubenstein, B. B., 181
Russell, Bertrand, 16, 69, 72, 86, 97, 98, 173, 311; and personality theory, 101–103, 108, 140, 143

Sahaykwisā, 10–11
Saint-Simon, Louis de Rouvroy, 204–205
Schrödinger, Erwin, 27, 28, 43
Sequoya, 158, 227

Shakespeare, William, 252, 253, 256, 269
Shaw, Ruth Faison, 80
Shimkin, D. B., 242
Snell, Bruno, 190
Sokrates, 92, 164
Solon, 165
Sophokles, 168
Sorokin, P. A., 24, 30, 33, 35, 36, 236, 237, 266
Sosibios, 168
Spinden, Herbert, 74
Spiro, Melford E., 212
Stalin, Joseph, 170
Strabon, 156n
Sumner, W. G., 218

Tarquinius, Sextus, 195n
Thales, 292
Themistokles, 149
Thomas, W. I., 224n
Thoukydides, 310
Timperley, H. J., 194n
Tolman, E. C., 113
Tolman, R. C., 32, 44–45
Trogus Pompeius, 184
Tyrtaios, 168

Vajda, Georges, 157, 241
Valerius Maximus, 192n
Varro, M. T., 210
Veblen, Osvald, 23
Veblen, Thorstein, 243
Volterra, Vito, 32, 42, 43

Wallis, Louis, 239
Weber, Ernst Heinrich, 53
Webster, Hutton, 35
Weyl, Hermann, 24, 38
White, W. A., 21
Wolff, H. G., 59

Xenophanes, 265
Xenophon, 165, 192n

Young, Kimball, 224

Index of Geographical
Names and Peoples

Achaian: Atreids, 161; identity, 161, 164; period, 162
Africa, 228, 235; "Afro" hairstyle, 155; practices regarding female genitals among tribes in, 156–157; ownership of fertile cows in, 221. *See also* Bushmen; Hottentots; Ik tribe
Aleut, 79
American Revolution, 232, 299
Americans: neurotic and normal, 75; modal personality of, 100–103, 105, 106, 108–111, 119–120; ethnic identity of, 148, 172; Southern, 167, 220; and dissociative acculturation, 242; geographical mobility of, 278; and immigrants, 278–280. *See also* Blacks, American; Indians, American; United States
Annamites, 141, 229
Apache Indians, 232, 238
Arabs, 158, 229, 239, 243, 293; Persianization of, 235; dissociative acculturation of relative to Jews and Christians, 241. *See also* Mohammedans
Aranda. *See* Arunta
Arizona, 273
Armenians, 159
Arunta, 142, 202, 289
Aryans, 139; "honorary," 139, 242
Assyria, 239
Athenians, 144, 146, 149, 168, 171, 242; ethnic identity of, 161–165; republicanism of, 179
Athens, 275; Greekness of, 162; plague in, 310
Attike, 162, 169

Australian natives, 194, 197, 205. *See also* Arunta
Austria, 148, 160

Babylonia, 239
Bantu, 155
Barbarians, 161
Betsileo, 106
Blacks, American, 142, 155, 220–221
Boer War, 232
Bohemian (Czech) aristocrats, 148
Brazil, 221
Burma, 233
Bushmen, 154–155, 220
Byblos, 239
Byzantium, 259

California, 273
Canaan, 155, 157, 239–240
Cape York Eskimo, 30, 141n
Capua, 235
Carthage, 239
Catholics, 122, 148, 201n
Central Asia, 299
Chassidim, 158
Cherokee Indians, writing system of, 158, 227
Cheyenne Indians, 75
China, 81n, 235; manufacture of porcelain in, 226. *See also* Gin Ling College, Shanghai.
Chinese, 235; pigtail as token of ethnic identity of, 158; marriage of "Chinese Twins," 204; invention of gunpowder by, 237
Christians, 157, 241
Circum-Pacific groups, 80

Colorado River, 198, 274
Comanche Indians, 43
Communists, 125, 283
Cretans, 103n, 140-141, 145
Cubans, 143
Cyprus, 239
Czech (Bohemian) aristocrats, 148

Dorians, 161-164, 190
Dutch, former colonial laws of, 221

Echetos, 192n
Egypt, 178, 292
Epeiros (Epirus), 192n-193n
Ephesians, 156n
Eskimo of Cape York, 30, 141n
Ethiopia, 239
Europe, 226, 229, 278; cultural borrowing in, 227; science of, 283; psychiatrists from, in the U.S., 280

Fiji, 23, 78
Florence, merchants of, 229
France, 31, 168, 235, 280
French and Indian Wars, 232
Frenchmen, 109, 168, 237; typical, 98, 101, 102, 108, 143; French Jews, 158-159; physicists, 267; "Bohemian," 280

Genoese, 221
Germanic tribes, 235
Germans, 104, 267. *See also* Nazis
Germany, 139, 219, 227, 231, 280; military forces of, 170, 232-233
Gin-Ling College, Shanghai, 194n
Great Britain, 138, 229, 230; military forces of, 232-233; "Oxford accent" in, 243
Greeks, 104n; language of, 5n; ancient, 92-93, 153, 159, 161, 178, 184, 192n; Levantine, 159; literature of, 159, 171n, 190-191, 252n, 289; city-states of, 162-163, 165; homosexuality in literature of, 190-191; and European culture, 227, 236; and negative dissociative acculturation, 243; and "battle of the iota," 260; and the "contest of shamans" motif, 262; gods of, 266; thought models of, 266; science of, 268-269, 292-293. *See also* Athenians; Cretans;

Dorians; Helots; Korinthians; Spartans
Greenwich Village, 275, 294
Gypsy music, 161

Hebrews (including Israelites), 219; sources of dietary laws of, 155-156; kingship among, 232; sources of sex morality in religion of, 239-240. *See also* Israel; Jews
Helots, 144, 157, 161, 165, 169, 221. *See also* Spartans
Hopi Indians, 90, 143, 238, 239; notion of "un-Hopi" among, 90, 244
"Hottentot" apron, 157
Hottentots, 114
Hungarian Revolution of 1956, 116, 122-133
Hungarians: motivations of Hungarian freedom fighters, 116, 122-133; ethnic identity of, 146-148, 156, 160-161; Catholic aristocrats as, 148; language of, 154; kymass-drinking by, 156; and gypsy music, 161; traditional Turanian origin of, 299
Hungary, 147-148; Austrianization of, 148

Ik tribe, 310, 311
Indians, American, 43, 51, 242; and dissociative acculturation, 238-239. *See also* Apache Indians; Hopi Indians; Mohave Indians; Plains Indians; *and other specific tribes or nations*
Indochina. *See* Moi tribes; Rhadé Moi; Sedang Moi
Ishtar cult, 239
Israel, 142, 159, 172, 236, 239. *See also* Hebrews; Jews
Israelites. *See* Hebrews
Italian-Americans, 148
Italy, 220
Ithake, 192n

Japanese: *sumo* wrestlers, 81n; as "honorary Aryans," 139, 242; in war, 194n, 233; and Westernization, 230-231
Jews, 147, 157, 159; and Nazis, 104, 125-126, 139, 158; Chassidic, 142, 158; ethnic personality of, 142;

Israeli, 142; and Arabs, 158, 241; ethnic identity of, 158, 171–172; and Star of David, 158; and relevant class identity, 172; and dissociative acculturation, 239, 243; and the biblical thought model, 290. *See also* Hebrews; Israel

Kallatiai of India, 243
Kenya, 156
Keraki, 205
Kesar Island, 30
Khoisan women, 157. *See also* Bushmen; Hottentots
Kiowa, 205
Korinthians, 162

Leuktra, 164
Levantine Greek, 159

Macedonians, 93
Madagascar, 219
Malay, 55–56, 219, 221, 228–229
Malta, 239
Manchu, 158, 235
Maori, 75, 79, 82, 179n, 259
Masai, 78
Mecca, 228, 245
Melanesians, 155
Melos, 162
Menomini Indians, 287
Mentawei Islanders, 219
Midianites, 219, 239
Milesians, 292
Moab, 239
Moguls, 235
Mohammedans, 55, 158, 221, 235, 241. *See also* Arabs
Mohave Indians, 90, 91, 98, 103–105, 113, 147, 150, 168, 179n, 249; as witches, 10–11, 119, 200; cultural mandates of, 119; ethnic personality of, 146; ethnic identity of, 151–152; sex and marriage among, 183, 184, 188–189, 197–201, 209; divorce among, 198, 199; as shamans, 249–263; anus pain group of illnesses among, 251, 256–257, 260, 261; psychiatric ideas of, 273–276; creation myth of, 274–275; theory of depression among, 276
Moi tribes, 154. *See also* Rhadé Moi; Sedang Moi

Mongols, 55, 235
Muria, 240n

Nabathea, 239
Naga, 184
Navaho Indians, 238
Nazis, 104, 125, 130, 139, 147, 158, 174, 229, 235; and Jews, 158, 172; and acculturation, 233–234, 241–242; sciolism of, 283. *See also* Germans; Germany
New York (city and state of), 37, 184, 208
Nordics, 219
North America, "contest of shamans" motif in, 262

Palestine, 239
Pawnee Indians, 43
Pelasgians, 162
Peloponnesian War, 162, 163, 168
Perioikians, 169
Persians, 79, 167, 241, 311
Philippines, 228
Philistines, 239
Phoenicia, 239
Phokis, 163
Pima-Papago Indians, 239
Pitcairn Island, 30
Plains Indians, 168, 193, 222, 255n; marriage customs among, 208–209; Ghost Dance religion of, 242–243
Poles, 158
Polynesians, 227
Portuguese, 221
Pueblo Indians, 239

Rhadé Moi, 209n
Romans, 104, 125, 159–160, 171, 192n, 235, 241; European cultural borrowings from, 227, 236
Rumania, 147–148
Russia, 230
Russians: and Hungarian freedom fighters, 125, 129, 130; and ethnic identity, 170, 172

Sakai of Malaya, 228–229
Salamis, 242
Sardis, 194
Sedang Moi of Indochina, ix, 79, 80, 103, 104, 141n, 165–166, 183n, 195n,

229; pseudo-scientific theories of, 270–273
Semiramis, 194
Semites, 239
Shanghai, 194n
Shoshoni, Wind-River, 242, 243
Siberia, 262
Sicily, 239
Silk Road, 221
Skythians, 157
Smyrniots, 194
Spain, 235
Spartans, 94, 104, 221; as a class, 136; ethnic personality of, 142, 144, 146, 149, 151; ethnic identity of, 145, 146–147, 150, 152–154, 157, 160–165, 168–171, 174; sayings of, 149, 151, 160. *See also* Helots
Sphakteria, 164
Sweden, 184

Tanala, 219, 222
Thebans, 153, 162
Thebes, 164
Tibet, 228
Trobriand Islanders, 202, 240n, 266
Turan, 299

United States, 30; Constitution of, 39, 121–122; notion of "un-American"

in, 90, 244; society of, 122; courts of, 124; western frontier of, 126; sex attitudes in, 210, 222; military forces of, 220, 232–234; and the Westernization of Japan, 230; Deep South of, 231; "American Way of Life" in, 234, 278, 280; role of "adjustment" in, 277; psychoanalysis in, 282. *See also* Americans; Blacks, American; Indians, American

Vandals, 235
Venetians, 221
Versailles, Treaty of, 219
Vienna, 67, 148; neurotics of, 63, 65, 75; middle class of, 66
Visigoths, 235

White Anglo-Saxon Protestant (WASP), 148
Witoto Indians, 196n

Yahi, 234
Yuma Indians, 168
Yuman tribes, 198, 239
Yurok, 150, 208

Zafimaniry Tanala, 219. *See also* Tanala
Zuni Indians, 239

General Index

"A" and "any," distinction between, 97n, 109

Abduction, 211; and pursuit, simulated, 196

Abortion, 64–65, 67, 70; typology of practices pertaining to, 77–79; motivations for, 81–83, 177n; methods of among Menomini Indian women, 287

Abstract summation, 89–93

Abtötungsprinzip (principle of destruction), 9, 10, 13, 14, 16, 18, 25

Acculturation, 74, 218, 221; defined, 216–217. *See also* Antagonistic acculturation

Acte gratuit, 6

Action: traditional patterns of, 82; conjugate, or cooperative, or parallel, 114; criminal and legitimate, 178–179

Actualization, 131–132, 134; subjective, 76; of ethnic personality, 143–144, 150; and ethnic identity, 151

Adaptability, 43

Adjustment, 277–281; using cultural material for neurotic ends, 261; as opposed to sanity, 276, 307, 309

Adoption: of human beings by a spirit, 272; of means (*see* Means)

Affectivity, 58

"Afro" hairstyle, 155

Age differences, and marriage among the Mohave, 198, 200–201

Aggression, anal, 192n

Alienness, 280. *See also* Immigrants

"All" and "every," distinction between, 110

Alloplastic activities, 157, 158, 244–245

Alloplastic adjustment, 244n–245n

American Revolution, 232, 299

Amoeba, 57

Analytic variables, 97, 99

Animals, and modal personality, 104. *See also* Dogs

Anomie, 236, 308, 310

Antagonistic acculturation, 75, 157–158, 216–246; cause and function of resistance in, 221–225; resistances to borrowing and lending in, 218–221; and stimulus diffusion, 225–228; dissociative negative acculturation, 225, 228, 237–245; defensive isolation and, 228–229; types of, 228–245; and adoption of new means, 230–237

Anteriority, imputed, 303

Anticipation, and pre-experience, 298

Anti-instinctuality, 291

Anti-method, 18

Anti-type, 239

Anus, 187; vaginalization of, 189, 206–207, 212; myth-fantasy of human beings without, 81. *See also Hiwey lak*

Anxiety, and countertransference, 180n

Archetypes, theory of, 75

Areal climax, 162

Assimilation, 217

Asymmetrical relationship, 23n

Atomic theories, 268

Atrocities, 192n

Autoplastic: behavior, 157, 244; sociocultural change, 245; adjustment, 245n

Bakchai (Euripides), 139
"Barter, silent," 225, 228–229
Barter of women, 193, 203, 208. *See also* Circulation of women; Talion, law of
"Battle of the iota," 260
Behavior, 6, 14, 178; experimental, 10, analysis of, 38; prevalent concrete modes of, 90; rationalization of, 93; conceptual schemes pertaining to, 95; explanations of, 97; relationship between psychological and social analyses of, 116–122; and ethnic personality, 140, 143, 152; ideal model of, 141; and ethnic identity, 152, 160, 169
Beliefs, and fantasies, 82
Bilanisme, 204
Biochemical unifying level, 59
"Biological paleo-psychology," 181
Biologistic thought model, 289
Biology, 3n; and the principle of complementarity, 9–10, 16
Biopsychological theories, 21
Birth process, and orgasm, 182
Bisexuality, 190
Blinding, 193n, 194
Blitzkrieg, 232
Blood circulation, Sedang awareness of, 272–273
Bodies: laws of, 40; ideal rigid, 42
Böttcherstrasse, the German periodical, 173
Bouffée délierante, 200–201
Bride: price, 196; service to parents of, 196, 198, 211; of Christ, 201n; deflowering of, 203. *See also* Circulation of women

Calculus of probability, 36, 37, 44, 77
Cardinal number, and identity, 137
Castration, 192, 193n; symbolic, 192, 196, 197, 206
Causality, 26–28; functional, 27; principle of, 72; probabilitarian theories of, 309
Celibacy, 201n
Central nervous system, 56–58, 61
Chain reaction, 55, 56
Chance, nature of, 36
Change, 30; defining of, 23–24; direction of, 29; anomic, 306
Chemotherapy, and psychical ill-

nesses, 286–288
Chronoholistic system, 50, 52, 53
Circular reasoning, 115
Circulation of women, 177, 179; role of brother and of husband in, 191–212. *See also* Barter of women; Bride; Exchange of women
Class, 103n, 110; and personality, 107–108; mathematical distinguished from social, 136; and the individual, 137–138; "relevance" of, 139; identities, 167–174; and adjustment, 279
Classification: of the sciences of Man, 3–18; of sense data by science, 36; initial devices for, 82
Clinical thought model, 289–292
Clitoridectomy, 156
Closed system, 8, 173
Co-emergence: of marriage and kinship, 211; of society/culture and human psyche, 308
Coherence: of the sequence of ideas, 6; of the sequence of behaviors, 6; of a theoretical system, 15; of a conceptual scheme, 23
Collection of systems, 32
Collective: mentality, 21; representation, 21, 90, 281; distinctiveness, 170; identities, 174
Communism, 124, 129
Compendences, artificial, 268
Complementarity, 1–2; of sociological and psychological discourse, 3, 6–8, 10–11, 119–120; principle of, 9, 14–16, 65, 72, 307; relationship, 12–13, 18, 25, 39, 81, 110; culture and personality as a conceptual scheme, 96; of two modal personality models, 131, 134–135; and motivation, 132; of ethnic personality and ethnic identity, 151; and bases of kinship, 211–212
Compensation of the bride's family, 209
Concentration camps, 310
Conceptual schemes: of personality, 100; vs. mechanical models, 267
Configurations of personality, 107–108
Conformity: extreme, 126; in America, 277, 279, 280
Congruences, biologically inexplicable, 115

Consciousness, 10, 74, 76, 206
Conspicuousness, 243
Constitution of the United States, 39, 121-122
Constraint: defined, 6; observer as a source of, 6, 10
Conventional operation, 24
Convulsions: hystero-epileptic, 268; Mohave theory of, 273-275
Coordinates, "attached" to individuals, 40-42
Cosmology, 284
"Counter-mores," 243, 244
Counter-Oedipal attitudes, 290
Counter-prestation, 196
Countertransference of the observer, 95n
Counter-type (*Gegentypus*), 244
Counting vs. measuring, 33
Cousins, marriage of, 199
Covert culture, 90, 222, 226, 243
Creative myth, Mohave, 274-275
Creative dissent, 279
Creativity, 6n, 12
Creed of the Apostles, 122
Crisis situation, and cultural borrowing, 221-222
Criterion of yield, 5
Critical mass, and stress, 53-55
Cultural: history, 32; fact, 48; practices and corresponding fantasies, 63-64, 76-77, 79-82; alternatives, 64; implementation, 74, 76, 79; ethos, 76; mandates, 119; internal traits, 155-163; inertia, 218; mentalities, 236; values, "misuse" of, 237; type-casting, 280; communication, 297; thought models (*see* Thought models, cultural)
Culturalism, 87, 88, 114, 116, 280
Culture, 13, 33, 45, 94n, 280, 310; and the unconscious, 63-83; studies of, 87, 88, 92n; defined, 88; and personality studies, 89, 95, 106-107, 109, 131-133; implicit and explicit, 90; mediators of, 91-92; pre-reified abstraction of, 92; change, 217, 227 (*see also* Acculturation; Antagonistic acculturation); latent patterns, 243; conflict, 278; historical thought model, 289. *See also* Covert culture; Overt culture
Cumulative vulnerabilities, 53

Curing powers and songs, 257-259
Custom(s), 4, 39, 82, 297, 298; as a social gravitational field, 41; and selective implementation, 169; positive, 178; opposite, 179; and shamanism, 261-262

Day residue, and dreams, 250, 254
Dead, coitus with shade of the, 200
Death: fictitious, of Mohave fiancé, 199; premature, 199n, 200; burning the house after, 285n
Death instinct, primary, 8n, 277, 288-294
Decentralizing system, 61
Deculturalization of science, 292-294
Dedekind cut, 53, 61
Dedifferentiation, 279
Deduction, 81
Defense, shamanism as a, 261
Defensive isolation, and antagonistic acculturation, 228-229
Democracy, and social flexibility, 43
Depression, Mohave theory of, 276
Descriptive information, 297-298
Destruction: of living matter, 33; principle of (see *Abtötungsprinzip*)
Deuteronomy, 240
Deviants, deculturated or transculturated, 280
Deviative imitation, 157
Dictatorship, and social rigidity, 43
Dietary laws, Hebrew, 156
Differential equations, 43, 50
Differentiation, 4; ostentatious, 243; in America, 279
Diffusion, 216-217, 221; theory of, 74-76, 245; resistance to, 218, 243; of goals, 234
Direction: concept of, 28; of change, 29; of time, 29
"Disappearance" of the object of study, 14-15
Disciplines, autonomy of, 3
Discontinuity of individual processes, 25
Dissociative ethnic identity, 173
Dissociative negative acculturation, 225, 228, 237-245
Distance, measuring of, 34
Divine guidance, 25
Divorce, Mohave, 198, 199
Dogs: feces-eating among the Sedang

Moi, 80; in the Mohave culture, 104; and the notion of incest, 210
"Double discourse," 1–2, 15, 16, 119
Double weddings, 203
Doubt, self-serving, 87
Dreams, 190, 204, 206, 306; of women during menstrual cycles, 181–182; and exchange of women, 185–186; and magical powers, 249–251, 253–256, 260, 263; fights in, 255–256, 261–262; of a Plains Indian, 255n; pathogenic, 258; learning in, 263, 276; myths condensed in, 263; Freud's theory of, 288; "timeless" aspect of, 303–304
Durkheim's law, 31–32

Earthworm, nervous system of, 57, 58
Economic man, 42, 114–115, 120n
Ego, 6, 48, 267; temporal, 6, 137, 309; and abortion, 64; functions, 121; support, 291; syntonic acts, 126, 128, 129
Ego Ideal, 6, 39, 48, 121, 122, 144, 147
Elementargedanken, theory of, 74
Emergence, theory of, 21, 38, 45
Empathy, and motivation, 124
Endogenous causes of stress: and internalized Superego, 48–49; and distinction between "person" and "environment," 49–50; sources of, 51–52, 54, 61; internal accumulation model of, 53–56
English: alphabet, 158; language, 266, 278
Ensembles, theory of, 32
Entropy. *See* Thermodynamics, second law of
Environment, 49–51
Equality: and the measuring process, 34; idea of, 210
Equilibrium, 30, 42, 188n; of a system, 31, social, 45
Ergodic hypothesis, 32, 63, 70
Ersatz products, 227
Estrogen, 181
Ethical thought model, 289
Ethnic distinctiveness, 223
Ethnic identity, 136–174; and double meaning of identity, 136–140; vs. ethnic personality, 140–153; model, 152; and trait instancing, 153; formation and manifestation of, 153–165;

dissociative, 156, 173; "self" and "ascribed" mystique in, 163–165; double, 164; and group identities, 165–174; hypercathected, 170–171, 174; incorporation of ideologies into, 172
Ethnic personality, 76, 120; vs. ethnic identity, 140–153; dissociative-differentiating origins of traits of, 144; and Mohave shamanism, 262
Ethnic typicality, 143
Ethnos, 141, 142, 143, 164, 172, 173
Evolution, 43
Exchange of women, 192–194, 196–197, 211; unconscious meaning of, 185–191. *See also* Circulation of women
"Exhibition": of ethnic personality, 143, 144; of ethnic identity, 150
Exile, fugitive, 104n
Exogenous ("outside"), 48, 50, 51, 54, 57, 60, 61
Exogenous causes of stress: pre-amplified and pre-structured stimuli as, 56–57; sources of, 61
Expediency (*commodité*), 100
"Explaining away," 13
Explanation: and frame of reference, 14; excessive, 14–15; of a natural process, 22; the term, 87
Explanations: of behavior, 97, 118; complementary, 151n (*see also* Complementarity)
Externality, of the observer, 6

Facial expression, 144
Family: complexes, 192, 202; fixations, 198; and marriage, 200, 204
Fantasies, wishes, and impulses, duplicated elsewhere by customs, 63–64, 76–77, 79–82
Fantasy, 81; repressed, and real behavior, 178
"Farting vagina," 185, 187, 188, 206, 207
Father: killing the surrogates of, 125, 127, 130, 132; and the Oedipal conflict, 189
Feces-eating monsters, 80
Feedback mechanisms, 129, 132
Females: labia of, 156–157; juvenile sexual delinquency of, 195n; desynchronization of sexuality of, 183.

See also Sexual drive; Women
Feminization, symbolic, 192, 194, 196, 206
Field: theories, 21; concept, 42
Finger painting, 80
Force, 8n, 37; social, 40; and social gravitational fields, 41
Foresight, 308
Form persistence, 227
Free associations, 70, 79
Free-path method, 38
Free will, 25
Frustration-aggression hypothesis, 288
Functional interchangeability, 166-167
Future, 56; pertinence of socialization learning to, 299-303, 305-308, 310-311

Gedankenexperimente. See "Thought experiments"
Gemeinschaft vs. *Gesellschaft*, 105
General Adaptation Syndrome (G.A.S.), 50
Generals, military usefulness of, 139
Generations, 202-203; and the Unconscious, 184; American first and second, 278
Generosity, of Yuman tribes, 198
Genetic makeup: of social insects, 5; anomalous, 138
Gens-name, transmission of among the Mohave, 199n
Geometry, 23, 33; of J. Bólyai, 44; of N. Lobachevski, 44; Euclidean, 46, 284, 302; Riemannian, 284-285; and "economy of effort," 302
Gestalt, 61; theories, 21; psychology, 54
Ghetto territory, 310
Ghost Dance, 242-243
Ghosts, seductive, 276
Goals: pseudo-diffusion of, 230-232; theory of, 233; intermediate, 233-237; moving away from, 301-302
God the Father, 260
Gods, Olympian, 266. *See also* Divine guidance
Grammar, generative, 12
Gratification: from collective action, 127-130, 132-134; renunciation of immediate, 308
Gravitational field, 40-41
Greek tragedies, 4, 5
Gregariousness, 4, 5

Group: and explanations concerning it, 7; "mind," 21; society as a type of, 38-39; in the mathematical sense, 39-41; behavior of, 117; small, 117-119; identities, 165-174
Guilt feelings, 125, 127-128
Gypsy music, 161

Haber nitrogen-fixation process, 227
Halo meaning, 252, 253, 266, 293
"Happening," 309
Here and now (H/N), 298-306, 310-311
Hereditary system, 43, 45-46
Heredity, 33, 43
Heterosexual compensation, 189, 207
Heterosexual problem, the, 211
History, 29, 160, 311; cultural, 73; vs. chronicle, 309-310
Hiwey lak (Mohave anus pain group of illnesses), 251, 256-257, 260; specialists of, 256-257, 261
Holy Grail, 306
Homeostasis, 61
Homing instinct of animals, 306
Homosexuality: symbolic, 188, 190, 206-207; in Greek literature, 190-191; latent, 204, 205, 208, 210-211; as perversion, 209; and kinship, 209-210; due to deprivation, 209n; lacking in animals, 210, 211n; in the Hebrew religion, 240
"Hottentot apron," 157
Human beings (*Homo sapiens*), 60, 98, 178; as a gregarious species, 4, 5; variability of, 76; without an anus, in myth-fantasy, 80-81; and individuation, 137; behavior of, 140; personality of, 141; identity of, 145, 171
Human Relations Area Files, 77-78
Humiliation by coitus, 194-195
Husband-buying, 209n
Hysteresis, 43

Id, 49n, 64, 267
Identification mechanism, 224
Identity: recognition of and change in, 24; double meaning of, 136-140; defined, 137, 138; individual, 167, 171, 174; "assistant," 174; "crisis," 174. *See also* Ethnic Identity
Illness, caused by stress, 59, 61
Illusion of precision, 44

Imitation in reverse, 157
Immigrants, 278-280
Impotency, 185
Imputed characteristics, 114
Incest, 79, 180-181; among the Mohave, 183, 199, 200-201, 209; in Sweden, 184; in human societies, 202; quasi-incest and marriage of Siamese twins, 204; in anecdotes, 207
Incorporation process in cultural borrowing, 244
Indeterminacy: principle of, 9, 16-17, 39, 45, 72; the term, 72
Individual: and society, 4-5, 20-21, 23; explanations concerning, 7; concept of, 23, 45; and the environment, 49; practices and norms of, 93; behavior of, 95, 117; concrete, 107; sociological vs. psychological approaches to, 118-119; study of, 122; absolute uniqueness of, 137; integrity of the, 223; motives of (see Motivation)
Individual processes, 25-26, 33
Individuality: social implementation of, 165-166; and class identities, 169-170
Individualization: of the generalized shamanistic defense, 261; vs. adjustment in America, 279
Induction, 81, 82, 83
Inductive generalizations, 97; and ethnic personality, 140-150
Infinite divisibility of matter, 273
Infinity, 273
Information, pertinence of, 299
Infra-neural (biochemical) unifying level, 59
"In-group," 153, 244; and "out-group," 223-224
Insanity, plea of, 124
Insects, social, 5
"Inside." See Endogenous causes of stress
Instinct: in humans, 4, 49n, 169, 183n; in animals, 300, 306. See also Anti-instinctuality
Insulin therapy, 286
Integro-differential analysis, 32, 43, 50
Interdisciplinarity, 2
Interests: theory of, 233; common, 234
Internality of the observer, 6

Interpretation methods, in culture-and-personality studies, 131
Interpretative nihilism, 69
"Intervening opportunity," 233
Interviewing techniques, 133
Introjection, 224; and negative suggestion, 244
Invariance: of the affective content in variants of a myth, 12; of structures, 13
Invention, independent, 74
Inversion: of a problem, 67; of the second law of thermodynamics, 72
"Inward-bound" itinerary, 305
Irrational number, 53n
Irregular clocks, 35
Irreversible processes, 25, 28-30, 33
Isolation, 225, 245

Jahvism, 240
Jealousy, 202, 204, 210
"Jewish-Marxist-pluto-democracy," 241
Jordan curve, 35n, 49, 50, 60, 61

Kinetics, 23, 36, 92
Kingship, 232; of Zeus, 266
Kinship, 78; origin of the notion of, 177-212; Oedipus complex as inseparable from, 180-184; and the unconscious meaning of the exchange of women, 185-191; role of the brother and of the husband in the circulation of women, 191-212; and the Unconscious, 201-203
Koran, 245
Koro neurosis, 81n
Kymass-drinking, 156

Law, 26, 39, 41; defined, 28; statistical, 28
Learning: of songs and myths, 259, 263; future pertinence of relative to socialization/enculturation, 300-309, 311; behavior, 301
Least path: method of, 38; theory of, 41, 45
Liars, Cretans as, 140-141, 145
Limited possibilities, principle of, 73, 76
"Limiting cases," 44
Love, romantic, 200

Maladjustment, 278–280
Malingering, 291
Mammals, sexual behavior of, 210
Margin of normal functioning, 59–60
Marriage: customs, 184–186, 191n, 200–201; rites, 196–199, 209; as a transaction between men, 201, 204, 208; and latent homosexuality, 211
Marseillaise, The, 170
Mass, and gravitational field, 40
Masturbation, 274–275
Mathematical biophysics, 53n
Mathematical types, theory of, 16, 87, 101
Mathematics, 292–293
Matrilineal societies, 199n, 209n, 266
Meaning, 61; attributed, 59; latent, 78; meta-semantic, 253
Means, adoption of, without adoption of goals, 228, 230, 232–237, 242–246
Means-end schema, and antagonistic acculturation, 225, 226, 230, 237
Mechanical clock, 36
Mechanical models, as thought models, 267
Mechanics, 7, 26; classical, 117, 118, 284, 285; statistical, 8, 9, 28, 29, 33, 37, 38, 44, 45, 118, 284, 285; theoretical, 8, 9, 42
Mechanism, 25
Medical ecology, 60
Menopause, 183
Menstrual cycle, 181–182
Menstrual rite, 258
Mental disorders: theory of organic basis of, 276; psychogenic view of, 281
Mentalists, 3
Metalinguists, 266
Metaphysical reality, 20, 36
"Method in madness," 269
Methodology, 63, 65–71, 87; and complementarism, 18; method of contrasts, 21–22; method of the least path, 38; method of transformations, 38–39; of culture and personality studies, 88; physicalistic, 284
Military prowess, 159
Military technology, 217, 220, 232–233
Miscarriage, 179n
Misconduct, 254; patterns of, 142, 243, 279
Missionaries, 156

"Mock compliance," 250
Modal personality, 102–109; theory of, 100; models of, 113–135
Model: conjugate and non-conjugate, 114; explanatory, of man, 121; ideal, 142, 147, 149; ethnic identity, 151; negative, 157. See also Modal personality, models of
Moral masochism, theory of, 290–291
Morals: as restraint, 39; as a social gravitational field, 41
Morphine, reactions to, 52
Morphological differentiation, and sexual communication, 4
Mother, symbolic cannibalizing of, 183n
Mother-in-law stereotype, 119
Motility, 58
Motion, 24; relative, 25; concept of, 45
Motivation, 25, 127; instrumental, 11, 129–134; operant, 11, 130–134; and cultural reinforcement, 119; collective, 124; imputed, 124, 131; via common sense, 124, 131; subjective, 125–127; unconscious, 126; personal, and collective action, 128–129, 133
Mourning, Mohave theory of, 276
Mouth, "vaginalization" of, 189. See also Anus
Mystique: "self" and "ascribed," 163, 164; and individualism, 279
Mythological cultural model, 289
Myths, in Mohave culture, 249–250, 253–258, 263

Narcissism, 193, 260; of small differences, 223, 259
Nature-nurture controversy, 99, 118
Negative suggestion, 243–244
Neo-Freudians, 116
Nerve conductivity, theory of, 270–271
Neurosis, 75, 81n; among the Mohave, 198, 260–263. See also Viennese neurotics
Nomothetic information, 297, 298
Non-complementarism, 18
Nonconformism, obsessive, 279
Non-conjugate model, 114
Nonpredicative statements, 39
Norms, 89, 90, 93, 94
Nuclear family, 120
Numbers, laws of, 40

Numerology, 293

Observed, the, 3, 4, 15
Observer, the, 6-7, 10, 17, 141
Obstetrician, Mohave, 260
"Occult" phenomena, 291
Oedipus complex, 81, 202, 204-205; universality of, 75; role of, in combat behavior, 130; and kinship, 180-191; and homosexuality, 207, 209, 211; lacking in animals, 210; Occidental preoccupation with, 290
Old Testament, 183n, 239; Genesis, 197
"One-point memory," 43
Oral drives, separated from sexual drives, 183n
Order, 23; of individuals, 24, 42; of social positions, 29; of succession of events, 33; concept of, 45; the term, 309
Ordinal number, and identity, 137
Organicity, 281-288
Organismic theory, 21
Organisms, archaic, 57-58
Orgasm, 10, 182
Original sin, 142
Osmosis, 60
Other, self and, 49-50
"Out-group," 244, 246; and "in-group," 223-224
"Outward-bound," itinerary, 305
Overdetermination, 1
Overlapping, area of, 107
Overt culture, 90, 222, 243
Overvaluation, 262-263

Paleopsychological speculation, 75
Parallel action, 114
Paranoid tendencies, of Mohave shamans, 261-262
Participation, 127, 132
Patents, 219, 220, 221
Paternity, biological, 202
Path: of a system, 32; of displacement, 38
Pedagogical leniency, 291
Penis: inversion of, 80, 81n; *rectus*, 155; fish as symbol of, 189n
Performance, and ethnic identity, 145, 146, 149
Person, 24, 49; concept of, 310. *See also* Individual

Personality: culture and personality studies, 86-110, 131-133; and the reification of culture, 92; basic, 94, 102n; definitions of, 95; as a conceptual scheme, 95, 101, 108; "status," 102n, 103; medieval, 106; concrete, and modal personality, 107, 109. *See also* Modal personality
Pertinence: differentiated from relevance, 299-300; of socialization training to the future, 299-303, 305-308, 310-311
Phase, of a state, 30-31
Phenomena, reversible and irreversible, 117
Phlogiston theory of heat, 267
Physicalistic thought model, 288
Physical traits, and ethnic identity, 154
Physics: and "physicalism," 16; non-relativistic, 34; social prestige of, 283-285
Pigs: feces eaten by, 80; and eating pork, 155-156
Place names, 255
Plague, Athenian, 310
Plasticity, 137
Platonic idealism, 88, 135
Pluridisciplinarity, 2
Polygamous tendencies, 204
Polymastic animals and deity, 156n
Polysegmentation of society, 31
Population studies, 43
Porcelain manufacture, and stimulus diffusion, 226
Posteriority, imputed, 303-304
Practice, 297; and theory, 90, 93; and norm, 93, 94
Pre-amplification of environmental impact, 52, 55-56
Preconscious, 206
Predestination, 25
Pre-experience (P/E), 298-299; "pull," 304
"Preparation" (a mutilated laboratory animal), 10n, 14
Pre-structured stimuli, 56-57
Primary death instinct. *See* Death instinct, primary
Primogeniture, 137n
Probability, 48-49; mathematical, 8; degrees of, 28; value, 30; coefficients, 36, 37; analysis in terms of, 38; and sociological discourse, 45

Progesterone, 182
Projection, 224, 244
Property, Yuman attitude toward, 198
Prostitutes, 205; of Shanghai, 194n; reformed, 201n
Prostitution, in the Hebrew religion, 240
"Pseudobiologia phantastica," 75, 181
Pseudo-nonconformism, 279
"Psyche," 13
Psychiatrists: immigrant, 278, 280; stereotypes of, 281–282; jokes about, 282; and organicity, 282–283
Psychiatry: primitive, 269–276; modern, 276–277 (*see* also Organicity)
Psychic unity of mankind, 64, 74–77
Psychoanalysis, 81, 139, 282; and complementarity, 12, 16; and the meaning of symptoms, 17–18; validity of, 65–68, 75; and the psychic unity of mankind, 75; reculturalization of, 293–294
"Psychological fallacy," 89
Psychologistic lure, 135
Psychology, 2–3, 5–7, 77, 110, 122, 133, 135; and the principle of complementarity, 9–10, 13–18; and sociology, 109, 121; and modal personality, 113–114; and society and culture, 115, 122
Psychopathic personality, 49n. *See also* Mental disorders
Psychosomaticians, 60–61
Psychotics, seductiveness of, 272
Puberty: efforts to delay, 183; rite, 258
Purchase of women, 196, 211

Quanta and quantum theory, 9, 11, 17, 25, 39, 41, 51–53, 60

Racial unconscious, theory of, 75
Rape, 193, 195, 196n
Rationalizations, 132
Rauwolfia serpentina, 286–287
Raw fact, 10–11, 14
Reaction formation, 223, 240, 241, 244
Reactions: total, 57; discriminating and non-discriminating, 58; polysystemic and segmental, 59; subjective psychological, 127; "Eureka," 299
Readjustment, creative, 277, 309
Reality: principle, 6; testing, 290

Rebellion, 236
Reciprocal: statuses, 105; prestations, 106, 196–197
Reciprocity, 179
Reculturalization, 293–294
Reductionism, 3, 14, 130, 132
Referral or relevance, 299, 304
Refugees, Hungarian, 116
Regeneration, 59
Regression, 242
Regularities, 26–28, 33
Reification of culture, 90–92
Rejection of adoption, 225
Rejection, structured, of structures, 12, 13
Relationships: transitive, asymmetrical, 23; types of, in human society, 166–167; "logico-meaningful," 237
Relativity, theory of, 35, 267
Relevance of classes, 139
Renaissance, 227
Repression, 227
Reptiles, prehistoric, 58
Resistance, to cultural borrowing or lending, 218–225, 245. *See also* Antagonistic acculturation
Reverse adjustment, compulsive, 279
Reversibility of individual processes, 25
Revolution: Hungarian, 116, 122–133; American, 232, 299
Reward, 299–301
Rice cultivation, 219
Rigidity: of an organism, 57; of a society, 94
Rite de passage theory of marriage, 209–210
Ritual, 160; over-elaboration of, 197; Mohave, 250–251, 253–254, 257–259; oral, 259
Ritualism, 236
"Road of the rice spirits," 270–271
Role playing, and ethnic identity, 149, 150, 160
"Romania," 235
Rumors, study of the spread of, 260

"Sakai," meaning of, 229
Sample, adequate, 79
Sanctions, vs. moral values, 39
Sanity, as opposed to adjustment, 307, 309
Scalping, 193

Scheinproblem (pseudo-problem), 22
Schizophrenics, 195n; studied in psychiatric hospital, 97n
Science: cultural prestige of exact, 283-288, 293; deculturalization and reculturalization of, 292-294
Sciolism, 283, 293
Sea anemone, 57
Secret police (A.V.O.), 125, 129
Selection: of innate structures, 13; of segments of a total repertoire, 169-170
Selective sensitiveness, 51
Self: as observer, 10; and Other, 49-50; sister as substitute for, 187; uniqueness of the, 223; actualization of, 308. *See also* Individual; Individuality
Self-ethnographers, 140, 145
Self-model, and ethnic identity, 142
Sequentiality, sense of, and dreams, 303
Serendipity, 298, 300
Sermon on the Mount, 222
Sets, 97, 100
Sexual drive, human, 4-5; and maternity, 181-183; separated from oral drives, 183n
Sexual misbehavior, punishment for, 193n
Sexual presentation, by weak male primates, 210n, 211n
Sexuality, female, and Oedipus complex, 181-184
Shamans, 220; Mohave, 249-260, 276; Siberian, 256; and shamanism as a defense, 260-263; motif of "contest" of, 262; beliefs about, 268, 274-275; Greek, 292. *See also* Witchcraft
Shame, 127
Shock, allergic (anaphylactic), 50
Siamese twins, 204
Sibling rivalry, 276
Simultaneity, relativistic interpretation of, 34
"Slippages," 191n
Smallpox, 51-52
Social: communication, 4; status, 7, 167; roles, 14; gravitational field, 21, 40, 41; processes, 24-26, 30, 42, 44, 45, 128, 132, 134; structure of a state, 29; positions, 29-30, 195n; mobility, 30, 45; time, 33-36; space, 38, 44, 45; force, 40; mass, 40, 45;

lag, 43; laws, 45; psychology, 89, 120; movements and processes, 126; mandates, 130-132; science, 135; values, 193; crisis, 238; negativism, 261-263, 279; reflexes, 307-309
Social Science Research Council, 216
Socialization/enculturation (S/C), 297-300, 306-311
Society, 13, 39, 179; defined, 7, 23, 24; polysegmented, 31, 94, 105; concept of, 20, 33, 42, 44, 310; rigidity of and change in, 42-43; not an emergent, 45, 94n. *See also* Social
Socio-cultural: fact, 48; teachability, 115; "realities," 122; change, 245, 310; multi-dimensional space, 302-303, 305; drift, 311
Sociologistic pitfall, 135
Sociology: discourse of, 2-3, 6-7, 11, 14, 24, 45, 48-49; and psychology, 5, 9, 109, 110; observer as a source of constraint in, 6; and complementarity, 10, 13; approaches to central problem of, 21-22; and equal intervals, 34-35; scope of, 44-45; basic concepts of, 45; and scientific method, 46; and external events, 60; and modal personality, 113-114; of knowledge, 265-266
Soldiers, professional, 161-162
Song of Songs, 202
Songs, in Mohave culture, 249-261, 263
Son-in-law, 196
Souls, transferable, 270-271
Space, 34; curved, 41, 45; socio-cultural, 302-303
Specifications: and individual processes, 26; of an equilibrium, 31
Spy, 147, 148
Stability of a state, 30
Star of David, 158
States, 29-30
Statics, 36
Statistical: induction, 27; macroparameters, 43; hereditary statistical mechanics, 44; analysis, 70
"Stat. human," 116
"Stat. rat" (statistical rat), 14, 115-116
Stereotypes: hostile, 90; of mothers-in-law, 120; of physicians, 281
Stimulus diffusion, 158, 226-229; defined, 225-226

Stovarsol, 237
Stress: endogenous and exogenous sources of, 48-61; between the individual and the environment, 49; reaction to, 50, 57, 61; and trauma, 51; and capacity to dis-amplify impacts, 51-52; total and segmental systemic reactions to, 57-59; illness caused by, 59, 61; and negative suggestion, 244
Strychnine, reactions to, 52
Sublimation, 210, 307, 308
Suicide, 69; attempted, 69n; vicarious, 119, 199-200; of Lucretia, 195n; symbolic, 200; funeral, 276
Sumo wrestlers, 81n
Superego, 6, 39, 48, 91; internalized, 49; sadistic, 49n, 290; and abortion, 64; and society, 121, 122; and ethnic personality, 144; and ethnic identity, 147, 152
"Super-past," creation of, 242
Suppression: of social contact, 228-229; of cultural items, 229
Symbolic communication, 4
Symbols, transformation of, 12
Symmetry, 188n, 204, 205, 210
Symptoms, and complementarity, 17-18
System within a total system, 58

Taboos: deliberate violation of, 79, 82; and positive custom, 178
Tabula rasa, 81
Talion, law of, 186-188, 190-191, 203, 204, 206-207
Tanks, 232-233
Techniques, adoption of, 245-246
Telepathy, 291, 293
Termites as a social species, 4
Testosterone, 195n
Theoretical system, non-self-contradictory character of, 15
Theories: complementarity of, 13; and excessive explanations, 14-15; and practice, 90, 93
Thermodynamics, 8; second law of, 28-29, 33, 72, 173, 288-289
Thought: invariant structure of, 12; and language, 266
"Thought experiments" (*Gedankenexperimente*), 13, 120-121
Thought models, cultural, 265-294;

and social thought models, 266-267; and scientific thought models, 267-268, 283-288, 292-294; influence of on psychiatric theories, 269-294; in primitive psychiatric theories, 269-276; in modern psychiatric theories, 276-294; in theories of organic causation of mental disorders, 281-288; in theory of primary death instinct, 288-292
Three bodies, problem of, 9, 118
Time: temporal structures and succedaneous causality, 26; direction of, 29; defined, 33, 309; "absolute" vs. "physical," 33; measurement of, 34; thermodynamic, 35; social and physical, 35-36; pre-amplification and the future, 56; temporal ensemble, 109; in dreams, 303-304; history vs. chronicle, 309-310
Time, and socialization/enculturation, 297-311; pre-experience as symbolic anticipation, 298-299; concepts of relevance and pertinence differentiated, 299-300; the future pertinence of socialization learning, 299-303, 305-308, 310-311
Tissues, specialization of, 58
Topology, 42, 49, 77
Totality of qualities, 102, 143
Tradition, 33
Traitor, concept of, 147, 148
Transference phenomena, 274
Transformation(s), 12; point-to-point, 42; groups of, 45
Translation: semantic, 251-252, 257; exegetic, 252-253, 257-258; meta-semantic, 252-253, 257-258
Trauma, 51
Trial and error (T/E), 298-302, 306, 310
Tropisms, 4
Tumānp'à Utáūt song cycle, 255, 259, 261
Type: relationship, 166; solution, 261; conflicts, 261-262; experiences, 274
Types, theory of, 102, 261n
Typicality: and ethnic identity, 147; of Spartan sayings, 149, 151, 160
Typology, 77-79, 83
Tyrannophobia, 179
Tyranny, 178-179

Ultimogeniture, 137n
"Uncle Tom" Afro-American ethnic personality model, 142
Unconscious, the, 205–206; and culture, 63–83; and incest, 184; and kinship, 201–203; logic of, 269
Unidirectional processes, 33

Vagina, "oralizing" and "analizing" of, 189. *See also* Anus; "Farting vagina"
Value judgment, 142
Values, 115; systems of, 134; cultural, 237
Vengeance, desire for, 204
Vertretung, 18; the term, 17
Vicious circles, 15, 20, 94n, 102, 109
Viennese neurotics, 63, 65, 75
Vitalism, 25
Voyeurism, 204
Vulnerabilities, cumulative, 52

Weber-Fechner law, 53
Weddings, and barter, 203–204
Westernization: of Hungary, 156; of Japan, 230–231; of Germany, 231
Wife-sharing, 188
Wissenssoziological factors, 71
Witchcraft: Mohave, 200, 249, 256–260, 262–263; Arunta, 289. *See also* Shamans
Women: as athletes, 138; pregnant, 182–183. *See also* Bride; Circulation of women; Exchange of women; Females; Prostitutes
Working hypothesis, 20, 22
World War: First, 229, 232; Second, 233

Zone maniable, 52